technology

 Other titles in this
series include:

Food: A Reader for Writers,
Danielle Aquiline and Deborah Holdstein
(ISBN: 9780199385683)

Humor: A Reader for Writers,
Kathleen Volk Miller and Marion Wrenn
(ISBN: 9780199362684)

Poverty/Privilege: A Reader for Writers,
Connie Mick
(ISBN: 9780199361250)

Culture: A Reader for Writers,
John Mauk
(ISBN: 9780199947225)

Language: A Reader for Writers,
Gita DasBender
(ISBN: 9780199947485)

Sustainability: A Reader for Writers,
Carl Herndl
(ISBN: 9780199947508)

Identity: A Reader for Writers,
John Scenters-Zapico
(ISBN: 9780199947461)

Globalization: A Reader for Writers,
Maria Jerskey
(ISBN: 9780199947522)

technology

A READER *for* WRITERS

Johannah Rodgers

The New York City College of Technology/
The City University of New York

New York Oxford
Oxford University Press

Oxford University Press, Inc., publishes works that further Oxford University's
objective of excellence in research, scholarship, and education.

Oxford   New York
Auckland   Cape Town   Dar es Salaam   Hong Kong   Karachi
Kuala Lumpur   Madrid   Melbourne   Mexico City   Nairobi
New Delhi   Shanghai   Taipei   Toronto

With offices in
Argentina   Austria   Brazil   Chile   Czech Republic   France   Greece
Guatemala   Hungary   Italy   Japan   Poland   Portugal   Singapore
South Korea   Switzerland   Thailand   Turkey   Ukraine   Vietnam

For titles covered by Section 112 of the US Higher Education Opportunity Act,
please visit www.oup.com/us/he for the latest information about
pricing and alternate formats.

Published by Oxford University Press, Inc.
198 Madison Avenue, New York, New York 10016
http://www.oup.com

Library of Congress Cataloging-in-Publication Data
Rodgers, Johannah, author.
   Technology : a reader for writers / Johannah Rodgers, The New York City
College of Technology/The City University of New York.
      pages cm
   ISBN: 9780199340736
  1. Technical literature. I. Title.
   T10.7.R53 2014
   600--dc23
                                                        2014033949

Printing number: 9 8 7 6 5 4 3 2

Printed in the United States of America
on acid-free paper

brief table of contents

contents

"Defining technology in its complexity is as difficult as grasping the essence of politics."

"Technology is a word that mystifies as much as it explains ... In both popular and scholarly usage, the meanings of technology are deeply contradictory, almost perversely so."

"Few 'millennials'—or the generation aged between 18 and 33—can remember a time when technology has not been a fundamental part of their lives. Not only does it answer their questions, but, through social media, it also gives them the ability to alter the way in which they are perceived by their peers and the greater world around them."

"As for the hazardous character of the concept of technology, here I need only say that I am not thinking about weaponry or the physical damage wrought by the use of any particular technologies. The hazards I have in mind are conceptual, not physical."

Kevin Kelly, **"What Technology Wants"** *The Technium Blog* 2009   20

"We don't always have to do what technology wants, but I think we need to begin with what it wants so that we can work with these forces instead of against them."

Neil Postman, **"Five Things We Need to Know About Technological Change"** Lecture 1998   26

"The first idea is that all technological change is a trade-off. I like to call it a Faustian bargain. Technology giveth and technology taketh away."

2   Imagining Worlds: Does Science Fiction Inform Our Technological Reality?   37

Robert J. Sawyer, **"The Purpose of Science Fiction"** *Slate.com* 2011   39

"Those wishing to get in on the ground floor of discussing where technology is leading us would do well to heed Alvin Toffler's advice by cracking open a good science-fiction book and joining the conversation."

Neal Stephenson, **"Innovation Starvation"** *World Policy Journal* 2011   42

"In early 2011, I participated in a conference called Future Tense, where I lamented the decline of the manned space program, then pivoted to energy, indicating that the real issue isn't about rockets. It's our far broader inability as a society to execute on the big stuff. I had, through some kind of blind luck, struck a nerve. The audience at Future Tense was more confident than I that science fiction had relevance—even utility—in addressing the problem."

Jon Turney, **"Imagining Technology"** *NESTA* 2013   50

"Every technology, already realized or merely sketched, is always already embedded in stories. They run from the explanation of its basic operation, to its place in a collection of futuristic scenarios . . . "

"Physical law tells us that many things are impossible given existing technology, but the ever-expanding frontier of scientific knowledge shows us how to do many things of which we would never have dreamed. Writing stories within the rules of the universe as we know it and yet discovering fantastic possibilities of new ways of life is the central endeavor of the hard SF writer. SF writers prefer to give us truth, rather than reality. SF represents what the future could be like, although we know that the future will look nothing like it."

"[Y]esterday's future—our present day—is a blend of the predictable and the only slightly surprising. Still, a hundred and fifty years ago, the claim that people would do away with horses in the street, and spend their holidays flying through the air while packed like hens would have seemed mad. The real future of 50 years hence is likely to be just that wrenchingly strange."

"Part of the pleasure of reading old science fiction is precisely this: with the special powers vested in you by historical hindsight, you can compare the playfully visionary forecasts with what actually took place."

"Many highly accomplished scientists originally became interested in science through exposure to science fiction."

"Tethered to technology, we are shaken when that world 'unplugged' does not signify, does not satisfy. After an evening of avatar-to-avatar talk in a networked game, we feel, at one moment, in possession of a full social life and, in the next, curiously isolated, in tenuous complicity with strangers."

"There were lots of reasons why we pulled the plug on my family's electronic media for six months . . . or, I should say, why I did, because heaven knows my children would have sooner volunteered to go without food, water or hair products."

"All media of communication are a direct by-product of our sad inability to communicate directly from mind to mind."

"Instead of having the designer think through all the moral and political implications of technology use before it reaches users—an impossible task— we must find a way to get users to do some of that thinking themselves."

"What we really want are machines that can go a step further, endowed not only with the soundest codes of ethics that our best contemporary philosophers can devise, but also with the possibility of machines making their own moral progress, bringing them past our own limited early-twenty-first century idea of morality."

"For decades the golden rule in robotics has been that the more lifelike a creation, the more likely it crosses the line from cute to creepy. But questions are being raised as to whether this is really true."

"As the media theorist Marshall McLuhan pointed out in the 1960s, media are not just passive channels of information. They supply the stuff of thought, but they also shape the process of thought. And what the Net seems to be doing is chipping away my capacity for concentration and contemplation. My mind now expects to take in information the way the Net distributes it: in a swiftly moving stream of particles. Once I was a scuba diver in the sea of words. Now I zip along the surface like a guy on a Jet Ski."

"[D]igital media link over a billion people into the same network. This linking together in turn lets us tap our cognitive surplus, the trillion hours a year of free time the educated population of the planet has to spend doing things they care about."

"From Star Wars Kid to Maru the cat, what causes videos to go viral? And what does the success of the ephemera that washes across the internet say about us?"

"If the computer games which exist now had existed back in 1979 I would not have read any books, I think; I would not have seen writing as an adequate entertainment; I would not have seen going outdoors as sufficiently interesting to bother with."

"Wikipedia is today the gateway through which millions of people now seek access to knowledge which not long ago was only available using tools constructed and maintained by professional scholars."

"When we hear about the death of the book, it might be a good idea to ask what 'the book' is. Are we talking about people ceasing to read books, or about what they read the books on—paper or a screen?"

"Technology is transforming American education, for good and for ill."

"The academic achievement gap takes root in early childhood and is related to the formal and informal learning ecologies that kids navigate throughout life. Different parenting practices and household resources mean that middle-income kids enter kindergarten with richer language skills and greater exposure to books than their low-income counterparts. Throughout schooling these early learning divides expand. What role, if any, do digital and mobile media platforms play in America's learning divides?"

"A new phenomenon requires a new name, and so MOOC—massive open online course—has now entered the lexicon. So far, MOOCs have been true to the first 'o' in the acronym: Anyone can take these courses for free. Many people outside academia—including *New York Times* columnists David Brooks and Thomas L. Friedman—are gushing that MOOCs are the best thing to happen to learning since movable type. Inside academia, however, they have been met with widespread skepticism."

"Professors who care about public education should not produce products that will replace professors, dismantle departments, and provide a diminished education for students in public universities."

"The first step toward understanding how video games can—and, we argue, will—transform education is changing the widely shared perspective that games are 'mere entertainment.'"

"Technology—no matter how well designed—is only a magnifier of human intent and capacity. It is not a substitute."

"If you believe the hype, technology is going to help us end global poverty. Advances have indeed made a huge difference in the lives of the poor, but there's also a healthy amount of skepticism out there."

"We're used to treating information as free, but the price we pay for the illusion of 'free' is only workable so long as most of the overall economy *isn't* about information."

"Need a crash course in digital capitalism? Easy: you just need to understand four concepts—margins, volume, inequality and employment. And if you need more detail, just add the following adjectives: thin, vast, huge and poor."

"[The Internet] is terrific at the diffusion of innovation, interdisciplinary collaboration, seamlessly matching up buyers and sellers, and the logistical functions of the dating world. But weak ties seldom lead to high-risk activism."

"The fact remains that the Internet represents an extremely rare opportunity. For one thing, it's a meta-medium that can assume many shapes. Because it's becoming a tool that billions of people use, it could help people of the world work together to address their shared concerns."

"Medical technology offers us in many cases a devil's bargain: longer life, but with reduced mental capacity; freedom from depression, together with freedom from creativity or spirit; therapies that blur the line between what we achieve on our own and what we achieve because of the levels of various chemicals in our brains."

"What if there are no imminent, much less foreseeable cures to some of the most common and most lethal diseases? What if, in individual cases, not all diseases should be fought? What if we are refusing to confront the painful likelihood that our biological nature is not nearly as resilient or open to endless improvement as we have long believed?"

"A revolution in technology that is based on the primacy of individuals mandates a revolution by consumers in order for new medicine to take hold."

"As with most difficulties in global health care, lack of adequate technology is not the biggest problem. We already have a great warming technology: a mother's skin. But even in high-income countries we do not consistently use it."

"Anthropogenic climate change represents one of the greatest and swiftest transformations the earth has experienced."

rhetorical contents

analysis

argument

compare and contrast

personal

research

classification

graphic

preface

In the twenty-first century, technologies are not only all around us in the form of gadgets and digital devices, but *technology* itself is a term and a phenomenon that we read about and refer to on a daily basis. A quick search on the NYTimes.com website reveals that technology promises to transform institutions as colossal and seemingly permanent as education, medicine, and finance, and practices as basic and important as how we relate to and communicate with each other and how we read. And yet, at the center of all of these grand proclamations is this term *technology*, which is one that is very rarely defined and which is a term that, in all likelihood, few of us have spent much time trying to define. What is technology? This is, in fact, not at all an easy question to answer. What is more, the more we use this word, the more we may assume that we—and everyone else—simply know the answer to this question. Hidden in plain sight, this term *technology* raises numerous questions that only multiply as the term itself is increasingly understood as being part of some already existing and assumed "common knowledge."

However complex the process of defining and understanding technology may be, this is undoubtedly a very timely and worthwhile endeavor. For, as technologies are presented to us as increasingly crucial to our economic and social well-being, potentially transformative in their scope, and possibly threatening to traditional institutions, structures, and practices, the more important it is that we understand what it is that we are actually talking and writing and thinking about when we refer to this thing, whatever it is, called technology. Technology is, in fact, many things. It is tools and devices, processes, systems, and practices. According to the historian Ruth Schwartz Cowan, technologies are both the ways and the means by which things get done and through which humans shape and manipulate their environment. In other words, technologies truly are everywhere. What is more, the meanings and implications of these technologies are both diverse and profound.

While there are therefore many compelling reasons to study and think and write about technology, I can think of few more convincing than the one presented by Langdon Winner in his 1997 essay "Technomania." Reflecting on the obsession with technology gripping many in the United States in the late 1990s, Winner wrote:

> Today's neatly packaged innovations in computer networking, office automation, factory production, telecommunications, reproductive technology and genetic engineering contain all the moral dilemmas and political choices that have ever engaged philosophers, statesmen and ordinary working people. Will the world we are making be better than the one we have known before? Will it secure our freedom or curtail it? Will it enlarge social justice or limit it? Will it protect the biosphere or further assault it?

How today's "technomania" compares to that of the past is open to question. However, most will agree that some kind of mania is still very much with us and seems to today have reached only greater levels of intensity. And yet, even in his critique of this "technomania," Winner offers a number of reasons to delve into the study of technologies. For it is by studying them, he suggests, that we will begin to understand not only what our social and cultural priorities are, but how these relate to and inform various political and economic systems that ultimately shape society and affect humans and the environment. In other words, by thinking and writing about technology, we critically reflect on ourselves as individuals and as a society.

There may be few words more overused and less understood today than the word *technology*. While this issue is one that is addressed by many of the readings in this anthology, it is also one—for better or worse—that is further complicated by the title of this anthology. Although entitled *Technology: A Reader for Writers*, this anthology might more accurately be called *Information and Communications Technologies (ICT): A Reader for Writers*, since the readings contained in it focus almost exclusively on these specific technologies. This is no accident, of course, since the word *technology* is most often used in the early twenty-first century to refer to ICT, and it is therefore an especially appropriate topic for any composition course that is based on themes of writing and technology, and that is therefore concerned with media, communication, and literacy studies. Chapters 1 and 2 present a framework for thinking about issues related to defining and thinking about technology somewhat broadly; the rest of the chapters focus exclusively on ICT in the context of various disciplines: psychology and social science, literacy and cultural studies, education, political economy, and healthcare.

By its very nature, this anthology is interdisciplinary, containing a wide range of readings from various disciplines, sources, and experts. Why? Simply stated, technologies do not exist in a vacuum. Rather, they are inextricably woven into every aspect of society and culture. To investigate the subject of technology is then to undertake a study of societies and their values, beliefs, and institutions. By focusing on one specific technological sector, it is my hope that students can then transfer some of the knowledge and understanding gained through this inquiry to the study of other technologies and technological sectors. ICT is not necessarily the most important contemporary technology, but it is certainly the one that is most talked about and written about at the moment. It therefore seems a good place for students to begin thinking and writing about technologies and some of the many issues related to them.

Technology: A Reader for Writers is part of a series of brief single-topic readers from Oxford University Press designed for today's college writing courses. Each reader in this series approaches a topic of contemporary conversation from multiple perspectives:

- **Timely** Most selections were originally published in 2010 or later.
- **Global** Sources and voices from around the world are included.
- **Diverse** Selections come from a range of nontraditional and alternate print and online media, as well as representative mainstream sources.
- **Curated** Every author of a volume in this series is a teacher-scholar whose experience in the writing classroom as well as expertise in a volume's specific subject area informs his or her choices of readings.

In addition to the rich array of perspectives on topical (even urgent) issues addressed in each reader, each volume features an abundance of different genres and styles—from the academic research paper to the pithy Twitter argument. Useful but non-intrusive pedagogy includes the following:

- **Chapter introductions** provide a brief overview of the chapter's theme and a sense of how the chapter's selections relate both to the overarching theme and to each other.
- **Headnotes** introduce each reading by providing concise information about its original publication, and pose an open-ended question that encourages students to explore their prior knowledge of (or opinions about) some aspect of the selection's content.
- **"Analyze" and "Explore" questions** after each reading scaffold and support student reading for comprehension as well as rhetorical considerations, providing prompts for reflection, classroom discussion, and brief writing assignments.
- **"Forging Connections" and "Looking Further" prompts** after each chapter encourage critical thinking by asking students to compare perspectives and strategies among readings both within the chapter and with readings in other chapters, suggesting writing assignments that engage students with larger conversations in the academy, the community, and the media.
- **An appendix on "Researching and Writing About Technology"** guides student inquiry and research in a digital environment. Co-authored by a research librarian and a writing program director, this appendix provides real-world, transferable strategies for locating, assessing, synthesizing, and citing sources in support of an argument.

about the author

Johannah Rodgers is Assistant Professor in English at the City University of New York's New York City College of Technology. She has studied literature, rhetoric, and philosophy at Stanford University, Oxford University, Yale University, and at The City University of New York (CUNY). She has also studied the business and marketing of technologies first-hand while working in Silicon Valley as a research analyst. She holds degrees in Comparative Literature (B.A., Stanford University), Fiction

Writing (M.F.A., The City College of New York), and English/Rhetoric (Ph.D., The Graduate Center, CUNY). Her research interests relate to the history, technology, and anthropology of literacies, relationships between speaking and writing, and the use of writing as a symbolic system across disciplines and media. Her stories, essays, scholarly articles, and reviews have been published in various journals and magazines, including *The Brooklyn Rail, Bookforum, Fence, The Journal of Basic Writing*, and *Women's Studies Quarterly*. She is the author of the digital fiction project DNA (www.dnanovel.com; mimeograph, 2014), and the book *sentences* (Red Dust, 2007), as well as several ebooks about college writing, which can be accessed via her website www.whatiswriting.org.

acknowledgments

Every book is a collaboration, anthologies even more so than some other kinds. I cannot sufficiently thank my editor, Frederick Speers, and the contributors to this anthology for their work and for their support of this project. I also extend my gratitude to those involved in the design, production, editing, and marketing of this book. There are many writers, journalists, and scholars whose work informed and influenced this book, but whose writings, for various reasons, could not ultimately be included. Although too numerous to mention, a few must be singled out: Langdon Winner, David E. Nye, Ruth Schwartz Cowan, Carolyn Marvin, Wiebe E. Bijker, Donald MacKenzie, Judy Wajcman, Johanna Drucker, Lisa Gitleman, Herbert Marcuse, John Brockman, Steven Johnson, Stuart Moulthrop, and the editor of the SF blog. Donald Breckenridge and the cats (Oscar, Mishka, and Minou) supported me and my work on a daily basis. I extend my deep gratitude to them. I also thank all of my colleagues at the college and within CUNY, in particular Caroline Hellman, Aaron Barlow, Carole Harris, and Nina Bannett for their ongoing support of and interest in this project. I must also thank all of my many teachers, particularly Hans Gumbrecht, Robert Hullot-Kentor, Tom Ligotti, Mary Pedley, Jacques Karamanoukian, David Marshall, Angus Fletcher, Sondra Perl, Ira Shor, and Mark Mirsky; my former colleagues at R. B. Webber, especially Jeff Webber, Joseph Brilando, Stephen Plume, Rob Meinhardt, Reed Foster, Roger Merrill, Sheila Zelinger, and Steven Jordan; and several friends and family members, Jill Magi, Jonny Farrow, Michelle Memran, Elissa Linow, Beth Rosenberg, Stephanie Hirschman, Robert Landon, Rob Einaudi, Irene Stapleford, Jared Stark, Adam Gwosdof, Fred Spitz, Rachel Rosenzweig, Tom Dunham, Todd Pierce, Jessica Porter, Matthew McGuire, Mary Rodgers, Geraldine Peterson, and Peter and Nan Nolan. This book is dedicated to all of the students I have had the pleasure of working with and to my late colleague and friend Charles Hirsch, whose death in 2013 has left the world and us all a bit poorer. "Glory be to God for dappled things," he said to me on the first day I met him, quoting Gerard Manley Hopkins in a moment that was, as usual with Charles, filled with humor, wit, irony, absurdity, and truth. Thank you, Charles, for teaching me so much about technology and writing and teaching and life. Although I know you would have offered a few criticisms, I hope you and others may enjoy this book.

The author and editors of this book would also like to extend our heartfelt thanks to the following academics who provided valuable feedback on this anthology during its development:

Gwen Argersinger, Mesa Community College; **Greg Bachar**, Seattle Central Community College; **Allison Bryan**, Atlantic Cape Community College; **Nandan Choksi**, Broward College; **Douglas Crawford-Parker**, University of Kansas; **Carol DeBoer-Langworthy**, Brown University; **Jacqueline DiChiara**, Fairleigh Dickinson University and Bergen Community College; **Mike Dubose**, University of Toledo; **Michael Duvall**, College of Charleston; **Sharynn Etheridge**, Claflin University; **Cheryl Finley**, University of California – Merced; **Rod Freeman**, Estrella Mountain College; **Angela Fulk**, Buffalo State College; **Dane Galloway**, Ozarks Technical Community College; **Chris Gerben**, Stanford University; **Nora Gold**, Baruch College; **Theresa Hunt**, Rutgers University; **Joseph Justice**, South Plains College; **Michael Klein**, James Madison University; **Pete Kunze**, Florida State University; **Kara Mae**, Northeastern University; **Michael Martin**, Marygrove College; **James McWard**, Johnson County Community College; **Dorothy Minor**, Tulsa Community College; **Christy Rieger**, Mercyhurst University; **Mark Stevens**, Southern Polytechnic State University; **Rebecca Saulsbury**, Florida Southern College; **KT Shaver**, California State University–Long Beach; and **Michel Walker**, Copper Mountain College.

Which Came First, Technology or Society?

Technology is—and has always been—all around us. It is a fundamental part of what it means to be human and how society functions. However, technology is also, as the writers in this chapter remind us, a term and a concept that few of us fully comprehend. Of the many issues involved in understanding what technology is, the first complication arises in relation to our contemporary use of the term as one that refers primarily to computers and cell phones. In fact, the word *technology* refers to much more than the information and communications technologies (ICT) represented by devices like these. Technology is also—to name just a few other examples—scissors, highways, nail polish, photocopiers, automobiles, and supercolliders. Furthermore, technology encompasses not only artifacts, or things, but also processes and systems, which are sometimes mechanical, sometimes digital, and often human and creative. Finally, although today we may think, talk, use, read, and write about this term *technology* on a daily basis, this broad awareness and interest in technology is very recent. As several writers in this chapter note, even though technology is as old as human history, the term *technology* itself did not come into common usage until the mid-twentieth century.

In his book *Keywords*, the cultural critic Raymond Williams proposes that "some important social and historical processes occur within language." This phenomenon may be nowhere more evident in the present day than in this word *technology*. As a word that most of us refer to with great frequency, and as one that we now read about just about everywhere, technology is one of those words that, as Eric Schatzberg comments in his essay in this chapter, quickly begins to "mean everything and nothing." And yet the importance of this word and how it is used cannot be overlooked. As Leo Marx comments in his essay in this chapter, "such keywords often serve as markers, or chronological sign-posts, of subtle, virtually unremarked, yet ultimately far-reaching changes in culture and society." That the meanings of words may be unstable and important is both reassuring and disturbing news for writers. Such a state reflects the potential power of writing as much as it reflects many of the problems associated with it. The fact that this word *technology* is one that can mean and refer to so many different things is certainly part and parcel of why there is so much to say, and to write, about it.

All the writers in this chapter are interested in considering the many different things that technology is and has been—both as a word and as a concept—and how these definitions relate to and help us to understand technology's relationships with culture and society. Professor of Science, Technology, and Society Thomas P. Hughes reminds us of the many complications involved in defining *technology* and how it did not emerge as a term for describing the mechanic arts until the middle of the twentieth century. Posing the question outright in his essay "What Is Technology?" academic Eric Schatzberg looks at definitions of the word in both popular and scholarly usage and the relationships between the two. Journalist Sarah

Murray explores how Millennials, or the generation born after 1980, currently assess the impact of communications technologies on culture and society. Historian of Science and Technology Leo Marx proposes that the concept of technology itself, even more than the lethal weapons and bombs made from various technologies, may be hazardous. Futurist Kevin Kelly compares technology to a living organism and defines it as an entity with its own desires in his article "What Technology Wants." Finally, media theorist and cultural critic Neil Postman reflects on the "Five Things We Need to Know About Technological Change" in an essay that considers the ways and means in which technology always simultaneously "giveth" and "taketh away."

Thomas P. Hughes
"Defining Technology"

Thomas P. Hughes is Mellon Professor of the History and Sociology of Science, Emeritus at the University of Pennsylvania. He is also Visiting Professor at the Massachusetts Institute of Technology and Stanford University. He has been writing, thinking, and teaching courses about technology for several decades. With a background in history and engineering, his writings on technology combine both scholarly and practical perspectives. He is the author of dozens of books and articles, including *Rescuing Prometheus* (Pantheon, 1998); *American Genesis* (Penguin 1990), which was a Pulitzer Prize finalist; and *Lewis Mumford: Public Intellectual* (Oxford University Press 1990), which he edited with Agatha Hughes. The following essay is excerpted from his most recent book, *Human-Built World: How to Think About Technology and Culture* (Chicago 2004). In this essay, Hughes explores the complexity involved in defining *technology* and considers the relationships between the history of the word and its use in contemporary society.

What does the word *technology* mean to you? What are your sources for this definition?

Defining technology in its complexity is as difficult as grasping the essence of politics. Few experienced politicians and political scientists attempt to define politics. Few experienced practitioners, historians, and social scientists try to inclusively define technology. Usually, technology and politics are defined by countless examples taken from the present and past. In the case of technology, it is usually presented in a context of usage, such as communications, transportation, energy, or production.

The word "technology" came into common use during the twentieth century, especially after World War II. Before then, the "practical arts," "applied science," and "engineering" were commonly used to designate what today is usually called technology. The *Oxford English Dictionary* finds the word "technology" being used as early as the seventeenth century, but then mostly to designate a discourse or treatise on the industrial or practical arts. In the nineteenth century, it designated the practical arts collectively.

> "Defining technology in its complexity is as difficult as grasping the essence of politics."

In 1831 Jacob Bigelow, a Harvard professor, used the word in the title of his book *Elements of Technology . . . on the Application of the Sciences to the Useful Arts.* He remarked that the word could be found in some older dictionaries and was beginning to be used by practical men. He used "technology" and the "practical arts" almost interchangeably, but distinguished them by associating technology with the application of science to the practical, or useful, arts. For him, technology involved not only artifacts, but also the processes that bring them into being. These processes involve invention and human ingenuity. In contrast, for Bigelow, the sciences consisted of discovered principles, ones that exist independently of humans. The sciences are discovered, not invented.

I also see technology as a creative process involving human ingenuity. Emphasis upon making, creativity, and ingenuity can be traced back to *teks,* an Indo-European root of the word "technology." *Teks* meant to fabricate or to weave. In the Greek, *tektōn* referred to a carpenter or builder and *tekhnē* to an art, craft, or skill. All of these early meanings suggest a process of making, even of creation. In the Middle Ages, the mechanical arts of weaving, weapon making, navigation, agriculture, and hunting involved building, fabrication, and other productive activities, not simply artifacts.

5   Landscape architect Anne Whiston Spirn's definition of landscape in *The Granite Garden: Urban Nature and Human Design* (1984) suggests a

way of thinking about technology. For her, landscape connects people and a place, and it involves the shaping of the land by people and people by the land. The land is not simply scenery; it is both the natural, or the given, and the human-built. It includes buildings as well as trees, rocks, mountains, lakes, and seas. I see technology as a means to shape the landscape.

As noted, "technology" was infrequently used until the late twentieth century. When a group of about twenty American historians and social scientists formed the Society for the History of Technology in 1958, they debated whether the society should be known by the familiar word "engineering" or the unfamiliar one "technology." They decided upon the latter, believing "technology," though the less used and less well-defined term, to be a more inclusive term than "engineering," an activity that it subsumes.

So historians of technology today are applying the word to activities and things in the past not then known as technology, but that are similar to activities and things in the present that are called technology. For example, machines in the nineteenth century and mills in the medieval period are called technology today, but they were not so designated by contemporaries, who called them simply machines and mills.

In 1959 the Society for the History of Technology began publication of a quarterly journal entitled *Technology and Culture*. The bewildering variety of things and systems referred to as technology in the journal's first two decades reveals technology's complex character. Rockets, steam and internal combustion engines, machine tools, textiles, computers, telegraphs, telephones, paper, telemetry, photography, radio, metals, weapons, chemicals, land transport, production systems, agricultural machines, water transport, tools, and instruments all appear as technology in the journal's pages. Yet the various kinds of technology noted in *Technology and Culture* have a common denominator—most can be associated with the creative activities, individual and collective, of craftsmen, mechanics, inventors, engineers, designers, and scientists. By limiting technology to their creative activities, I can avoid an unbounded definition that would include, say, the technology of cooking and coaching, as widespread as they may be.

Having taught the history of technology for decades and having faced the difficulties of defining it in detail, I have resorted to an overarching definition, one that covers how I use the term generally. I see technology as craftsmen, mechanics, inventors, engineers, designers, and scientists using tools, machines, and knowledge to create and control a human-built world consisting of artifacts and systems associated mostly with the traditional fields of civil, mechanical, electrical, mining, materials, and chemical engineering. In the twentieth and twenty-first centuries, however, the artifacts and systems also become associated with newer fields of engineering, such as aeronautical, industrial, computer, and environmental engineering, as well as bioengineering.

10   Besides seeing technology associated with engineering, I also consider it being used as a tool and as a source of symbols by many architects and artists. This view of technology allows me to stress the aesthetic dimensions of technology, which unfortunately have been neglected in the training of engineers, scientists, and others engaged with technology.

My background helps explain why I have chosen a definition emphasizing creativity and control. Before earning a Ph.D. in modern European history, I received a degree in mechanical and electrical engineering. In the 1950s, I found engineering and related technology at their best to be creative endeavors. Not uncritical of their social effects, I still considered them potentially a positive force and expressed a tempered enthusiasm for them and their practitioners.

Since then, I have learned about the Janus face of technology from counterculture critics, environmentalists, and environmental historians. Yet the traces of my enthusiasm still come through in my publications, especially this one. Hence my defining technology as a creative activity, hence my willingness to sympathetically portray those who have seen technology as evidence of a divine spark, and hence my interest in those who consider the machine a means to make a better world. Yet this sympathetic view is qualified by what I have learned from critics of technology.

Analyze

1. Hughes begins his essay by writing, "defining technology in its complexity is as difficult as grasping the essence of politics." Explain the difficulties involved in defining politics. How might these relate to the complications involved in defining technology? How apt is this comparison? What may such a comparison suggest about the various ways in which technology is defined and discussed?

2. According to Hughes, why was the word *technology* infrequently used until the late twentieth century?

3. Who is Anne Whiston Spirn? What are some of the reasons why Hughes mentions her definition of landscape in his essay?

Explore

1. How much have you thought about this word *technology*? What was your definition of it prior to reading Hughes's essay? Has your definition changed after reading this essay? Why or why not? Write one paragraph in response to each question.

2. In your own words, and based on what you have learned from this essay, write your own working definition of *technology* using the one Hughes presents near the end of his essay as a model.

3. At the end of his essay, Hughes refers to the "Janus face of technology." If you are not familiar with what this reference to the Roman god Janus means, look it up. In one or two paragraphs reflect on how Janus relates to the issues Hughes raises in relation to defining technology and his discussion of technology.

Eric Schatzberg
"What Is Technology?"

Eric Schatzberg is Professor of History of Science at the University of Wisconsin–Madison and Director of the Robert F. & Jean E. Holtz Center for Science and Technology Studies. He is working on a book on the history of the word *technology* and is using his blog, "Rethinking Technology" (http://rethinktechnology.wordpress.com/), as a place to explore and write about ideas related to this book. Offering readers some context for why he is writing a book about just one word, Schatzberg explains that while "Everyone knows that technology is an ubiquitous concept of our late-modern age . . . the term is also vague and poorly understood." In this essay, originally published as a blog post, Schatzberg discusses the diverse and sometimes contradictory meanings of the word to draw attention to the importance of its history and current status, as well as "to challenge the way the term gets used to obscure the role of conscious human choice in shaping our material culture."

What are some of the ways you use the word *technology* in your everyday life? Does this word always mean the same thing when you use it?

I'm writing a history of the concept of *technology*. (I use the convention of italicizing *technology* when talking about the term itself rather than what the term refers to in the world.) Why am I writing a book about one word? Well, most people would agree it's a pretty important word, central to the discourse of late modernity. As this Google Ngram shows, in frequency *technology* has become as important as science.

But frequency doesn't tell the whole story. *Technology* is a word that mystifies as much as it explains. In the memorable words of the online comic strip character Strong Bad, "the word technology means magic. It's basically anything that's really cool that you don't know how it works. And if it breaks, you have to buy a new one."

This is parody, of course. It works because Strong Bad captures how most people indeed relate to what we think of as *technology*. But this relationship expresses a deep irony. In one of its core meanings, *technology* is the epitome of rational human activity, what philosophers call "instrumental action," use of the most effective means to achieve a given end. (I'll be critiquing this definition of *technology* in my book, but that's a subject for a future post.) Yet to most users, the products of this rational action are as mysterious as transubstantiation of the Eucharist into the body of Christ.

That's just one example of how messed up the concept of *technology* is. But it's not an isolated example. In both popular and scholarly usage, the meanings of *technology* are deeply contradictory, almost perversely so. The concept embraces ideas and things, the recent and the ancient, everything and therefore nothing. One leading reference work in the 1950s defined *technology* unhelpfully as "how things are commonly done or made,"

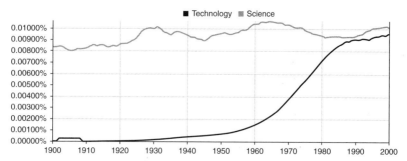

Figure 1.1   A Google Ngram showing the frequency of the words "technology" and "science" used in publicly searchable documents.

a definition that could apply to every form of human activity, from prayer to defecation. In contrast, popular usage limits *technology* primarily to digital electronics. This usage is common in elite discourse too, for example "instructional technology," which refers almost exclusively to educational use of digital tools. Similarly, the "technology" web page of the *New York Times* describes itself as covering "the Internet, telecommunications, wireless applications, electronics, science, computers, e-mail and the Web" (this is in metadata). But if we limit *technology* to digital devices, the term would be useless for explaining the role of machines, tools, skills, practical knowledge, and related theories in shaping human history.

Is this a problem? It is if we take *technology* seriously as a concept for   5 understanding our modern world.

Analyze

1. Why does Schatzberg include the Google Ngram in his article? How does it relate to and support the argument he presents?
2. What examples does Schatzberg give to illustrate the ways in which various meanings of the word *technology* are "deeply contradictory"?
3. Explain why Schatzberg asserts that limiting technology to digital devices is a problem if we are to fully understand the meanings of this term *technology*.
4. Schatzberg employs a religious metaphor in this essay. Is this effective in supporting the points he is making regarding technology and magic and how difficult the word *technology* is to define? Why or why not? What are some other images he could have used to make this point? Explain why these images would have been more or less effective.

Explore

1. Look up the word *technology* in two different dictionaries, for instance *Merriam-Webster's* and *Dictionary.com*. Transcribe the definitions, making sure to cite your sources. Then, look up and carefully read the "Definition and usage" section for the entry on "Technology" on *Wikipedia*. What similarities exist across these entries? What differences? In a short essay, explain how and in what ways each entry and the differences amongst them relate to several key points made by Schatzberg in his essay.

2. Review the headlines on the current NYTimes.com "Technology" section (http://www.nytimes.com/pages/technology/index.html). Make two lists: one of five to ten technologies listed and a second of the sociocultural and economic issues being written about in relation to these technologies. Based on these lists, write your own definition of technology. Working with two or three of your classmates, compare and contrast the definitions each of you have developed. Then, discuss how these definitions relate to several issues discussed in Schatzberg's essay.

3. In the course of one day, make a note of every time you either use or hear the word *technology*, keeping track of when, where, and in what context the word comes up. Analyze the data you've collected. In what ways are the uses of this word similar or different? Is it possible to place the different uses of the word into categories? What might these be? Spend ten minutes free writing about your findings. Then, write a one-page analysis of the different uses and categories associated with this word.

Sarah Murray
"Transition: Technology Puts Power in the Hands of Many"

Sarah Murray is a writer and journalist whose work focuses on sustainable development and the relationships among business, society, and the environment. Her articles cover a range of topics, including environmental sustainability, technology, and international development. You can access and read more of her articles on her website, http://sarahmurray.info/journalism/. In this essay, Murray reviews the findings of several recent surveys of "Millennials," or the generation born since 1980, to discuss the ways in which technology relates to this generation's current perspectives on social relations and economics.

In what ways have the use of online tools and smart devices affected your own social, professional, and economic outlook?

Few "millennials"—or the generation aged between 18 and 33—can remember a time when technology has not been a fundamental part of their lives. Not only does it answer their questions, but, through social media, it also gives them the ability to alter the way in which they are perceived by their peers and the greater world around them. Online tools and smart devices have empowered the generation born since 1980 in a way few previous technologies have done.

"Technology has played a huge role in how they're different from the generation that came before them," says Jean Case, chief executive of the Case Foundation, which she and her husband Steve Case, AOL's co-founder, created in 1997.

This generation sees technology as leveling the playing field. In the FT-Telefónica Global Millennials Survey of 18- to 30-year olds almost 70 per cent of respondents said "technology creates more opportunities for all" as opposed to "a select few."

This belief has brought tremendous confidence to the world's first generation of digital natives, despite facing the worst economic outlook since the great depression.

"We have all these incredible gadgets that connect us to the world," says   5
Paul Taylor, executive vice-president of the Pew Research Centre and director of its Social & Demographic Trends project. "But for them, it's the wallpaper of their lives and it allows them to place themselves at the centre of the universe."

With a Facebook page or a Twitter presence, millennials can broadcast their views, ideas and creative output globally—and potentially find an audience of millions. "That is enormously empowering," says Mr. Taylor. "That, as much as anything, contributes to their confidence."

While technology might help them feel at the centre of the universe, its ability to connect millennials to other communities across the world has also created in many a desire to help solve big global problems. "They're idealists and their level of engagement with the things they care about is extraordinary," says Ms. Case. She cites research the foundation conducted revealing that millennials want to do more than simply give to causes they care about. Some 44 per cent wanted to know how their donations were used and 41 per cent, when giving, also wanted to know about volunteer opportunities.

"This is a different level of engagement from young people than we've traditionally seen," she says.

Again, technology is playing a role. Supporting this philanthropic impulse are non-profit websites that match charities with volunteers or allow donors to track small donations and receive feedback from recipients. Meanwhile, the sense of how millennials can contribute as individuals is increasing as traditional ways of working are eroded and technology replaces not just manual labour but also intellectual capital.

10   "Artificial intelligence, algorithms and the web mean that all the repetitive jobs are going away," says Bill Drayton, founder of Ashoka, the social entrepreneurship organization. "The new value is in contributing to change." Millennials' belief in their ability to effect change varies across the world. The Telefónica survey found Latin Americans had the strongest sense that they could make a difference globally, at 62 per cent, compared with 40 per cent of all respondents.

This belief increases when considering their own environment, with 62 per cent of all surveyed saying they could make a difference locally.

What this highlights is a shift in the way leadership is viewed. Millennials' trust in traditional institutions and leaders is declining. More than half the respondents did not think governments reflected their beliefs and values. Instead, they put more faith in the wisdom of the crowd, accessed via social media. Millennials trust each other and turn to their peers when they have questions to answer. "There's a two-way connection and anyone can talk to anyone in the world," says Mr. Taylor.

Yet the confidence and connectivity that technology has brought this generation can also be accompanied by stresses and doubts.

"The old model of organisation, where a few people choreograph what everyone else does is failing and instead you have fluid, open architecture with synapses running in every direction," says Mr. Drayton. This means that, to survive and thrive, millennials believe they must rely less on institutions and more on themselves and their peers.

15   One thing that may help millennials navigate this new fluid, open environment is that, as a 2010 Pew Research Centre study revealed, they are more receptive to change than older generations.

The study, which polled millennials in the US, found them more tolerant of immigrants than their elders, with almost 6-in-10 saying that immigrants strengthened the country.

While religious extremism is on the rise among young people in certain communities, many are more religiously tolerant than their elders, with

76 per cent of those polled by Telefónica saying they were open to religions and beliefs outside their own.

Mr. Taylor sees this particularly at work among US millennials, among whom attitudes to interracial marriage and sexual identity are changing rapidly. "In the US, one thing that's notable is their acceptance of diversity," he says. "There's a lot of social change that's connected to this generation."

Of course, for the millions of young people without jobs, any tolerance, openness and confidence in their ability to effect change is tempered by the grim prospect of being unable to make the transition from school to the workplace or to afford to buy a home or eventually retire.

Given the growing gaps in employment prospects and wealth levels   20 among young people worldwide, differences in attitude between the haves and have-nots are likely to increase, too.

However, given the millennials' desire to help solve problems, they may well play a prominent role in building a more stable economy and an equitable society.

Ms Case is optimistic. "These people will change the world, and they have opportunities to do that," she says. "We have a segment being left behind. But I'm hoping that the generation with the opportunities will pay attention to their peers without."

What the youth have to say:
Nicholas Davies, 23, Student Official, United Kingdom

> "While recession has had a huge effect on the number and range of   25
> jobs available to graduates, that is no reason to be pessimistic about
> the future. I will always strive for my ideal future, and persistence
> will get me there one day."

Pablo Rodríguez Sánchez, 27, Communications Co-ordinator, Mexico

> "Our generation today faces a void: our governments have failed us;
> companies have failed us too. We have a crisis of credibility towards
> institutions. We have come to realise we are the protagonists of the
> 21st century. Our generation is starting to wake up and create the
> solutions of our own problems."

Oghenefego Isikwenu, 29, Consultant, Kenya

> "My future will be much better than that of my parents' generation thanks to better education. An innovative group of young Africans are actively involved in making a positive impact in their fields. But security is a big concern. With unemployment increasing more young people have no option but to go into crime."

30   Dana Sobh, 19, Student, Lebanon

> "The future seems a little intimidating. You can't tell whether the actions of today are leading to success or destruction. I'm constantly haunted by thoughts such as 'Did I choose the right career path?' However, the economic climate might get better by the time I graduate."

Analyze

1. Write a one-paragraph summary of Murray's article.
2. What is Murray's argument? What claims does she use to support her thesis?
3. One key finding that Murray reports is that "This generation sees technology as leveling the playing field." What does she include as being part of this "leveling"? From your perspective, is leveling one of the effects technology has had in society? Why or why not?
4. Take another look at the end of the article, where Murray includes quotes from youth around the world. What do you notice about these? What are some common threads that run through them? If you were to add your own quotation to this list, what would you say?

Explore

1. Murray proposes that "Online tools and smart devices have empowered the generation born since 1980 in a way few previous technologies have done." Write one page reflecting on whether and how this has been your experience. Then, write one page considering whether, based on this reflection, you agree with Murray.

2. One of the reports referenced in the article is the FT-Telefónica Global Millennials Survey (http://survey.telefonica.com/survey-findings/). You can read this and other surveys related to the article, including "The Social Side of the Internet" (http://casefoundation.org/topic/social-media/publications?page=1) on the Internet. Locate one of these surveys or reports. Summarize what you've read and then compare that to Murray's claims based on the same study. Is your reading of this survey or study the same as Murray's or different? Write a short essay reflecting those similarities and differences.

3. Research one of the following devices—telegraph, telephone, or radio—and the effects it had on young people when it came into common use. Write a letter to Murray explaining your findings and how she might incorporate this historical perspective into a future article.

Leo Marx
"Technology: The Emergence of a Hazardous Concept"

Leo Marx is Senior Lecturer and Kenan Professor of American Cultural History Emeritus in the Massachusetts Institute of Technology's Program in Science, Technology, and Society (STS). His work, which has been foundational to the field of STS worldwide, examines the relationship between technology and culture in nineteenth- and twentieth-century America. He is the author of *The Machine in the Garden: Technology and the Pastoral Ideal in America* (1964); *The Pilot and the Passenger: Essays on Literature, Technology, and Culture in America* (1988); editor (with Merritt Roe Smith) of *Does Technology Drive History? The Dilemma of Technological Determinism* (1994); and editor (with Bruce Mazlish) of *Progress: Fact or Illusion?* (1996). In this excerpt from a longer essay, Marx reviews the history of the term *technology* and its meanings in contemporary culture and society.

Have you ever thought of technology as hazardous? Why or why not?

New Concepts as Historical Markers

The history of technology is one of those subjects that most people know more about than they realize. Long before the academy recognized it as a specialized field of scholarly inquiry, American schools were routinely disseminating a sketchy outline of that history to millions of pupils. We learned about James Watt and the steam engine, Eli Whitney and the cotton gin, and about other great inventors and their inventions. Even more important, we were led to assume that innovation in the mechanic arts is a—perhaps the—driving force of human history. The theme was omnipresent in my childhood experience. I met it in the graphic charts and illustrations in my copy of *The Book of Knowledge*, a popular children's encyclopedia, and in the alluring dioramas of Early Man in the New York Museum of Natural History. These exhibits represented the advance of civilization as a sequence of the inventions in the mechanic arts with which *Homo sapiens* gained a unique power over nature. This comforting theme remains popular today and is insinuated by all kinds of historical narrative. Here, for example, is a passage from an anthropological study of apes and the origins of human violence:

> Our own ancestors from this line [of woodland apes] began shaping stone tools and relying much more consistently on meat around 2 million years ago. They tamed fire perhaps 1.5 million years ago. They developed human language at some unknown later time, perhaps 150,000 years ago. They invented agriculture 10,000 years ago. They made gunpowder around 1,000 years ago, and motor vehicles a century ago.[2]

This typical summary of human history from stone age tools to Ford cars illustrates the shared "scientific" understanding, circa 2010, of the history of technology. But one arresting if scarcely noted aspect of the story is the belated emergence of the word used to name the very rubric—the kind of thing—that allegedly drives our history. The word is *technology*. The fact is that during all but the very last few seconds, as it were, of the ten millennia of recorded human history encapsulated in this account, the concept of technology—as we know it today—did not exist. The word *technology*,

"… the essence of technology is by no means anything technological."
—Martin Heidegger[1]

which joined the Greek root, *techne* (an art or craft) with the suffix *ology* (a branch of learning), first entered the English language in the seventeenth century. At that time, in keeping with its etymology, a technology was a branch of learning, or discourse, or treatise concerned with the mechanic arts. As Eric Schatzberg has demonstrated in a seminal essay, the word then referred to a field of study, not an object of study.[3] But the word, even in that now archaic sense, was a rarity in nineteenth-century America. By 1861, to be sure, it was accorded a somewhat greater prominence by the founders of the Massachusetts Institute of Technology, but they also were invoking the limited sense of the term to mean higher technical education. As for technology in the now familiar sense of the word—the mechanic arts collectively—it did not catch on in America until around 1900, when a few influential writers, notably Thorstein Veblen and Charles Beard, responding to German usage in the social sciences, accorded technology a pivotal role in shaping modern industrial society. But even then, the use of the word remained largely confined to academic and intellectual circles; it did not gain truly popular currency until the 1930s.

But why, one might ask, is the history of this word important? The answer, from the viewpoint of a cultural historian, is that the emergence of a keyword in public discourse—whether a newly coined word or an old word invested with new meaning—may prove to be an illuminating historical event. Such keywords often serve as markers, or chronological signposts, of subtle, virtually unremarked, yet ultimately far-reaching changes in culture and society. Recall, for example, Alexis de Tocqueville's tacit admission, in *Democracy in America*, that in order to do his subject justice he was compelled to coin the (French) word *individualisme*, "a novel expression to which a novel idea has given birth"; or Raymond Williams's famous discovery, in writing *Culture and Society*, of the striking interdependence (or reflexivity) in the relations between certain keywords and fundamental changes in society and culture. Williams had set out to examine the transformation of culture coincident with the advent of industrial capitalism in Britain, but he found that the concept of culture itself, along with such other pivotal concepts of the era as class, industry, democracy, and art, was a product of—indeed had been invested with its new meaning by—the very changes he proposed to analyze. Not only had those changes lent currency to the concept of culture, but they had simultaneously changed its meaning. I believe that a similar process marked the emergence of technology as a keyword in the lexicon we rely on to chart the changing character of contemporary society and culture.[4]

But how, then, are we to identify the specific changes that prompted the emergence of technology—the concept, the word, the purported thing itself? My assumption is that those changes, whatever they were, created a semantic—indeed, a conceptual—void, which is to say, an awareness of certain novel developments in society and culture for which no adequate name had yet become available. It was this void, presumably, that the word *technology*, in its new and extended meaning, eventually would fill. It would prove to be preferable—a more apt signifier—for the new agents of change than any of its precursors, received terms such as the mechanic (or useful or practical or industrial) arts, or invention, improvement, machine, machinery, or mechanism. In a seminal essay of 1829, Thomas Carlyle had posed a variant of my question: if one had to sum up the oncoming age in a word, he asked, what might it be? His unequivocal answer was: machinery. "It is the Age of Machinery," he wrote, "in every outward and inward sense of that word."[5] During the next half century, however, machinery—like the alternatives just mentioned—turned out to be unsuitable. But why? Why did technology prove to be preferable? To answer the question, we need to identify the specific character of the concurrent changes in the mechanic arts—not only the changes within those arts, but also the changes in the interrelations between them and the rest of society and culture.

5   As for the hazardous character of the concept of technology, here I need only say that I am not thinking about weaponry or the physical damage wrought by the use of any particular technologies. The hazards I have in mind are conceptual, not physical. They stem from the meanings conveyed by the concept technology itself, and from the peculiar role it enables us to confer on the mechanic arts as an ostensibly discrete entity—one capable of becoming a virtually autonomous, all-encompassing agent of change.

NOTES

1. Martin Heidegger, *The Question Concerning Technology and Other Essays,* trans. William Lovett (New York, 1977), 4.

2. Richard Wrangham and Dale Peterson, *Demonic Males: Apes and the Origins of Human Violence* (New York, 1996), 61.

3. Erik Schatzberg, "Technik Comes to America: Changing Meanings of Technology before 1930," *Technology and Culture* 47 (2006): 486–512. The first use of the amplified sense of the word, referring to the mechanic arts themselves, according to the *Oxford English Dictionary* (OED), was in 1859; variants of the older meaning of technology—e.g., technik, technique, etc.—also

had appeared in German, Swedish, French, and Spanish in the late eighteenth century.

4. Alexis de Tocqueville, *Democracy in America*, trans. Phillips Bradley (New York, 1946), II:98 (the OED credits the Henry Reeve translation of 1835 with the first use of the word in English); Raymond Williams, *Culture and Society, 1780–1950* (New York: 1983), xiii–xviii; *Keywords: A Vocabulary of Culture and Society* (New York, 1985), 11–26 and 315–16.

5. Thomas Carlyle, "Signs of the Times," *Edinburgh Review* (1829), reprinted in *Selected Writings*, ed. Alan Shelston (New York, 1971), 64. Carlyle, incidentally, is credited with the first use of the word *industrialism*, in *Sartor Resartus* (1831).

Analyze

1. Explain the reasons why Marx believes that "the history of technology is one of those subjects that people know more about than they realize."

2. According to Marx, why is the history of a word important? Why might the history of the word *technology* be particularly important to understanding it as a term and concept?

3. Marx's essay is written for an academic audience. What are some terms he uses that are directed toward such an audience? List five of these terms and look up their definitions. Has your understanding of the passage in which these terms appeared changed based on your increased understanding of these terms? Explain why or why not this is the case.

4. Near the end of the essay, Marx comments on the differences between the terms *machinery* and *technology*. Explain why and how he distinguishes these two words. What connotations does each one of these words have for you?

Explore

1. Marx begins his essay by explaining that throughout his early education, he was taught that the mechanic arts were a "driving force" in human history. Were you likewise taught this? If yes, describe some specific instances and examples of such teaching. If not, what were you taught about the mechanic arts? How does what you were taught differ from what Marx was taught?

2. Marx claims that human power over nature is "insinuated by all kinds of historical narrative," including the very brief narrative cited in his article. Explain how, in the narrative quoted, human domination over nature is expressed explicitly and implicitly. Some of the issues you may want to look at include word choice, selection of evidence, and paragraph structure.

3. Epigraphs can have several different functions in essays, and Marx's use of the German philosopher Martin Heidegger's writing on technology as an epigraph to his essay fulfills several: to give a very brief introduction to the argument of the essay, to establish that the author has done his research in the field, and to place one work in dialogue with another. In a short essay, explain your understanding and interpretation of the epigraph and how Marx's argument relates to it. At the end of your essay, explain why, given the choice to select an epigraph for the essay, you would select the current epigraph or some other one that you believe would better reflect and illustrate the arguments presented in the essay.

4. What you've read is an excerpt from a longer essay. Find the complete essay either on the Internet or in a library database and read the rest of it. Create an outline of how Marx's essay is structured. In a two- or three-page essay, explain how the ideas introduced in this excerpt relate to those discussed later in the article.

Kevin Kelly
"What Technology Wants"

Kevin Kelly is the founding executive editor of *Wired* magazine and a former editor/publisher of *The Whole Earth Catalog*. A journalist and blogger, he is a frequent contributor to several publications, including *Edge*, an online publication that gathers and publishes the views of leading cultural critics, artists, and academics on topics related to culture, society, and technology. Although originally written as a blog post, the following essay, "What Technology Wants," was later published as part of Kelly's 2011 book of the same title. A longtime resident of Silicon Valley, Kelly's views are often seen as being informed by the concerns not only of futurists, but also of entrepreneurs and business leaders. In this essay, Kelly proposes that it is time we started to understand the wants and needs of technology itself.

Do you believe that technology can want things? Why or why not?

Your dog wants to go outside. Your cat wants to be scratched. Birds want mates. Worms want moisture. Bacteria want food.

The wants of a microscopic single-celled organism are less than the wants of you or me, but all organisms share a few fundamental desires: to survive, to grow. The wants of a protozoan are unconscious, unarticulated, and more like an urge, or even tendency. A bacterium tends to drift toward nutrients with no awareness of its needs. There is no room beneath its membrane for a will as we know it, yet in a dim way it chooses to satisfy its wants by heading one way and not another.

Perhaps not much room is needed to want. The astrophysicist Freeman Dyson claims that we should view the smallest known bits of organized matter—quantum particles—as making choices. For millions of years a particle will exist and then suddenly it decays. Why then? Dyson says that from the individual particle's viewpoint, this moment can only look like a choice, a satisfaction of a want. It is only on the scale of statistics with millions of particles that a particle's choice shapes up as a predictable radiation half-life. But even individual human wants and desires average out to weirdly predictable laws in aggregate.

If a little one-celled protozoan—a very small package—can have a choice, if a flea has urges, if a starfish has a bias towards certain things, if a mouse can want, then so can the growing, complexifying technological assemblage we have surrounded ourselves with. Its complexity is approaching the complexity of a microscopic organism. This tissue consists (so far) of billions of dwellings, millions of factories, billions of hectares of land modified by plant and animal breeding, trillion of motors, thousands of dammed rivers and artificial lakes, hundreds of millions of automobiles coursing along like cells, a quadrillion computer chips, millions of miles of wire, and it consumes 16 terawatts of power.

None of these parts operate independently. No mechanical system can function by itself. Each bit of technology requires the viability and growth of all the rest of technology to keep going. There is no communication

5

without the nerves of electricity. There is no electricity without the veins of coal mining, uranium mining, or damming of rivers, or even the mining of precious metals to make solar panels. There is no metabolism of factories without the ingest of food from domesticated plants and animals, and no circulation of goods without vehicles. This global-scaled network of systems, subsystems, machines, pipes, roads, wires, conveyor belts, automobiles, servers and routers, institutions, laws, calculators, sensors, works of art, archives, activators, collective memory, and power generators—this whole grand system of interrelated and interdependent pieces forms a very primitive organism-like system. Call it the technium.

The technium is the sphere of visible technology and intangible organizations that form what we think of as modern culture. It is the current accumulation of all that humans have created. For the last 1,000 years, this technosphere has grown about 1.5% per year. It marks the difference between our lives now, versus 10,000 years ago. Our society is as dependent on this technological system as nature itself. Yet, like all systems it has its own agenda. Like all organisms the technium also wants.

To head off any confusion, the technium is not conscious (at this point). Its wants are not deliberations, but rather tendencies. Leanings. Urges. Trajectories. By the nature of self-reinforcing feedback loops, any large system will tend to lean in certain directions more than others. The sum total of millions of amplifying relationships, circuits, and networks of influence is to push the total in one direction more than another. Every owner of a large complicated machine can appreciate this tendency. Your machine will "want" to stall in certain conditions, or want to "run away" in others. Left to its own devices, complex systems will gravitate to specific states. In mathematical terms this is called the convergence upon "strange attractors"—sort of gravity wells that pull in a complex system toward this state no matter where it starts.

Of course we humans want certain things from the technium, but at the same time there is an inherent bias in the technium outside of our wants. Beyond our desires, there is a tendency within the technium that—all other things being equal—favors certain solutions. Technology will head in certain directions because physics, mathematics, and realities of innovation constrain possibilities. Imagine other worlds of alien civilizations. Once they discover electricity, their electronics will share some, but not all, attributes with our electrical devices. That which they share can be counted as the inherent agenda of electrical technology. Throughout the galaxy any civilization that invents nuclear power will hit upon a small set of workable solutions: that set is the inherent "agenda" of technology.

It would be wonderful if we could survey all alien technological civilizations to extract the common tendencies in technological growth. A large number of technological evolutions would reveal the culture-free dynamics beneath them all. Since we have a solitary sample of one technium back on Earth, we have fewer methods of unraveling inherent system bias in technology. Three lines of evidence present themselves:

1. We can look back in history to when technological development was more culturally isolated. The pathways of technology in early China, South America, Africa, and Western Europe came about with only minimal cross-over influence. Examination of their parallel developmental sequences can reveal inherent biases.

2. More importantly, the major predecessor system to technology is organic life. Many of the dynamics of evolution and syntropy extend from living organisms into artificial systems, primarily because they share similar disequilibrial states. We can see the direction of technology in the direction of life and evolution (that is if you accept evolution has a bias as I do).

3. The long-term history of our single technium shows high-level patterns which we can project forward. We can ignore individual inventions and chart long-term flows which enable them. Much as we might want the compressed history of a growing creature and guess where it goes next. If the organism is a caterpillar we are out of luck; if it is a worm, it will succeed.

So, looking at the evolution of life and the long-term histories of past technologies, what are the long-term trajectories of the technium? What does technology want?

Possibilities

To increase diversity

To maximize freedom/choices

To expand the space of the possible

Efficiencies

To increase specialization/uniqueness

To increase power density

To increase density of meaning

20   To engage all matter and energy

To reach ubiquity and free-ness

To become beautiful

Complexity

To increase complexity

To increase social co-dependency

25   To increase self-referential nature

To align with nature

Evolvability

To accelerate evolvability

To play the infinite game

In general the long-term bias of technology is to increase the diversity of artifacts, methods, techniques. More ways, more choices. Over time technological advances invent more energy efficient methods, and gravitate to technologies which compress the most information and knowledge into a given space or weight. Also over time, more and more matter on the planet will be touched by technological processes. Also, technologies tend toward ubiquity and cheapness. They also tend towards new levels of complexity (though many will get simpler, too). Over time technologies require more surrounding technologies in order to be discovered and to operate; some technologies become eusocial—a distributed existence—in which they are inert when solitary. In the long run, technology increases the speed at which it evolves and encourages its own means of invention to change. It aims to keep the game of change going.

What this means is that when the future trajectory of a particular field   30
of technology is in doubt, "all things being equal" you can guess several
things about where it is headed:

- The varieties of whatever will increase. Those varieties that give
  humans more free choices will prevail.
- Technologies will start out general in their first version, and spe-
  cialize over time. Going niche will always be going with the flow.
  There is almost no end to how specialized (and tiny) some niches
  can get.
- You can safely anticipate higher energy efficiency, more compact meaning and everything getting smarter.
- All are headed to ubiquity and free. What flips when everyone has
  one? What happens when it is free?
- Any highly evolved form becomes beautiful, which can be its own   35
  attraction.
- Over time the fastest moving technology will become more social,
  more co-dependent, more ecological, more deeply entwined with other
  technologies. Many technologies require scaffolding tech to be born
  first.
- The trend is toward enabling technologies which become tools for in-
  venting new technologies easier, faster, cheaper.
- High tech needs clean water, clean air, reliable energy just as much as
  humans want the same.

These are just some of the things technology wants. We don't always
have to do what technology wants, but I think we need to begin with what
it wants so that we can work with these forces instead of against them.

Analyze

1. What is Kelly's definition of "the technium"? Why is this concept important to his argument?
2. Who is the audience for this essay? What is your basis for making that
   assessment?
3. Kelly makes several analogies between living organisms and technology throughout his essay. Why is this important to his argument?

Explore

1. Kelly's essay appears to represent a view informed by what some critics would call "technological determinism." Look up this phrase and transcribe its definitions from one or more sources. Based on your findings, explain why you agree or disagree that Kelly's views might be described as such.

2. Kelly makes the claim that in assessing the future of "the technium" it may be possible to "ignore individual inventions and chart long-term flows which enable them." And yet, many historians of technology would argue that each and every invention is shaped by social and cultural factors. Do some research on an invention—for instance, the refrigerator. How might this example be used to support or contest Kelly's argument?

3. Near the end of his essay, Kelly makes a comparison between caterpillars and worms. Research the biological differences between caterpillars and worms. Using this research, explain how Kelly uses these two organisms as examples to support his argument.

Neil Postman
"Five Things We Need to Know About Technological Change"

Neil Postman (March 8, 1931–October 5, 2003) was an American author, media theorist, and cultural critic who was a professor in New York University's Steinhardt School of Education. Best known for his 1985 book *Amusing Ourselves to Death*, in which he considers the impact of television on public discourse, he also wrote several other books and articles about education, technology, and relationships between media and communications and sociocultural practices and institutions. Although Postman's writings often address communications technologies that may seem somewhat dated, many critics have noted how applicable many of Postman's findings related to the culture of television are to today's "digital age." In this essay, Postman reflects on the social impact of technology and the things he has learned about technology from being involved in the study of media and communications for many decades.

Has a specific technology changed the way in which you engage in a specific activity or complete a specific task? What have you gained from using this technology? What has been lost?

First Idea

The first idea is that all technological change is a trade-off. I like to call it a Faustian bargain. Technology giveth and technology taketh away. This means that for every advantage a new technology offers, there is always a corresponding disadvantage. The disadvantage may exceed in importance the advantage, or the advantage may well be worth the cost. Now, this may seem to be a rather obvious idea, but you would be surprised at how many people believe that new technologies are unmixed blessings. You need only think of the enthusiasms with which most people approach their understanding of computers. Ask anyone who knows something about computers to talk about them, and you will find that they will, unabashedly and relentlessly, extol the wonders of computers. You will also find that in most cases they will completely neglect to mention any of the liabilities of computers. This is a dangerous imbalance, since the greater the wonders of a technology, the greater will be its negative consequences.

Think of the automobile, which for all of its obvious advantages, has poisoned our air, choked our cities, and degraded the beauty of our natural landscape. Or you might reflect on the paradox of medical technology which brings wondrous cures but is, at the same time, a demonstrable cause of certain diseases and disabilities, and has played a significant role in reducing the diagnostic skills of physicians. It is also well to recall that for all of the intellectual and social benefits provided by the printing press, its costs were equally monumental. The printing press gave the Western world prose, but it made poetry into an exotic and elitist form of communication. It gave us inductive science, but it reduced religious sensibility to a form of fanciful superstition. Printing gave us the modern conception of nationhood, but in so doing turned patriotism into a sordid if not lethal emotion. We might even say that the printing of the Bible in vernacular languages introduced the impression that God was an Englishman or a German or a Frenchman—that is to say, printing reduced God to the dimensions of a local potentate.

Perhaps the best way I can express this idea is to say that the question, "What will a new technology do?" is no more important than the question, "What will a new technology undo?" Indeed, the latter question is more important, precisely because it is asked so infrequently. One might say, then, that a sophisticated perspective on technological change includes one's being skeptical of Utopian and Messianic visions drawn by those who have no sense of history or of the precarious balances on which culture depends. In fact, if it were up to me, I would forbid anyone from talking about the new information technologies unless the person can demonstrate that he or she knows something about the social and psychic effects of the alphabet, the mechanical clock, the printing press, and telegraphy. In other words, knows something about the costs of great technologies.

Idea Number One, then, is that culture always pays a price for technology.

Second Idea

5   This leads to the second idea, which is that the advantages and disadvantages of new technologies are never distributed evenly among the population. This means that every new technology benefits some and harms others. There are even some who are not affected at all. Consider again the case of the printing press in the 16th century, of which Martin Luther said it was "God's highest and extremest act of grace, whereby the business of the gospel is driven forward." By placing the word of God on every Christian's kitchen table, the mass-produced book undermined the authority of the church hierarchy, and hastened the breakup of the Holy Roman See. The Protestants of that time cheered this development. The Catholics were enraged and distraught. Since I am a Jew, had I lived at that time, I probably wouldn't have given a damn one way or another, since it would make no difference whether a pogrom was inspired by Martin Luther or Pope Leo X. Some gain, some lose, a few remain as they were.

Let us take as another example, television, although here I should add at once that in the case of television there are very few indeed who are not affected in one way or another. In America, where television has taken hold more deeply than anywhere else, there are many people who find it a blessing, not least those who have achieved high-paying, gratifying careers in television as executives, technicians, directors, newscasters and entertainers. On the other hand, and in the long run, television may bring an end to the careers of school teachers since school was an invention of the printing press and must stand or fall on the issue of how much importance the printed word will have in the future. There is no chance, of course, that television will go away but school teachers who are enthusiastic about its presence always call to my mind an image of some turn-of-the-century blacksmith who not only is singing the praises of the automobile but who also believes that his business will be enhanced by it. We know now that his business was not enhanced by it; it was rendered obsolete by it, as perhaps an intelligent blacksmith would have known.

The questions, then, that are never far from the mind of a person who is knowledgeable about technological change are these: Who specifically benefits from the development of a new technology? Which groups, what type of person, what kind of industry will be favored? And, of course, which groups of people will thereby be harmed?

These questions should certainly be on our minds when we think about computer technology. There is no doubt that the computer has been and will continue to be advantageous to large-scale organizations like the military or airline companies or banks or tax collecting institutions. And it is equally clear that the computer is now indispensable to high-level researchers in physics and other natural sciences. But to what extent has computer technology been an advantage to the masses of people? To steel workers, vegetable store owners, automobile mechanics, musicians, bakers, bricklayers, dentists, yes, theologians, and most of the rest into whose lives the computer now intrudes? These people have had their private matters made more accessible to powerful institutions. They are more easily tracked and controlled; they are subjected to more examinations, and are increasingly mystified by the decisions made about them. They are more than ever reduced to mere numerical objects. They are being buried by junk mail. They are easy targets for advertising agencies and political institutions.

In a word, these people are losers in the great computer revolution.   10 The winners, which include among others computer companies, multi-national corporations and the nation state, will, of course, encourage the losers to be enthusiastic about computer technology. That is the way of winners, and so in the beginning they told the losers that with personal computers the average person can balance a checkbook more neatly, keep better track of recipes, and make more logical shopping lists. Then they told them that computers will make it possible to vote at home, shop at home, get all the entertainment they wish at home, and thus make community life unnecessary. And now, of course, the winners speak constantly of the Age of Information, always implying that the more information we have, the better we will be in solving significant problems—not only personal ones but large-scale social problems, as well. But how true is this? If there are children starving in the world—and there are—it is not because of insufficient information. We have known for a long time how to produce enough food to feed every child on the planet. How is it that we let so many of them starve? If there is violence on our streets, it is not because we have insufficient information. If women are abused, if divorce and pornography and mental illness are increasing, none of it has anything to do with insufficient information. I dare say it is because something else is missing, and I don't think I have to tell this audience what it is. Who knows? This age of information may turn out to be a curse if we are blinded by it so that we cannot see truly where our problems lie. That is why it is always necessary for us to ask of those who speak enthusiastically of computer technology, why do you do this? What interests do you represent? To whom are you hoping to give power? From whom will you be withholding power?

I do not mean to attribute unsavory, let alone sinister motives to anyone. I say only that since technology favors some people and harms others, these are questions that must always be asked. And so, that there are always winners and losers in technological change is the second idea.

Third Idea

Here is the third. Embedded in every technology there is a powerful idea, sometimes two or three powerful ideas. These ideas are often hidden from our view because they are of a somewhat abstract nature. But this should not be taken to mean that they do not have practical consequences.

Perhaps you are familiar with the old adage that says: To a man with a hammer, everything looks like a nail. We may extend that truism: To a person with a pencil, everything looks like a sentence. To a person with a TV camera, everything looks like an image. To a person with a computer, everything looks like data. I do not think we need to take these aphorisms literally. But what they call to our attention is that every technology has a prejudice. Like language itself, it predisposes us to favor and value certain perspectives and accomplishments. In a culture without writing, human memory is of the greatest importance, as are the proverbs, sayings and songs which contain the accumulated oral wisdom of centuries. That is why Solomon was thought to be the wisest of men. In Kings I we are told he knew 3,000 proverbs. But in a culture with writing, such feats of memory are considered a waste of time, and proverbs are merely irrelevant fancies.

The writing person favors logical organization and systematic analysis, not proverbs. The telegraphic person values speed, not introspection. The television person values immediacy, not history. And computer people, what shall we say of them? Perhaps we can say that the computer person values information, not knowledge, certainly not wisdom. Indeed, in the computer age, the concept of wisdom may vanish altogether.

The third idea, then, is that every technology has a philosophy which is   15
given expression in how the technology makes people use their minds, in what it makes us do with our bodies, in how it codifies the world, in which of our senses it amplifies, in which of our emotional and intellectual tendencies it disregards. This idea is the sum and substance of what the great Catholic prophet Marshall McLuhan meant when he coined the famous sentence, "The medium is the message."

Fourth Idea

Here is the fourth idea: Technological change is not additive; it is ecological. I can explain this best by an analogy. What happens if we place a drop of red dye into a beaker of clear water? Do we have clear water plus a spot of red dye? Obviously not. We have a new coloration to every molecule of water. That is what I mean by ecological change. A new medium does not add something; it changes everything. In the year 1500, after the printing press was invented, you did not have old Europe plus the printing press. You had a different Europe. After television, America was not America plus television. Television gave a new coloration to every political campaign, to every home, to every school, to every church, to every industry, and so on.

That is why we must be cautious about technological innovation. The consequences of technological change are always vast, often unpredictable and largely irreversible. That is also why we must be suspicious of capitalists. Capitalists are by definition not only personal risk takers but, more to the point, cultural risk takers. The most creative and daring of them hope to exploit new technologies to the fullest, and do not much care what traditions are overthrown in the process or whether or not a culture is prepared to function without such traditions. Capitalists are, in a word, radicals. In America, our most significant radicals have always been capitalists—men like Bell, Edison, Ford, Carnegie, Sarnoff, Goldwyn. These men obliterated the 19th century, and created the 20th, which is why it is a mystery to me that capitalists are thought to be conservative. Perhaps it is because they are inclined to wear dark suits and grey ties.

I trust you understand that in saying all this, I am making no argument for socialism. I say only that capitalists need to be carefully watched and disciplined. To be sure, they talk of family, marriage, piety, and honor but if allowed to exploit new technology to its fullest economic potential, they may undo the institutions that make such ideas possible. And here I might just give two examples of this point, taken from the American encounter with technology. The first concerns education. Who, we may ask, has had the greatest impact on American education in this century? If you are thinking of John Dewey or any other education philosopher, I must say you are quite wrong. The greatest impact has been made by quiet men in grey suits in a suburb of New York City called Princeton, New Jersey. There, they developed and promoted the technology known as the standardized test, such as IQ tests, the SATs and the GREs. Their tests redefined what we mean by learning, and have resulted in our reorganizing the curriculum to accommodate the tests.

A second example concerns our politics. It is clear by now that the people who have had the most radical effect on American politics in our time are not political ideologues or student protesters with long hair and copies of Karl Marx under their arms. The radicals who have changed the nature of politics in America are entrepreneurs in dark suits and grey ties who manage the large television industry in America. They did not mean to turn political discourse into a form of entertainment. They did not mean to make it impossible for an overweight person to run for high political office. They did not mean to reduce political campaigning to a 30-second TV commercial. All they were trying to do is to make television into a vast and unsleeping money machine. That they destroyed substantive political discourse in the process does not concern them.

Fifth Idea

I come now to the fifth and final idea, which is that media tend to become   20
mythic. I use this word in the sense in which it was used by the French
literary critic, Roland Barthes. He used the word "myth" to refer to a
common tendency to think of our technological creations as if they were
God-given, as if they were a part of the natural order of things. I have on
occasion asked my students if they know when the alphabet was invented.
The question astonishes them. It is as if I asked them when clouds and trees
were invented. The alphabet, they believe, was not something that was invented. It just is. It is this way with many products of human culture but
with none more consistently than technology. Cars, planes, TV, movies,
newspapers—they have achieved mythic status because they are perceived
as gifts of nature, not as artifacts produced in a specific political and historical context.

When a technology becomes mythic, it is always dangerous because it is
then accepted as it is, and is therefore not easily susceptible to modification
or control. If you should propose to the average American that television
broadcasting should not begin until 5 PM and should cease at 11 PM, or
propose that there should be no television commercials, he will think the
idea ridiculous. But not because he disagrees with your cultural agenda. He
will think it ridiculous because he assumes you are proposing that something in nature be changed; as if you are suggesting that the sun should rise
at 10 AM instead of at 6.

Whenever I think about the capacity of technology to become mythic,
I call to mind the remark made by Pope John Paul II. He said, "Science can
purify religion from error and superstition. Religion can purify science
from idolatry and false absolutes."

What I am saying is that our enthusiasm for technology can turn into a
form of idolatry and our belief in its beneficence can be a false absolute. The
best way to view technology is as a strange intruder, to remember that technology is not part of God's plan but a product of human creativity and
hubris, and that its capacity for good or evil rests entirely on human awareness of what it does for us and to us.

Conclusion

25   And so, these are my five ideas about technological change. First, that we always pay a price for technology; the greater the technology, the greater the price. Second, that there are always winners and losers, and that the winners always try to persuade the losers that they are really winners. Third, that there is embedded in every great technology an epistemological, political or social prejudice. Sometimes that bias is greatly to our advantage. Sometimes it is not. The printing press annihilated the oral tradition; telegraphy annihilated space; television has humiliated the word; the computer, perhaps, will degrade community life. And so on. Fourth, technological change is not additive; it is ecological, which means, it changes everything and is, therefore, too important to be left entirely in the hands of Bill Gates. And fifth, technology tends to become mythic; that is, perceived as part of the natural order of things, and therefore tends to control more of our lives than is good for us.

If we had more time, I could supply some additional important things about technological change but I will stand by these for the moment, and will close with this thought. In the past, we experienced technological change in the manner of sleep-walkers. Our unspoken slogan has been "technology *über alles*," and we have been willing to shape our lives to fit the requirements of technology, not the requirements of culture. This is a form of stupidity, especially in an age of vast technological change. We need to proceed with our eyes wide open so that we may use technology rather than be used by it.

Analyze

1. Postman's first idea is that "all technological change is a trade-off." What specific technologies does he then discuss to explain this idea, and what does he point out about these specific technologies?
2. Postman refers to technology as a "Faustian bargain." Who was Faust, and what is a Faustian bargain?
3. How does Postman define "ecological change" compared to "additive change"? Why does he believe technological change is ecological and not additive?

Explore

1. Although Postman gives concrete examples to support the claims he makes in his discussion of the first and second things that we need to know about technological change, he does not do so for the fourth. Based on your experience, what might be appropriate examples to use in support of his fourth claim? Write a paragraph explaining how each relates to or illustrates the point he is making.

2. Rewrite Postman's five ideas in your own words. Look over them. If you were to present these five ideas, would you choose the order Postman did, or would you order them differently? Explain your rationale for this choice. Would you remove any of the ideas? Why? Would you add any? Why?

3. This essay was originally delivered as a lecture. There are specific attributes of the text as written that reflect this fact. What are they? Do these strengthen or weaken the piece as a written argument? Explain.

4. This talk was delivered in 1998. If Postman were delivering this talk today, what changes might he need to make to it? Explain what some of these changes might be and why they would be necessary.

5. Postman wrote this talk for an audience of engineers in the twentieth century. Rewrite this talk for an audience of your peers in the twenty-first century.

Forging Connections

1. In a short essay, reflect on some of the issues that Hughes, Schatzberg, and/or Marx discuss in relation to definitions of *technology*. What are some of the complications involved in defining this word? Why, according to one or more of these authors, do people often use the word *technology* without fully understanding it? Afterward, reread Murray's essay, and write one or two pages reflecting on how one or two specific issues discussed by Hughes, Schatzberg, and/or Marx are evident in Murray's essay.

2. Both Hughes and Schatzberg are academics, and both of these short essays are examples of academic prose. However, you will notice how different the style and tone of Hughes's piece are from Schatzberg's. Although this difference can be explained in part by differences between the writing style of each author, some of these differences emerge

from the fact that Hughes's essay was published in a book published by an academic press and Schatzberg's essay was published on a blog. What are some particular differences in the tone and writing style of these two pieces? Cite specific examples from both texts to support your claims. What are the advantages and disadvantages of each? Which do you prefer? Why?

3. Unlike Schatzberg, who claims that technology cannot be understood only as information and communications technologies (ICT), Kelly is very comfortable connecting ICT to all other technologies, including transportation, mining, energy generation, and food production. Which view are you more inclined to side with? Why?

4. Invite Marx and Kelly to debate the issues of how technology is defined and how it functions. Using quoted language from their two articles, place the two authors' arguments and the claims used to support them in dialogue. What emerges?

Looking Further

1. Hughes writes at the end of his essay about the "Janus face of technology," referring to the fact that every technology will have both positive and negative consequences. Several other authors in this anthology address this issue (Diane Ravitch, Allan Collins, Kentaro Toyama, Daniel Callahan). Select one of these essays and, in a three- to five-page essay, describe how the "Janus face of technology" relates to the changes—both positive and negative—that technologies promise to bring to education, global development, or health care.

2. In his "second idea" about technological change, Postman writes that "the advantages and disadvantages of new technologies are never distributed evenly among the population." Although Postman describes briefly how this idea relates to specific technologies, he does not discuss the specific advantages and disadvantages that accrue from those technologies. Some other authors in this anthology do. In a short essay, explain how Postman's idea is related to the issues discussed in Kentaro Toyama's essay and in S. Craig Watkins's essay.

2

Imagining Worlds:
Does Science Fiction Inform Our Technological Reality?

If someone mentions the word *technology* in the same breath as the word *literature,* chances are, most people are going to think of the literary genre of science fiction (SF). Although all literature is concerned with technology, there is, in fact, a long history connecting science and technology to the literary genre of SF. Both those who write SF and read SF are often involved in some way with the study of science and technology in the real world. Furthermore, certain scientific and technological inventions were imagined in SF before they became a reality: Jules Verne wrote about underwater and airborne travel long before submarines and airplanes existed, and Martin Cooper, director of research and development at Motorola, often mentions the *Star Trek* communicator as his inspiration for the design of mobile phones in the early 1970s. According to Cooper, a wireless communication device such as that used in the television series "was not fantasy to us" but rather "an objective."

Scientists to this day look to SF to consider what the writer Michio Kaku describes as "the physics of the impossible." However, there are many reasons beyond the shared interests of scientists and SF writers to explain why SF is a unique lens through which to assess definitions and discussions of science and technology. First, by distancing readers from the realities of the day to day, SF enables them to view technologies not as inevitable, as they sometimes can seem, but as an extension of larger sociocultural issues. Then, by posing "what if" questions not only about the future but also, implicitly, about how we are living today, SF allows readers to think through the consequences of technology in a way writing based solely on facts may not.

Mapping, describing, and understanding the relationships between SF and reality is, of course, complex, often even more so than it may be in other genres of literary fiction. As the SF writer and scientist Gregory Benford explains, "Fiction is (let's be frank) lies—beautiful lies, maybe, intoxicating, uplifting, enormously suggestive—but lies, nonetheless. So 'science fiction' is a contradiction. Is it Lies about the Truth? Or the deeper Truth about Lies?" What Benford is drawing attention to is the fact that while the realism found in SF is—like all literary realism—created through a selective combination of fiction and fact, the equation between these two terms and how they function is quite distinct. SF writers create fictional worlds based on an extrapolation of reality and then represent an altered reality in such a manner that readers experience those worlds as realistic. As a result, SF navigates the line between fiction and reality in a manner distinct from other genres of fictional prose.

All of the writers in this chapter are interested in exploring relationships between technology and SF. However, each approaches the question from a slightly different perspective. Robert J. Sawyer proposes that SF may have more to say about science than, at times, science itself does. Neal Stephenson reflects on the possible relationships between SF and technological innovation. Jon Turney argues that stories and narratives may be as much a part of technological artifacts and processes as they are part of SF. In an essay that considers the characteristics of SF as a genre and the unique place of "hard"

SF as a subgenre, Kathryn Cramer reminds us of the unique relationships that exist between the realities of science and the imagined worlds of SF. Damien Broderick looks at today's and yesterday's futures and how technology relates to both. Wendy Lesser, in a review of one of Isaac Asimov's novels, reflects on her own reading of SF and how SF is both part of the age in which it is written and about futures that may come into being much earlier than anyone thought possible. Finally, the physicist Michio Kaku considers not only the relationships between SF and science but the scientific possibilities—and current scientific realities—of the "impossible."

Robert J. Sawyer
"The Purpose of Science Fiction"

Robert J. Sawyer is a Canadian SF writer who is the author of over two dozen novels. The recipient of numerous awards and fellowships, he has been the recipient of the Hugo, Nebula, and Aurora Awards for best SF novel of the year. His most recent novels include *Red Planet Blues: Murder on the Mean Streets of Mars* (2014), *Triggers* (2012), and *Wonder* (2011), the third volume in his critically acclaimed WWW Trilogy. In this essay, Sawyer reflects on the things that SF can teach us and why, at times, it may be able to do so better than real-world science can.

What do you think the purpose of SF is?

M ary Shelley's 1818 novel *Frankenstein, or the Modern Prometheus*, is generally considered the first work of science fiction. It explores, in scientific terms, the notion of synthetic life: Dr. Victor Frankenstein studies the chemical breakdown that occurs after death so he can reverse it to animate nonliving matter. Like so many other works of science fiction that followed, Shelley's story is a cautionary tale: It raises profound questions about who should have the right to create living things and what responsibility the creators should have to their creations and to society.

Think about that: Mary Shelley put these questions on the table almost two centuries ago—41 years before Darwin published *The Origin of Species* and 135 years before Crick and Watson figured out the structure of DNA.

Is it any wonder that Alvin Toffler, one of the first futurists, called reading science fiction the only preventive medicine for future shock?

Isaac Asimov, the great American science fiction writer, defined the genre thus: "Science fiction is the branch of literature that deals with the responses of human beings to changes in science and technology." The societal impact of what is being cooked up in labs is always foremost in the science fiction writer's mind. H.G. Wells grappled with creating chimera life forms in *The Island of Doctor Moreau* (1896), Aldous Huxley gave us a heads-up on modified humans in *Brave New World* (1932), and Michael Crichton's final science-fiction novel, *Next* (2006), brought the issues of gene splicing and recombinant DNA to a mass audience.

"Science fiction is the WikiLeaks of science, getting word to the public about what cutting-edge research really means."

What's valuable about this for societies is that science-fiction writers explore these issues in ways that working scientists simply can't. Some years ago, for a documentary for Discovery Channel Canada, I interviewed neurobiologist Joe Tsien, who had created superintelligent mice in his lab at Princeton—something he freely spoke about when the cameras were off. But as soon as we started rolling, and I asked him about the creation of smarter mice, he made a "cut" gesture. "We can talk about the mice having better memories but not about them being smarter. The public will be all over me if they think we're making animals more intelligent."

5   But science-fiction writers do get to talk about the real meaning of research. We're not beholden to skittish funding bodies and so are free to speculate about the full range of impacts that new technologies might have— not just the upsides but the downsides, too. And we always look at the human impact rather than couching research in vague, nonthreatening terms.

We also aren't bound by nondisclosure agreements, the way so many commercial and government scientists are. Indeed, a year before the first atomic bomb was built, the FBI demanded that the magazine *Astounding Science Fiction* recall its March 1944 issue, which contained a story by Cleve Cartmill detailing how a uranium-fission bomb might be built. Science-fiction writers began the public discourse about the actual effects of nuclear weapons (see for instance Judith Merril's classic 1948 story "That Only a Mother," which deals with gene damage caused by radiation). We also were among the first to weigh in on the dangers of nuclear power (see for example Lester del Rey's 1956 novel *Nerves*). Science fiction is the

WikiLeaks of science, getting word to the public about what cutting-edge research really means.

And we come with the credentials to do this work. Many science-fiction writers, such as Gregory Benford, are working scientists. Many others, such as Joe Haldeman, have advanced degrees in science. Others, like me, have backgrounds in science and technology journalism. Our recent works have tackled such issues as the management of global climate change (Kim Stanley Robinson's *Forty Signs of Rain* and its sequels), biological terrorism (Paolo Bacigalupi's *The Windup Girl*), and the privacy of online information and China's attempts to control its citizens' access to the World Wide Web (my own *WWW:Wake* and its sequels).

Print science-fiction writers often do consulting for government bodies. A group of science-fiction writers called SIGMA frequently advises the Department of Homeland Security about technology issues, and Jack McDevitt and I recently were consulted by NASA about the search for intelligence in the cosmos.

At the core of science fiction is the notion of extrapolation, of asking, "If this goes on, where will it lead?" And, unlike most scientists who think in relatively short time frames—getting to the next funding deadline, or readying a product to bring to market—we think on much longer scales: not just months and years, but decades and centuries.

That said, our job is not to predict the future. Rather, it's to suggest all the possible futures—so that society can make informed decisions about where we want to go. George Orwell's science-fiction classic *Nineteen Eighty-Four* wasn't a failure because the future it predicted failed to come to pass. Rather, it was a resounding success because it helped us prevent that future. Those wishing to get in on the ground floor of discussing where technology is leading us would do well to heed Alvin Toffler's advice by cracking open a good science-fiction book and joining the conversation.

10

Analyze

1. Sawyer mentions Mary Shelley's novel *Frankenstein, or the Modern Prometheus* in the first sentence of his article. Why does he refer to this novel and how does it relate to his larger argument regarding the purpose and importance of SF?

2. How did the writer Isaac Asimov define the genre of SF? How closely does this match Sawyer's definition of the genre?

3. According to Sawyer, what specific constraints do scientists work under that SF writers need not be concerned with?

4. Throughout the article, Sawyer explains the several different ways in which SF writers are involved with science. Make a list of these.

Explore

1. How well does the title of Sawyer's essay represent the content of his essay? In one page, assess the ways in which this title does and does not adequately represent the content of the essay. Afterward, free write about what the article is about and consider some other possible titles that would be appropriate for it.

2. Sawyer makes some very provocative claims in this essay. Briefly summarize his argument and make an outline of the claims he uses to support it. Write a two-page overview of Sawyer's essay explaining how his claims relate to and support his thesis.

3. Look up the myth of Prometheus, making sure to cite your source(s). In your own words, explain the ways in which this myth relates to definitions and discussions of technology in the present day. Then, in one page, reflect on how Sawyer's reference to the myth relates to his argument about the purpose of science fiction.

Neal Stephenson
"Innovation Starvation"

Neal Stephenson is the author of over a dozen novels, which span a range of genres, including SF, historical fiction, and cyberpunk. The recipient of numerous science fiction awards, including the Hugo Prize, the Prometheus Award, the Locus Prize, and the Clarke Award, Stephenson's most recent novel is *Reamde*, a techno-thriller that has been praised by critics both for its readability and its technical sophistication. A former game designer, Stephenson has long been interested in space exploration, a subject that he has explored not only in his fiction, but also by working with contemporary companies and organizations related to the future of space travel. In this essay, Stephenson considers how innovation happens and the place of SF and new technologies in relation to society's ability to "get big things done."

In your vision of the future, what types of large-scale projects could you imagine being developed to "solve age-old problems?"

My lifespan encompasses the era when the United States of America was capable of launching human beings into space. Some of my earliest memories are of sitting on a braided rug before a hulking black-and-white television, watching the early Gemini missions. This summer, at the age of 51—not even old—I watched on a flatscreen as the last Space Shuttle lifted off the pad. I have followed the dwindling of the space program with sadness, even bitterness. Where's my donut-shaped space station? Where's my ticket to Mars? Until recently, though, I have kept my feelings to myself. Space exploration has always had its detractors. To complain about its demise is to expose oneself to attack from those who have no sympathy that an affluent, middle-aged white American has not lived to see his boyhood fantasies fulfilled.

Still, I worry that our inability to match the achievements of the 1960s space program might be symptomatic of a general failure of our society to get big things done. My parents and grandparents witnessed the creation of the airplane, the automobile, nuclear energy, and the computer to name only a few. Scientists and engineers who came of age during the first half of the 20th century could look forward to building things that would solve age-old problems, transform the landscape, build the economy, and provide jobs for the burgeoning middle class that was the basis for our stable democracy.

The Deepwater Horizon oil spill of 2010 crystallized my feeling that we have lost our ability to get important things done. The OPEC oil shock was in 1973—almost 40 years ago. It was obvious then that it was crazy for the United States to let itself be held economic hostage to the kinds of countries where oil was being produced. It led to Jimmy Carter's proposal for the development of an enormous synthetic fuels industry on American soil. Whatever one might think of the merits of the Carter presidency or of this particular proposal, it was, at least, a serious effort to come to grips with the problem.

Little has been heard in that vein since. We've been talking about wind farms, tidal power, and solar power for decades. Some progress has been made in those areas, but energy is still all about oil. In my city, Seattle, a 35-year-old plan to run a light rail line across Lake Washington is now being blocked by a citizen initiative. Thwarted or endlessly delayed in its efforts to build things, the city plods ahead with a project to paint bicycle lanes on the pavement of thoroughfares.

5   In early 2011, I participated in a conference called Future Tense, where I lamented the decline of the manned space program, then pivoted to energy, indicating that the real issue isn't about rockets. It's our far broader inability as a society to execute on the big stuff. I had, through some kind of blind luck, struck a nerve. The audience at Future Tense was more confident than I that science fiction [SF] had relevance—even utility—in addressing the problem. I heard two theories as to why:

1. The Inspiration Theory. SF inspires people to choose science and engineering as careers. This much is undoubtedly true, and somewhat obvious.
2. The Hieroglyph Theory. Good SF supplies a plausible, fully thought-out picture of an alternate reality in which some sort of compelling innovation has taken place. A good SF universe has a coherence and internal logic that makes sense to scientists and engineers. Examples include Isaac Asimov's robots, Robert Heinlein's rocket ships, and William Gibson's cyberspace. As Jim Karkanias of Microsoft Research puts it, such icons serve as hieroglyphs—simple, recognizable symbols on whose significance everyone agrees.

Researchers and engineers have found themselves concentrating on more and more narrowly focused topics as science and technology have become more complex. A large technology company or lab might employ hundreds or thousands of persons, each of whom can address only a thin slice of the overall problem. Communication among them can become a mare's nest of email threads and PowerPoints. The fondness that many such people have for SF reflects, in part, the usefulness of an over-arching narrative that supplies them and their colleagues with a shared vision. Coordinating their efforts through a command-and-control management system is a little like trying to run a modern economy out of a Politburo. Letting them work toward an agreed-on goal is something more like a free and largely self-coordinated market of ideas.

Spanning the Ages

SF has changed over the span of time I am talking about—from the 1950s (the era of the development of nuclear power, jet airplanes, the space race, and the computer) to now. Speaking broadly, the techno-optimism of the Golden Age of SF has given way to fiction written in a generally darker, more skeptical and ambiguous tone. I myself have tended to write a lot about hackers—trickster archetypes who exploit the arcane capabilities of complex systems devised by faceless others.

Believing we have all the technology we'll ever need, we seek to draw   10
attention to its destructive side effects. This seems foolish now that we find ourselves saddled with technologies like Japan's ramshackle 1960's-vintage reactors at Fukushima when we have the possibility of clean nuclear fusion on the horizon. The imperative to develop new technologies and implement them on a heroic scale no longer seems like the childish preoccupation of a few nerds with slide rules. It's the only way for the human race to escape from its current predicaments. Too bad we've forgotten how to do it.

"You're the ones who've been slacking off!" proclaims Michael Crow, president of Arizona State University (and one of the other speakers at Future Tense). He refers, of course, to SF writers. The scientists and engineers, he seems to be saying, are ready and looking for things to do. Time for the SF writers to start pulling their weight and supplying big visions that make sense. Hence the Hieroglyph project, an effort to produce an anthology of new SF that will be in some ways a conscious throwback to the practical techno-optimism of the Golden Age.

Spaceborne Civilizations

China is frequently cited as a country now executing on Big Stuff, and there's no doubt they are constructing dams, high-speed rail systems, and rockets at an extraordinary clip. But those are not fundamentally innovative. Their space program, like all other countries' (including our own), is just parroting work that was done 50 years ago by the Soviets and the Americans. A truly innovative program would involve taking risks (and accepting failures) to pioneer some of the alternative space launch technologies that have been advanced by researchers all over the world during the decades dominated by rockets.

Imagine a factory mass-producing small vehicles, about as big and complicated as refrigerators, which roll off the end of an assembly line, are loaded with space-bound cargo, and topped off with non-polluting liquid hydrogen fuel, then exposed to intense concentrated heat from an array of ground-based lasers or microwave antennas. Heated to temperatures beyond what can be achieved through a chemical reaction, the hydrogen erupts from a nozzle on the base of the device and sends it rocketing into the air. Tracked through its flight by the lasers or microwaves, the vehicle soars into orbit, carrying a larger payload for its size than a chemical rocket could ever manage, but the complexity, expense, and jobs remain grounded. For decades, this has been the vision of such researchers as physicists Jordin Kare and Kevin Parkin. A similar idea, using a pulsed ground-based laser to blast propellant from the backside of a space vehicle, was being talked about by Arthur Kantrowitz, Freeman Dyson, and other eminent physicists in the early 1960s.

If that sounds too complicated, then consider the 2003 proposal of Geoff Landis and Vincent Denis to construct a 20-kilometer-high tower using simple steel trusses. Conventional rockets launched from its top would be able to carry twice as much payload as comparable ones launched from ground level. There is even abundant research, dating all the way back to Konstantin Tsiolkovsky, the father of astronautics beginning in the late 19th century, to show that a simple tether—a long rope, tumbling end-over-end while orbiting the earth—could be used to scoop payloads out of the upper atmosphere and haul them up into orbit without the need for engines of any kind. Energy would be pumped into the system using an electrodynamic process with no moving parts.

15   All are promising ideas—just the sort that used to get an earlier generation of scientists and engineers fired up about actually building something.

But to grasp just how far our current mindset is from being able to attempt innovation on such a scale, consider the fate of the space shuttle's external tanks [ETs]. Dwarfing the vehicle itself, the ET was the largest and most prominent feature of the space shuttle as it stood on the pad. It remained attached to the shuttle—or perhaps it makes as much sense to say that the shuttle remained attached to it—long after the two strap-on boosters had fallen away. The ET and the shuttle remained connected all the way out of the atmosphere and into space. Only after the system had attained orbital velocity was the tank jettisoned and allowed to fall into the atmosphere, where it was destroyed on re-entry.

At a modest marginal cost, the ETs could have been kept in orbit indefinitely. The mass of the ET at separation, including residual propellants, was about twice that of the largest possible Shuttle payload. Not destroying them would have roughly tripled the total mass launched into orbit by the Shuttle. ETs could have been connected to build units that would have humbled today's International Space Station. The residual oxygen and hydrogen sloshing around in them could have been combined to generate electricity and produce tons of water, a commodity that is vastly expensive and desirable in space. But in spite of hard work and passionate advocacy by space experts who wished to see the tanks put to use, NASA—for reasons both technical and political—sent each of them to fiery destruction in the atmosphere. Viewed as a parable, it has much to tell us about the difficulties of innovating in other spheres.

Executing the Big Stuff

Innovation can't happen without accepting the risk that it might fail. The vast and radical innovations of the mid-20th century took place in a world that, in retrospect, looks insanely dangerous and unstable. Possible outcomes that the modern mind identifies as serious risks might not have been taken seriously—supposing they were noticed at all—by people habituated to the Depression, the World Wars, and the Cold War, in times when seat belts, antibiotics, and many vaccines did not exist. Competition between the Western democracies and the communist powers obliged the former to push their scientists and engineers to the limits of what they could imagine and supplied a sort of safety net in the event that their initial efforts did not pay off. A grizzled NASA veteran once told me that the Apollo moon landings were communism's greatest achievement.

In his recent book *Adapt: Why Success Always Starts with Failure*, Tim Harford outlines Charles Darwin's discovery of a vast array of distinct species in the Galapagos Islands—a state of affairs that contrasts with the picture seen on large continents, where evolutionary experiments tend to get pulled back toward a sort of ecological consensus by interbreeding. "Galapagan isolation" vs. the "nervous corporate hierarchy" is the contrast staked out by Harford in assessing the ability of an organization to innovate.

Most people who work in corporations or academia have witnessed something like the following: A number of engineers are sitting together in a room, bouncing ideas off each other. Out of the discussion emerges a new concept that seems promising. Then some laptop-wielding person in the corner, having performed a quick Google search, announces that this "new" idea is, in fact, an old one—or at least vaguely similar—and has already been tried. 20

Either it failed, or it succeeded. If it failed, then no manager who wants to keep his or her job will approve spending money trying to revive it. If it succeeded, then it's patented and entry to the market is presumed to be unattainable, since the first people who thought of it will have "first-mover advantage" and will have created "barriers to entry." The number of seemingly promising ideas that have been crushed in this way must number in the millions.

What if that person in the corner hadn't been able to do a Google search? It might have required weeks of library research to uncover evidence that the idea wasn't entirely new—and after a long and toilsome slog through many books, tracking down many references, some relevant, some not. When the precedent was finally unearthed, it might not have seemed like such a direct precedent after all. There might be reasons why it would be worth taking a second crack at the idea, perhaps hybridizing it with innovations from other fields. Hence the virtues of Galapagan isolation.

The counterpart to Galapagan isolation is the struggle for survival on a large continent, where firmly established ecosystems tend to blur and swamp new adaptations. Jaron Lanier, a computer scientist, composer, visual artist, and author of the recent book *You are Not a Gadget: A Manifesto*, has some insights about the unintended consequences of the Internet—the informational equivalent of a large continent—on our ability to take risks. In the pre-net era, managers were forced to make decisions based on what they knew to be limited information. Today, by contrast, data flows to managers in real time from countless sources that could not even be imagined a couple of generations ago, and powerful computers process, organize, and display the data in ways that are as far beyond the hand-drawn graph-paper plots of my youth as modern video games are to tic-tac-toe. In a world where decision-makers are so close to being omniscient, it's easy to see risk as a quaint artifact of a primitive and dangerous past.

The illusion of eliminating uncertainty from corporate decision-making is not merely a question of management style or personal preference. In the legal environment that has developed around publicly traded corporations, managers are strongly discouraged from shouldering any risks that they know about—or, in the opinion of some future jury, should have known about—even if they have a hunch that the gamble might pay off in the long run. There is no such thing as "long run" in industries driven by the next quarterly report. The possibility of some innovation making money is just that—a mere possibility that will not have time to materialize before the subpoenas from minority shareholder lawsuits begin to roll in.

Today's belief in ineluctable certainty is the true innovation-killer of our age. In this environment, the best an audacious manager can do is to develop small improvements to existing systems—climbing the hill, as it were, toward a local maximum, trimming fat, eking out the occasional tiny innovation—like city planners painting bicycle lanes on the streets as a gesture toward solving our energy problems. Any strategy that involves crossing a valley—accepting short-term losses to reach a higher hill in the distance—will soon be brought to a halt by the demands of a system that celebrates short-term gains and tolerates stagnation, but condemns anything else as failure. In short, a world where big stuff can never get done.

Analyze

1. Explain why, for Stephenson, "The Deepwater Horizon oil spill of 2010 crystallized [his] feeling that we have lost our ability to get important things done."
2. When and what was the Future Tense conference? How was Stephenson's talk received there?
3. What are the two theories Stephenson mentions to describe the relationships that exist between science and SF?
4. Who was Konstantin Tsiolkovsky? Why does Stephenson mention him in his essay?

Explore

1. In your own words, explain The Inspiration Theory and The Hieroglyph Theory. Although Stephenson distinguishes between the two theories, they share many attributes. Explain how the two theories are related to one another. Then, based on Stephenson's essay, assess whether he appears to be advocating for one theory over another.
2. Neal Stephenson was born in 1960 and, in this essay, he draws attention to the fact that his ideas about technology and its potential applications have been shaped by his generational perspectives. Write a letter to Stephenson explaining how your ideas about technology and its potential applications have been shaped by your generational perspective. Then, explain why you agree or disagree with various propositions he makes in the essay and how your generational perspective may be a factor in your response.

3. Neal Stephenson points to the 2010 Deepwater Horizon oil spill as an event that "crystallized [his] feeling that we have lost our ability to get important things done." Do some research into this oil spill. What happened? What were the consequences? Prepare a presentation for your class explaining why the Deepwater Horizon spill was a significant event and how it relates to Stephenson's comments on the need for greater innovation in technological development in energy production and transportation systems.

Jon Turney
"Imagining Technology"

Jon Turney is a British science writer and editor. He is the author of several books, including *The Rough Guide to the Future* (2010), *Medicine and Health Science Trends* (2001), and *Frankenstein's Footsteps: Science, Genetics and Popular Culture* (1998). He is also the co-author of *Harvey's Heart: The Discovery of Blood Circulation Science* (2001), the co-editor of *Not Art: Ten Scientists' Diaries* (2003), and the author of several reports, including one for the British Heart Foundation's anniversary in 2012. The following essay is excerpted from the report *Imagining Technology* (2013), which was commissioned by Nesta, an innovation charity based in Great Britain. In this essay, part of a longer report dedicated to exploring whether "imagining technologies and societies in which they are used make[s] innovation more or less likely," Turney discusses technology's relationships to SF and SF's relationships to technology.

What stories do you tell yourself about technology? What stories do specific technological devices tell you?

Technology's Place in Science Fiction

The brief for this working paper is to appraise science fiction's influence on technological development. Science fiction—henceforth SF—does look like a good place to seek such influence. It is a genre with fuzzy boundaries, so it is fruitless to look for a watertight definition of SF (or even, perhaps, "science" and "fiction"). But one which critics agree is useful is an old formulation by Darko Suvin. He defined SF as "a literary genre whose necessary and sufficient conditions are the presence and interaction of estrangement and cognition, and whose main formal device is *an imaginative framework alternative to the author's empirical environment*" (my emphasis). Another world, a future world, or a different version of this world, in other words.

Suvin goes on to suggest that an SF story has atleast one *"novum"*—a feature which defines a key difference between the reader's everyday world and the world being portrayed. They come in a variety of forms, but in a large portion of SF the novum has a scientific origin. Well, that is not quite right. Despite the label, as critic and SF novelist Adam Roberts observes, "the great majority of SF written in the nineteenth and twentieth centuries is actually 'extrapolated technology fiction'." Hence, the novum is generally technological. Generalisation is hazardous, as Roberts emphasises, but he suggests that "We find tools and machines at the core of most science fiction: such that spaceships, robots, time-machines and virtual technology (computers and virtual realities) are the four most commonly occurring tropes of the field."

There is more to the technology of science fiction than this. And there is more to science fiction than technology. The generalisation is broadly right, though. That means SF as a whole is an important arena for imagining the effects of technologies, existing and yet to come. Its imagined worlds are ones in which life is enabled or constrained by technologies in ways we have not yet seen in our world. Whether we do see them realised may then be influenced by the role technologies play in these alternate realities.

The influence is strengthened by the fact that many SF authors love technology, and many technologists love SF. The latter may be a love that dare not speak its name, though. Science fiction has sometimes been dismissed as a juvenile literature—the Golden Age of SF is always 14, it has been said. And it is still not quite respectable (less so, perhaps, in the UK than in other Anglophone countries). Written SF has always been riven by tensions between an urge to grow beyond its roots in pulp fiction and a wish to celebrate them. While printed SF has been increasingly accepted as sufficiently literary to be worth discussing with literary critical tools, the image of SF in general as crude and not quite grown up has been perpetuated to some extent by its growing cultural presence in films, comic books and computer games.

5   Whether or not this image is justified, crude and not quite grown up
fictions can still have great power, and popularity. They provide some of the
most readily accessible images of possible technologies and figure continually in public discussion of those technologies. At the same time, their dubious (to some) cultural standing influences the rhetoric of those discussions.
What is, or is not, considered science fiction—as opposed to, for example,
"serious" speculation, extrapolation, or technological goal-setting—is often
the subject of boundary disputes energised by an inferiority, or superiority,
complex.

Science Fiction's Place in Technology

Technology is more than just clever stuff. It is about ways of doing things,
as well as the gadgets and devices, the artifacts, that often stand in for technology in public discussion. As with science fiction, definitions abound,
and it is more fruitful to consider what they have in common than to try
and arrive at a definitive version.

A useful survey by two innovation scholars, James Fleck and John Howells,
finds that taking all definitions together suggests considering a "technology
complex," rather than technology per se. Any example includes, in varying
combinations, a basic function, an energy source, and artifacts or hardware.
But it also extends to such things as layouts, procedures, skills, work organisation, management techniques, capital, industry structures, social relations and
culture. They add up to what others have called a socio-technical system. For
Fleck and Howells, the main thing about the technology complex is that artifacts always operate as part of human activity in a social context. This suggests
that working out what effects a new technology might have, or how it might
fit into future ways of life, involves exploring a very large space of possibilities.
The kind of space, in fact, that fiction is good at exploring.

This affinity is underlined by another way of putting this notion of the
technology complex. Every technology begins in the imagination, and
needs a description of what it will achieve. Along with the technical speci-
fication of a new invention, there is a built-in narrative. Every patent tells a
story. Make this device, or follow this process, and certain things will be
possible— things not seen before.

The twinning of technologies with stories is emphasised by historian of
technology David Nye. Conceiving a tool entails thinking in time and

imagining change, he says. Tools are aids to future action. "A tool always implies at least one small story."

As technological development has become more conscious, and sys- 10 tematic, these stories have grown more elaborate. Every technology, already realised or merely sketched, is always already embedded in stories. They run from the explanation of its basic operation, to its place in a collection of futuristic scenarios, whether those scenarios are business plans, paths to national economic competitiveness, environmental good deeds, effective military strategies, or simply advertisements for aids to domestic comfort.

Just as technologies have always come with stories, there have long been fictional stories about technology. Prometheus, Daedalus and Icarus still symbolise the perils and rewards of innovation. Like technology itself, the stories we tell about it have evolved. As the effects of technological change became more obvious, science fiction was one powerful cultural response. It forms a large subset of the stories about technology we have accumulated, which can be separated conceptually (though not always in practice) from the stories inherent in plans for technological development.

Analyze

1. According to Turney, what are the reasons why SF as a genre, is, in the opinion of some, "still not quite respectable?"
2. What is a "novum" and why is it important to Turney's definition and discussion of SF?
3. Turney writes, "Every patent tells a story." Explain what he means by this and how it relates to his argument about the relationships between technology and science fiction.

Explore

1. Turney proposes that "every technology, already realized or merely sketched, is always embedded in stories." Write a short narrative from the perspective of a tool or technological device that you use on a daily basis, for instance an iPhone, a pen, a bike, or a refrigerator. What might these devices or tools be thinking? What stories could these tools or devices relate with regard to how they are used or what they may know about us based on how we use them?

2. In the first paragraph of his essay, Turney cites the literary critic Darko Suvin's definition of SF as a genre. Rewrite this definition in your own words. Then, looking at how Turney interprets and rephrases this definition, compare and contrast the three: Suvin's, your own, and Turney's.

3. In a two-page response essay, review and reflect on two sections from Turney's essay, "Technology's Place in Science Fiction" and "Science Fiction's Place in Technology." What did you learn from each? Which section do you believe is most persuasive? Why?

Kathryn Cramer
"On Science and Science Fiction"

Kathryn Cramer is an American SF writer, editor, and literary critic. The author of numerous award-winning SF books and stories, she has also co-edited approximately 30 anthologies related to science fiction and is a founding editor of *The New York Review of Science Fiction*. Currently an editor at Project Hieroglyph, a Web-based space for writers, scientists, artists, and engineers to collaborate on visions of the near future, she is also the editor of the forthcoming book *Hieroglyph: Stories and Blueprints for a Better Future* (2014). In this essay, Cramer reflects on SF as a genre and hard SF as a subgenre, exploring questions related to the relationships between science and SF.

How do you think science relates to SF?

M. C. Escher remarked in his essay "The Impossible" that "Whoever wants to portray something that does not exist has to obey certain rules." The majority of science fiction stories are not plausible extrapolations upon our current situation, using available information; rather they are Escheresque impossible objects which use the principles of science in much the same way that Escher used rules of geometric symmetry—the rules give form to the impossible imaginative content.

Science fiction allows us to understand and experience our past, present, and future, in terms of an imagined future. Like the conventions of perspective in drawing, which allow us to extrapolate railroads from two convergent lines crossed by a lot of parallel line segments, the conventions of science fiction allow us to imagine a physical world beyond the frame of the scenes described. All science fiction about the future, no matter how rigorously constructed, must build its future from fragments of the past and present; the futures we construct are as much a part of the present as we ourselves are; although they will never really be the future, they can represent it.

Physical law tells us that many things are impossible given existing technology, but the ever-expanding frontier of scientific knowledge shows us how to do many things of which we would never have dreamed. Writing stories within the rules of the universe as we know it and yet discovering fantastic possibilities of new ways of life is the central endeavor of the hard science fiction writer. Science fiction writers prefer to give us truth, rather than reality. Science fiction represents what the future could be like, although we know that the future will look nothing like it. Science fiction allows us to know about our future, although when we meet it we may not recognize it.

There has been a persistent view that "hard" science fiction is somehow the core and center of the science fiction field; that all other science fiction orbits around this center; and that the characteristic of this core is a particular attitude toward science and technology. What we habitually call "hard" science fiction is more precisely technophilic science fiction, an attitude which Poul Anderson described in the 1970s: "Science, technology, material achievement and the rest are basically good. In them lies a necessary if not sufficient condition for the improvement of man's lot, even his mental and spiritual lot." He also differentiated the hard science fiction story from other varieties of science fiction: "A hard science story bases itself upon real, present-day science or technology and carries these further with a minimum of imaginary forces, materials or laws of nature." One is more likely to identify a story as "hard" science fiction—regardless of the amount of actual science it contains—if the narrative voice is pragmatic, deterministic, and matter-of-fact about the many high-tech artifacts among which the story takes place, and if the future (or clearly alternate present or past) in which the protagonist lives is primarily the result of significant technological change from the here-and-now. Through repetition we have come to identify this narrative voice as "futuristic."

5   Like utopian fiction, science fiction grew out of the desire to create and predict the possibility of a better world. In science fiction, this better world will be created and predicted through science and technology: scientific exploration and technological innovation are political acts leading to world salvation. But without the tradition of the folk-tale, science fiction, should it exist at all, would be a literature of didactic tracts, blueprints for "utopia." Fortunately, the enlightened, rationalistic, utopian impulse collided with the irrational, romantic, fanciful folk story-telling tradition.

In addition to its connection to the folk-tale, science fiction has another important connection to pre-literate culture. Before the Reformation, when only the clergy were allowed to read the Bible, the laity looked to religious art not for representations of daily reality, but for revelations of the principles underlying reality—to discover the sacred texts. Science fiction is the religious art of science. While of course anyone who can read today is as entitled to read scientific texts as they are to read the Bible, the habits of "reading" religious art have carried forward to the way we read science fiction. We read science fiction not for representations of our daily lives, but for revelation of the principles behind everyday experience—the cosmic order. As young teenagers we may have read science fiction to learn about science itself. As adults, we probably already know most of the science, perhaps better than many of the authors whose works we read, but science linked to story-telling gives us an emotional experience difficult to replicate while confronting mundane reality alone, without the company of a book.

Since the founding of the science fiction field in the nineteen-twenties, science has been the guiding force of science fiction, and to some extent science fiction has been able to reciprocate. Could there have been a space program without science fiction? While the robots that make cars in Japanese factories bear precious little resemblance to those in *I, Robot*, they might not now exist were it not for Isaac Asimov and company. Several generations of scientists and engineers have grown up reading science fiction, learning that there is such thing as science, and if they work hard in school they can play too—science fiction influenced the career choices of such scientists as Carl Sagan and the late Gerald Feinberg. A number of science fiction readers turned scientist have later in life become science fiction writers: Fred Hoyle, Gene Wolfe, John Cramer, Carl Sagan, Gregory Benford, Robert L. Forward, and Don Kingsbury, just to name a few. Despite this connection between science and science fiction, the nature of this connection remains largely unexplored.

The early defense of science fiction emphasized the wonders of science and the sensation that they arouse in the reader—at its best, science fiction tends to be about the emotional experience of discovering what is true, often represented by scientific discoveries of great consequence. In traditional hard science fiction, the story is to be taken very literally, insisting on it more strongly than any other kind of English-language fiction.

However, over the last couple of decades not enough attention has been paid to those virtues that science fiction derives from its unique relationship with science. During this time, the relationship between science and science fiction has been de-emphasized in favor of the relationship between science fiction and literature. By now a significant portion of the field's practitioners prefer to call science fiction "speculative fiction," because the social position of a "futurist" is more desirable than that of a "science fiction writer." From this view, speculative fiction, which addresses not just the past and present, but also the glorious, mysterious future, is a much broader field than "mainstream" (the science fiction world's dismissive term for non-science fiction) set in the currently-known or historically-known world, usually involving only those characters and situations that we conceive of as appropriate to a realistic account. Thus defined, mainstream [science fiction] is a subset of science fiction, and the greats of literature are, intentionally or not, merely speculative fiction writers without much talent for speculation.

Although John W. Campbell promoted this view of science fiction,   10 stripped of Campbell's technologically oriented futurism it takes on a different meaning: science is marginalized in favor of social extrapolation. While the prose style of the average science fiction story has improved, many of the best writers have been distracted from the task of working out their own syntheses of science and fiction, and so it goes: out go the paragraphs giving clear evidence that the writer spent all day calculating the nature and quality of eclipses on a planet with five moons, and in come paragraphs of carefully observed description of the protagonist's moods, signifying the writer's sincere obeisance to the conservative but currently fashionable belief that all good stories are "character driven."

Hard science fiction also interacts with the technologies and accompanying institutions that produce and distribute it. In the twenty years since the death of John W. Campbell, much has happened to obscure his technophilic vision of science fiction. The hard science fiction attitude became a salable commodity on its own, separable from scientific content. Particularly during the Reagan years, "hard science fiction" evolved into right wing power fantasies about military hardware, tales of men killing things with big machines, fantasies that had very little to do with scientific thought or theory.

In that era, the majority of the most talented younger science fiction writers were quite uninterested in writing about science, precisely because what was generally perceived as hard science fiction was rapidly degenerating into political allegory. In the midst of this, many writers were still writing good hard science fiction: Isaac Asimov, Arthur C. Clarke, Charles Sheffield, Joe Haldeman, Donald Kingsbury, Gregory Benford, Greg Bear, Paul Preuss, and Joan Slonsczewski. Simultaneously, certain of the cyberpunk writers, Bruce Sterling, William Gibson, and Rudy Rucker, were bending certain tropes of hard science fiction to their postmodern project. A number of good hard science fiction stories have appeared in the past few years by such writers as Geoffrey Landis, Connie Willis, George Alec Effinger, and Lois McMaster Bujold.

The 1983 Eaton Conference on hard science fiction conference brought together literary critics and "writer/scientists" Robert L. Forward, David Brin, Gregory Benford. They discussed many aspects of the effect of hard science fiction, but judging by the published proceedings of the conference, some basic connections between science and fiction remained obscure.

Having served on panels on hard science fiction at conventions, I had noticed certain rhetorical patterns in the claims hard science fiction writers made for hard science fiction. Whenever possible, they minimize the differences between very hard science fiction and science itself. For example, David Brin, in his essay "Running Out of Speculative Niches: A Crisis for Hard SF?" astutely observes that in a hard science fiction story, "'science' itself . . . is a major character" (8). He goes on to describe how something rather like peer review transpires among hard science fiction writers. While I acknowledge that this sort of interactive reading occurs among hard science fiction writers and among writers in other genres and subgenres, the general drift of Brin's essay in the Eaton Conference Proceedings, and for that matter Forward's, entitled "When Science Writes the Fiction," and Benford's, entitled "Is There a Technological Fix for the Human Condition?", is that science and hard science fiction are very similar. This perception of the similarity of science and hard science fiction is manifest in Benford's definition of hard science fiction in that essay:

15   My minimum definition of hard science fiction demands that it highly prize fidelity to the physical facts of the universe, while constructing a new objective "reality" within a fictional matrix. It is not

enough to merely use science as integral to the narrative . . . Science fiction must use science in a speculative fashion. The physical sciences are the most capable of detailed prediction (and thus falsification by experiment), so they are perceived in fiction as more reliable indicators of future possibilities, or stable grounds for orderly speculation.

But, as mathematician Henri Poincaré pointed out, only a small of minority of the human race experiences mathematics pleasurably. So, while mathematics is the bones holding up the scientific animal, the science must be "de-boned" before it can be used in fiction, because the majority of readers, even hard science fiction readers, will tolerate very few equations in a work of fiction. Even the anthology *Mathenauts*, edited by Rudy Rucker, contains, to my count, only four equations, and of those, none are beyond the ken of a high school freshman.

Although some hard science fiction writers take the same attitude as Leonardo Da Vinci, who claimed in his essay "On Painting and Science" that "No human inquiry can call itself a true science if it is not confirmed by mathematical proofs," and expect that the scientifically literate reader will whip out her calculator and discover that all the math behind appearances works out, as often as not it doesn't. In this sense science and hard science fiction are very different.

Hard science fiction is a lively and diverse literature that attempts to get at the power and wonder of science, to articulate the sensation of discovering the true and the real. Stories like "The Singing Diamond" by Robert Forward and "Surface Tension" by James Blish hit the reader with a shot-gun blast of ideas; at the right moment, under the right circumstances, reading a story like that can capture the feeling of making a major discovery.

Hard science fiction is about the aesthetics of knowledge, even knowledge of the most disturbing, overwhelming kind—that which is bigger than one's loving or hating it. In Philip Latham's "The Xi Effect," Edgar Allen Poe's "Descent in the Maelstrom," and Arthur C. Clarke's "Transit of Earth" this knowledge is deadly, but its revelation is numinous. Hard science fiction is at its core beyond questions of optimism and pessimism, beyond questions of technology and application. Hard science fiction recognizes wonder as the finest human emotion.

20   As most science fiction readers already know, hard science fiction has an identifiable feel, a particular kind of narrative voice, the right attitude. This attitude is respectful of the principles underlying the practice of science, not unlike the reverence one should display when entering the chapel. A rationalist cosmology accompanies this attitude: a cosmology based on the belief that the literal facts of a situation are more important than any interpretation. The anti-mysticism of hard science fiction is a point of pride for science fiction writers (and scientists of similar mindset) who see science as a replacement for religion and superstition.

In his essay on metaphor, entitled "On Truth and Falsity in their Extra-moral Sense," the philosopher Friedrich Nietzsche describes what he feels to be the literal, factual, non-metaphorical situation of humanity, which might easily serve as a description of the hard science fiction cosmography:

> In some remote corner of the universe, effused into innumerable solar-systems, there was once a star upon which clever animals invented cognition. It was the haughtiest, most mendacious moment in the history of this world, but yet only a moment. After Nature had taken breath awhile the star congealed and the clever animals had to die.

The lifespan of our sun is but the briefest moment in the history of the universe; everything we value will vanish soon unless we spread ourselves across the universe, or unless there have been, are, or will be other intelligent life forms out there. Hard science fiction writers try to find a way out of this dilemma. Hard science fiction uses the rules of a deterministic universe to show us that our fate is not yet sealed. As Hal Clement remarked in conversation, in hard science fiction, the universe itself is the antagonist.

Hard science fiction's problem-solving attitude toward our inevitable extinction has three corollaries: (1) no precondition of viable intelligent life is irreplaceable, given enough scientific knowledge, (2) the replacement of things needed to sustain life is necessary, desirable, and promotes the long-term survival of our species, (3) the scientific should replace the unscientific. Nietzsche's pronouncement that "the clever animals had to die" is a depressing thought for the realist; but for the hard science fiction rationalist, it is an exciting challenge! Hard science fiction's strong connection to physics—one of the last systems of classical idealism to retain its intellectual validity—allows hard science fiction to continue to take on the most all-encompassing aspect of the human condition, our survival as a species. The technophilic wing of the science fiction community treasures the thought that because of our interest in and enthusiasm for technological innovation, we may just be the next stage of human evolution. This notion leads to one of hard science fiction's paradoxes: if our faith in science replaces religious faith, science is coopted into becoming a religion, which, of course, would be unscientific. The work of Arthur C. Clarke best shows the tension between science and religion within hard science fiction: some editions of his novel Childhood's End carried the disclaimer that the opinions in the book were "not those of the author." His Christmas hard science fiction story "The Star" also shows this tension: the story "explains" the Star of Bethlehem in hard science fiction terms, a scientific and technological notion replaces a religious one; yet, were it not for Christianity, this replacement would lack meaning.

The primacy of the sense of wonder in science fiction poses a direct challenge to religion: does the wonder of science and the natural world as experienced through science fiction replace religious awe? It is perhaps no coincidence that a similar controversy has emerged in the New Age movement over whether or not true enlightenment can be attained through the use of meditation machines—are electric revelations authentic? If not, how can we tell the difference?

The idea that in the future better and more scientific things will replace all the things we currently need and use—a cosmic belief in an ever-improving standard of living—constitute what I call the replacement principle of science fiction. Robert Heinlein's "It's Great to Be Back" expresses this idea in strong terms: a family returning to Earth after years on of living on the Moon discovers that their nostalgia for the lushness of Earth and the richness of its societies was misguided sentimentality. Frederick Pohl's "Day Million" describes a society in which most of what we know has been replaced by something more futuristic, but he makes less attempt at salesmanship. While atomic light bulbs no longer seem like such a good idea, the notion of living in an L5 colony, traveling to another planet, and communicating with an extraterrestrial intelligence still enchant us. If "slow glass" as described in Bob Shaw's "Light of Other Days" were commercially available, many of us would buy it. And we remain fascinated by such technologies as cloning (see Ursula K. Le Guin's "Nine Lives") and time travel (see Ian Watson's "Very Slow Time Machine"). The big ideas of hard science fiction are more ambitious than the creation of any single device. Hard science fiction shows us many alternate places to live: space stations, other planets, undersea communities, and so on: hard science fiction takes the position that we should have the knowledge and technology to create, from the building blocks of the universe, everything we need to have rich and happy lives, so as to end our child-like dependence on the Earth and what nature gives us.

Though some hard science fiction writers claim that their future worlds and situations never violate physical law, and therefore just might happen, most science fiction scenarios are at least implausible, often wildly so, and many are outright impossible. The long-standing controversy over whether science fiction writers should use faster-than-light travel in their stories exposes the various conflicting demands upon the writer: because of science fiction's utopian goal of saving humanity from extinction, it is a game that must be played by the rules; it will do no good to beg for favors from the uncaring universe. Eliminating faster-than-light travel from possibility does rather limit our options: we're all dressed up with no place to go. And yet, we must become a self-made species, become the fittest, so we can survive the inevitable death of our sun.

Analyze

1. How does Cramer define "hard science fiction?" How does "hard science fiction" differ from what she calls "science fiction?"
2. What are the differences between SF and speculative fiction, according to Cramer?
3. For what reasons, according to Cramer, were younger SF writers uninterested in writing about science during the Reagan era?
4. What is the "replacement theory" in SF?

Explore

1. Cramer begins her essay with a quote from an essay by the artist M. C. Escher. If you are not familiar with Escher's work, find an image of one of his works on the Web. After you have done so, and based on what you have learned about Escher's work from looking at this image, write one page reflecting on how Escher's work relates to the point Cramer is making in her first paragraph about the relationships between science and SF.

2. Cramer writes, "all science fiction about the future, no matter how rigorously constructed, must build its future from fragments of the past and present." In your own words, explain the point Cramer is making. Then, reflecting on Cramer's sentence and your rewording of this sentence, write a two-page essay explaining why this is a particularly important point to consider when thinking about SF and its relationships to science and technology in the real world.
3. Although Cramer does not choose to use section headings in her essay, the essay clearly falls into distinct sections. As you reread this essay, consider where you would place section breaks. Once you have finished rereading the essay, go back and give a subtitle to each section based on what it is about. Finally, in one or two pages explain your rationale for choosing these section breaks and section titles.

Damien Broderick
"Stranger Than You Can Imagine"

Damien Broderick is an Australian SF and science writer. The author of more than a dozen books, Broderick has also edited over 50 books and was the founding SF editor of the Australian popular-science magazine *Cosmos*. A graduate of the Ph.D. program in Literary Studies at Deakin University, Australia, Broderick completed a dissertation studying relationships among SF, literature, and science. Before moving to San Antonio, Texas, where he now resides, Broderick was for several years a Senior Fellow in the School of Culture and Communication at the University of Melbourne. In this essay, Broderick considers the ways in which technology has and has not allowed us to realize the future predicted in various SF novels and how the future of our present may be very different from the future of the past.

When you think about the future, what do you envision? Why?

Personal jet packs! Weekend trips to Mars! Domed cities beneath the sea! No more time-consuming food, just neat nutrition pills!

That was the future, or part of it, expected by the popular imagination; fuelled by science-fiction comics, movies, and lurid pulp stories reaching back to the 1930s. So when the 21st century began, and we were still stuck here in suburban gridlock, watching attractive airheads getting kicked off the island and bored nobodies doing nothing for hours a day on *Big Brother*, everyone became very cynical about the future. How dull it was! Meanwhile, the new future, the real future, looked like a nightmare of greenhouse scorchers and drought, or shocking, unexpected flooding. Space shuttles fell out of the sky in blazing ruin. Clones were expected any day, but many pious people feared they would have no souls. Darwin had gone out of fashion in the heartland of Western power, the United States. And astrologers now outnumbered astronomers.

It is not so surprising that the future has not turned out like the comic books. After all, nobody expects 21st century law enforcement to be run by masked avengers wearing capes and driving in jet-propelled Batmobiles. Real astronauts don't do their work repairing the Hubble space telescope in satin tights and brass bikinis, with glass bubbles over their heads, despite decades of comics portraying them this way.

The real future crept up on us, in the form of mobile phones (a surprise technology actually predicted in comics such as *Dick Tracy* and the 1960s television program *Star Trek*); portable laptops at affordable prices with vastly more grunt than the computers used to send men to the moon; and computer-generated movies that portray wild 1940s science-fiction horror and space soap-opera scenes in exceptional, believable detail thanks to just such computers. And of course, DVDs, commuter cars built around microelectronics, café lattes, Pilates exercises, and airport bookstores clogged with vapid self-help manuals.

5   In other words, yesterday's future—our present day—is a blend of the predictable and the only slightly surprising. Still, a hundred and fifty years ago, the claim that people would do away with horses in the street, and spend their holidays flying through the air while packed like hens would have seemed mad. The real future of 50 years hence is likely to be just that wrenchingly strange.

And the reason for that strangeness—strictly unpredictable in detail from where we sit here and now—is an accelerating rate of change. It's driving certain key technologies forward in a wild rush, especially computing power.

Taking this insight literally leads to a very perplexing forecast: the singularity, as it's been called, or the spike. It's an ever-soaring curve on the graph of change, dragging us upward through a series of drastic dislocations in work and play; the very shape of our minds and bodies; the world we inhabit.

Here's a jolting change greater than anything we've seen so far in history: by the middle of this century it's possible, even probable, that the relentless ageing of our bodies will be halted by advances in biological understanding plus remarkable new medical interventions. However slowly these health improvements start out, they will carry their beneficiaries forward, step-by-step, year after year, to an era where everyone who chooses has the option of rejuvenation and indefinitely extended youth.

Until now, as the playwright Tom Stoppard has noted wryly, "age is a very high price to pay for maturity." The end result of the Human Genome Project and its successors will see the abolition of that terrible and once inevitable price. After all, the egg cells from which each of us grew were as old as our mother, yet those comparatively old cells later matured and built brand spanking new babies. Is there any reason why we can't learn the secrets of the egg cells that ensure healthy youngsters, and then apply those lessons to keep all our adult cells, and the tissues they comprise, healthy and youthful?

There might be moral objections to eternal youth. Just as blustering attempts were once made to prohibit anaesthetics during childbirth, since its pain was imagined to be a punishment imposed by God, so the debilities of age and the finality of death could be considered a necessary part of life, imposed by the deity's wisdom. It's illuminating to recall how many other natural conditions we duck by using technology such as glasses, central heating, dental anaesthetics and tampons. It seems that the changes we're told God wants us to avoid are often those that haven't happened yet. Once we get used to them, once they become part of our lives, moralists discover belatedly that God really doesn't mind after all.

But the singularity will not stop at physical immortality (if that convergence of technologies isn't blocked by war, political caution, or the ruination of the planet by unsustainable industrial and agricultural approaches).

As machines get smarter, they won't just take over the burdens of toil, they will enhance us as well . . . literally. The promise of virtual reality may have stalled as we wait for computer power to double and redouble every year or so—a proliferation that gives us a thousand times as much power every decade, and a million times after two decades, a billion after three. Two or three decades hence, a benign version of the world of *The Matrix* is feasible. Augmented by billions of nanomachines smaller than brain cells, we could have the opportunity to link our thoughts and emotions directly, one person to another, in a kind of machine telepathy. We might roam through rich imaginary spaces and landscapes that make today's supposedly awesome special-effects movies seem as convincing as a child's crayon drawings.

Some might choose to upload their personalities into a totally constructed reality, perhaps even migrate there, adventurous denizens of a wholly new frontier. Living that way, we might be able to copy ourselves numerous times, our variant selves remaining linked in an electronic version of the way nature now links our twin brain hemispheres. One copy, or more, might remain safely archived for back-up, others might roam the depths of space in cheap, tiny starships designed to carry our nano-selves at nearly the speed of light into the deep night—even at the cost of losing their connection to the core self, at least until they return home.

But these are merely my projections beyond the opaque wall of the singularity, a place we can go only in imagination—for now. Even so, what we dream today will be the merest shadow of tomorrow's reality. Let's hope the under-funded research programs working toward extended youthful lifespan succeed in time for us, personally, to share in that great adventure.

Analyze

1. Why, according to Broderick, are most people "cynical about the future" in the twenty-first century?
2. According to Broderick, why has today's reality not turned out to be "like the comic books?"
3. How does Broderick describe and define "the singularity?"

Explore

1. Using an online search engine, locate an image that visually represents the future Broderick describes as being part of the "popular imagination." Then, locate an image that visually represents the reality of the twenty-first century as depicted in Broderick's essay. Finally, locate an image that visually represents the "real future" described by

Broderick. Could one of the three images be used to visually represent Broderick's description of the future after the singularity? If not, locate an image that would visually represent the future Broderick describes after the singularity. Write a well-developed paragraph explaining how each image you have located relates to the passage in Broderick's essay it is illustrating.

2. In a short essay, explain how the title of Broderick's essay fits well with both the reality of the twenty-first century and Broderick's vision for the future after the singularity.

3. While Broderick admits that people have become "very cynical about the future" based on the realities of the twenty-first century, he also speculates in his essay that the future of today will be quite different from yesterday's future. In a two- or three-page essay, explain his reasons for being more optimistic about the future of the present compared with the future of the past. Then, explain why you agree or disagree with his assessment.

Wendy Lesser
"Unearthly Powers"

Wendy Lesser is an American writer and editor. The author of several fiction and nonfiction books, she is also the founding editor of *The Threepenny Review*, a quarterly review of arts and society published out of San Francisco. A cultural critic and frequent book reviewer, her most recent book, *Why I Read: The Serious Pleasure of Books* (2014), recounts her experiences as a reader and what she has learned as a result. In the following essay, first published in *The Threepenny Review*, Lesser reviews one of Isaac Asimov's novels, *Endless Eternity*, reflecting on her own reading of SF as a youth and the ways in which the present may be turning out to be very much like the one Asimov depicted in his novel.

Is there a technology that you use regularly today that reminds you of a technology you may have once read about in an SF story, or seen in a film or on TV?

The world we inhabit is one in which weekly newsmagazines, printed on paper in columns of type, are considered primitive and profoundly obsolescent; in which an entire bookshelf of bound volumes can be stored in a gadget the size of a fingertip; in which a mechanical device that is only about four inches long and a fraction of an inch thick can record whatever we like, play it back to us through a tiny earpiece, and rest comfortably in a pocket when not in use; in which space flight has been invented but is rarely used by humans, who have lost interest in it after the initial decades of excitement; in which hand-held or easily portable computers are a commonplace item; in which literature can hardly be distinguished from film in the public mind; and in which some members of society long fruitlessly for a past era when all such developments were unknown and almost inconceivable.

We *do*, in fact, live in such a world, but I mean something else. The above description, detail by detail, exactly characterizes the world of Isaac Asimov's *The End of Eternity,* a science-fiction novel set mainly in the 482nd, 575th, and 2456th centuries. What is remarkable is that Asimov's book first appeared in print in 1955.

For those of you who were not around then (and I barely was—I was three at the time), let me assure you that none of the present-day realities mentioned in my first paragraph was even a mote in a scientist's eye. In 1955, the year my family moved to Palo Alto, my father had just started working for IBM, where he helped develop the huge mainframe computer that would eventually become the great-great-great-grandfather of Macs and PCs alike. By 1966 or 1967, when I began reading Isaac Asimov novels, a version of that mainframe had recently become available for use in a few high-school computing classes, so that some of us in the Palo Alto school system were taught how to inscribe the punch-cards that fed into the mechanical maw—a process so inhuman and alienating and difficult, so resolutely *digital* in its outlook, that I was determined never to have anything to do with computers again. This resolve disintegrated in about 1983, when I purchased my first "personal computer," a boxy Kaypro whose 64-kilobyte RAM was laughably minute by today's standards, but whose CPU was nonetheless more powerful (or so the salesman told me) than the massive computer that first flew a man to the moon in 1969.

And this is not to speak of laptops, cell phones, flashdrives, iPods, DVDs, Kindles, and all the other devices which only came into widespread use in the last decade or two. Asimov thought all this would take many centuries; instead, it took less than two generations. Yet if he was wrong about the timing, he was fantastically right about not only the inventions themselves, but the effect they would have on society.

Part of the pleasure of reading old science fiction is precisely this: with the special powers vested in you by historical hindsight, you can compare the playfully visionary forecasts with what actually took place. This puts you rather in the position of Asimov's "Eternals," the characters in *The End of Eternity* who stand outside of time, observing and controlling the vast majority who still live within it. The Eternals, contrary to what their name suggests, do not live forever; they age and die just as normal people do. But they have such extensive powers of technical analysis (their highest-ranked functionaries are called Computers, who are superior to Sociologists, who are above Technicians) that they are capable of predicting what will happen to any individual human or group of humans. And because they also have at their beck-and-call an easy form of time travel—consisting of "kettles" that whizz along preset pathways in the fourth dimension, taking them many centuries "upwhen" or "downwhen"—they can actually enter into history at specific points in time and repeatedly change it. These so-called Reality Changes might involve something as small as moving a container from one shelf to another, or as large as engineering the deaths of a dozen people in a crash. The aim is always to produce the Maximum Desired Response (M.D.R.) with the Minimum Necessary Change (M.N.C.): to insure, in short, that the unpleasant or anti-social or generally disruptive event does not occur, and thus to keep mankind in a state of comfortable if slightly dull equilibrium.

Though technology is what makes this kind of reality-control possible, only a human being is capable of finding exactly the right moment and method of change. "Mechanical computing would not do," Asimov's typically invisible, intangible narrator tells us. "The largest Computaplex ever built, manned by the cleverest and most experienced Senior Computer ever born, could do no better than to indicate the ranges in which the M.N.C. might be found. It was then the Technician, glancing over the data, who decided on an exact point in that range. A good Technician was rarely wrong. A top Technician was never wrong." And then, in the kind of portentous single-sentence paragraph in which science fiction delights, Asimov adds: "Harlan was never wrong."

Harlan is our hero, a man whose "homewhen," or time of origin, is the 95th century, but who as a teenager was lifted out of Time to become one of the Eternals. (Forgive me—the capitals are all Asimov's.) Like all

5

Eternals, he can never go back to his own century, not only because the rules forbid it, but because if he went back he would, like Jimmy Stewart in *It's a Wonderful Life,* find everything horribly changed; he would learn that he had never had a home or a mother or an existence of any kind, because the ongoing series of Reality Changes (some, perhaps, implemented by himself) would have wiped him off the record. So instead he travels light, moving from one century to another, putting in the fix as needed, obeying his superiors, and only occasionally wondering why life is structured the way it is and whether Eternity really lasts forever. (Apparently it doesn't: even the Eternals cannot get into the "hidden" centuries between the 70,000th and the 150,000th, and when they enter the system after that, all they find is a dead, uninhabited, featureless world.)

I won't go any further into the plot of this novel. If you have never been a science-fiction fan, I will long since have lost you anyway. But if you ever were a fan—as I was, quite obsessively, in my teens—you cannot do better than to return to the works of Isaac Asimov. Cheesy as the love story inevitably is, and inconsistent as some of the time-related logic turns out to be (why, for instance, does Harlan have to cancel an appointment in the 575th century in order to go to the 3000th and see a man who is "free this afternoon," when normal logic tells us he could have gone and returned in a matter of minutes, or even seconds?), the essential storyline has a deeply compelling quality that is—to me, at least—irresistible. As I approached the end of this novel, I found myself agitatedly turning pages in the way I always do in the last hundred pages of a Henry James novel (even, I'll confess, a Henry James novel I have read before). And, as in a James novel, the propulsive force is a desire to find out how things turn out for these deeply knowing but finally helpless characters, who are up against moral dilemmas they can't easily solve, and who are impeded in their attempted solutions by people who are socially and economically more powerful than they are.

The End of Eternity may be one of Asimov's better novels, but it follows the same essential pattern as all his others, as I discovered when I went back recently to reread *Foundation's Edge* and *The Robots of Dawn*. Like all obsessive writers, Isaac Asimov is a victim of the repetition compulsion, reproducing a single novel over and over again in all its myriad forms. His goes something like this: An individual with good powers of analysis and logic, as well as a great deal of modestly worn courage, confronts a gigantic system that is out to thwart him because he threatens, wittingly or unwittingly, to bring about its downfall. In the course of his efforts, he has to rely on other people without knowing for sure which ones are his friends or lovers and which his enemies or betrayers. He is good at crossing cultural boundaries and even interacting with other life forms (some of Asimov's most touching relationships are those between human and robot), but he retains a stubborn, almost curmudgeonly affection for the values and sensations of his own home place. Generally this place is Earth, and even when it is not, he and his entire culture have a kind of residual nostalgia—though also a civilized man's anti-primitive aversion, or an adult's anti-infantile one—for that long-lost homeland, that long-gone birthplace of the human race.

One of the advantages of looking back on Asimov's work from the remove of several decades, not to mention the turn of a century, is that one can see how deeply enmeshed he was in the history of his own time. He was the child of Russian emigrants who left the Soviet Union for America in 1923, just three years after their son Isaac was born; and one can, if one chooses, view his whole science-fiction oeuvre as a recapitulation of the Soviet experiment and the Cold War reaction to it. Yet these novels, although they wear their anti-totalitarian garb as prominently as Orwell's ever did, are unlikely ever to be kidnapped by the right, for the simple reason that all the individualistic, novelty-mongering American virtues are countered in Asimov's work—and sometimes outweighed—by their opposites: that is, a belief in collective effort, a passion for history, and an ineradicable pessimism about the prospects for human progress. For Asimov, super-civilization and technological achievement always go hand-in-hand with a general softening or attenuation of the human spirit, and it is only by getting back to basics (or intuition, or felt sensation) that people can continue to move ahead. It is an essentially nostalgic view, and as such it is profoundly Russian, however much Asimov may have felt himself to be a fully fledged citizen of his new country.

The author's note attached to the 2010 reissue of *The End of Eternity* tells us that Isaac Asimov, in addition to writing vast quantities of science fiction, "taught biochemistry at Boston University School of Medicine and wrote detective stories and nonfiction books on Shakespeare, the Gilbert and Sullivan operettas, biochemistry, and the environment. He died in 1992." But if we go back a mere quarter of a century or so, to the 1984 Ballantine paperback of *The Robots of Dawn*, we can locate ourselves at a moment when the author himself (not to mention Ballantine Books) was still with us. In the author's note to that book, we learn that "at the present time, he has published over 260 books, distributed through every major division of the Dewey system of library classification, and shows no signs of slowing up. He remains as youthful, as lively, and as lovable as ever, and grows more handsome with each year. You can be sure that this is so since he has written this little essay himself and his devotion to absolute objectivity is notorious." If you are one of those people who, like myself, remains committed to the primitive, cellulose-based habits of reading, the pages on which you read this will be yellowed and flaking; but the voice will be as strong and as vitally alive as ever. Now, *that's* what I call time travel.

Analyze

1. Make a list of the inventions mentioned by Lesser in the first paragraph and explain how each has been realized, either by pointing to a specific technology or some historical event enabled by a specific technology.

2. According to Lesser, what does the term "homewhen" refer to in Asimov's novel?

3. List some of the reasons why Lesser assesses Asimov's *The End of Eternity* as one of the author's "better novels."

Explore

1. Do a rhetorical analysis of Lesser's essay in order to respond to the following questions: Who may be the intended audience for this essay? What is Lesser's purpose in writing this essay? Cite specific evidence from the essay to support your reasons for assessing the intended audience, or audiences, and purpose, or purposes.

2. Although primarily a review essay, Lesser also seems to be writing a personal essay or memoir. Examine how Lesser's essay combines elements of both genres—the review essay and the memoir. As a class, discuss the ways in which her incorporation of elements of a personal essay help her readers better understand the points she makes about Asimov's novel.

3. Lesser writes, "One of the advantages of looking back on Asimov's work from the remove of several decades, not to mention the turn of a century, is that one can see how deeply enmeshed he was in the history

of his own time." In a short essay, describe how the technologies and cultural issues being discussed in Lesser's own essay reflect the concerns of someone writing in 2010.

4. Write a review of Lesser's review, making sure to choose a specific audience and publication for your essay. Would you recommend that people read Lesser's essay? Why or why not?

Michio Kaku
"Physics of the Impossible"

Michio Kaku is the Henry Semat Professor of Theoretical Physics at the City University of New York's Graduate Center. A leader in the field of theoretical physics, he is the author of several popular science books, including *Parallel Worlds, Visions, Beyond Einstein, Hyperspace,* and *Physics of the Impossible*—the basis for his Science Channel TV show, *Sci Fi Science: Physics of the Impossible.* His most recent book, published in 2012, is *Physics of the Future: How Science Will Shape Human Destiny and Our Daily Lives by the Year 2100.* A co-founder of string field theory, Kaku is a working scientist who has expressed his interest in continuing the work of Albert Einstein to "unite the four fundamental forces of nature into a single grand unified theory of everything." In this essay, excerpted from his book *Physics of the Impossible*, Kaku reflects on his early fascination with SF, how this interest related to his pursuit of a career as a scientist, and the relationships between science and SF.

What is something that is today, from a scientific perspective, considered impossible that you would like to study in order to understand whether the impossible might someday be possible?

One day, would it be possible to walk through walls? To build starships that can travel faster than the speed of light? To read other people's minds? To become invisible? To move objects with the power of our minds? To transport our bodies instantly through outer space?

Since I was a child, I've always been fascinated by these questions. Like many physicists, when I was growing up, I was mesmerized by the possibility of time travel, ray guns, force fields, parallel universes, and the like. Magic, fantasy, science fiction were all a gigantic playground for my imagination. They began my lifelong love affair with the impossible.

I remember watching the old *Flash Gordon* reruns on TV. Every Saturday, I was glued to the TV set, marveling at the adventures of Flash, Dr. Zarkov, and Dale Arden and their dazzling array of futuristic technology: the rocket ships, invisibility shields, ray guns, and cities in the sky. I never missed a week. The program opened up an entirely new world for me. I was thrilled by the thought of one day rocketing to an alien planet and exploring its strange terrain. Being pulled into the orbit of these fantastic inventions I knew that my own destiny was somehow wrapped up with the marvels of the science that the show promised.

As it turns out, I was not alone. Many highly accomplished scientists originally became interested in science through exposure to science fiction. The great astronomer Edwin Hubble was fascinated by the works of Jules Verne. As a result of reading Verne's work, Hubble abandoned a promising career in law, and, disobeying his father's wishes, set off on a career in science. He eventually became the greatest astronomer of the twentieth century. Carl Sagan, noted astronomer and bestselling author, found his imagination set afire by reading Edgar Rice Burroughs's John Carter of Mars novels. Like John Carter, he dreamed of one day exploring the sands of Mars.

5   I was just a child the day when Albert Einstein died, but I remember people talking about his life, and death, in hushed tones. The next day I saw in the newspapers a picture of his desk, with the unfinished manuscript of his greatest, unfinished work. I asked myself, What could be so important that the greatest scientist of our time could not finish it? The article claimed that Einstein had an impossible dream, a problem so difficult that it was not possible for a mortal to finish it. It took me years to find out what that manuscript was about: a grand, unifying "theory of everything." His dream—which consumed the last three decades of his life—helped me to focus my own imagination. I wanted, in some small way, to be part of the effort to complete Einstein's work, to unify the laws of physics into a single theory.

As I grew older I began to realize that although Flash Gordon was the hero and always got the girl, it was the scientist who actually made the TV series work. Without Dr. Zarkov, there would be no rocket ship, no trips to Mongo, no saving Earth. Heroics aside, without science there is no science fiction.

I came to realize that these tales were simply impossible in terms of the science involved, just flights of the imagination. Growing up meant putting away such fantasy. In real life, I was told, one had to abandon the impossible and embrace the practical.

However, I concluded that if I was to continue my fascination with the impossible, the key was through the realm of physics. Without a solid background in advanced physics, I would be forever speculating about futuristic technologies without understanding whether or not they were possible. I realized I needed to immerse myself in advanced mathematics and learn theoretical physics. So that is what I did.

In high school for my science fair project I assembled an atom smasher in my mom's garage. I went to the Westinghouse company and gathered 400 pounds of scrap transformer steel. Over Christmas I wound 22 miles of copper wire on the high school football field. Eventually I built a 2.3-million-electron-volt betatron particle accelerator, which consumed 6 kilowatts of power (the entire output of my house) and generated a magnetic field of 20,000 times the Earth's magnetic field. The goal was to generate a beam of gamma rays powerful enough to create antimatter.

My science fair project took me to the National Science Fair and eventually fulfilled my dream, winning a scholarship to Harvard, where I could finally pursue my goal of becoming a theoretical physicist and follow in the footsteps of my role model, Albert Einstein.   10

Today I receive e-mails from science fiction writers and screen-writers asking me to help them sharpen their own tales by exploring the limits of the laws of physics.

The "Impossible" Is Relative

As a physicist, I have learned that the "impossible" is often a relative term. Growing up, I remember my teacher one day walking up to the map of the Earth on the wall and pointing out the coastlines of South America and Africa. Wasn't it an odd coincidence, she said, that the two coastlines fit together, almost like a jigsaw puzzle? Some scientists, she said, speculated that perhaps they were once part of the same, vast continent. But that was silly. No force could possibly push two gigantic continents apart. Such thinking was impossible, she concluded.

Later that year we studied the dinosaurs. Wasn't it strange, our teacher told us, that the dinosaurs dominated the Earth for millions of years, and then one day they all vanished? No one knew why they had all died off. Some paleontologists thought that maybe a meteor from space had killed them, but that was impossible, more in the realm of science fiction.

Today we now know that through plate tectonics the continents do move, and that 65 million years ago a gigantic meteor measuring six miles across most likely did obliterate the dinosaurs and much of life on Earth. In my own short lifetime I have seen the seemingly impossible become established scientific fact over and over again. So is it impossible to think we might one day be able to teleport ourselves from one place to another, or build a spaceship that will one day take us light-years away to the stars?

15   Normally such feats would be considered impossible by today's physicists. Might they become possible within a few centuries? Or in ten thousand years, when our technology is more advanced? Or in a million years? To put it another way, if we were to somehow encounter a civilization a million years more advanced than ours, would their everyday technology appear to be "magic" to us? That, at its heart, is one of the central questions running through this book; just because something is "impossible" today, will it remain impossible centuries or millions of years into the future?

Given the remarkable advances in science in the past century, especially the creation of the quantum theory and general relativity, it is now possible to give rough estimates of when, if ever, some of these fantastic technologies may be realized. With the coming of even more advanced theories, such as string theory, even concepts bordering on science fiction, such as time travel and parallel universes, are now being re-evaluated by physicists. Think back 150 years to those technological advances that were declared "impossible" by scientists at the time and that have now become part of our everyday lives. Jules Verne wrote a novel in 1863, *Paris in the Twentieth Century,* which was locked away and forgotten for over a century until it was accidentally discovered by his great-grandson and published for the first time in 1994. In it Verne predicted what Paris might look like in the year 1960. His novel was filled with technology that was clearly considered impossible in the nineteenth century, including fax machines, a world-wide communications network, glass skyscrapers, gas-powered automobiles, and high-speed elevated trains.

Not surprisingly, Verne could make such stunningly accurate predictions because he was immersed in the world of science, picking the brains of scientists around him. A deep appreciation for the fundamentals of science allowed him to make such startling predictions.

Sadly, some of the greatest scientists of the nineteenth century took the opposite position and declared any number of technologies to be hopelessly impossible. Lord Kelvin, perhaps the most prominent physicist of the Victorian era (he is buried next to Isaac Newton in Westminster Abbey), declared that "heavier than air" devices such as the airplane were impossible. He thought X-rays were a hoax and that radio had no future. Lord Rutherford, who discovered the nucleus of the atom, dismissed the possibility of building an atomic bomb, comparing it to "moonshine." Chemists of the nineteenth century declared the search for the philosopher's stone, a fabled substance that can turn lead into gold, a scientific dead end. Nineteenth-century chemistry was based on the fundamental immutability of the elements, like lead. Yet with today's atom smashers, we can, in principle, turn lead atoms into gold. Think how fantastic today's televisions, computers, and Internet would have seemed at the turn of the twentieth century.

More recently, black holes were once considered to be science fiction. Einstein himself wrote a paper in 1939 that "proved" that black holes could never form. Yet today the Hubble Space Telescope and the Chandra X-ray telescope have revealed thousands of black holes in space.

The reason that these technologies were deemed "impossibilities" is that   20
the basic laws of physics and science were not known in the nineteenth century and the early part of the twentieth. Given the huge gaps in the understanding of science at the time, especially at the atomic level, it's no wonder such advances were considered impossible.

Studying the Impossible

Ironically, the serious study of the impossible has frequently opened up rich and entirely unexpected domains of science. For example, over the centuries the frustrating and futile search for a "perpetual motion machine" led physicists to conclude that such a machine was impossible, forcing them to postulate the conservation of energy and the three laws of thermodynamics. Thus the futile search to build perpetual motion machines helped to open up the entirely new field of thermodynamics, which in part laid the foundation of the steam engine, the machine age, and modern industrial society.

At the end of the nineteenth century, scientists decided that it was "impossible" for the Earth to be billions of years old. Lord Kelvin declared flatly that a molten Earth would cool down in 20 to 40 million years, contradicting the geologists and Darwinian biologists who claimed that the Earth might be billions of years old. The impossible was finally proven to be possible with the discovery of the nuclear force by Madame Curie and others, showing how the center of the Earth, heated by radioactive decay, could indeed be kept molten for billions of years.

We ignore the impossible at our peril. In the 1920s and 1930s Robert Goddard, the founder of modern rocketry, was the subject of intense criticism by those who thought that rockets could never travel in outer space. They sarcastically called his pursuit Goddard's Folly. In 1921 the editors of the *New York Times* railed against Dr. Goddard's work: "Professor Goddard does not know the relation between action and reaction and the need to have something better than a vacuum against which to react. He seems to lack the basic knowledge ladled out daily in high schools." Rockets were impossible, the editors huffed, because there was no air to push against in outer space. Sadly, one head of state did understand the implications of Goddard's "impossible" rockets—Adolf Hitler. During World War II, Germany's barrage of impossibly advanced V-2 rockets rained death and destruction on London, almost bringing it to its knees.

Studying the impossible may have also changed the course of world history. In the 1950s it was widely believed, even by Einstein, that an atomic bomb was "impossible." Physicists knew that there was a tremendous amount of energy locked deep inside the atom's nucleus, according to Einstein's equation $E = mc^2$, but the energy released by a single nucleus was too insignificant to consider. But atomic physicist Leó Szilárd remembered reading the 1914 H. G. Wells novel, *The World Set Free,* in which Wells predicted the development of the atomic bomb. In the book he stated that the secret of the atomic bomb would be solved by a physicist in 1933. By chance Szilárd stumbled upon this book in 1932. Spurred on by the novel, in 1933, precisely as predicted by Wells some two decades earlier, he hit upon the idea of magnifying the power of a single atom via a chain reaction, so that the energy of splitting a single uranium nucleus could be magnified by many trillions. Szilárd then set into motion a series of key experiments and secret negotiations between Einstein and President Franklin Roosevelt that would lead to the Manhattan Project, which built the atomic bomb.

25   Time and again we see that the study of the impossible has opened up entirely new vistas, pushing the boundaries of physics and chemistry and

forcing scientists to redefine what they mean by "impossible." As Sir William Osier once said, "The philosophies of one age have become the absurdities of the next, and the foolishness of yesterday has become the wisdom of tomorrow."

Many physicists subscribe to the famous dictum of T. H. White, who wrote in *The Once and Future King,* "Anything that is not forbidden, is mandatory!" In physics we find evidence of this all the time. Unless there is a law of physics explicitly preventing a new phenomenon, we eventually find that it exists. (This has happened several times in the search for new subatomic particles. By probing the limits of what is forbidden, physicists have often unexpectedly discovered new laws of physics.) A corollary to T. H. White's statement might well be, "Anything that is not impossible, is mandatory!"

For example, cosmologist Stephen Hawking tried to prove that time travel was impossible by finding a new law of physics that would forbid it, which he called the "chronology protection conjecture." Unfortunately, after many years of hard work he was unable to prove this principle. In fact, to the contrary, physicists have now demonstrated that a law that prevents time travel is beyond our present-day mathematics. Today, because there is no law of physics preventing the existence of time machines, physicists have had to take their possibility very seriously.

Already one "impossible" technology is now proving to be possible: the notion of teleportation (at least at the level of atoms). Even a few years ago physicists would have said that sending or beaming an object from one point to another violated the laws of quantum physics. The writers of the original *Star Trek* television series, in fact, were so stung by the criticism from physicists that they added "Heisenberg compensators" to explain their teleporters in order to address this flaw. Today, because of a recent breakthrough, physicists can teleport atoms across a room or photons under the Danube River.

Analyze

1. Who is Flash Gordon, and why does Kaku mention the television show based on his character in the introduction to his essay?
2. Explain the point Kaku is making by discussing the example of plate tectonics.
3. Why does Kaku end his essay with a paragraph about teleportation? How does this paragraph relate to several key points he makes throughout the essay?

Explore

1. Watch an episode of *Star Trek*, making a note of every technological tool that is used in the episode and its functions. Then, make a list of these technologies and explain how each is related to, or reflected in, technologies that we use today. Review and discuss these lists as a class, paying particular attention to the different ways in which technologies from the television show relate to the technologies we use today.

2. Watch the first episode of Kaku's television show *Physics of the Impossible* on YouTube. As you watch the episode, write a description of what you are watching, keeping track of what happens in the episode and the themes and issues presented. After watching the episode, write a three- to five-page essay comparing and contrasting the experience of reading the essay and watching the video. In the essay, explain some of the similar themes and issues discussed. Compare and contrast the ways in which similar themes and issues are presented in the video and in the essay. Reflect on your response to the video and to the essay, as well as on the similarities and differences between what you learned from each.

3. Quantum Mechanics and the Theory of Relativity appear to both be very important in Kaku's discussion of the possibility of realizing in reality technologies that were once thought to be "impossible." Do some research on Quantum Mechanics and the Theory of Relativity. Explain briefly what each is, and in a short essay explain how these theories and Kaku's discussions of them relate to time travel.

Forging Connections

1. Each author in this chapter takes some position with regard to how SF relates to the future, the present, and the past. In a three- to five-page essay, compare and contrast the ways in which two of the authors in this chapter discuss SF's relationship to the future, present, and past. Based on this comparison, explain how your understanding of SF and its purposes may have changed.

2. In his essay, Neal Stephenson lays out two broad theories, The Inspiration Theory and The Hieroglyph Theory, which can be used to describe the complex relationships between science and SF. Choose two essays in this chapter and explain why each seems to be characterized more by The Inspiration Theory, The Hieroglyph Theory, or some combination of both.

Looking Further

1. Several authors in this anthology refer to the relationships between technology and myth, both in terms of how "mythical" contemporary thinking about technology can be, as well as in terms of the ways in which classical myths about technology as recounted in the myths of Prometheus, Daedalus, and Icarus help us better understand how technologies function. Look up the myths of Prometheus, Daedalus, and Icarus. Compare and contrast these. Then, consider how the themes and issues raised by one relate to one or more of the essays in this collection.

2. In discussing the relationships between technologies and stories, Jon Turney quotes the historian of technology David Nye, who wrote, "a tool always implies at least one small story." Such stories, Turney explains, are found both in "the explanation of [the tool's] basic operation" and in "its place in a collection of futuristic scenarios." Choose a specific tool, either mechanical or digital. Then, write a short story (three to five pages) about the tool in which you incorporate a description of its current day-to-day uses and imagine and describe its possible applications. Afterwards, reflect on how your short fiction may have changed your understanding of the real-world functions of this tool and its social significance.

3

(Dis)Connecting in a Digital Age: What Does It Mean to Be Human in an Age of Social Media and "Intelligent" Machines?

Do you prefer socializing with your friends online or in person? Ten years ago, such a question would have been one that very few of us could answer. Today, it is one that all of us have to seriously consider. Isn't it easier and more convenient to interact with people via social media applications than in person? But what happens when the majority of the time you spend socializing with others takes place in virtual rather than actual worlds? Furthermore, as we rely more and more on digital networks to relate to one another and on automated machines to perform various tasks, how should we design and program these technologies to make sure we are acting in the best interests of humans? While thinking machines and robots may sound like science fiction, the reality is that robotic devices like driverless cars are already legal in certain states. As a result, a number of ethical issues related to how we will use and relate to "thinking machines" arise, as do issues related to the consequences of our increasing use of devices and social media to mediate our relationships with other humans today.

The authors in this chapter all consider the social, cultural, and psychological implications of humans' increasing reliance on technologies for various tasks and functions, particularly interacting with one another. In her essay "Alone Together," psychologist Sherry Turkle probes the possible consequences of our reliance on "sociable" machines and how this reliance may affect actual human-to-human interaction. Journalist Susan Maushart reports on the effects of a six-month ban on her children's use of social media in her essay "When My Kids Unplugged." Cartoonist and graphic novelist Scott McCloud speculates that regardless of which specific media and technologies we use to communicate with, they are all acting as substitutes for our sad inability to communicate mind to mind. In his essay "Machines of Laughter and Forgetting" the cultural critic Evgeny Morozov asks not what the effects of our increasing use of technologies may be, but how humans might redesign technologies to make all of us more aware of their functions and the consequences of those functions. Psychologist Gary

Marcus, in his essay "Moral Machines," reports on increasingly automated technologies, such as Google's driverless cars, and how these technologies will require us to develop new ethical frameworks. Finally, Rose Eveleth reports on current theories related to humanoid robot development in her essay "Robots: Is the Uncanny Valley Real?"

Sherry Turkle
"Alone Together"

Sherry Turkle is a Professor in the Science, Technology, and Society Program at the Massachusetts Institute of Technology (MIT) and the founder and current director of the MIT Initiative on Technology and Self. Her research, which combines sociological and psychological perspectives on technology and its uses, has been read and circulated widely. She has written numerous books and articles, including *Life on the Screen: Identity in the Age of the Internet* (1995) and *Simulation and Its Discontents* (2009). Turkle's work is unique in its ability to address both academic and general audiences. In this essay, excerpted from her 2012 book *Alone Together: Why We Expect More from Technology and Less from Each Other,* Turkle reports on the findings from her most recent research, which considers the potential benefits and drawbacks of increased human interaction with robots and machines.

Has social media changed the ways in which you communicate with your friends and family members? How?

Computers no longer wait for humans to project meaning onto them. Now, sociable robots meet our gaze, speak to us, and learn to recognize us. They ask us to take care of them; in response, we imagine that they might care for us in return. Indeed, among the most talked about robotic designs are in the area of care and companionship. In summer 2010, there are enthusiastic reports in the *New York Times* and the *Wall Street Journal* on robotic teachers, companions, and therapists. And Microsoft

"Technology reshapes the landscape of our emotional lives, but is it offering us the lives we want to lead?"

demonstrates a virtual human, Milo, that recognizes the people it interacts with and whose personality is sculpted by them. Tellingly, in the video that introduces Milo to the public, a young man begins by playing games with Milo in a virtual garden; by the end of the demonstration, things have heated up—he confides in Milo after being told off by his parents.[1]

We are challenged to ask what such things augur. Some people are looking for robots to clean rugs and help with the laundry. Others hope for a mechanical bride. As sociable robots propose themselves as substitutes for people, new networked devices offer us machine-mediated relationships with each other, another kind of substitution. We romance the robot and become inseparable from our smartphones. As this happens, we remake ourselves and our relationships with each other through our new intimacy with machines. People talk about Web access on their BlackBerries as "the place for hope" in life, the place where loneliness can be defeated. A woman in her late sixties describes her new iPhone: "It's like having a little Times Square in my pocketbook. All lights. All the people I could meet." People are lonely. The network is seductive. But if we are always on, we may deny ourselves the rewards of solitude.

As I listen for what stands behind this moment, I hear a certain fatigue with the difficulties of life with people. We insert robots into every narrative of human frailty. People make too many demands; robot demands would be of a more manageable sort. People disappoint; robots will not. When people talk about relationships with robots, they talk about cheating husbands, wives who fake orgasms, and children who take drugs. They talk about how hard it is to understand family and friends. I am at first surprised by these comments. Their clear intent is to bring people down a notch. A forty-four-year-old woman says, "After all, we never know how another person really feels. People put on a good face. Robots would be safer." A thirty-year-old man remarks, "I'd rather talk to a robot. Friends can be exhausting. The robot will always be there for me. And whenever I'm done, I can walk away."

The idea of sociable robots suggests that we might navigate intimacy by skirting it. People seem comforted by the belief that if we alienate or fail each other, robots will be there, programmed to provide simulations of love.[2] Our population is aging; there will be robots to take care of us. Our children are neglected; robots will tend to them. We are too exhausted to deal with each other in adversity; robots will have the energy. Robots won't be judgmental. We will be accommodated. An older woman says of her robot dog, "It is better than a real dog.... It won't do dangerous things, and it won't betray you....Also, it won't die suddenly and abandon you and make you very sad."[3]

The elderly are the first to have companionate robots aggressively marketed to them, but young people also see the merits of robotic companionship. These days, teenagers have sexual adulthood thrust upon them before they are ready to deal with the complexities of relationships. They are drawn to the comfort of connection without the demands of intimacy. This may lead them to a hookup—sex without commitment or even caring. Or it may lead to an online romance—companionship that can always be interrupted. Not surprisingly, teenagers are drawn to love stories in which full intimacy cannot occur—here I think of current passions for films and novels about high school vampires who cannot sexually consummate relationships for fear of hurting those they love. And teenagers are drawn to the idea of technological communion. They talk easily of robots that would be safe and predictable companions.[4]

These young people have grown up with sociable robot pets, the companions of their playrooms, which portrayed emotion, said they cared, and asked to be cared for.[5] We are psychologically programmed not only to nurture what we love but to love what we nurture. So even simple artificial creatures can provoke heartfelt attachment. Many teenagers anticipate that the robot toys of their childhood will give way to full-fledged machine companions. In the psychoanalytic tradition, a symptom addresses a conflict but distracts us from understanding or resolving it; a dream expresses a wish.[6] Sociable robots serve as both symptom and dream: as a symptom, they promise a way to sidestep conflicts about intimacy; as a dream, they express a wish for relationships with limits, a way to be both together and alone.[7]

Some people even talk about robots as providing respite from feeling overwhelmed by technology. In Japan, companionate robots are specifically marketed as a way to seduce people out of cyberspace; robots plant a new flag in the physical real. If the problem is that too much technology has made us busy and anxious, the solution will be another technology that will organize, amuse, and relax us. So, although historically robots provoked anxieties about technology out of control, these days they are more likely to represent the reassuring idea that in a world of problems, science will offer solutions.[8] Robots have become a twenty-first-century deus ex machina. Putting hope in robots expresses an enduring technological optimism, a belief that as other things go wrong, science will go right. In a complicated world, robots seem a simple salvation. It is like calling in the cavalry.

But this is not a book about robots. Rather, it is about how we are changed as technology offers us substitutes for connecting with each other face-to-face. We are offered robots and a whole world of machine-mediated relationships on networked devices. As we instant-message, e-mail, text, and Twitter, technology redraws the boundaries between intimacy and solitude. We talk of getting "rid" of our e-mails, as though these notes are so much excess baggage. Teenagers avoid making telephone calls, fearful that they "reveal too much." They would rather text than talk. Adults, too, choose keyboards over the human voice. It is more efficient, they say. Things that happen in "real time" take too much time. Tethered to technology, we are shaken when that world "unplugged" does not signify, does not satisfy. After an evening of avatar-to-avatar talk in a networked game, we feel, at one moment, in possession of a full social life and, in the next, curiously isolated, in tenuous complicity with strangers. We build a following on Facebook or MySpace and wonder to what degree our followers are friends. We recreate ourselves as online personae and give ourselves new bodies, homes, jobs, and romances. Yet, suddenly, in the half-light of virtual community, we may feel utterly alone. As we distribute ourselves, we may abandon ourselves. Sometimes people experience no sense of having communicated after hours of connection. And they report feelings of closeness when they are paying little attention. In all of this, there is a nagging question: Does virtual intimacy degrade our experience of the other kind and, indeed, of all encounters, of any kind?

Connectivity and Its Discontents

Online connections were first conceived as a substitute for face-to-face contact, when the latter was for some reason impractical: Don't have time to make a phone call? Shoot off a text message. But very quickly, the text message became the connection of choice. We discovered the network—the world of connectivity—to be uniquely suited to the overworked and over-scheduled life it makes possible. And now we look to the network to defend us against loneliness even as we use it to control the intensity of our connections. Technology makes it easy to communicate when we wish and to disengage at will.

A few years ago at a dinner party in Paris, I met Ellen, an ambitious, elegant young woman in her early thirties, thrilled to be working at her dream job in advertising. Once a week, she would call her grandmother in Philadelphia using Skype, an Internet service that functions as a telephone with a Web camera. Before Skype, Ellen's calls to her grandmother were costly and brief. With Skype, the calls are free and give the compelling sense that the other person is present—Skype is an almost real-time video link. Ellen could now call more frequently: "Twice a week and I stay on the call for an hour," she told me. It should have been rewarding; instead, when I met her, Ellen was unhappy. She knew that her grandmother was unaware that Skype allows surreptitious multitasking. Her grandmother could see Ellen's face on the screen but not her hands. Ellen admitted to me, "I do my e-mail during the calls. I'm not really paying attention to our conversation."

Ellen's multitasking removed her to another place. She felt her grandmother was talking to someone who was not really there. During their Skype conversations, Ellen and her grandmother were more connected than they had ever been before, but at the same time, each was alone. Ellen felt guilty and confused: she knew that her grandmother was happy, even if their intimacy was now, for Ellen, another task among multitasks.

I have often observed this distinctive confusion: these days, whether you are online or not, it is easy for people to end up unsure if they are closer together or further apart. I remember my own sense of disorientation the first time I realized that I was "alone together." I had traveled an exhausting thirty-six hours to attend a conference on advanced robotic technology held in central Japan. The packed grand ballroom was Wi-Fi enabled: the speaker was using the Web for his presentation, laptops were open throughout the audience, fingers were flying, and there was a sense of great concentration and intensity. But not many in the audience were attending to the speaker. Most people seemed to be doing their e-mail, downloading files, and surfing the Net. The man next to me was searching for a *New Yorker* cartoon to illustrate his upcoming presentation. Every once in a while, audience members gave the speaker some attention, lowering their laptop screens in a kind of curtsy, a gesture of courtesy.

Outside, in the hallways, the people milling around me were looking past me to virtual others. They were on their laptops and their phones, connecting to colleagues at the conference going on around them and to others around the globe. There but not there. Of course, clusters of people chatted with each other, making dinner plans, "networking" in that old sense of the word, the one that implies having a coffee or sharing a meal. But at this conference, it was clear that what people mostly want from public space is to be alone with their personal networks. It is good to come together physically, but it is more important to stay tethered to our devices. I thought of how Sigmund Freud considered the power of communities both to shape and to subvert us, and a psychoanalytic pun came to mind: "connectivity and its discontents."

The phrase comes back to me months later as I interview management consultants who seem to have lost touch with their best instincts for what makes them competitive. They complain about the BlackBerry revolution, yet accept it as inevitable while decrying it as corrosive. They say they used to talk to each other as they waited to give presentations or took taxis to the airport; now they spend that time doing e-mail. Some tell me they are making better use of their "downtime," but they argue without conviction. The time that they once used to talk as they waited for appointments or drove to the airport was never downtime. It was the time when far-flung global teams solidified relationships and refined ideas.

In corporations, among friends, and within academic departments, people readily admit that they would rather leave a voicemail or send an e-mail than talk face-to-face. Some who say "I live my life on my BlackBerry" are forthright about avoiding the "real-time" commitment of a phone call. The new technologies allow us to "dial down" human contact, to titrate its nature and extent. I recently overheard a conversation in a restaurant between two women. "No one answers the phone in our house anymore," the first woman proclaimed with some consternation. "It used to be that the kids would race to pick up the phone. Now they are up in their rooms, knowing no one is going to call them, and texting and going on Facebook or whatever instead." Parents with teenage children will be nodding at this very familiar story in recognition and perhaps a sense of wonderment that this has happened, and so quickly. And teenagers will simply be saying, "Well, what's your point?"

A thirteen-year-old tells me she "hates the phone and never listens to voicemail." Texting offers just the right amount of access, just the right amount of control. She is a modern Goldilocks: for her, texting puts people not too close, not too far, but at just the right distance. The world is now full of modern Goldilockses, people who take comfort in being in touch with a lot of people whom they also keep at bay. A twenty-one-year-old college student reflects on the new balance: "I don't use my phone for calls any more. I don't have the time to just go on and on. I like texting, Twitter, looking at someone's Facebook wall. I learn what I need to know."

Randy, twenty-seven, has a younger sister—a Goldilocks who got her distances wrong. Randy is an American lawyer now working in California. His family lives in New York, and he flies to the East Coast to see them three or four times a year. When I meet Randy, his sister Nora, twenty-four, had just announced her engagement and wedding date via e-mail to a list of friends and family. "That," Randy says to me bitterly, "is how I got the news." He doesn't know if he is more angry or hurt. "It doesn't feel right that she didn't call," he says. "I was getting ready for a trip home. Couldn't she have told me then? She's my sister, but I didn't have a private moment when she told me in person. Or at least a call, just the two of us. When I told her I was upset, she sort of understood, but laughed and said that she and her fiancé just wanted to do things simply, as simply as possible. I feel very far away from her."

Nora did not mean to offend her brother. She saw e-mail as efficient and did not see beyond. We have long turned to technology to make us more efficient in work; now Nora illustrates how we want it to make us more efficient in our private lives. But when technology engineers intimacy, relationships can be reduced to mere connections. And then, easy connection becomes redefined as intimacy. Put otherwise, cyberintimacies slide into cybersolitudes.

And with constant connection comes new anxieties of disconnection, a kind of panic. Even Randy, who longs for a phone call from Nora on such an important matter as her wedding, is never without his BlackBerry. He holds it in his hands during our entire conversation. Once, he puts it in his pocket. A few moments later, it comes out, fingered like a talisman. In interviews with young and old, I find people genuinely terrified of being cut off from the "grid." People say that the loss of a cell phone can "feel like a death." One television producer in her mid-forties tells me that without her smartphone, "I felt like I had lost my mind." Whether or not our devices are in use, without them we feel disconnected, adrift. A danger even to ourselves, we insist on our right to send text messages while driving our cars and object to rules that would limit the practice.[9]

Only a decade ago, I would have been mystified that fifteen-year-olds in my urban neighborhood, a neighborhood of parks and shopping malls, of front stoops and coffee shops, would feel the need to send and receive close to six thousand messages a month via portable digital devices or that best friends would assume that when they visited, it would usually be on the virtual real estate of Facebook.[10] It might have seemed intrusive, if not illegal, that my mobile phone would tell me the location of all my acquaintances within a ten-mile radius.[11] But these days we are accustomed to all this. Life in a media bubble has come to seem natural. So has the end of a certain public etiquette: on the street, we speak into the invisible microphones on our mobile phones and appear to be talking to ourselves. We share intimacies with the air as though unconcerned about who can hear us or the details of our physical surroundings.

I once described the computer as a second self, a mirror of mind. Now the metaphor no longer goes far enough. Our new devices provide space for the emergence of a new state of the self, itself, split between the screen and the physical real, wired into existence through technology.

Teenagers tell me they sleep with their cell phone, and even when it isn't on their person, when it has been banished to the school locker, for instance, they know when their phone is vibrating. The technology has become like a phantom limb, it is so much a part of them. These young people are among the first to grow up with an expectation of continuous connection: always on, and always on them. And they are among the first to grow up not necessarily thinking of simulation as second best. All of this makes them fluent with technology but brings a set of new insecurities. They nurture friendships on social-networking sites and then wonder if they are among friends. They are connected all day but are not sure if they have communicated. They become confused about companionship. Can they find it in their lives on the screen? Could they find it with a robot? Their digitized friendships—played out with emoticon emotions, so often predicated on rapid response rather than reflection—may prepare them, at times through nothing more than their superficiality, for relationships that could bring superficiality to a higher power, that is, for relationships with the inanimate. They come to accept lower expectations for connection and, finally, the idea that robot friendships could be sufficient unto the day.

Overwhelmed by the volume and velocity of our lives, we turn to technology to help us find time. But technology makes us busier than ever and ever more in search of retreat. Gradually, we come to see our online life as life itself. We come to see what robots offer as relationship. The simplification of relationship is no longer a source of complaint. It becomes what we want. These seem the gathering clouds of a perfect storm.

Technology reshapes the landscape of our emotional lives, but is it offering us the lives we want to lead? Many roboticists are enthusiastic about having robots tend to our children and our aging parents, for instance. Are these psychologically, socially, and ethically acceptable propositions? What are our responsibilities here? And are we comfortable with virtual environments that propose themselves not as places for recreation but as new worlds to live in? What do we have, now that we have what we say we want—now that we have what technology makes easy?[12] This is the time to begin these conversations, together. It is too late to leave the future to the futurists.

NOTES

1. Benedict Carey and John Markoff, "Students, Meet Your New Teacher, Mr. Robot," *New York Times,* July 10, 2010, www.nytimes.com/2010/07/11/science/11 robots.html (accessed July 10, 2010); Anne Tergeson and Miho Inada, "It's Not a Stuffed Animal, It's a $6,000 Medical Device," *Wall Street Journal,* June 21, 2010, http://online.wsj.com/article/SB10001424052748704463504575301051844937276.html (accessed August 10, 2010); Jonathan Fildes, "'Virtual Human' Milo Comes Out to Play at TED in Oxford," *BBC News,* July 13, 2010, www.bbc.co.uk/news/10623423 (accessed July 13, 2010); Amy Harmon, "A Soft Spot for Circuitry: Robot Machines as Companions," *New York Times,* July 4, 2010, www.nytimes.com/2010/07/05/science/05robot.html?pagewanted=all (accessed July 4, 2010); Emily Veach, "A Robot That Helps You Diet," *Wall Street Journal,* July 20, 2010, http://online.wsj.com/article/SB10001424052 748704682604575369981478383568.html (accessed July 20, 2010).

2. The way here is paved by erotic images of female robots used to sell refrigerators, washing machines, shaving cream, and vodka. See, for example, the campaign for Svedka Vodka (Steve Hall, "Svedka Launches Futuristic, Un-PC Campaign," Andrants.com, September 20, 2005, www.adrants.com/2005/09/svedka-launches-futuristic-unpc.php [accessed September 1, 2009]) and Phillip's shaving system ("Feel the Erotic Union of Man and Shavebot," AdFreak.com, August 21, 2007, http://adweek.blogs.com/ad freak/2007/08/feel-the-erotic.html [accessed September 1, 2009]).

3. Sharon Moshavi, "Putting on the Dog in Japan," *Boston Globe,* June 17, 1999, A1.

4. As preteens, the young women of the first Google generation (born roughly from 1987 to 1993) wore clothing widely referred to as "baby harlot"; they listened to songs about explicit sex well before puberty. Their boomer parents had few ideas about where to draw lines, having spent their own adolescences

declaring the lines irrelevant. Boomer parents grew up rejecting parental rules, but knowing that there were rules. One might say it is the job of teenagers to complain about constraints and the job of parents to insist on them, even if the rules are not obeyed. Rules, even unheeded, suggest that twelve to fifteen are not good ages to be emotionally and sexually enmeshed.

Today's teenagers cannot easily articulate any rules about sexual conduct except for those that will keep them "safe." Safety refers to not getting venereal diseases or AIDS. Safety refers to not getting pregnant. And on these matters teenagers are eloquent, unembarrassed, and startlingly well informed. But teenagers are overwhelmed with how unsafe they feel in relationships. A robot to talk to is appealing—even if currently unavailable—as are situations that provide feelings of closeness without emotional demands. I have said that rampant fantasies of vampire lovers (closeness with constraints on sexuality) bear a family resemblance to ideas about robot lovers (sex without intimacy, perfect). And closeness without the possibility of physical intimacy and eroticized encounters that can be switched off in an instant—these are the affordances of online encounters. Online romance expresses the aesthetic of the robotic moment. From a certain perspective, they are a way of preparing for it. On the psychology of adolescents' desire for relationships with constraint, I am indebted to conversations with child and adolescent psychoanalyst Monica Horovitz in August 2009.

5. Commenting on the insatiable desire for robot pets during the 2009 holiday season, a researcher on social trends comments, "A toy trend would be something that reflects the broader society, that tells you where society is going, something society needs." Gerald Celente, founder of the Trends Research Institute, cited in Brad Tuttle, "Toy Craze Explained: A Zhu Zhu Pet Hamster Is Like a 'Viral Infection,' " *Time,* December 9, 2009, http://money.blogs.time.com/2009/12/07/toy-craze-explained-a-zhu-zhu-pet-hamster-is-like-a-viral-infection (accessed December 9, 2009).

6. For classic psychodynamic formulations of the meaning of symptoms, see Sigmund Freud, "The Unconscious," in *The Standard Edition of Sigmund Freud,* ed. and trans. James Strachey et al. (London: Hogarth Press, 1953–1974), 14:159–204; "Introductory Lectures on Psychoanalysis," in *The Standard Edition,* vols. 15 and 16; "From the History of an Infantile Neurosis," in *The Standard Edition,* 17:1–122; "Inhibitions, Symptoms, and Anxiety," in *The Standard Edition,* 20:75–172; and Sigmund Freud and Joseph Breuer, "Studies on Hysteria," in *The Standard Edition,* 2:48–106. For Freud on dreams as wishes, see "The Interpretation of Dreams," in *The Standard Edition,* vol. IV.

7. For an argument about the pleasures of limited worlds in another technological realm, see Natasha Schüll's work on gambling, *Addiction by Design: Machine Gambling in Las Vegas* (Princeton, NJ: Princeton University Press, forthcoming).

8. See, for example, Bill Gates, "A Robot in Every Home," *Scientific American,* January 2007, www.scientificamerican.com/article.cfm?id=a-robot-in-every-home (accessed September 2, 2009).

9. See, for example, Matt Richtel, "In Study, Texting Lifts Crash Risk by Large Margin," *New York Times,* July 27, 2009, www.nytimes.com/2009/07/28/ technology/28texting.html (accessed September 1, 2009). On the pressure that friends and family members put on drivers who text, see "Driver Texting Now an Issue in Back Seat," *New York Times,* September 9, 2009, www.nytimes.com/ 2009/09/09/technology/09 distracted.html (accessed September 9, 2009). As I complete this book, Oprah Winfrey has made texting while driving a personal crusade, encouraging people across America to sign an online pledge to not text and drive. See "Oprah's No Phone Zone," Oprah.com, www.oprah .com/packages/no-phone-zone.html (accessed May 30, 2010).

10. The teenage national average as of January 2010 is closer to thirty-five hundred; my affluent, urban neighborhood has a far higher number. Roger Entner, "Under-aged Texting: Usage and Actual Cost," Nielson.com, January 27, 2010,http://blog.nielsen.com/nielsenwire/online_mobile/under-aged-texting-usage-and-actual-cost (accessed May 30, 2010). On texting's impact on teenage life, see Katie Hafner, "Texting May Be Taking Its Toll," *New York Times,* May 25, 2009, www.nytimes.com/2009/05/26/health/26teen.html?_r=2& 8dpc (accessed July 21, 2009).

11. To find friends in the neighborhood, Loopt for the iPhone is a popular "app."

12. A witty experiment suggests that Facebook "friends" won't even show up when you invite them to a party. Hal Niedzviecki, "Facebook in a Crowd," *New York Times,* October 24, 2008, www.nytimes.com/2008/10/26/ magazine/26lives-t.html (accessed July 27, 2010).

Analyze

1. Who is Milo?
2. What are some reasons why several individuals involved in Turkle's study reported preferring to interact with robots instead of humans?
3. Explain why Turkle makes a reference to vampires and how it relates to her argument about young people's relationships to technology.
4. What is a *deus ex machina*? Why does Turkle suggest that robots may be one?

Explore

1. Turkle ends her essay with a research question. She writes, "Does virtual intimacy degrade our experience of the other kind and, indeed, of all encounters, of any kind?" Based on your personal experience, answer this question by comparing and contrasting the sense of connection you experience with others after a virtual versus an in-person social encounter.

2. In the 2014 movie *Her*, a man has a relationship with an iPhone. Watch the trailer for this movie on the Web. Afterwards, write a description of the trailer in which you carefully explain what happens in the trailer for an audience who has not seen the trailer. Then, analyze the trailer, explaining what specific issues discussed by Turkle in her essay also appear to be evident in the movie trailer. Compare the experience of reading about these issues in Turkle's essay compared with seeing these issues dramatized in the film trailer. Finally, write a short essay in which you explain how seeing the film trailer did or did not change your understanding of Turkle's essay and the import of the issues discussed in the essay.

3. Using an Internet search engine, locate an image that you believe could be used to illustrate Turkle's essay. Then, in one or two pages, explain why you chose the image, what particular themes from Turkle's essay appear to be related to the image, and how the image may help readers better understand what Turkle's essay is about.

Susan Maushart
"When My Kids Unplugged"

Susan Maushart is an American author and journalist who lives and works in both the United States and Australia. A frequent contributor on issues related to motherhood, marriage, and media to both print and television news outlets, Maushart is the author of the books *The Winter of Our Disconnect: How Three Totally Wired Teenagers (and a Mother Who Slept with Her iPhone) Pulled the Plug on Their Technology and Lived to Tell the Tale* (2011) and *Wifework: What Marriage Really Means for Women* (2002). In this essay, originally published on Salon.com, Maushart describes the reasons why she pulled the plug on her children's use of social media for six months and the results of the experiment.

Have you ever taken a break from social media? What happened?

There were lots of reasons why we pulled the plug on my family's electronic media for six months . . . or, I should say, why I did, because heaven knows my children would have sooner volunteered to go without food, water or hair products. At ages fourteen, fifteen and eighteen, my daughters and my son don't use media. They *inhabit* media. And they do so exactly as a fish inhabits a pond. Gracefully. Unblinkingly. And utterly without consciousness or curiosity as to how they got there. Over a period of years, I watched and worried as our media began to function as a force field separating my children from what my son, only half-ironically, called RL (Real Life). But to be honest, the teenagers weren't the only ones with dependency issues. Although a recent arrival to the global village, I'd been known to abuse information too.

And clearly, we weren't alone. Zeynep Tufekci, who teaches sociology to students at the University of Maryland, is convinced that social-networking media are making us more, not less, accountable for our actions. "We're going back to a more normal place, historically," she observes—a place not unlike a small town, where everybody knows your business, whether you want them to or not. Identity theft is no longer the issue, Tufekci argues—but preserving anonymity may well be. "You know that old cartoon? On the Internet, nobody knows you're a dog? On the Internet today, everybody knows you're a dog. If you don't want people to know you're a dog, you'd better stay away from a keyboard."

Other observers worry that our meaningful relationships are being nudged aside by one-sided "parasocial" connections, such as my fourteen-year-old daughter Sussy's relationship with Taylor Swift or Zooey Deschanel: "Peripheral people in our network whose intimate details we follow closely online, even while they . . . are basically unaware we exist," in the words of Danah Boyd, a fellow at Harvard's Berkman Center for Internet and Society. Social media have enabled an explosion of what anthropologists call "weak ties." But whither the strong ones? The deep ones?

And speaking of getting real, Flickr cofounder Caterina Fake—and no, I am not making that up—admitted recently that the ease of online sharing has made her slack about getting together with friends the old-fashioned way, in high-resolution reality. "These technologies allow you to be much more broadly friendly, but you just spread yourself much more thinly over many more people," she explained. And who wants to raise a stack of pancake people (to use playwright Richard Foreman's term for those who are becoming—as it were—flattened by Facebook)? My worst fear as a parent was that my kids might lose an alternative frame of reference—that growing up as Digital Natives, they would swallow the pancake paradigm whole and forget there were more nourishing ways for friends and family to connect.

5   One particular evening my daughter Sussy and I hunkered down in front of the fire with the boxes of family photos ("Whoa. Look at all those hard copies!" she cried) for a veritable festival of face-to-Facebooking was a good case in point. We devoured thousands of images, laughing, hooting, or blinking in wonderment just as we would have done online. But sitting side by side, passing pictures from one set of hands to another, created a different energy. We didn't simply consume the images, or allow them to consume us. Rather, they became catapults, triggers for stories and recollections, for the exchange of family and cultural history far greater than the sum of the individual parts. "Yes, darling, Grammy was a hottie back in sixty-nine," I agreed, my eyes bright with unshed tears. "No, I'm pretty sure that was her real hair."

An impromptu glee club I encountered on one summer night around the piano evoked similar longings: more than a nostalgia for the real, it was a déjà vu about the real, I reflected, as the playlist skidded freakily from "The Jungle Book" to Death Cab for Cutie and back again. "I had no idea [your friend] could play the piano!" I exclaimed to my eighteen-year-old daughter Anni after the group dispersed that night. "To be honest, neither did I," she admitted.

"Was it okay? I mean, you all looked like you were having fun . . ." I trailed off.

"Fun?" she spat back. "You must be joking! It was awesome."

10   My fifteen-year-old son Bill's exile from MSN, Facebook, and his anime stash propelled him out of the door faster than a bullet from one of his beloved first-person shooter games. My dread was that he would simply make a beeline for his friend's house. And he did too—at first. Within a week or two, his separation anxiety seemed to dissipate. He started spending more time at the beach and pool, catching up with friends he hadn't connected with since primary school. Matt, for instance, who was now a serious trumpet player, and Tom, the older brother of Bill's gaming buddy Pat, who had recently taken up jazz piano. They were both studying with the same teacher, a saxophonist named Paul Andrews, Bill reported. And so began

the prelude to his renewed interest in the saxophone. Any chance that he could start lessons again? he asked me soon afterward.

I pretended to consider it—no sense ruining everything by showing my approval—and agreed to a "trial lesson." I came in at the end of it, just in time to see Andrews nod his head curtly.

> "So, tell me. What do you want to be?"
>
> "A musician," Bill replied without hesitation.
>
> ("WTF?" I was screaming internally.)
>
> "Uh huh." Andrews nodded again. "Well, practice, focus, listen,   15
> learn . . . and you can be."

Up to that point, Bill had barely picked up his instrument in two years. From that point, he has hardly put it down.

In the ensuing weeks and months after that pivotal first lesson, I watched my son evolve like a human Pokémon from a surly, back-talking gamer to a surly back-talking musician in-the-making. (LOL.) To this day, Bill insists that it wasn't the technology ban that changed him. It was the friends, and the teacher they'd led him to. "Ah. I see," I reply.

> "The technology ban was nothing but a trigger," he adds, a little less certainly.
>
> "Ah, a trigger," I echo. (Bang, bang! I think to myself. Got 'im!)

Sussy ended up switching friendship groups too. Loss of Facebook (not to   20 mention loss of MSN and MySpace) seemed to increase her focus generally; at the same time, it put her out of the loop with her old friends. "With Jen and Cat and that kind of group, you figure stuff out on the computer, like sleepovers and stuff," she explained to me. These invitations happened spontaneously, usually on the spur of the moment, in fact, with little or no notice. If you blinked—or, more to the point, if you went offline—you missed them. The girls in Sussy's new group at school didn't operate like that. "We planned a sleepover a week in advance!" she told me proudly, and slightly incredulously.

Sussy's coping mechanisms differed from Anni's and Bill's significantly. The older kids took the opportunity to go out more—shopping, visiting, or clubbing in Anni's case, and hanging out at the pool or jamming in somebody's garage in Bill's. Sussy had fewer friends who lived in the neighborhood, so she faced major transportation issues. Her best girlfriend, my goddaughter Maddi, lived in Melbourne. Her closest boy chum, Andy, had just moved with his family to England.

Partly for these reasons, her overall media time budget probably remained unchanged.

She clung to the landline like a drowning teenager to a life raft. After school, she'd install herself in the family room, echoey and airplane-hangar-like now that it had been clear-felled of its media and their bulky accoutrements, and hold court before an unseen audience for two or three hours at a clip. She assured me that both Maddi and Andy had their parents' permission to ring her as often as they liked; it seems they had magic Internet landlines that made long-distance calls for free, "Or just about."

"What if you need to ring them?" I wanted to know.

25   "Easy. I just send them a signal—I ring once or twice and then hang up. Really, Mum, we've got it all figured out."

Many people have asked me if there was ever a moment during the electronic media blackout when I was tempted to quit. Not counting April 25, the day I received a phone bill for $1,123.26, I can honestly say, no. Not at all.

Digital Immigrants use technology to achieve specific ends. Digital Natives breathe technology in order to . . . well, breathe. To exist. Before, Sussy had pretty much lived online. Now she was pretty much living on the phone. Cleverly, she also used it to gain access to banned media. "Google 'Nick Jonas'!" she'd bark into the phone to Maddi, when the need to know the details of Miley Cyrus' relationship status grew unbearably urgent, or, "Check my Facebook!" (the girls regularly, and companionably, hacked each other's accounts anyhow), or, "Message Andy and tell him to ring me at eight my time." Maddi was now more than a best friend. She was Sussy's personal remote outsourcer, carrying out her digital bidding with terrifying dispatch.

Their relationship changed in less obvious ways, too, during those marathon conversations, and so did her connection with Andy. "On MSN, you're kind of almost waving at people. You get introduced, and it's like hi and LOL and ILY and stuff . . . but you never really get to know them," she explained to me. "On the phone, it's totally different. It's like D&M [deep and meaningful]. You get close. You get tight."

Analyze

1. Maushart explains that her children don't "use media," they "inhabit media." How does she then define the term *inhabit*? Why would she choose to make the distinction between *using* and *inhabiting* in her description of her children's relationship to social media?
2. What, according to Maushart, are "parasocial" connections? Why may these be cause for some parental concern?
3. What was Maushart's greatest fear regarding her children growing up as "digital natives"?

Explore

1. Look up the phrase "digital immigrant" on a search engine. Review the images from the search results. Choose one that you believe best illustrates the term as defined by Maushart. Then, choose one that best illustrates our own definition of the term. In an essay, explain how you define the term "digital immigrant" and how this compares to Maushart's definition, why you selected the image that you did for Maushart's definition, and how this image compares and contrasts to the image you chose to illustrate your own definition of the term.
2. Do some research on the terms "digital native" and "digital immigrant" and the definitions of these terms. Based on your search, write a short essay explaining why you consider yourself a "digital native" or a "digital immigrant," and how your use of three to five specific technologies reflects your decision to categorize yourself as such.
3. Develop a short interview guide to find out more about technology usage patterns. For instance, pose questions about how often a user uses a particular social media application and for what purposes he or she uses it. Interview someone whom you consider a "digital native." Then, using the same set of questions, interview someone whom you consider to be a "digital immigrant." Based on your findings from these interviews, write a short essay comparing and contrasting the characteristics and technology usage patterns of a digital native and a digital immigrant. How do these findings relate and compare to those reported in Maushart's essay?

Scott McCloud
"Media and Communication"

Scott McCloud is an American cartoonist and theorist of comics. The founder of the international 24-Hour Comics movement, he is also the author of the influential Bill of Rights for Comics Creators. In his books *Understanding Comics* (1994) and *Making Comics* (2006), McCloud takes the subject and theory of graphic communication as his subject matter, exploring the history, place, and status of comics in relation to other communications media. In this excerpt from *Understanding Comics*, McCloud explains how communication functions and varies by medium.

What is your preferred medium of communication? Why?

SAD, OF COURSE, BECAUSE NEARLY ALL PROBLEMS IN HUMAN HISTORY *STEM* FROM THAT INABILITY.

EACH *MEDIUM* (THE TERM COMES FROM THE LATIN WORD MEANING *MIDDLE*) SERVES AS A BRIDGE *BETWEEN* MINDS.

SPOKEN WORD

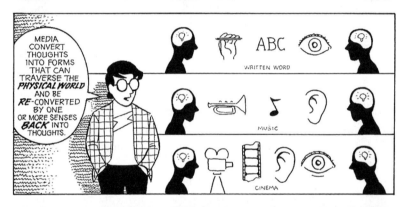

MEDIA CONVERT THOUGHTS INTO FORMS THAT CAN TRAVERSE THE *PHYSICAL WORLD* AND BE *RE-*CONVERTED BY ONE OR MORE SENSES *BACK* INTO THOUGHTS.

WRITTEN WORD

MUSIC

CINEMA

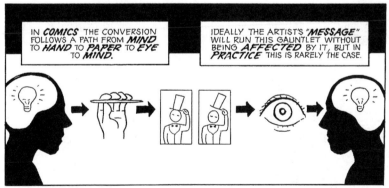

IN *COMICS* THE CONVERSION FOLLOWS A PATH FROM *MIND* TO *HAND* TO *PAPER* TO *EYE* TO *MIND.*

IDEALLY THE ARTIST'S *"MESSAGE"* WILL RUN THIS GAUNTLET WITHOUT BEING *AFFECTED* BY IT, BUT IN *PRACTICE* THIS IS RARELY THE CASE.

Analyze

1. How many different types of communication media are represented by McCloud in his graphic essay? List them.
2. According to McCloud, what is the etymology of the word *medium*? Explain how a medium serves as a bridge between minds.
3. Explain what is being illustrated and explained in the fourth panel of the graphic essay.

Explore

1. Prior to reading McCloud's description, how did you think communication happened? How has your understanding of communication as a process changed based on reading McCloud's description? Write a one-page response to each of these questions.
2. In the fourth panel of his graphic essay, McCloud carefully breaks down the steps through which the sender of a message produces that message. However, he does not as carefully describe the ways in which the receiver of the message understands that message. Using either words or pictures, describe in more depth the processes that take place as a receiver of a message receives, understands, and interprets the message being sent.
3. Working in groups, research the various technologies and media that are involved in communicating via a social media website such as Facebook. Then, update the fifth panel of McCloud's graphic essay to depict the communication processes that occur using social media.

Evgeny Morozov
"Machines of Laughter and Forgetting"

Evgeny Morozov is a journalist who was born in Belarus and whose work on technology, democracy, and society has been published in a wide range of publications. The author of the books *The Net Delusion: The Dark Side of Internet Freedom* (2012) and, most recently, *To Save Everything, Click Here: The Folly of Technological Solutionism* (2014), Morozov has been a visiting scholar at Stanford University and a Schwartz fellow at the New America Foundation. A contributing editor to *Foreign Policy* and *Boston Review*, he is currently completing a Ph.D. in the History of Science at Harvard University. In this essay, originally published as an article in the *New York Times*, Morozov considers why it is commonly believed that technologies should be invisible, and what happens if technologies not only become visible but are used to challenge various patterns of thinking and behavior.

Can you think of ways in which a technological device that you frequently use could be modified to actively challenge your daily patterns of living and thinking?

U ntil very recently, technology had a clear, if boring, purpose: by taking care of the Little Things, it enabled us, its human masters, to focus on the Big Things. "Unless there are slaves to do the ugly, horrible, uninteresting work, culture and contemplation become almost impossible," proclaimed that noted connoisseur of contemplation Oscar Wilde.

Fortunately, he added a charming clarification: "Human slavery is wrong, insecure and demoralizing. On mechanical slavery, on the slavery of the machine, the future of the world depends."

Wilde was not alone. "Civilization," wrote the philosopher and mathematician Alfred North Whitehead in 1911, "advances by extending the number of important operations which we can perform without thinking about them." Whitehead was writing about mathematics, but technology, with its reliance on formula and algorithms, easily fits his dictum as well.

On this account, technology can save us a lot of cognitive effort, for "thinking" needs to happen only once, at the design stage. We'll surround ourselves with gadgets and artifacts that will do exactly what they are meant to do—and they'll do it in a frictionless, invisible way. "The ideal system so buries the technology that the user is not even aware of its presence," announced the design guru Donald Norman in his landmark 1998 book, "The Invisible Computer." But is that what we really want?

The hidden truth about many attempts to "bury" technology is that they 5 embody an amoral and unsustainable vision. Pick any electrical appliance in your kitchen. The odds are that you have no idea how much electricity it consumes, let alone how it compares to other appliances and households. This ignorance is neither natural nor inevitable; it stems from a conscious decision by the designer of that kitchen appliance to free up your "cognitive resources" so that you can unleash your inner Oscar Wilde on "contemplating" other things. Multiply such ignorance by a few billion, and global warming no longer looks like a mystery.

Whitehead, it seems, was either wrong or extremely selective: on many important issues, civilization only destroys itself by extending the number of important operations that we can perform without thinking about them. On many issues, we want more thinking, not less.

Take privacy. Opening browser tabs is easy, as is using our Facebook account to navigate from site to site. In fact, we often do so unthinkingly. Given that our online tools and platforms are built in a way to make our browsing experience as frictionless as possible, is it any surprise that so much of our personal information is disclosed without our ever realizing it?

This, too, is not inevitable: designed differently, our digital infrastructure could provide many more opportunities for reflection. In a recent paper, a group of Cornell researchers proposed that our browsers could bombard us with strange but provocative messages to make us alert to the very information infrastructure that some designers have done their best to conceal. Imagine being told that "you visited 592 Web sites this week. That's .5 times the number of Web pages on the whole Internet in 1994!"

The goal here is not to hit us with a piece of statistics—sheer numbers rarely lead to complex narratives—but to tell a story that can get us thinking about things we'd rather not be thinking about. So let us not give in to technophobia just yet: we should not go back to doing everything by hand just because it can lead to more thinking.

10   Rather, we must distribute the thinking process equally. Instead of having the designer think through all the moral and political implications of technology use before it reaches users—an impossible task—we must find a way to get users to do some of that thinking themselves.

Alas, most designers, following Wilde, think of technologies as nothing more than mechanical slaves that must maximize efficiency. But some are realizing that technologies don't have to be just trivial problem-solvers: they can also be subversive troublemakers, making us question our habits and received ideas.

Recently, designers in Germany built devices—"transformational products," they call them—that engage users in "conversations without words." My favorite is a caterpillar-shaped extension cord. If any of the devices plugged into it are left in standby mode, the "caterpillar" starts twisting as if it were in pain.

Does it do what normal extension cords do? Yes. But it also awakens users to the fact that the cord is simply the endpoint of a complex socio-technical system with its own politics and ethics. Before, designers have tried to conceal that system. In the future, designers will be obliged to make it visible.

While devices-as-problem-solvers seek to avoid friction, devices-as-troublemakers seek to create an "aesthetic of friction" that engages users in new ways. Will such extra seconds of thought—nay, contemplation—slow down civilization? They well might. But who said that stopping to catch a breath on our way to the abyss is not a sensible strategy?

Analyze

1. Explain the connection Morozov is making between Oscar Wilde's quote about slavery, Donald Norman's pronouncement about ideal design, and Alfred Lord Whitehead's comment about the advancement of civilization. How are these related? How do they relate to Morozov's argument?

2. Morozov advocates that thinking be distributed more equally between designers and users. Why?

3. In your own words, explain how the extension cord described by Morozov functions, and why it is an example of a "transformational product."

Explore

1. Do some research on an electrical device or appliance that you use daily. How much electricity does it consume? From what source is that electricity generated? How much does the electricity cost on a daily and monthly basis? Based on your research, and making use of one of several Web-based carbon footprint calculators, calculate the carbon footprint of the device or appliance. Write a two-page report explaining your findings and how these may or may not affect your future usage of this device or appliance.

2. Look up the paper by Cornell researchers referenced in Morozov's essay. Do a rhetorical analysis of the report, considering who the

audience is for this report and how the language and structure of the report make that clear. In a short essay, compare the language in the report and its findings to Morozov's article. How do they differ? What similarities exist?

3. Consider how a technological device that you use on a daily basis could be redesigned as a "transformational product." Write a proposal describing the current functions of this device, the proposed changes to the device, and the potential benefits to users of its redesign as a transformational product.

Gary Marcus
"Moral Machines"

Gary Marcus is a Professor of Psychology at New York University (NYU) and director of the NYU Center for Language and Music (CLAM), where he studies evolution, language, and cognitive development. He is the author of several books on cognition and the development of mind; the most recent is *Guitar Zero: The New Musician and the Science of Learning*. In this essay, originally published as a *New Yorker* blog post, Marcus considers the ethical issues that will arise as machines become more "intelligent" and the steps that must be taken to address these issues.

On what do you base your own system of ethics?

Google's driver-less cars are already street-legal in three states, California, Florida, and Nevada, and someday similar devices may not just be possible but mandatory. Eventually (though not yet) automated vehicles will be able to drive better, and more safely than you can; no drinking, no distraction, better reflexes, and better awareness (via networking) of other vehicles. Within two or three decades the difference between automated driving and human driving will be so great you may not be legally allowed to drive your own car, and even if you are allowed, it would be immoral of you to drive, because the risk of you hurting yourself or another person will be far greater than if you allowed a machine to do the work.

That moment will be significant not just because it will signal the end of one more human niche, but because it will signal the beginning of another: the era in which it will no longer be optional for machines to have ethical systems. Your car is speeding along a bridge at fifty miles per hour when an errant school bus carrying forty innocent children crosses its path. Should your car swerve, possibly risking the life of its owner (you), in order to save the children, or keep going, putting all forty kids at risk? If the decision must be made in milliseconds, the computer will have to make the call.

These issues may be even more pressing when it comes to military robots. When, if ever, might it be ethical to send robots in the place of soldiers? Robot soldiers might not only be faster, stronger, and more reliable than human beings, they would also be immune from panic and sleep-deprivation, and never be overcome with a desire for vengeance. Yet, as The Human Rights Watch noted in a widely-publicized report earlier this week, robot soldiers would also be utterly devoid of human compassion, and could easily wreak unprecedented devastation in the hands of a Stalin or Pol Pot. Anyone who has seen the opening scenes of *RoboCop* knows why we have misgivings about robots being soldiers, or cops.

But what should we do about it? The solution proposed by Human Rights Watch—an outright ban on "the development, production, and use of fully autonomous weapons"—seems wildly unrealistic. The Pentagon is likely to be loath to give up its enormous investment in robotic soldiers (in the words of Peter W. Singer, "Predator [drones] are merely the first generation"), and few parents would prefer to send their own sons (or daughters) into combat if robots were an alternative.

With or without robotic soldiers, what we really need is a sound way to   5
teach our machines to be ethical. The trouble is that we have almost no idea how to do that. Many discussions start with three famous laws from Isaac Asimov:

1. A robot may not injure a human being or, through inaction, allow a human being to come to harm.

2. A robot must obey the orders given to it by human beings, except where such orders would conflict with the first law.
3. A robot must protect its own existence as long as such protection does not conflict with the first or second laws.

The trouble with these seemingly sound laws is threefold. The first is technical: at least for now, we couldn't program a machine with Asimov's laws if we tried. As yet, we haven't figured out how to build a machine that fully comprehends the concept of "dinner," much less something as abstract as "harm" or "protection." Likewise, we are a long way from constructing a robot that can fully anticipate the consequences of any of its actions (or inactions). For now, a robot is lucky if it can predict would happen if it dropped a glass of water. A.I. has a long way to go before laws as abstract as Asimov's could realistically be encoded in software.

10   Second, even if we could figure out how to do the programming, the rules might be too restrictive. The first and second laws, for example, preclude robots from ever harming other humans, but most people would make exceptions for robots that could eliminate potential human targets that were a clear and present danger to others. Only a true ideologue would want to stop a robotic sniper from taking down a hostage-taker or Columbine killer.

Meanwhile, Asimov's laws themselves might not be fair—to robots. As the computer scientist Kevin Korb has pointed out, Asimov's laws effectively treat robots like slaves. Perhaps that is acceptable for now, but it could become morally questionable (and more difficult to enforce) as machines become smarter and possibly more self-aware.

The laws of Asimov are hardly the only approach to machine ethics, but many others are equally fraught. An all-powerful computer that was programmed to maximize human pleasure, for example, might consign us all to an intravenous dopamine drip; an automated car that aimed to minimize harm would never leave the driveway. Almost any easy solution that one might imagine leads to some variation or another on the Sorcerer's Apprentice, a genie that's given us what we've asked for, rather than what we truly desire. A tiny cadre of brave-hearted souls at Oxford, Yale, and the Berkeley California Singularity Institute are working on these problems, but the annual amount of money being spent on developing machine morality is tiny.

The thought that haunts me the most is that that human ethics themselves are only a work-in-progress. We still confront situations for which we don't have well-developed codes (e.g., in the case of assisted suicide) and need not look far into the past to find cases where our own codes were dubious, or worse (e.g., laws that permitted slavery and segregation). What we really want are machines that can go a step further, endowed not only with the soundest codes of ethics that our best contemporary philosophers can devise, but also with the possibility of machines making their own moral progress, bringing them past our own limited early-twenty-first century idea of morality.

Building machines with a conscience is a big job, and one that will require the coordinated efforts of philosophers, computer scientists, legislators, and lawyers. And, as Colin Allen, a pioneer in machine ethics, put it, "We don't want to get to the point where we should have had this discussion twenty years ago." As machines become faster, more intelligent, and more powerful, the need to endow them with a sense of morality becomes more and more urgent.

"Ethical subroutines" may sound like science fiction, but once upon a time, so did self-driving cars.   15

Analyze

1. According to Marcus, why may it be in the future immoral for someone to decide to drive his or her own car?
2. Explain the ethical dilemma Marcus describes in relation to driverless cars.
3. What are Asimov's three laws regarding robots? What are the problems with these three laws, according to Marcus?
4. What is the thought that "still haunts" Marcus? Why?

Explore

1. Rewrite Asimov's three laws to address the issues Marcus raises with regard to their possibly being too restrictive or flawed. After rewriting the laws, write a short essay explaining how the changes you made address the issues raised by Marcus.
2. Isaac Asimov's three laws of robotics were written in 1942. Asimov would later add a fourth law to the list that was intended to precede the other three laws: "A robot may not harm humanity, or, by inaction,

allow humanity to come to harm." Write a short essay explaining why or why not Asimov's fourth law may address some of the issues raised by Marcus with regard to the first three laws.

3. Look up the phrase "Sorcerer's Apprentice." In a short essay, explain how driverless cars may be an example of the phenomenon described by the phrase.

4. Working in small groups, do a search for the #Robotsandyou hashtag on Twitter. Review the last week's posts. What appear to be the major issues being discussed in the posts? Look up one of the articles referenced by one of the posts. Prepare a presentation for your class explaining how this article relates to various issues discussed in Marcus's essay.

Rose Eveleth
"Robots: Is the Uncanny Valley Real?"

Rose Eveleth is an American science writer and producer for several media outlets. A frequent blog contributor to *Smart Planet*, she has produced science podcasts for the *Story Collider* and the *New York Times*. In this essay, originally published in the Technology Section of the British Broadcasting Corporation (BBC) website, Eveleth assesses the current status of "the uncanny valley," a phenomenon identified in the 1970s by Japanese roboticist Masahiro Mori that posits that the more lifelike an animated or robotic creation may be, the more likely humans are to find it creepy.

Would you prefer that, in the future, as robots become more common, they look and act more like humans or machines? Why?

For decades the golden rule in robotics has been that the more lifelike a creation, the more likely it crosses the line from cute to creepy. But questions are being raised as to whether this is really true.

Mick Walters opens a door in his lab and points his computer's camera towards the small, blurry, tan-colored object he has just revealed. "This is Kaspar Two," he says. As the Skype connection catches up, an image of a robot in a baseball hat, a blue button-down shirt and striped socks appears. Kaspar Two is a robot child. He's not even on, just sitting slumped over. Even though the image is somewhat fuzzy, Kaspar Two is able to give me that feeling, that nagging sense of unease. "I must admit," says Walters, "when I first actually built Kaspar, I did think he was a bit uncanny."

Kaspar has been created at University of Hertfordshire, UK to help children with autism understand how to read emotions and engage with other people, but it falls into what's often called "the uncanny valley." From humanoid robot heads to super-realistic prosthetic hands, the uncanny valley is where robots that give us the creeps live. It is the range between obvious cartoons and discernibly real people, where things look almost lifelike, and yet not quite believable. Peering into the uncanny valley is an uncomfortable experience. Its residents, like Kaspar, have a way of eliciting feelings of disgust, fear or dread.

For almost 30 years, the concept of the uncanny valley has acted as a golden rule for roboticists and animators. From Pixar to puppets, creating characters that are too lifelike was thought to be the kiss of death for any project. But now the concept itself is coming under scrutiny like never before. What exactly we are feeling and why we feel this way are questions that have finally found their way under the microscope. And some researchers are asking whether the uncanny valley exists at all.

What's in a Name?

The first time many people encountered the concept of the uncanny valley   5
was in 2001 with the movie *Final Fantasy: The Spirits Within*. Today, it is known as one of the first photorealistic computer animated films, but at the time not everyone was impressed. The groundbreaking graphics made many movie-goers uncomfortable, and the film flopped, losing Columbia Pictures $52 million. The faces were too human, too close to real life. "At first it's fun to watch the characters," film critic Peter Travers wrote in *Rolling Stone*. "But then you notice a coldness in the eyes, a mechanical quality in the movements."

A link between what is almost human and what is creepy was proposed long before *Final Fantasy*, however. The phrase "uncanny valley" is widely accepted to have originated in 1970, with the publication of an academic paper by roboticist Masahiro Mori in an obscure journal called *Energy*. Mori's original paper was in Japanese. Contrary to popular belief, his original title "Bukimi No Tani" only roughly translates into the phrase it has made famous. A more accurate translation is "valley of eeriness."

This matters because it demonstrates the problem with the uncanny valley: it is an inherently woolly idea. When researchers try to study the phenomenon, they often have a hard time pinning down what an uncanny response actually looks like. The main graph in Mori's paper has been mis-translated many times, leaving many people unsure what he really meant. Mori used the Japanese word "shinwakan" on the y-axis, a word that has no direct translation into English. The most common interpretation is "like-ability," but not all translators agree about that. Other suggestions include "familiarity," "affinity," and "comfort level."

Perhaps the most surprising thing about the concept's history, though, isn't the translation troubles, nor the debate over what is being represented on his graph, but how long it took for that debate to arise. Mori's paper didn't include any measurements. It was more an essay than a study. Yet, despite broad dissemination, the uncanny valley avoided scientific scrutiny until the early 2000's, when graphics and animatronics like *Final Fantasy* started giving people the creeps. As scientists started to explore Mori's graph, they began to ask whether real data would reveal the same pattern.

Spot of Bother

A few studies have asserted that the whole thing doesn't exist. In one study, David Hanson of Hanson Robotics, in Plano, Texas, and his colleagues showed participants images of two different robots that were animated to simulate human-like facial expressions. The survey simply asked the partici-pants what they thought of the experience. The vast majority (73%) liked the human-like robots. In fact, not one person stated that these robots dis-turbed them.

10   Hanson and his team then showed the participants a continuum of images, starting with a picture of Princess Jasmine taken from the Disney movie *Aladdin*. Over the course of six images, Jasmine's face slowly morphed into that of actress Jennifer Love Hewitt. The idea of these facial progression studies is to try to observe the dip in likeability that Mori pre-dicted between an obviously cartoon image and an obviously human one. The participants were asked to rank the acceptability of each picture in the series. But, again, rather than see a dip in the scores in the middle of the

range—as the uncanny valley would predict—none of the images seemed to bother anyone.

Why this happened isn't clear, and not everyone thinks Hanson's experiment is robust. Many other studies have shown the opposite. For example, Edward Schneider's lab at SUNY Potsdam in New York collected 75 existing characters from video games and animation, including Hello Kitty, Mickey Mouse, Snoopy and Lara Croft. They asked participants how human and how attractive (or repulsive) they perceived each character to be. In this case, the researchers did find a dip in likeability in the middle of the series, roughly where the ogres from World of Warcraft sit.

Moreover, a team lead by Karl MacDorman at Indiana University conducted an experiment similar to Hanson's, using a progression of images in which a robot face slowly morphs into a human one. They, too, found a U-shaped dip in likeability in the middle of their 11-image series.

However, among the labs that have observed the uncanny valley, there is strong debate about its shape. Christoph Bartneck, a robotics researcher at Canterbury University in New Zealand, says that, based on his studies, a valley might be the wrong geological metaphor altogether. "As far as we can tell," he says, "it looks more like a cliff." Essentially, he says, at the point where robots achieve extreme human-likeness, but remain discernibly unhuman, their likeability plummets. And people only start to like them again when they become so human-like that they escape detection.

To make things even more complicated, there's nothing that proves the uncanny valley reflects gradations of the same reaction. It could be a handful of reactions to different aspects of having a varying degree of human-likeness. When MacDorman showed his subjects videos of many different robots, the responses followed no clear pattern. "The results do not indicate a single uncanny valley for a particular range of human-likeness," MacDorman wrote in the paper. "Rather, they suggest that human-likeness is only one of perhaps many factors influencing the extent to which a robot is perceived as being strange, familiar, or eerie."

Basic Instincts

Questions about what reaction (or reactions) cause the uncanny valley (or, indeed, the uncanny cliff) quickly lead to other questions about why we react at all. 15

There are a few explanations that might account for our strange aversion to humanoid robots. One is that not being able to tell whether something is human or not can be a deeply unsettling feeling in itself. Artists and directors take advantage of this all the time for dramatic effect. The dread that viewers feel while trying to figure out who is a zombie, or Cylon, or alien might be the very same dread they feel when faced with a very realistic robot.

Another explanation focuses on the disconnect between how realistic something looks, and how well it moves. There's always been a lag time between how quickly designers can make things look like people, and how quickly engineers can make them move like us. If a figure that you thought was human started to move jerkily, you would recoil. Similarly, if you were to shake a robot's hand while expecting a human touch, but instead felt cold rubber, you would be caught off guard. An unexpected break in humanness can be an unpleasant shock, one that sets off fearful and distrustful instincts. "Whenever we see something move, and we're not familiar with the mechanism of movement, it grabs our attention," says Andrew Olney, a psychologist at the University of Memphis who works on designing intelligent robots. "If your coffee cup started slowly moving across the table, that would kind of freak you out a bit."

Finally, a third theory turns to evolution. It suggests that if a robot looks like a human, but moves unnaturally, our brains subconsciously classify what we're seeing as someone with a disease. This is the same explanation proposed for most feelings of disgust. When we stand near something like faeces, rotting flesh, or a jerking robot, we experience a sudden urge to get away from it so as to avoid catching the infections it may harbour. Some preliminary research in rhesus monkeys suggests that these animals share an uncanny valley-like response, indicating that they have perhaps adapted to the same evolutionary pressure in the same way as us.

Ultimate Challenge

We are, of course, becoming more accustomed to robots and avatars in everyday life. Between games like Last of Us and movies like *Avatar*, we see computer-generated images of people all the time. Mori's original examples of uncanny objects, like a wooden prosthetic hand, probably wouldn't raise an eyebrow today because they are so obviously fake. *Final Fantasy* no longer triggers unsettling feelings among younger viewers, who are used to games like Crysis and Witcher 2. The shift in expectations has been going on all along—and might well continue until technology is good enough to fool us.

This trend sets up a roboticist's ultimate challenge: to be the first person to build a robot that is indistinguishably human to other humans. It is a challenge that Hiroshi Ishiguro, one of the world's leading humanoid roboticists, believes he will one day meet. Some of his humanoid robots already interact with people, and some robot designers treat them as if they were human. When one roboticist named Peter Kahn visited Karl MacDorman's human-computer interaction lab at Indiana University and wanted to take apart Ishiguro's Repliee Q1Expo, a petite Japanese humanoid-woman in a pink blazer, he first turned to his wife and asked, "May I touch her?" 20

But not everyone is convinced that we'll engineer our way out of the uncanny valley, or that it is a good thing if we do. While what makes us uncomfortable is likely to shift, the presence of discomfort won't, they argue. Potentially, it could get worse. "You can imagine cases, for example, maybe 50 years down the road, someone might be in a relationship with an android and not know it," says MacDorman. "But if there were an accident and some of the mechanical underpinnings are exposed, that would be uncanny. It would be uncanny in a different way."

Analyze

1. What is Kaspar Two and why does Eveleth refer to it in her introduction?
2. What is the "uncanny valley"? When was the term invented? By whom?
3. What were the findings of Hanson's study? Why are these important to Eveleth's essay?
4. What are a few explanations cited by Eveleth for human aversion to humanoid robots? What is Repliee Q1Expo? Why does Eveleth refer to it in her conclusion?

Explore

1. Locate and watch the movie trailer for *Final Fantasy: The Spirits Within* on the Web. Compare your reactions to this trailer with those

reported by Eveleth. Then, write one or two pages discussing why your reactions were similar or dissimilar to her findings, making sure to consider some reasons why your experience may have been similar to or different from those reported.

2. Eveleth lists three explanations that may "account for our strange aversion to humanoid robots." Summarize each of these. Then, in a short essay, reflect on which you believe may be the most relevant and the reasons why you believe this to be the case.

3. In a short essay, explain why you do or don't believe that the term "uncanny valley" is the most appropriate one to describe the phenomenon that Masahiro Mori and other roboticists have observed. In what ways does this term accurately represent the phenomenon? In what ways might this not be the most appropriate term to describe the phenomenon? What term might be more appropriate or accurate to describe the phenomenon?

Forging Connections

1. Several issues raised by Sherry Turkle in her essay "Alone Together" are also addressed in Susan Maushart's essay. In a short essay, explain what these shared issues are, and reflect on how Maushart's findings from her experiment relate to some questions posed and issues raised by Turkle.

2. Placing Evgeny Morozov's essay and Gary Marcus's essay in dialogue, consider how disruptive technologies might be used in the development of a new machine ethics. Write a short essay explaining how these essays can be connected to one another and how disruptive technologies might be used to help address some of the ethical issues discussed by Marcus.

Looking Further

1. Marcus cites Asimov's Three Laws of Robotics in his essay "Moral Machines" as being a place where many discussions of machine ethics begin. Asimov wrote the three laws as part of his 1942 short story "Runaround." Locate a copy of this story on the Web or in your college library. Read the story and write a short essay explaining what it is about and why the three laws are included in the story. Then, compare

Asimov's use of the laws in the story to Marcus's use of the laws in his essay. Do they appear to be used for similar purposes? Why or why not?

2. Both Malcolm Gladwell (Chapter 6) and Susan Maushart write about the differences between "strong" and "weak" ties and express similar concerns about the fact that social media may allow for the cultivation of only "weak" ties. However, both authors are "digital immigrants," not "digital natives." As someone who has grown up using social media, write a letter to Gladwell or Maushart in which you explain why or why not you agree with his or her assessment that social media create "weak" ties. In your letter, make sure that you describe a specific relationship that has developed via social media and how this would be characterized as one with "weak" or "strong" ties.

4

Digital Literacies and Identities: How Is Technology Changing Readers and Writers?

While it is fairly uncommon to think about something as ancient as the alphabet as a technology, it is one. Nonetheless, as media theorist and cultural critic Neil

121

Postman points out in his essay from Chapter 1, when he would ask his students "when the alphabet was invented," the question "astonished" them. It was, he writes, "as if I asked them when clouds and trees were invented." Although the many technologies involved with reading and writing practices—the alphabet, pencils, pens, books, printing presses— may be so familiar to us as to seem almost "natural," they were all at one time new technologies that have had, and continue to have, numerous and profound effects. As the historian Ruth Schwartz Cohen explains in her book *A Social History of American Technology*, "even languages and the things that contain languages (such as books, letters, computer software, and student essays) are technologies: they are things that people have created so as to better control and manipulate the social environment."

The potential impact of information and communications technology (ICT) on literacy practices and the cognitive processes associated with them is one that, for many different reasons, has attracted a lot of attention in the media and is one that some critics believe may be cause for great concern. This results in part from the fact that literacies and the practices associated with them are intricately related to what it means to be human and to the complex networks through which socio-cultural practices are transmitted and recorded. But various information and communications technologies are also entwined with literacy practices and the many off-shoots of this: publishing, education, and scholarship. So much so that many have compared the changes happening now in our digital age with those that took place beginning in the fifteenth century with the advent of the printing press. Based on this analogy, the scale of the changes in literacy practices as a result of new digital technologies could be large and their effects profound. While it may be too early to really know what these changes may be, there is in the meantime a great deal to write and think about with regard to literacy practices and how various technologies— both old and new—are related to these practices.

In his essay "Is Google Making Us Stupid?" journalist Nicholas Carr reflects on how Internet and Web technologies may be affecting the ways in which we read and write. Addressing similar issues in his essay "Does Google Make You Smarter?" but proposing a somewhat different interpretation, professor and journalist Clay Shirky considers what may be gained from the increasing use of the Internet and Web technologies. Journalist Sam Leith in his essay "What Does It All Meme?" contemplates what the implications of the Internet may mean culturally. Writer Toby Litt ponders the history and future of reading in a world where video games may provide an immersive and entertaining substitute to the imaginary worlds of literary fiction. Historian William Cronon assesses Wikipedia in comparison to the *Encyclopedia Britannica*. Finally, novelist Ursula Le Guin, in her essay "The Death of the Book," questions whether those who see electronic media as the death of reading may be missing the bigger picture regarding the importance of reading in a digital age.

Nicholas Carr
"Is Google Making Us Stupid?"

Nicholas Carr is an American writer who writes books and articles on technology, business, and culture. His most recent book is entitled *The Big Switch: Rewiring the World from Edison to Google*, and his earlier book, *The Shallows: What the Internet Is Doing to Our Brains*, was a finalist for the 2011 Pulitzer Prize. In this essay, originally published in 2008 in *The Atlantic*, Carr considers the wide ranging effects, both positive and negative, of the World Wide Web on reading and writing practices, and considers its unique attributes and characteristics in relation to other important communications technologies, such as the printing press.

Has the Internet changed or altered the way you read things? How?

"**D**ave, stop. Stop, will you? Stop, Dave. Will you stop, Dave?" So the supercomputer HAL pleads with the implacable astronaut Dave Bowman in a famous and weirdly poignant scene toward the end of Stanley Kubrick's *2001: A Space Odyssey*. Bowman, having nearly been sent to a deep-space death by the malfunctioning machine, is calmly, coldly disconnecting the memory circuits that control its artificial brain. "Dave, my mind is going," HAL says, forlornly. "I can feel it. I can feel it."

> "The Internet promises to have particularly far-reaching effects on cognition."

I can feel it, too. Over the past few years I've had an uncomfortable sense that someone, or something, has been tinkering with my brain, remapping the neural circuitry, reprogramming the memory. My mind isn't going—so far as I can tell—but it's changing. I'm not thinking the way I used to think. I can feel it most strongly when I'm reading. Immersing myself in a book or a lengthy article used to be easy. My mind would get caught up in the narrative or the turns of the argument, and I'd spend hours strolling through long stretches of prose. That's rarely the case anymore. Now my concentration often starts to drift after two or three pages. I get fidgety, lose the thread, begin looking for something else to do. I feel as if I'm always dragging my wayward brain back to the text. The deep reading that used to come naturally has become a struggle.

I think I know what's going on. For more than a decade now, I've been spending a lot of time online, searching and surfing and sometimes adding to the great databases of the Internet. The Web has been a godsend to me as a writer. Research that once required days in the stacks or periodical rooms of libraries can now be done in minutes. A few Google searches, some quick clicks on hyperlinks, and I've got the telltale fact or pithy quote I was after. Even when I'm not working, I'm as likely as not to be foraging in the Web's info-thickets, reading and writing e-mails, scanning headlines and blog posts, watching videos and listening to podcasts, or just tripping from link to link to link. (Unlike footnotes, to which they're sometimes likened, hyperlinks don't merely point to related works; they propel you toward them.)

For me, as for others, the Net is becoming a universal medium, the conduit for most of the information that flows through my eyes and ears and into my mind. The advantages of having immediate access to such an incredibly rich store of information are many, and they've been widely described and duly applauded. "The perfect recall of silicon memory," *Wired's* Clive Thompson has written, "can be an enormous boon to thinking." But that boon comes at a price. As the media theorist Marshall McLuhan pointed out in the 1960s, media are not just passive channels of information. They supply the stuff of thought, but they also shape the process of thought. And what the Net seems to be doing is chipping away my capacity for concentration and contemplation. My mind now expects to take in information the way the Net distributes it: in a swiftly moving stream of particles. Once I was a scuba diver in the sea of words. Now I zip along the surface like a guy on a Jet Ski.

I'm not the only one. When I mention my troubles with reading to friends and acquaintances—literary types, most of them—many say they're having similar experiences. The more they use the Web, the more they have to fight to stay focused on long pieces of writing. Some of the bloggers I follow have also begun mentioning the phenomenon. Scott Karp, who writes a blog about online media, recently confessed that he has stopped reading books altogether. "I was a lit major in college, and used to be [a] voracious book reader," he wrote. "What happened?" He speculates on the answer: "What if I do all my reading on the web not so much because the way I read has changed, i.e. I'm just seeking convenience, but because the way I THINK has changed?"

Bruce Friedman, who blogs regularly about the use of computers in medicine, also has described how the Internet has altered his mental habits. "I now have almost totally lost the ability to read and absorb a longish article on the web or in print," he wrote earlier this year. A pathologist who has long been on the faculty of the University of Michigan Medical School, Friedman elaborated on his comment in a telephone conversation with me. His thinking, he said, has taken on a "staccato" quality, reflecting the way he quickly scans short passages of text from many sources online. "I can't read *War and Peace* anymore," he admitted. "I've lost the ability to do that. Even a blog post of more than three or four paragraphs is too much to absorb. I skim it."

Anecdotes alone don't prove much. And we still await the long-term neurological and psychological experiments that will provide a definitive picture of how Internet use affects cognition. But a recently published study of online research habits, conducted by scholars from University College London, suggests that we may well be in the midst of a sea change in the way we read and think. As part of the five-year research program, the scholars examined computer logs documenting the behavior of visitors to two popular research sites, one operated by the British Library and one by a U.K. educational consortium, that provide access to journal articles,

5

e-books, and other sources of written information. They found that people using the sites exhibited "a form of skimming activity," hopping from one source to another and rarely returning to any source they'd already visited. They typically read no more than one or two pages of an article or book before they would "bounce" out to another site. Sometimes they'd save a long article, but there's no evidence that they ever went back and actually read it. The authors of the study report:

> It is clear that users are not reading online in the traditional sense; indeed there are signs that new forms of "reading" are emerging as users "power browse" horizontally through titles, contents pages and abstracts going for quick wins. It almost seems that they go online to avoid reading in the traditional sense.

Thanks to the ubiquity of text on the Internet, not to mention the popularity of text-messaging on cell phones, we may well be reading more today than we did in the 1970s or 1980s, when television was our medium of choice. But it's a different kind of reading, and behind it lies a different kind of thinking—perhaps even a new sense of the self. "We are not only *what* we read," says Maryanne Wolf, a developmental psychologist at Tufts University and the author of *Proust and the Squid: The Story and Science of the Reading Brain*. "We are *how* we read." Wolf worries that the style of reading promoted by the Net, a style that puts "efficiency" and "immediacy" above all else, may be weakening our capacity for the kind of deep reading that emerged when an earlier technology, the printing press, made long and complex works of prose commonplace. When we read online, she says, we tend to become "mere decoders of information." Our ability to interpret text, to make the rich mental connections that form when we read deeply and without distraction, remains largely disengaged.

10   Reading, explains Wolf, is not an instinctive skill for human beings. It's not etched into our genes the way speech is. We have to teach our minds how to translate the symbolic characters we see into the language we understand. And the media or other technologies we use in learning and practicing the craft of reading play an important part in shaping the neural circuits inside our brains. Experiments demonstrate that readers of ideograms, such as the Chinese, develop a mental circuitry for reading that is very different from the circuitry found in those of us whose written language employs an alphabet. The variations extend across many regions of the brain, including

those that govern such essential cognitive functions as memory and the interpretation of visual and auditory stimuli. We can expect as well that the circuits woven by our use of the Net will be different from those woven by our reading of books and other printed works.

Sometime in 1882, Friedrich Nietzsche bought a typewriter—a Malling-Hansen Writing Ball, to be precise. His vision was failing, and keeping his eyes focused on a page had become exhausting and painful, often bringing on crushing headaches. He had been forced to curtail his writing, and he feared that he would soon have to give it up. The typewriter rescued him, at least for a time. Once he had mastered touch-typing, he was able to write with his eyes closed, using only the tips of his fingers. Words could once again flow from his mind to the page.

But the machine had a subtler effect on his work. One of Nietzsche's friends, a composer, noticed a change in the style of his writing. His already terse prose had become even tighter, more telegraphic. "Perhaps you will through this instrument even take to a new idiom," the friend wrote in a letter, noting that, in his own work, his "'thoughts' in music and language often depend on the quality of pen and paper."

"You are right," Nietzsche replied, "our writing equipment takes part in the forming of our thoughts." Under the sway of the machine, writes the German media scholar Friedrich A. Kittler, Nietzsche's prose "changed from arguments to aphorisms, from thoughts to puns, from rhetoric to telegram style."

The human brain is almost infinitely malleable. People used to think that our mental meshwork, the dense connections formed among the 100 billion or so neurons inside our skulls, was largely fixed by the time we reached adulthood. But brain researchers have discovered that that's not the case. James Olds, a professor of neuroscience who directs the Krasnow Institute for Advanced Study at George Mason University, says that even the adult mind "is very plastic." Nerve cells routinely break old connections and form new ones. "The brain," according to Olds, "has the ability to reprogram itself on the fly, altering the way it functions."

As we use what the sociologist Daniel Bell has called our "intellectual technologies"—the tools that extend our mental rather than our physical capacities—we inevitably begin to take on the qualities of those technologies. The mechanical clock, which came into common use in the 14th century, provides a compelling example. In *Technics and Civilization*, the historian and cultural critic Lewis Mumford described how the clock "disassociated time from human events and helped create the belief in an independent world of mathematically measurable sequences." The "abstract framework of divided time" became "the point of reference for both action and thought."

The clock's methodical ticking helped bring into being the scientific mind and the scientific man. But it also took something away. As the late MIT computer scientist Joseph Weizenbaum observed in his 1976 book, *Computer Power and Human Reason: From Judgment to Calculation*, the conception of the world that emerged from the widespread use of time-keeping instruments "remains an impoverished version of the older one, for it rests on a rejection of those direct experiences that formed the basis for, and indeed constituted, the old reality." In deciding when to eat, to work, to sleep, to rise, we stopped listening to our senses and started obeying the clock.

The process of adapting to new intellectual technologies is reflected in the changing metaphors we use to explain ourselves to ourselves. When the mechanical clock arrived, people began thinking of their brains as operating "like clockwork." Today, in the age of software, we have come to think of them as operating "like computers." But the changes, neuroscience tells us, go much deeper than metaphor. Thanks to our brain's plasticity, the adaptation occurs also at a biological level.

The Internet promises to have particularly far-reaching effects on cognition. In a paper published in 1936, the British mathematician Alan Turing proved that a digital computer, which at the time existed only as a theoretical machine, could be programmed to perform the function of any other information-processing device. And that's what we're seeing today. The Internet, an immeasurably powerful computing system, is subsuming most of our other intellectual technologies. It's becoming our map and our clock, our printing press and our typewriter, our calculator and our telephone, and our radio and TV.

When the Net absorbs a medium, that medium is re-created in the Net's image. It injects the medium's content with hyperlinks, blinking ads, and other digital gewgaws, and it surrounds the content with the content of all the other media it has absorbed. A new e-mail message, for instance, may announce its arrival as we're glancing over the latest headlines at a newspaper's site. The result is to scatter our attention and diffuse our concentration.

20   The Net's influence doesn't end at the edges of a computer screen, either. As people's minds become attuned to the crazy quilt of Internet media,

traditional media have to adapt to the audience's new expectations. Television programs add text crawls and pop-up ads, and magazines and newspapers shorten their articles, introduce capsule summaries, and crowd their pages with easy-to-browse info-snippets. When, in March of this year, *The New York Times* decided to devote the second and third pages of every edition to article abstracts, its design director, Tom Bodkin, explained that the "shortcuts" would give harried readers a quick "taste" of the day's news, sparing them the "less efficient" method of actually turning the pages and reading the articles. Old media have little choice but to play by the new-media rules.

Never has a communications system played so many roles in our lives— or exerted such broad influence over our thoughts—as the Internet does today. Yet, for all that's been written about the Net, there's been little consideration of how, exactly, it's reprogramming us. The Net's intellectual ethic remains obscure.

About the same time that Nietzsche started using his typewriter, an earnest young man named Frederick Winslow Taylor carried a stopwatch into the Midvale Steel plant in Philadelphia and began a historic series of experiments aimed at improving the efficiency of the plant's machinists. With the approval of Midvale's owners, he recruited a group of factory hands, set them to work on various metalworking machines, and recorded and timed their every movement as well as the operations of the machines. By breaking down every job into a sequence of small, discrete steps and then testing different ways of performing each one, Taylor created a set of precise instructions—an "algorithm," we might say today—for how each worker should work. Midvale's employees grumbled about the strict new regime, claiming that it turned them into little more than automatons, but the factory's productivity soared.

More than a hundred years after the invention of the steam engine, the Industrial Revolution had at last found its philosophy and its philosopher. Taylor's tight industrial choreography—his "system," as he liked to call it— was embraced by manufacturers throughout the country and, in time, around the world. Seeking maximum speed, maximum efficiency, and maximum output, factory owners used time-and-motion studies to organize their work and configure the jobs of their workers. The goal, as Taylor defined it in his celebrated 1911 treatise, *The Principles of Scientific Management*, was to identify and adopt, for every job, the "one best method" of work and thereby to effect "the gradual substitution of science for rule of thumb throughout the mechanic arts." Once his system was applied to all acts of manual labor, Taylor assured his followers, it would bring about a restructuring not only of industry but of society, creating a utopia of perfect efficiency. "In the past the man has been first," he declared; "in the future the system must be first."

Taylor's system is still very much with us; it remains the ethic of industrial manufacturing. And now, thanks to the growing power that computer engineers and software coders wield over our intellectual lives, Taylor's ethic is beginning to govern the realm of the mind as well. The Internet is a machine designed for the efficient and automated collection, transmission, and manipulation of information, and its legions of programmers are intent on finding the "one best method"—the perfect algorithm—to carry out every mental movement of what we've come to describe as "knowledge work."

25   Google's headquarters, in Mountain View, California—the Googleplex— is the Internet's high church, and the religion practiced inside its walls is Taylorism. Google, says its chief executive, Eric Schmidt, is "a company that's founded around the science of measurement," and it is striving to "systematize everything" it does. Drawing on the terabytes of behavioral data it collects through its search engine and other sites, it carries out thousands of experiments a day, according to the *Harvard Business Review*, and it uses the results to refine the algorithms that increasingly control how people find information and extract meaning from it. What Taylor did for the work of the hand, Google is doing for the work of the mind.

The company has declared that its mission is "to organize the world's information and make it universally accessible and useful." It seeks to develop "the perfect search engine," which it defines as something that "understands exactly what you mean and gives you back exactly what you want." In Google's view, information is a kind of commodity, a utilitarian resource that can be mined and processed with industrial efficiency. The more pieces of information we can "access" and the faster we can extract their gist, the more productive we become as thinkers.

Where does it end? Sergey Brin and Larry Page, the gifted young men who founded Google while pursuing doctoral degrees in computer science at Stanford, speak frequently of their desire to turn their search engine into an artificial intelligence, a HAL-like machine that might be connected directly to our brains. "The ultimate search engine is something as smart as people—or smarter," Page said in a speech a few years back. "For us, working on search is a way to work on artificial intelligence." In a 2004 interview with *Newsweek*, Brin said, "Certainly if you had all the world's information directly attached to your brain, or an artificial brain that was smarter than your brain, you'd be better off." Last year, Page told a convention of scientists that Google is "really trying to build artificial intelligence and to do it on a large scale."

Such an ambition is a natural one, even an admirable one, for a pair of math whizzes with vast quantities of cash at their disposal and a small army of computer scientists in their employ. A fundamentally scientific enterprise, Google is motivated by a desire to use technology, in Eric Schmidt's words, "to solve problems that have never been solved before," and artificial intelligence is the hardest problem out there. Why wouldn't Brin and Page want to be the ones to crack it?

Still, their easy assumption that we'd all "be better off" if our brains were supplemented, or even replaced, by an artificial intelligence is unsettling. It suggests a belief that intelligence is the output of a mechanical process, a series of discrete steps that can be isolated, measured, and optimized. In Google's world, the world we enter when we go online, there's little place for the fuzziness of contemplation. Ambiguity is not an opening for insight but a bug to be fixed. The human brain is just an outdated computer that needs a faster processor and a bigger hard drive.

The idea that our minds should operate as high-speed data-processing machines is not only built into the workings of the Internet, it is the network's reigning business model as well. The faster we surf across the Web—the more links we click and pages we view—the more opportunities Google and other companies gain to collect information about us and to feed us advertisements. Most of the proprietors of the commercial Internet have a financial stake in collecting the crumbs of data we leave behind as we flit from link to link—the more crumbs, the better. The last thing these companies want is to encourage leisurely reading or slow, concentrated thought. It's in their economic interest to drive us to distraction.

Maybe I'm just a worrywart. Just as there's a tendency to glorify technological progress, there's a countertendency to expect the worst of every new tool or machine. In Plato's *Phaedrus*, Socrates bemoaned the development of writing. He feared that, as people came to rely on the written word as a substitute for the knowledge they used to carry inside their heads, they would, in the words of one of the dialogue's characters, "cease to exercise their memory and become forgetful." And because they would be able to "receive a quantity of information without proper instruction," they would

30

"be thought very knowledgeable when they are for the most part quite ignorant." They would be "filled with the conceit of wisdom instead of real wisdom." Socrates wasn't wrong—the new technology did often have the effects he feared—but he was shortsighted. He couldn't foresee the many ways that writing and reading would serve to spread information, spur fresh ideas, and expand human knowledge (if not wisdom).

The arrival of Gutenberg's printing press, in the 15th century, set off another round of teeth gnashing. The Italian humanist Hieronimo Squarciafico worried that the easy availability of books would lead to intellectual laziness, making men "less studious" and weakening their minds. Others argued that cheaply printed books and broadsheets would undermine religious authority, demean the work of scholars and scribes, and spread sedition and debauchery. As New York University professor Clay Shirky notes, "Most of the arguments made against the printing press were correct, even prescient." But, again, the doomsayers were unable to imagine the myriad blessings that the printed word would deliver.

So, yes, you should be skeptical of my skepticism. Perhaps those who dismiss critics of the Internet as Luddites or nostalgists will be proved correct, and from our hyperactive, data-stoked minds will spring a golden age of intellectual discovery and universal wisdom. Then again, the Net isn't the alphabet, and although it may replace the printing press, it produces something altogether different. The kind of deep reading that a sequence of printed pages promotes is valuable not just for the knowledge we acquire from the author's words but for the intellectual vibrations those words set off within our own minds. In the quiet spaces opened up by the sustained, undistracted reading of a book, or by any other act of contemplation, for that matter, we make our own associations, draw our own inferences and analogies, foster our own ideas. Deep reading, as Maryanne Wolf argues, is indistinguishable from deep thinking.

If we lose those quiet spaces, or fill them up with "content," we will sacrifice something important not only in our selves but in our culture. In a recent essay, the playwright Richard Foreman eloquently described what's at stake:

35   I come from a tradition of Western culture, in which the ideal (my ideal) was the complex, dense and "cathedral-like" structure of the highly educated and articulate personality—a man or woman who carried inside themselves a personally constructed and unique version of the entire heritage of the West. [But now] I see within us all

(myself included) the replacement of complex inner density with a new kind of self—evolving under the pressure of information overload and the technology of the "instantly available."

As we are drained of our "inner repertory of dense cultural inheritance," Foreman concluded, we risk turning into "'pancake people'—spread wide and thin as we connect with that vast network of information accessed by the mere touch of a button."

I'm haunted by that scene in *2001*. What makes it so poignant, and so weird, is the computer's emotional response to the disassembly of its mind: its despair as one circuit after another goes dark, its childlike pleading with the astronaut—"I can feel it. I can feel it. I'm afraid"—and its final reversion to what can only be called a state of innocence. HAL's outpouring of feeling contrasts with the emotionlessness that characterizes the human figures in the film, who go about their business with an almost robotic efficiency. Their thoughts and actions feel scripted, as if they're following the steps of an algorithm. In the world of *2001*, people have become so machinelike that the most human character turns out to be a machine. That's the essence of Kubrick's dark prophecy: as we come to rely on computers to mediate our understanding of the world, it is our own intelligence that flattens into artificial intelligence.

Analyze

1. Carr enumerates both the positive and negative effects of using the Web in relation to his career as a writer. List these.
2. What does Nietzsche's typewriter have to do with Carr's argument about Google and the Internet?
3. Explain the relevance of Joseph Weizenbaum's comments on clocks and other timekeeping instruments to Carr's argument.
4. What is Taylorism and why is it important to Carr's discussion of technology's possible impact on reading processes?
5. Carr mentions the work of developmental psychologist Maryanne Wolf. Why?
6. Carr begins and ends his essay with a reference to *2001: A Space Odyssey*. If you are not familiar with that film and the novel by Arthur C. Clarke on which the movie was based, look both up. Then, explain some reasons why Carr may have introduced and concluded his essay with this reference.

Explore

1. One of Carr's central points in his essay relates to the fact that "the process of adapting to new intellectual technologies is reflected in the changing metaphors we use to explain ourselves to ourselves." Free write about the metaphors that you use to describe yourself and your thinking processes. Have these changed over time? How may these metaphors relate to the technologies you use or may once have used?

2. In her essay "How We Read: Close, Hyper, Machine," the academic N. Katherine Hayles critiques Carr's essay and explains the ways in which various types of reading can all exist at the same time. Look up a copy of Hayles's essay either in your college library or on the Web. Read the essay, making note of the many places where her essay is in dialogue with Carr's essay. Then, in a short essay, which you will present to your classmates, explain what Hayles's essay is about and how it can be compared and contrasted with Carr's essay.

3. In response to Carr's argument and the claims he uses to support his argument, write a three- to five-page essay in which you explain, based on your own experiences of using Google and other Web technologies in your writing and research processes, why you agree or disagree with Carr's argument and the claims he uses to support his argument. In your essay, make sure to cite and comment on textual evidence from Carr's essay.

cite Anthology

Clay Shirky
"Does the Internet Make You Smarter?"

Clay Shirky is an American writer, educator, and consultant who has been writing and thinking about the Internet since the mid-1990s. An Associate Professor at New York University (NYU) in Journalism and New Media Studies, Shirky's writings are currently focused on the Internet's effect in shifting media landscapes, the Internet economy and its effects on national culture, and open source software in post-PC network ecologies. His articles and essays have been published in a range of business and technology magazines and newspapers, and he is the author of several books, most recently *Cognitive Surplus: How Technology Makes Consumers Into Collaborators* (2011) and *Here Comes Everybody: The Power of Organizing Without Organizations* (2009). In this essay, Shirky argues that the Internet, contrary to widely held perceptions, does not make us dumber or more distracted but may actually be an engine behind a potential cognitive surplus.

Does using the Internet make you feel more or less intelligent? Why?

Digital media have made creating and disseminating text, sound, and images cheap, easy and global. The bulk of publicly available media is now created by people who understand little of the professional standards and practices for media.

Instead, these amateurs produce endless streams of mediocrity, eroding cultural norms about quality and acceptability, and leading to increasingly alarmed predictions of incipient chaos and intellectual collapse.

But of course, that's what always happens. Every increase in freedom to create or consume media, from paperback books to YouTube, alarms people accustomed to the restrictions of the old system, convincing them that the new media will make young people stupid. This fear dates back to at least the invention of movable type.

As Gutenberg's press spread through Europe, the Bible was translated into local languages, enabling direct encounters with the text; this was accompanied by a flood of contemporary literature, most of it mediocre. Vulgar versions of the Bible and distracting secular writings fueled religious unrest and civic confusion, leading to claims that the printing press, if not controlled, would lead to chaos and the dismemberment of European intellectual life.

These claims were, of course, correct. Print fueled the Protestant Reformation, which did indeed destroy the Church's pan-European hold on intellectual life. What the 16th-century foes of print didn't imagine—couldn't imagine—was what followed: We built new norms around newly abundant and contemporary literature. Novels, newspapers, scientific journals, the separation of fiction and non-fiction, all of these innovations were created during the collapse of the scribal system, and all had the effect of increasing, rather than decreasing, the intellectual range and output of society. 5

To take a famous example, the essential insight of the scientific revolution was peer review, the idea that science was a collaborative effort that included the feedback and participation of others. Peer review was a cultural institution that took the printing press for granted as a means of distributing research quickly and widely, but added the kind of cultural constraints that made it valuable.

We are living through a similar explosion of publishing capability today, where digital media link over a billion people into the same network. This linking together in turn lets us tap our cognitive surplus, the trillion hours a year of free time the educated population of the planet has to spend doing things they care about. In the 20th century, the bulk of that time was spent watching television, but our cognitive surplus is so enormous that diverting even a tiny fraction of time from consumption to participation can create enormous positive effects.

Wikipedia took the idea of peer review and applied it to volunteers on a global scale, becoming the most important English reference work in less than 10 years. Yet the cumulative time devoted to creating Wikipedia, something like 100 million hours of human thought, is expended by Americans every weekend, just watching ads. It only takes a fractional shift in the direction of participation to create remarkable new educational resources.

Similarly, open source software, created without managerial control of the workers or ownership of the product, has been critical to the spread of the Web. Searches for everything from supernovae to prime numbers now happen as giant, distributed efforts. Ushahidi, the Kenyan crisis mapping tool invented in 2008, now aggregates citizen reports about crises the world over. PatientsLikeMe, a website designed to accelerate medical research by getting patients to publicly share their health information, has assembled a larger group of sufferers of Lou Gehrig's disease than any pharmaceutical agency in history, by appealing to the shared sense of seeking medical progress.

10   Of course, not everything people care about is a high-minded project. Whenever media become more abundant, average quality falls quickly, while new institutional models for quality arise slowly. Today we have The World's Funniest Home Videos running 24/7 on YouTube, while the potentially world-changing uses of cognitive surplus are still early and special cases.

That always happens too. In the history of print, we got erotic novels 100 years before we got scientific journals, and complaints about distraction have been rampant; no less a beneficiary of the printing press than

Martin Luther complained, "The multitude of books is a great evil. There is no measure of limit to this fever for writing." Edgar Allan Poe, writing during another surge in publishing, concluded, "The enormous multiplication of books in every branch of knowledge is one of the greatest evils of this age; since it presents one of the most serious obstacles to the acquisition of correct information."

The response to distraction, then as now, was social structure. Reading is an unnatural act; we are no more evolved to read books than we are to use computers. Literate societies become literate by investing extraordinary resources, every year, training children to read. Now it's our turn to figure out what response we need to shape our use of digital tools.

Does the Internet Make You Dumber?

The case for digitally-driven stupidity assumes we'll fail to integrate digital freedoms into society as well as we integrated literacy. This assumption in turn rests on three beliefs: that the recent past was a glorious and irreplaceable high-water mark of intellectual attainment; that the present is only characterized by the silly stuff and not by the noble experiments; and that this generation of young people will fail to invent cultural norms that do for the Internet's abundance what the intellectuals of the 17th century did for print culture. There are likewise three reasons to think that the Internet will fuel the intellectual achievements of 21st-century society.

First, the rosy past of the pessimists was not, on closer examination, so rosy. The decade the pessimists want to return us to is the 1980s, the last period before society had any significant digital freedoms. Despite frequent genuflection to European novels, we actually spent a lot more time watching "Diff'rent Strokes" than reading Proust, prior to the Internet's spread. The Net, in fact, restores reading and writing as central activities in our culture.

The present is, as noted, characterized by lots of throwaway cultural   15
artifacts, but the nice thing about throwaway material is that it gets thrown away. This issue isn't whether there's lots of dumb stuff online—there is, just as there is lots of dumb stuff in bookstores. The issue is whether there are any ideas so good today that they will survive into the future. Several early uses of our cognitive surplus, like open source software, look like they will pass that test.

The past was not as golden, nor is the present as tawdry, as the pessimists suggest, but the only thing really worth arguing about is the future. It is our misfortune, as a historical generation, to live through the largest expansion in expressive capability in human history, a misfortune because abundance breaks more things than scarcity. We are now witnessing the rapid stress of older institutions accompanied by the slow and fitful development of cultural alternatives. Just as required education was a response to print, using the Internet well will require new cultural institutions as well, not just new technologies.

It is tempting to want *PatientsLikeMe* without the dumb videos, just as we might want scientific journals without the erotic novels, but that's not how media works. Increased freedom to create means increased freedom to create throwaway material, as well as freedom to indulge in the experimentation that eventually makes the good new stuff possible. There is no easy way to get through a media revolution of this magnitude; the task before us now is to experiment with new ways of using a medium that is social, ubiquitous and cheap, a medium that changes the landscape by distributing freedom of the press and freedom of assembly as widely as freedom of speech.

Analyze

1. According to Shirky, what was the "essential insight of the scientific revolution"? What were the effects of this insight?
2. Shirky compares Wikipedia with the scientific peer review process initiated with the invention of the printing press. Explain why this comparison is important to his argument.
3. How does Shirky define "cognitive surplus"? Why is this term central to his argument?
4. What are the three beliefs that Shirky cites as being behind the "digitally driven stupidity" case?

Explore

1. Central to Shirky's essay is the analogy he makes between the printing press and the Internet. Make two lists: one of the changes that Shirky mentions in relation to the printing press and one of the changes he mentions in relation to the Internet. Write a short essay assessing the strength of this analogy based on the evidence presented by Shirky.

2. Much of Shirky's argument regarding the potential for the collective cognitive surplus relates to his belief that the Internet is fundamentally different from television. Write a short essay comparing and contrasting how your use of Internet and Web technologies is similar or different to how you watch TV.

3. If, as many critics claim, the Web is a "meta-medium" that incorporates all of the media that came before it, how might this perspective affect Shirky's argument? In a three- to five-page essay, describe the many different media that are brought together by the Web and assess the extent to which Shirky acknowledges this perspective in his essay and the strength of Shirky's argument in the context of this perspective.

Sam Leith
"What Does It All Meme?"

Sam Leith is a British author and journalist. A frequent contributor to *The Spectator, The Wall Street Journal Europe,* and *The Guardian,* he has a regular column in the *Monday Evening Standard.* Leith has published several works of nonfiction: *Dead Pets, Sod's Law, You Talkin' to Me?,* and, most recently, *Words Like Loaded Pistols: Rhetoric From Aristotle to Obama* (2012). *The Coincidence Engine,* his first novel, was published in April 2011. In this essay, Leith reviews the origin and meanings of the term *meme* and considers the possible effects and consequences of instant media events for culture and society.

What is currently your favorite meme? Why?

H e lives in Japan. He's a straight-haired Scottish Fold, four years old, slightly rotund (his name means "round" in Japanese). Otherwise? Well, there's this thing he does where he jumps into an empty cardboard box. He jumps into all sorts of cardboard boxes. And out. Sometimes he climbs in a bin. Just for fun!

And Maru is famous. At the time of writing, YouTube videos of Maru have been viewed 100m times. He's the subject of a recent hardback book, *I Am Maru*. It consists of 95 glossy pages of photographs of Maru being a cat. In August, three weeks before its publication date, it was the number one cat book on Amazon UK.

Maru is just a cat. But he's also more than just a cat. Maru is a bellwether of the state of the culture. Maru is a meme.

If you have an email inbox you will, even if the term is unfamiliar, have come across what it denotes: the viral ephemera that washes across the internet, proliferates on Facebook walls and trends on Twitter. The internet is the most potent medium of mass communication in human history but we use it to exchange videos of cats jumping through cardboard boxes, old Rick Astley songs and pictures of a rabbit with a pancake.

5   The success of these memes prompts certain questions. Not least, what's wrong with us? But also, what do they tell us about our relationships with each other? And what is it that makes certain memes catch fire?

"That's the million-dollar question," says Don Caldwell, a reporter for the website *Know Your Meme*. "There's not an easy answer. I see them as filling ecological niches. There's the funny niche, the weird niche and the cuteness niche: Maru the cat has filled that section of the internet pretty well for himself."

"The success of a meme is like the reproductive success of an organism," he adds. "They have to be really well suited to their environment, and the environment of a meme is the cultural zeitgeist."

The word "meme" was originally minted in the analogue age by the scientist Richard Dawkins. In *The Selfish Gene* (1976), he proposed that natural selection could work on ideas (which would flourish or fail with us as their ecosystem) as well as genetic material, and chose the term as a counterpart to "gene": a meme as a unit of cultural transmission. Essentially, this means a contagious idea. The term is broad. Limericks can be a meme. The late 18th-century epidemic of copycat suicides by men in yellow trousers after the publication of Goethe's *The Sorrows of Young Werther* is a meme. Rioting is a meme. So memes, in this extended sense, existed before the internet and continue to exist outside it.

Latin tags and rhetorical commonplaces were memes; "Kilroy was here" was a meme; chain letters, before the arrival of the internet, were memes that behaved in a recognisably viral way. There were fax memes and email memes, such as the smutty private email sent by one Claire Swire that ended up being viewed by millions in 2000.

But internet culture, and the exceptional speed and ease of transmis- 10 sion online, represents a step-change. Early geneticists were attracted to fruit flies as research subjects because their extreme fecundity and short lifecycles meant many generations could be studied in a space of months. When it comes to memes, the internet is an immense colony of fruit flies living in fast-forward—with all the experimental data widely and instantly available.

Looking at this data, the one distinguishing feature would seem to be downright frivolity. Memes support the idea that the online world has blurred the distinction between work and play—that media has given way to social media. A giant culture of messing about has found its perfect technology. It's no coincidence that the biennial convention on internet meme culture, held at Massachusetts Institute of Technology since 2008, is called ROFLCon, after the common online acronym for "Rolling On the Floor Laughing."

In line with the evolutionary analogy, the memes that live longest tend to be those that are most adaptable. If the defining art form of the first part of the 20th century was collage, from the constellations of fragments in modernist poetry to the collided images of the plastic arts, that of the digital age is surely the remix or the mash-up. Video clips are spliced together; sound is sampled and repurposed; public domain images are overdubbed with catchphrases. *Downfall,* a German film made in 2004 showing the last days of Hitler, is appropriated to have the Führer ranting about Oasis splitting up; a sample of Gregg Wallace from *Masterchef* provides the hook for a techno track ("I like the base, base, biscuit base"). The term "exploitable" is, in this context, often used as a noun by those who make memes and describe their behaviour.

Jonah Peretti, founder of *Buzzfeed,* a website that keeps track of, promotes and reports what goes on in viral media, says: "We used to think of the world in sections like front-page news, the sports section, the business section, the entertainment section. But when you think about memes and a lot of web culture, things are not organised that way. They're organised by a sort of social logic. What kind of things do people like to do together? What kinds of things do people relate to? We organise our site by these emotional responses. So we don't have a sports section and an entertainment section: we have an LOL [laughing out loud!] section, a WTF [good heavens!] section, a geeky section and so on."

One of the most enduring and easily remixed meme genres is what users on internet forums call the "image macro"—that is, a picture with lettering across it—of which the best known is probably the LOLcat. There are now millions of these in circulation. The archetypal LOLcat—back in the dawn of time, ie 2007, was a fat-looking grey mog asking: "I can has cheezburger?" Subgenres sprang up, multiplied, divided and adapted. The Bible has been translated into LOLspeak and LOLwalruses are already old, old news.

15   Image macros may use a specific image and an associated running joke, or a phrasal template of the sort known as "snowclones": for example, "to X, or not to X"; "X is the new Y." Snowclones are catnip to the internet. A catchphrase from online wargames, "I'm in your base, killing your men" (and numerous misspelled alternatives), has spawned the snowclone, "I'm in ur X, Ying ur Z." You'll find it on LOLcats: "I'm in ur fridge, eating ur noms." Kanye West's famous interruption—"I'ma let you finish"—was another instant snowclone; "Yo Jesus, I'm real happy for you, and I'mma let you finish, but Allah had one of the best ideas of all time. Of all time!" And so forth.

A participatory element undoubtedly helps memes to spread—and to beget other memes. Peretti describes the rise of "Disaster Girl," which began life as an image of a little girl smiling impishly with a burning house in the background. "What we did at Buzzfeed was to cut her face out of the image and let people put it on top of any disaster. So she went in front of Bill and Monica's first meeting, Windows Vista, the Hindenburg . . . People already liked the image and were passing it around. But we made it easier for them to participate and make it their own."

Memes have penetrated the real world too. Whimsical crazes such as "planking"—where users, and increasingly celebrities including Justin Bieber and Katy Perry, photograph themselves lying flat in odd locations— or "extreme ironing" are activities undertaken so that the images of them can be uploaded to the internet. One of the most celebrated instances of a meme that straddles the online and offline worlds is the "flashmob," where a crowd of strangers appears spontaneously in a public space and, for example, breaks into a synchronised dance routine.

The first flashmob was convened in 2003 by Bill Wasik, a writer on technology and culture then working as a senior editor at *Harper's* magazine. "It really started as a prank or a joke," he says. "I'd become very interested in viral email and I thought it would be fun to do a show in New York where the audience would be gathered entirely by viral email. At a certain point, I realised I could be lazier and not come up with an idea for the show: the show would just be everybody coming out to the same place at the same time for no reason.

"I intended this to be a little New York experiment. Just a few weeks into it people were doing them all round the country and then all round the world. I had meant it to be viral in one way, where the emails would spread virally. But then it became viral on a completely other level."

Wasik's experience is a good example of the way in which online memes can be analysed. Memes circulate like jokes and, more often than not, *are* jokes. But while nobody seems to know where jokes come from, thanks to the elephantine memory of the internet it's often possible to trace memes back to the source. We can name Wasik as the inventor of the flashmob in a way we will never be able to name the man who first asked why the chicken crossed the road. That makes even the silliest meme potentially useful as a way of understanding the structures and behaviours of digital social networks.

Indeed, they already have their archivists. The website Know Your Meme started out as a spoofy online video show but is turning into something of a scholarly resource. It documents a whole range of viral phenomena, tracing them to their origins; following the spin-offs and sub-memes, and charting—through Google Insights analysis—the arc of popularity over time. Here is where you go to find out who Star Wars Kid was and what is up with this flying cat with a pop-tart instead of a body.

Don Caldwell of *Know Your Meme* doesn't entirely laugh off the suggestion that what the site is doing resembles Alan Lomax's fieldwork recording folk music in the middle of the past century. "I did my undergraduate degree in anthropology. I see value in documenting culture in this way, trying to understand how it works and how it spreads. What makes some ideas spread more than others?

"With the internet, we can document and witness ideas spreading at rates that we never saw before, for many more people—and you can just watch it happen. We approach a meme as if it has its own life—and we try to explain its life history."

In so fast-moving an environment, the life of even the strongest meme is poignantly short. Maru will still be climbing into cardboard boxes long after his autobiography has been remaindered.

25   When I ask Bill Wasik if any viral object has struck him as especially memorable, he says: "To me both the amazing thing and the disquieting thing about the internet as a medium for culture, entertainment and the transmission of meaning is just how many remarkable things pass through it every day, and how few of them persist in our minds. I feel like the internet resists the very question you're asking. Every day I am rapt by what I see there. The next day I've forgotten everything."

Analyze

1. In your own words, explain what a meme is. Compare this definition to Leith's definition.
2. Who was Richard Dawkins and why is he important to Leith's essay?
3. In what ways are the memes today different from pre-Internet memes?
4. What is ROFLcon?
5. How does BuzzFeed organize its website? Why?

Explore

1. Leith writes, "Memes circulate like jokes and, more often than not, are jokes. But while nobody seems to know where jokes come from, thanks to the elephantine memory of the internet it's often possible to trace memes back to the source." Choose two of the Top 10 Memes from the previous year on the Know Your Meme website (http://knowyour meme.com/blog/meme-review). Write a short essay in which you compare and contrast the two memes by describing them, where they originated, user interpretations and responses to them, and what cultural phenomenon or phenomena each meme—and the responses to it—may be a comment on. What similarities and differences exist between the two memes?
2. Leith ends his essay by quoting Bill Warik, who, on the subject of memes, noted with some sense of wonder how fascinating they are and yet that by "the next day I've forgotten everything [about them]." Describe a meme that you were once interested in. Why was it so exciting and important at the time? Explain why or why not you consider the meme important now. Reflecting on the time period when the meme was popular, what might that meme have to say about that particular sociocultural moment and what was happening at the time?

3. Leith's article was published in 2011 and, since then, some journalists have commented that Internet memes may no longer hold much interest for Internet users. Write an updated article in which you inform your contemporary audience of the state of Internet memes at the moment, describe their ongoing or declining importance, and discuss Leith's article and its 2011 analysis of Internet memes in relation to their current cultural status.

Toby Litt
"The Reader and Technology"

Toby Litt is a British writer. The author of numerous short stories and novels, Litt has recently been involved with writing a monthly comic book series, *Dead Boy Detectives*, which is based on characters from Neil Gaiman's *Sandman*, and has been collaboratively writing an opera. In this essay, originally published in the literary magazine *Granta*, Litt reflects on his childhood and upbringing and how the absence of video games may have had a profound effect on his decision to become a writer.

How has technology changed the ways in which you read and write?

My Futuristic Past

I was born on 20 August 1968—eleven months to the day before the first Apollo Moon Landing. The Space Age was always something to which I aspired rather than belonged.

For several years, between approximately 1976 and 1979, I wasn't interested in anything earthbound. The two most important films of my boyhood were *Star Wars*, which showed me where I wanted to be, and *Close Encounters of the Third Kind*, which showed me a possible means of getting there.

In preference to Ampthill, Bedfordshire in 1979, I would have taken any technological dystopia. There was no armed rebellion against Margaret Thatcher, and even if there had been it would not have involved laser guns.

A couple of years ago, I spent three months playing *World of Warcraft*— partly as research for a short story I was writing, mostly because I became addicted to it. This convinced me of one thing: If the computer games which exist now had existed back in 1979 I would not have read any books, I think; I would not have seen writing as an adequate entertainment; I would not have seen going outdoors as sufficiently interesting to bother with.

5   Similarly, I find it difficult to understand why any eleven-year-old of today would be sufficiently bored to turn inward for entertainment.

This raises the question as to how future writers will come about, without "silence, exile and cunning"—without the need for these things?

I was formed, as a writer, by the boredom of the place in which I lived. Philip Larkin said "not the place's fault"—but in my case, I think it was. And then, the being taken out of the first place into another place (boarding school) where I was unable to have any privacy. This developed a mania for privacy in me, which began to come out as poetry, as a diary. It's not that I didn't do these things before—they just became essentials for self-creating, self-preservation. That's how I read myself, anyway.

The Reader and Technology

Literature isn't alien to technology, literature is technological to begin with.

Literature depends on technology—a society needs to be able to do more than subsist before it produces a literature. An oral culture, yes, that is possible—but I am referring specifically to words on the page, words on the screen.

10   The internet connection offers all of us the constant temptation of snippets, of trivia. We don't live, as other writers did in the past, without these particular temptations. They had their own temptations: Byron wasn't undistracted. Yet there were greater acres of emptiness, surely. Travel took forever. Winters isolated. Boredom was there as a resource for daydreaming, trancing out.

I think writers will continue to occur but technology and its trivia will cause us to lose something, just as we lost something when we lost the classical education. We write worse because we cannot write classical prose.

Yet classical prose is useless for describing the world of 2012, the world that is there—ready to buzz—in your pocket or bag.

Our perceptions outrun the sedentary sentence by much too much; just as we listen to mp3s to hear what an album *would* sound like were we actually to sit down and listen to it, so we skim-read the classic books to get a sense of what they would be like were we to sit down and dwell on them.

Readers more accustomed to screens—web pages, iPhone displays—will scan a page of text for its contents, rather than experience it in a gradual linear top-left to bottom-right way. This will make for increased speed and decreased specificity. These readers will be half-distracted even as they read; their visual field will include other things than just the text, because they won't feel happy unless those things are there. A writer of long, doubling-back sentences such as Henry James will be incomprehensible to them. They won't be grammatically equipped to deal with him. They won't be neurologically capable of reading him. Their eyes will photograph fields rather than, as ours do, or did, follow tracks.

This scanning approach will have a bad effect on sentence structure. For these readers, the fact they are reading bassackwardly—constructed sequences of words won't matter. They won't even notice. As long as the content is there for them somewhere on the page, the job of writing will have been done.

Perhaps future writers will, therefore, create vague fields of possible   15 meaning; more Charles Olson than Ezra Pound. The exact sequence of sounds, the precise inflection of grammar—these things will seem prissy. We will be back to the eighteenth century, pre-Flaubert.

Isaac Babel's famous sentence from his story "Guy de Maupassant": "No iron spike can pierce a human heart as icily as a period in the right place"—prissy.

The Novel and Connectivity

The people novels have conventionally been written about are gradually ceasing to exist.

Novels have always belonged to aristocrats of time; not, I say, merely to aristocrats, although they have been disproportionately represented. Our perceptions outrun the sedentary sentence by much too much but to those subjects who have freedom of choice about how to act within time. The Fordist factory-line workers, performing a repetitive task all day, cannot interest the novel for more than a few moments whilst they are at work. It is only when the machine stops that the story begins. (David Foster Wallace's *The Pale King* attempts to make a novel out of the dead time of insanely repetitive deskwork; and it fails, at least in the form of it he left us.)

Proposition: "The human race is no longer sufficiently bored with life to be distracted by an art form as boring as the novel."

20   Perhaps novels will continue, but instead of the machine it will be the connectivity that stops, or becomes secondary.

What we're going to see more and more of is the pseudo-contemporary novel—in which characters are, for some reason, cut off from one another, technologically cut off. Already, many contemporary novels avoid the truly contemporary (which is hyperconnectivity).

The basic plots of Western Literature depend on separation by distance— Odysseus separated from Penelope; the *Odyssey* doesn't exist if Odysseus can catch an EasyJet flight home, or text Penelope's Blackberry. Joyce's *Ulysses* doesn't exist if Bloom can do his day's business from a laptop in a Temple Bar coffeeshop.

I don't want to overemphasize this. You could imagine a similar anxiety over how the telephone would undermine fiction. Perhaps it is just a matter of acceleration. But I don't think I am alone in already being weary of characters who make their great discoveries whilst sitting in front of a computer screen. If for example a character, by diligent online research and persistent emailing, finds out one day—after a ping in their inbox—who their father really is, isn't that a story hardly worth telling? Watching someone at a computer is dull. Watching someone play even the most exciting computer game is dull. You, reading this now, are not something any writer would want to write about for more than a sentence.

The Future

In the Preface to Volume 15 of the New York Edition, Henry James writes about "operative irony." It's a long quote, but try to stick with it because it may contain the whole future of the novel.

25   I have already mentioned the particular rebuke once addressed me on all this ground, the question of where on earth, where round-about us at this hour, I had "found" my Neil Paradays, my Ralph

Limberts, my Hugh Verekers and other such supersubtle fry. I was reminded then, as I have said, that these represented eminent cases fell to the ground, as by their foolish weight, unless I could give chapter and verse for the eminence. I was reduced to confessing I couldn't, and yet must repeat again here how little I was so abashed. On going over these I see, to our critical edification, exactly why—which was because I was able to plead that my postulates, my animating presences, were all, to their great enrichment, their intensification of value, ironic; the strength of applied irony being surely in the sincerities, the lucidities, the utilities that stand behind it. When it's not a campaign, of a sort, on behalf of the something better (better than the obnoxious, the provoking object) that blessedly, as is assumed, *might* be, it's not worth speaking of. But this is exactly what we mean by operative irony. It implies and projects the possible other case, the case rich and edifying where the actuality is pretentious and vain. So it plays its lamp; so, essentially, it carries that smokeless flame, which makes clear, with all the rest, the good cause that guides it. My application of which remarks is that the studies here collected have their justification in the ironic spirit, the spirit expressed by my being able to reply promptly enough to my friend: "If the life about us for the last thirty years refuses warrant for these examples, then so much the worse for that life. The *constatation* would be so deplorable that instead of making it we must dodge it: there are decencies that in the name of the general self-respect we must take for granted, there's a kind of rudimentary intellectual honour to which we must, in the interest of civilization, at least pretend." But I must really reproduce the whole passion of my retort.

In the future, *all* novels will invoke a kind of operative irony; post-Twitter, post-whatever-comes-after-what-comes-after-Twitter. Who are these "supersubtle fry," your characters, who have all this time in which to become rich, deep selfhoods? Where do you find these interesting subjects of yours?

Or, as Henry James appears to us, so we will appear to the readers of the near future: existing in a different, slow-flowing time that they will need to make an extreme effort of deceleration to access.

I think—as a result of all this—there will be great nostalgia for the pre-trivial age, not even to mention the pre-genetic manipulation age.

Literature can accommodate nostalgia, but only as a houseguest; if nostalgia becomes the landlord, architect and psychoanalyst, literature will have to evict itself.

Analyze

1. Explain the reasons Litt cites for stating "literature is technological to begin with."
2. According to Litt, how will scanning, as opposed to close reading, affect sentence structures?
3. Why, according to Litt, will all future novels "invoke a kind of operative irony"?

Explore

1. Litt proposes that he "was formed, as a writer, by the boredom of the place in which [he] lived," and then suggests that this sense of boredom may not be possible for young people today. Reflecting on your own experience growing up, free write about whether or not you were ever bored. If so, what did you do to counteract the sense of boredom? If not, explain why you were never bored. Finally, based on what you have written, explain why you agree or disagree with Litt's two propositions: first that writers are formed by boredom and second that "the human race is no longer sufficiently bored with life to be distracted by an art form as boring as the novel."
2. The American novelist Henry James is mentioned and quoted several times in Litt's essay. If you are not familiar with James's fiction, look up and read one of his short stories on the Web (all of his writings are in the public domain and although many are quite long two of his shorter stories are "The Real Thing" and "The Story in It"). After reading one short story, review the comments that Litt makes about James in his essay and the quotes by James included in the essay. Then, in an informal piece of writing, reflect on and respond to the following questions: What are some of the purposes that these references and quotations appear to serve in Litt's essay? Based on your reading of James's short story, do you agree with Litt's assessments of James's writing? Why or why not? Cite evidence from both Litt's essay and James's short story as textual evidence to support your points.

3. Consider the novel as a literary form and genre. It is generally over 200 pages, often focused on the psychology of individual characters, read by solitary readers with the time and space to dedicate to reading, and written by one individual. Based on what Litt writes about contemporary literacy practices and your understanding of those practices, write a short essay in which you argue for a specific art form/genre for the twenty-first century. How long is it? What is its content focused on? How is it written? How is it read? What might you call this new genre?

William Cronon
"Scholarly Authority in a Wikified World"

William Cronon is the Frederick Jackson Turner and Vilas Research Professor of History, Geography, and Environmental Studies at the University of Wisconsin–Madison. His research, which focuses on American environmental history and the history of the American West, seeks to understand the history of human interactions with the natural world. He is the author of the books *Changes in the Land: Indians, Colonists, and the Ecology of New England* (1983) and *Nature's Metropolis: Chicago and the Great West* (1991) and the editor of *Uncommon Ground: Rethinking the Human Place in Nature* (1996). In this essay, Cronon evaluates Wikipedia as a research source, considering its strengths, its weaknesses, and its overall quality compared to traditional printed encyclopedias.

Do you consider Wikipedia as reliable a research source as a printed encyclopedia? Why or why not?

Like most scholars, I was skeptical about Wikipedia when Jimmy Wales first launched the site back in 2001. The notion that unvetted volunteers cooperatively contributing to an online encyclopedia might produce a reference work of any real value seemed at best dubious—and, more likely, laughably absurd. Surely it would be riddled with errors. Surely its coverage would be ridiculously patchy. Surely it would lack the breadth, depth, and nuance of more traditional reference works like the venerable *Encyclopedia Britannica*.

My initial skepticism is now proof of how little I understood what Jimmy Wales grasped far better than I. Wikipedia exploded from an initial 20,000 articles in 18 languages during its first year to more than 19 million articles in 270 languages (3.8 million of them in English alone) written or edited by 82,000 active contributors. Whatever reservations one might still have about its overall quality, I don't believe there's much doubt that Wikipedia is the largest, most comprehensive, copiously detailed, stunningly useful encyclopedia in all of human history.

I myself use it on a daily basis, and am pretty sure most of my colleagues and students do too even if they won't admit it. It consistently ranks just behind Facebook, Google, YouTube, and Yahoo among the most visited sites on the Web, with 400 million unique visitors and 6 billion individual page views per month during 2011. For a small nonprofit organization with three dozen paid employees to achieve this kind of prominence against corporations with vastly more capital makes its achievement all the more astonishing.

More to the point, though, Wikipedia is today the gateway through which millions of people now seek access to knowledge which not long ago was only available using tools constructed and maintained by professional scholars. Whatever the reference tools we consulted—dictionaries, almanacs, encyclopedias, books of quotations, finding aids, bibliographies—we did so because their contents had been carefully scrutinized by professionals with appropriate scholarly training.

5   No longer. Wikipedia and its kin have changed all that, and those of us who inhabit the world of scholarship need to ponder the ongoing role of professional authority when traditional disciplines can no longer maintain the kind of intellectual monopolies that their members once took for granted. No one needs a PhD in a subject, or even a baccalaureate major, to contribute or modify Wikipedia entries. Although the wide-open Wiki world sometimes harbors howling errors, even outright fraud, the overall quality of Wikipedia content is remarkably good. If one's goal is quick consultation for information one can check in other ways, or a brief orientation to an unfamiliar topic, then it's hard to imagine a more serviceable tool than Wikipedia. I even have an app that downloads to my iPhone the entire English-language contents of the site—over four gigabytes—so I always have it at my fingertips even when I'm offline.

Don't get me wrong. I'm not saying that any encyclopedia entry is a substitute for the much deeper, richer, more integrated knowledge that has always been the goal of good scholarship. Like every teacher, I caution my students not to rely on encyclopedias when doing serious research. And despite the claims made by a controversial report in *Nature* back in December 2005 that scientific entries in Wikipedia and *Encyclopedia Britannica* were surprisingly comparable in their proclivity for errors, I generally agree with those who defend *Britannica* for its traditional excellence in scholarly nuance and quality of writing when compared with its online rival.

I'm not extolling the virtues of Wikipedia because I regard it as the epitome of scholarly synthesis. Of course not. But the contrast with *Encyclopedia Britannica* does point to the changing nature of scholarly authority in a digital age. *Britannica* was first published in Edinburgh in 1768, and promoted itself from 1824 forward (with the publication of the Supplement to the fourth, fifth, and sixth editions) by commissioning signed contributions by eminent scholars. The famous 11th edition, published in 1910–11, is widely regarded as the most distinguished of all. Historians who contributed entries included J. B. Bury on the Roman Empire, H. M. Chadwick on Anglo-Saxon England, James Harvey Robinson on the Reformation, A. F. Pollard on Tudor England, and Frederick Jackson Turner on U.S. history. Just a few of the historians who have contributed to editions since then include Jacques Barzun, Clayborne Carson, Linda Colley, Joseph Ellis, Eric Foner, John Keegan, James Lockhart, William McNeill, James McPherson, Allan Nevins, Jaroslav Pelikan, Henri Pirenne, Jonathan Spence, Romila Thapar, Arnold Toynbee, Sean Wilentz, and Gordon Wood. The scholarly authority of names like these helped make *Britannica* the gold standard of English-language encyclopedias for more than a century and a half.

Yet Wikipedia has now triumphed with no such reliance on named scholarly experts. Like much on the internet created in a mechanically templated multiauthored environment, it is at its best when presenting simple descriptive summaries and linear narratives broken down into predictable taxonomic subsections that can be composed and edited in modular units. Long, complicated interpretations exploring subtly interacting historical causes in carefully contextualized analyses or beautifully flowing narratives—these one will never find on Wikipedia.

What one *will* find is a breadth and intellectual scope that put even the largest traditional encyclopedias to shame. Unsurprisingly, Wikipedia blows away most competitors for topics involving scientific or technical information, not only because it attracts volunteers especially knowledgeable in these areas, but because it can give such topics all the space they need and revise them literally by the minute. Compare Wikipedia with *Britannica* on "Fermat's Last Theorem" and you'll see what I mean. On topics of current interest, including many environmental subjects central to my own work, Wikipedia has a nimbleness that even newspapers have trouble matching. Its entry on Hurricane Katrina, for instance, already filled many screens while the storm was still raging over New Orleans. (*Britannica*, in contrast, still offers only seven short paragraphs on the subject.) Even controversial topics that are famous for generating warring submissions by opposing sides often do a remarkably good job of migrating toward shared middle ground. Compare Wikipedia's entry on "abortion" or "abortion debate" with *Britannica*'s and ask yourself which does a better job.

10   Perhaps most importantly, Wikipedia provides an online home for people interested in histories long marginalized by the traditional academy. The old boundary between antiquarianism and professional history collapses in an online universe where people who love a particular subject can compile and share endless historical resources for its study in ways never possible before. Amateur genealogists have enabled the creation of document databases that quantitative historians of the 1960s could only fantasize. In my own field of environmental history, I've long told students that gardens and cooking, which have only recently begun to attract the academic attention they deserve, have been studied for generations by serious antiquarians and amateur scholars (many of them women) whose interests were marginalized by a male-dominated academy. In the wikified world of the Web, it's no longer possible to police these boundaries of academic respectability, and we may all be the better for it if only we can embrace this new openness without losing the commitment to rigor that the best amateurs and professionals have always shared more than the professionals have generally been willing to admit.

What is to be done?

If you can't beat 'em, join 'em. Scientists, engineers, and programmers have been contributing sophisticated entries to Wikipedia almost from the beginning. Two disciplines in particular—mathematics and music—have systematically sought to colonize Wikipedia on behalf of their scholarly communities. That's undoubtedly why Wikipedia's entry on Fermat's Last Theorem is so much better than *Britannica*'s, and why the Wikipedia entry for so many composers and other musical subjects is often so good.

Because the discipline of history is much harder to corral than these more technical subjects, and because it's nearly impossible to imagine organizing historians to provide editorial input for all relevant Wikipedia pages, it would undoubtedly be more productive to approach this challenge in a "wikier" way. There are few pages on Wikipedia that couldn't be enhanced with more historical content. There are few historical entries that wouldn't benefit from more scholarly input. And there are myriad historical entries that are missing altogether. Given the openness of Wikipedia's protocols, improvements like these can be made by historians no matter what their training or institutional setting. Indeed, some teachers now require students to draft or revise Wikipedia entries as class assignments.

All one needs is to open oneself to the possibilities and give up the comfort of credentialed expertise to contribute to the greatest encyclopedia the world has ever known—which again, I intend here mainly as a symbol for the Web itself.

We might start with the entry for the American Historical Association.   15 It's pretty inadequate, and would surely benefit from some scholarly revision.

Any volunteers?

Analyze

1. Why does Cronon choose to compare Wikipedia to *the Encyclopedia Britannica*, as opposed to some other print or online source?
2. What types of writing does Cronon believe are best suited to a "multi-authored environment" like Wikipedia? Why?
3. For what reasons, according to Cronon, does "Wikipedia blow away competitors for topics involving scientific and technical information"?
4. Cronon lists several strengths that Wikipedia possesses compared with traditional printed encyclopedias. What are they? What does he cite as some strength of printed encyclopedias?

Explore

1. Look up the entries for "Fermat's Theorem" and "Right to Die" on *Wikipedia*. Compare and contrast these two entries, paying particular attention to the differences between the two entries with respect to the

editorial messages included in each entry, the length of each entry, the notes included in each entry and the references. Based on this comparison, write a one-page assessment of your understanding of *Wikipedia* and its reliability prior to this investigation and your understanding of *Wikipedia* and its reliability after this investigation.

2. Look up the entry for "Fermat's Theorem" on Wikipedia and the same entry in a printed encyclopedia. Compare and contrast the two entries, paying particular attention to the differences between the two entries with respect to the length of each entry, the supplementary graphics included with each entry, the notes included in each entry, and the references. Based on this comparison, write a one-page assessment of your understanding of *Wikipedia* and its reliability prior to this investigation and your understanding of *Wikipedia* and its reliability after this investigation.

3. Cronon offers guidelines for the types of topics that are well suited to *Wikipedia* entries. Based on these guidelines, in a short essay describe one topic that would be well suited to *Wikipedia* and one that would not be. In the context of Cronon's guidelines and your understanding of them and these topics, explain why you chose each topic.

4. Although there are over four million entries in English on *Wikipedia*, there are still many entries that have yet to be written or completed. Those still in progress are referred to as "stubs." Look up one of the stubs on *Wikipedia* and write a draft of the entry.

Ursula K. Le Guin
"The Death of the Book"

Ursula K. Le Guin is an American writer. The author of over a dozen novels, including *The Earthsea Trilogy* and *The Left Hand of Darkness*, Le Guin is also a poet, an author of children's books, and a literary and social critic. The recipient of numerous awards for her science fiction novels, Le Guin continues to write book reviews and is a frequent contributor to her blog, www.ursulakleguin.com, where the following essay was first published. In this essay, Le Guin reflects on the nature of the book as printed and electronic object, proposing that ebooks may ultimately extend rather than curtail the projected lifespan of books.

Do you prefer reading books in print or on a screen? Why?

People love to talk about the death of whatever—the book, or history, or Nature, or God, or authentic Cajun cuisine. Eschatologically-minded people do, anyhow.

After I wrote that, I felt pleased with myself, but uneasy. I went and looked up eschatological. I knew it didn't mean what scatological means, even though they sound exactly alike except eschatological has one more syllable, but I thought it had to do only with death. I didn't realise it concerns not one thing but The Four Last Things: Death, Judgment, Heaven, and Hell. If it included scatology too, it would be practically the whole ball of wax.

Anyhow, the eschatologists' judgment is that the book is going to die and go to heaven or hell, leaving us to the mercy of Hollywood and our computer screens.

There certainly is something sick about the book industry, but it seems closely related to the sickness affecting every industry that, under pressure from a corporate owner, dumps product standards and long-range planning in favor of "predictable" sales and short-term profits.

As for books themselves, the changes in book technology are cataclysmic. Yet it seems to me that rather than dying, "the book" is growing— taking on a second form and shape, the ebook.   5

This is a vast, unplanned change that's as confusing, uncomfortable, and destructive as most unplanned changes. Certainly it's putting huge strain on all the familiar channels of book publication and acquisition, from the publishers, distributors, book stores, and libraries, to the reader who's afraid that the latest best seller, or perhaps all literature, will suddenly pass him by if he doesn't rush out and buy an electronic device to read it on.

But that's it, isn't it?—that's what books are about—reading?

Is reading obsolete, is the reader dead?

Dear reader: How are you doing? I am fairly obsolete, but by no means, at the moment, dead.

Dear reader: Are you reading at this moment? I am, because I'm writing   10 this, and it's very hard to write without reading, as you know if you ever tried it in the dark.

Dear reader: What are you reading on? I'm writing and reading on my computer, as I imagine you are. (At least, I hope you're reading what I'm writing, and aren't writing "What Tosh!" in the margin. Though I've always wanted to write "What Tosh!" in a margin ever since I read it years ago in the margin of a library book. It was such a good description of the book.)

Reading is undeniably one of the things people do on the computer. And also, on the various electronic devices that are capable of and may be looked upon as "for" telephoning, taking photographs, playing music and games, etc, people may spend a good while texting sweetiepie, or looking up recipes for authentic Cajun gumbo, or checking out the stock report—all of which involve reading. People use computers to play games or wander through picture galleries or watch movies, and to do computations and make spreadsheets and pie charts, and a few lucky ones get to draw pictures or compose music, and so on, but mostly, am I wrong? isn't an awful lot of what people do with computers either word-processing (writing) or processing words (reading)?

How much of anything can you do in the e-world *without* reading? The use of any computer above the toddler-entertainment level is dependent on at least some literacy in the user. Operations can be learned mechanically, but still, the main element of a keyboard is letters, and icons take you only so far. Texting may have replaced all other forms of verbality for some people, but texting is just a primitive form of writing: you can't do it unless you no u frm i, lol.

It looks to me as if people are in fact reading and writing more than they ever did. People who used to work and talk together now work each alone in a cubicle, writing and reading all day long on screen. Communication that used to be oral, face to face or on the telephone, is now written, emailed, and read.

15   None of that has much to do with book-reading, true; yet it's hard for me to see how the death of the book is to result from the overwhelming prevalence of a technology that makes reading a more invaluable skill than it ever was.

Ah, say the eschatologists, but it's competition from the wondrous, endless everything-else-you-can-do-on-your-iPad—competition is murdering the book!

Could be. Or it might just make readers more discriminating. A recent article in the *NY Times* ("Finding Your Book Interrupted . . . By the Tablet You Read It On" by Julie Bosman and Matt Richtel, March 4, 2012) quoted a woman in Los Angeles: "With so many distractions, my taste in books has really leveled up. . . . Recently, I gravitate to books that make me forget I have a world of entertainment at my fingertips. If the book's not good enough to do that, I guess my time is better spent." Her sentence ends oddly, but I think it means that she prefers reading an entertaining book to activating the world of entertainment with her fingertips. Why does she not consider books part of this world of entertainment? Maybe because the book, even when activated by her fingertips, entertains her without the moving, flickering, twitching, jumping, glittering, shouting, thumping, bellowing, screaming, blood-spattering, ear-splitting, etc, that we've been led to identify as entertainment. In any case, her point is clear: if a book's not as entertaining—on some level, not necessarily the same level—as the jumping, thumping, bleeding, etc, then why read it? Either activate the etc, or find a better book. As she puts it, level up.

When we hear about the death of the book, it might be a good idea to ask what "the book" is. Are we talking about people ceasing to read books, or about what they read the books on—paper or a screen?

Reading on a screen is certainly different from reading a page. I don't think we yet understand what the differences are. They may be considerable, but I doubt that they're so great as to justify giving the two kinds of reading different names, or saying that an ebook isn't a book at all.

If "the book" means only the book as physical object, its death, to some devotees of the Internet, may be a matter for rejoicing—hurray! we're rid of another nasty heavy bodily Thing with a copyright on it!—But mostly it's the occasion of lament and mourning. People to whom the physicality of the book printed on paper is important, sometimes more important than the contents—those who value them for their binding, paper, and typography, buy fine editions, make collections—and the many who simply take pleasure in holding and handling the book they're reading, are naturally distressed by the idea that the book on paper will be totally replaced by the immaterial text in a machine.

I can only suggest, don't agonize—organize! No matter how the corporations bluster and bully and bury us in advertising, the consumer always has the option of resistance. We don't get steamrollered by a new technology unless we lie down in front of the steamroller.

The steamroller is certainly on the move. Some kinds of printed book are already being replaced by ebooks. The mass market paperback edition is threatened by the low-cost ebook edition. Good news for those who like to

Substance

20

Organization

read on a screen, bad news for those who don't, or like to buy from Abebooks and A-libris or to pounce on 75-cent beat-up secondhand mysteries. But if the lovers of the material book are serious about valuing good binding and paper and design as essential to their reading pleasure, they will provide a visible, steady market for well-made hard-cover and paperback editions: which the book industry, if it has the sense of a sowbug, will meet. The question is whether the book industry does have the sense of a sowbug. Some of its behavior lately leads one to doubt. But let us hope. And there's always the "small publisher," the corporation-free independent, many of which are as canny as can be.

Other outcries about the death of the book have more to do with the direct competition with reading offered on the Internet. The book is being murdered by the etc at our fingertips.

Here "the book" usually refers to literature. At the moment, I think the DIY manual, or the cookbook, the guide to this or that, are the kinds of book most often replaced by information on a screen. The *Encyclopedia Britannica* just died, a victim, as it were, of Google. I don't think I'll bury our Eleventh Edition just yet, though; the information in it, being a product of its time (a hundred years ago), can be valuably different from that furnished by the search engine, which is also a product of its time. The annual encyclopedias of films/directors/actors were killed a few years ago by information sites on the Net—very good sites, though not as much fun to get lost in as the book was. We keep our 2003 edition because being ourselves ancient, we use it more efficiently than we do any site, and it's still useful and entertaining even if dead—more than you can say of the corpse of almost anything but a book.

25   I'm not sure why anyone, no matter how much they like to think about the End Times, believes that the *Iliad* or *Jane Eyre* or the *Bhagavad Gita* is dead or about to die. They have far more competition than they used to, yes; people may see the movie and think they know what the book is; they can be *dis*placed by the etc; but nothing can *re*place them. So long as people are taught to read (which may or may not happen in our underfunded schools), and particularly if they're taught what there is to read, and how to read it intelligently (extensions of the basic skill now often omitted in our underfunded schools), some of them will prefer reading to activating the etc. They will read books (on paper or on a screen) as literature.

And they will try to ensure that the books continue to exist, because continuity is an essential aspect of literature and knowledge. Books occupy time in a different way than most art and entertainment. In longevity perhaps only sculpture in stone outdoes them.

And here the issue of electronic and print on paper has to re-enter the discussion. On the permanence of what is in books, much of the *lasting* transmission of human culture still relies. It's possible that highest and most urgent value of the printed book may be its mere, solid, stolid permanence.

I'll be talking now not about "the book" in America in 2012 so much as about how things are all over the world in the many places where electricity may be available only to the rich, or intermittent, or non-existent; and how things may be in fifty years or five centuries, if we continue to degrade and destroy our habitat at the present rate.

The ease of reproducing an ebook and sending it all over the place can certainly secure its permanence, so long as the machine to read it on can be made and turned on. I think it's well to remember, though, that electric power is not to be counted on in quite the same way sunlight is.

Easy and infinite copy-ability also involves a certain risk. The text of the book on paper can't be altered without separately and individually altering every copy in existence, and alteration leaves unmistakable traces. With e-texts that have been altered, deliberately or by corruption (pirated texts are often incredibly corrupt), if the author is dead, establishing an original, authentic, correct text may be impossible. And the more piracies, abridgments, mash-ups, etc are tolerated, the less people will understand that textual integrity matters.   30

People to whom texts matter, such as readers of poetry or scientific monographs, know that the integrity of the text is essential. Our non-literate ancestors knew it. The three-year-old being read to demands it. *You must recite the words of the poem exactly as you learned them or it will lose its power—Daddy! You read it wrong! It says "did not" not "didn't!"*

The physical book may last for centuries; even a cheap paperback on pulp paper takes decades to degrade into unreadability. Continuous changes of technology, upgrades, corporate takeovers, leave behind them a debris of texts unreadable on any available machine. And an e-text has to be periodically recopied to keep it from degrading. People who archive them are reluctant to say how often, because it varies a great deal; but as anyone with email files over a few years old knows, the progress into entropy can be rapid. A university librarian told me that, as things are now, they expect to recopy every electronic text the library owns, every eight to ten years, indefinitely.

If we decided to replace the content of our libraries entirely with electronic archives, at this stage of the technology, a worst-case scenario would have informational and literary texts being altered without our consent or knowledge, reproduced or destroyed without our permission, rendered unreadable by the technology that printed them, and, unless regularly recopied and redistributed, fated within a few years or decades to turn inexorably into garble or simply blink out of existence.

But that's assuming the technology won't improve and stabilize. In any case, why should we go into either/or mode? It's seldom necessary and often destructive (look at Congress).

35   Maybe the e-reader and the electricity to run it will become available to everyone forever. That would be grand. But as things are or are likely to be, having books available in two different forms can only be a good thing, now and in the long run.

I do believe that, despite the temptations at our fingertips, there's an obstinate, durable minority of people who, having learned to read, will go on reading books, however and wherever they can find them, on pages or screens. And because people who read books mostly want to share them, and feel however obscurely that sharing them is important, they'll see to it that, however and wherever, the books are there for the next generation(s).

Human generations, that is—not technological generations. At the moment, the computer generation has shortened to about the life span of the gerbil, and might yet rival the fruitfly.

The life span of a book is more like that of the horse, or the human being, sometimes the oak, even the redwood. Which is why it seems a good idea, rather than mourning their death, to rejoice that books now have two ways of staying alive, getting passed on, enduring, instead of only one.

Analyze

1. What is eschatology? Why is this term relevant to Le Guin's essay?
2. Le Guin begins her essay by drawing attention to the phonetic similarity of the words eschatological and scatological. What may be some of her reasons for doing this?
3. Le Guin describes the effects of changes in book technology. List some of these.
4. What is the point Le Guin is making about texting? How does she make this point?

5. Why, according to Le Guin, may the "death" of the book as a physical object "be a matter for rejoicing"?
6. According to Le Guin, which genres of books may be replaced first by electronic editions?
7. Why do electronic copies of books need to be recopied on a regular basis?

Explore

1. Assess Le Guin's argument. What is her thesis? What claims does she use to support this thesis? What rhetorical strategies does she employ to make her argument?
2. Write Le Guin a letter explaining why you agree or disagree with her argument, making sure to concisely restate your understanding of her argument and the claims she uses to support it.
3. Personal ethnography involves keeping a record of your own actions and reactions to a specific situation or event. Write a two-page personal ethnography studying how you read a printed book. Then, write a two-page personal ethnography studying how you read text on a screen. Compare and contrast these. Then, based on your findings, write two pages connecting these to Le Guin's comments about reading printed books and reading on screens.

Forging Connections

1. Nicholas Carr and Ursula K. Le Guin appear to take different positions regarding the extent to which information and communications technologies may be changing or altering reading practices. In a blog post, explain their respective positions regarding this issue and the evidence each uses to support his or her position. Which do you find more persuasive? Why? Which is most in line with your own experience of reading with the aid of new technologies?
2. Both Nicholas Carr and Toby Litt recount their experiences with reading and writing in their essays. Write a three- to five-page essay in which you reflect on one or more of the following: how you learned to write, how you learned to read, how you used to read and write a lot and why you later stopped doing those things as much, how technology has changed the ways in which you read and write. If you were

particularly inspired by Litt or Carr's essay, you might want to consider writing an essay modeled on one of their essays, or consider incorporating a short response to one of those essays into your essay.

Looking Further

1. Neil Postman writes, "when a technology becomes mythic, it is always dangerous because it is then accepted as it is, and is therefore not easily susceptible to modification or control." Examine the ways in which Nicholas Carr writes about Internet technology in his essay "Is Google Making Us Stupid?" Does Carr's article portray Internet technology as "mythic" and thereby somehow outside of human control? In a two to three page essay, explain why or why not you believe this to be the case, using textual evidence from Carr's essay to support your argument. Then, consider how Carr's argument about reading and writing practices and Internet technology might change if he defined Internet technology not as a "given," but as an evolving technology that could be controlled and modified to better serve the needs of readers and writers.

2. Many academics and journalists have compared the advent of the printing press in the fifteenth century and its effects on literacy and publishing practices with those taking place today as a result of Internet and Web technologies. Locate several specific instances of this comparison in the essays in this chapter. In an essay, explain the context in which the analogy is made in each essay and its purpose. Based on these comparisons, your experience of using Internet and Web technologies for reading and writing practices, and what you've observed of how these technologies may be changing these practices, explain why or why not you believe an analogy can or should be made between the printing press and Internet and Web technologies.

5

Digital Education:
What Can Technology Teach Us?

"Promise and Peril" is the title of Diane Ravitch's 2013 essay on recent applications of information and communications technology (ICT) in education— and it is a title that aptly describes many of the issues involved in thinking about the topic of technology and education. For, while various technological applications in education may hold great promise—might online courseware applications bring affordable high-quality education to the entire world?—even such apparently idealistic projects raise a host of other questions and concerns related to how educational systems function and how learning occurs. Although some may hope that certain ICT applications could be a potential "silver bullet" to resolve issues related to education both nationally and globally, the realities involved in adopting these applications are much more complex. With regard to a system like education, one that functions often more ecologically than like a machine, the introduction of new tools, no matter how technologically advanced, may have a wide variety of consequences.

All of the authors in this chapter consider how and why information and communications technologies are being used in education today and what some of the effects of this use might be. Diane Ravitch, in her essay "Promise and Peril," considers how it is impossible to generalize regarding the use of technology in education since some applications have had very positive effects while others appear much more threatening. In his essay "Mobile Phones, Digital Media, and America's Learning Divide," academic S. Craig Watkins writes about the ways in which technology may not be so much changing things in education as reflecting how much things stay the same: The digital divide between those who have access to specific types of technology and those who don't reflects the learning divide that has existed for more than a century in the United States. Andrew Delbanco compares current technological initiatives related to education to those from the past in his article "MOOCs of Hazard," proposing that many nontechnological factors related to the state of higher education today may make today's technological projects succeed in a way those from the past did not. Responding to the reality of MOOCs in higher education, members of the Philosophy Department at San Jose State University lay out the educational and social justice issues at stake in their adoption in their "Open Letter to Michel Sandel [Regarding His JusticeX MOOC]." Finally, in "Video Games and the Future of Learning," David Williamson Shaffer, Kurt Squire, Richard Halverson, and James Paul Gee consider the ways in which video games incorporate many features of ideal learning environments.

Diane Ravitch
"Promise and Peril"

Diane Ravitch is Research Professor of Education at New York University. She is the author of more than twenty books. Her most recent include *Reign of Error: The Hoax of the Privatization Movement and the Danger to America's Public Schools* (2013) and *The Death and Life of the Great American School System: How Testing and Choice Are Undermining Education* (2010). The recipient of numerous awards, including the Delta Kappa Gamma Educators' Award, and the Distinguished Service Award from the National Association of Secondary School Principals in 2011, Ravitch also publishes work frequently on her website, which received 8.3 million page views in 2013. In this essay Ravitch considers the promise and perils of technology as it is currently being used in education.

What have been the effects—both positive and negative—of various technological tools on your educational experience?

Technology is transforming American education, for good and for ill. The good comes from the ingenious ways that teachers encourage their students to engage in science projects, learn about history by seeing the events for themselves and explore their own ideas on the Internet. There are literally thousands of Internet-savvy teachers who regularly exchange ideas about enlivening classrooms to heighten student engagement in learning.

> "Technology is transforming American education, for good and for ill."

The ill comes in many insidious forms.

One of the malign manifestations of the new technology is for-profit online charter schools, sometimes called virtual academies. These K-12 schools recruit heavily and spend many millions of taxpayer dollars on advertising. They typically collect state tuition for each student, which is removed from the local public schools' budget. They claim to offer customized, personalized education, but that's just rhetoric. They have high dropout rates, low test scores and low graduation rates. Some have annual attrition rates of 50 percent. But so long as the virtual schools keep luring new students, they are very profitable for their owners and investors.

Another dubious use of technology is to grade essays. Major testing companies such as Pearson and McGraw-Hill are using software to score written test answers. Machines can grade faster than teachers, but they cannot evaluate factual statements or the imaginative use of language. A student may write that World War II began in 1839, and the machine won't object. Students will learn to write according to the formula that the machine likes, at the expense of accuracy, creativity and imagination. Worse, the teacher will abandon the important job of reading what his or her students write and will be less informed about how they think. That is a loss for the quality of education. Frankly, it is a problem with online assessment in general, as the job of testing is shifted from the teacher to a distant corporation; the last round of state testing saw computer breakdowns in several states. In addition, it is only a matter of time until students hack into the tests.

5   The most worrisome use of technology is to accumulate and store personal, confidential data about every public school student. The Bill & Melinda Gates Foundation put up close to $100 million to create the Shared Learning Collaborative, now called inBloom, with partners Wireless Generation (owned by Rupert Murdoch's News Corporation) and Carnegie Corporation. It will gather student data from several districts and states, including New York, Georgia, Delaware, Kentucky and Louisiana (some of these states are reconsidering because of objections from parents). The data will be stored on a cloud managed by Amazon. On the cloud will be students' names, addresses, grades, test scores, disability status, attendance, program participation and many other details about students that teachers and schools are not allowed to release.

Who needs all this personal information, and why is it being shared? Advocates say that the goal is to create better products for individual students. Critics believe that the information will be given or sold to vendors, who will use it to market products to children and their parents. No one knows whether the data will be secure; snoops frequently hack into databases and clouds.

Until recently, the release of personal student data without parental consent would have been prohibited by a 1974 federal law known as FERPA (the Family Educational Rights and Privacy Act). In 2011, however, the U.S. Department of Education revised the FERPA regulations, making this data project legal. The electronic Privacy Information Center (EPIC) has sued the

Department of Education in federal court for watering down FERPA and allowing students' data to be released to third parties without parental consent.

Here is the conundrum: teachers see technology as a tool to inspire student learning; entrepreneurs see it as a way to standardize teaching, to replace teachers, to make money and to market new products. Which vision will prevail?

Analyze

1. What, according to Ravitch, are some innovative uses of technology by teachers?
2. What three uses of technology in education does Ravitch express concern about?
3. What are the stated and proposed benefits of each of the three?
4. What are the specific drawbacks of each according to Ravitch?
5. What is FERPA and how does its repeal relate to the inBloom initiative?
6. According to Ravitch, what is "the conundrum"?

Explore

1. Review the three dubious uses of technology that Ravitch discusses in her article. In a short essay, explain which of the three you believe is of greatest concern. Why?
2. In response to Ravitch's essay, reflect on what has been one of your best and one of your worst educational experiences involving technology. In one or two pages, describe each. Then, read over what you have written and compare these experiences to one another. What distinguishes them? What factors contributed to the success of one experience? What factors contributed to the lack of success of the other?
3. The emergence of for-profit online charter schools and machine-grading are two specific concerns expressed by Ravitch in relation to technology and education. Do some research on one of these issues. Then, based on your research, write a letter to Ravitch in which you describe your findings, your sources for these findings, and how your findings either confirm or contest her concerns about online charter schools or machine-grading.

S. Craig Watkins
"Mobile Phones, Digital Media, and America's Learning Divide"

S. Craig Watkins is Associate Professor in the Radio-Television-Film and African American Studies Departments at the University of Texas, Austin, and a member of the MacArthur Foundation's research network on Connected Learning. He is the author of the books *Representing: Hip Hop Culture and the Production of Black Cinema* (1998), *Hip Hop Matters: Politics, Pop Culture and the Struggle for the Soul of a Movement* (2005), and, most recently, *The Young and the Digital: What the Migration to Social Network Sites, Games and Anytime, Anywhere Media Means to Our Future* (2009). Additional information about the book and Watkins' research can be accessed at his blog, http://theyoungandthedigital.com. In the following essay, originally published on dmlcentral.net, a collaborative blog published by the Digital Media and Learning Research Hub, Watkins analyzes relationships between the "digital divide" and the "learning divide" in the United States and ways in which mobile technologies might be used to narrow both.

Have you ever used your mobile phone for educational or research purposes? If so, how? If no, why not?

During a recent research-related visit to New York City I decided to take a stroll down 125th Street in Harlem. Among the assortment of shops and vendors on the famous stretch that is home to the legendary Apollo Theater were an abundance of mobile phone providers. Even a few of the street vendors offered mobile phone accessories such as cases, covers, and car adaptors. It struck me that while you could easily purchase a mobile phone on 125th Street you could not purchase a desktop or laptop computer. Not that long ago the assumption that African Americans were a viable market for mobile phones did not exist.

As far back as 2007 data started to emerge that suggested that black and Latino households were much more likely to go online via a mobile phone than a desktop or laptop computer. We are also learning that a surging number of poor households are choosing to go with a mobile phone over a landline, largely because they cannot afford both.

My fieldwork is consistently suggesting that the future of black and Latino digital lives are linked, for better or worse, to mobile devices. The growing appeal of the mobile phone among African Americans and Latinos has not gone unnoticed by the press. In fact, several news outlets have even reported that mobile phones may be closing the digital divide. Is this true? Is there any evidence, empirical or anecdotal, that mobile is closing the digital divide?

Enduring Inequalities

The answer to that question depends on how you define the digital divide. For example, if you define the digital divide as largely a question of access to technology then the answer, arguably, is yes. Internet-capable phones, to the degree that poor and working-class communities can afford them, certainly bridge the access gap. In 2009 the Pew Internet & American Life Project reported that African Americans were more likely than any other racial or ethnic group to go online via a mobile phone. But what if you define the divide in terms of participation rather than access? Is it possible that mobile devices are reproducing some of America's most enduring inequalities? Truth is, there are some large gaps in our knowledge that make answering this last question difficult. But here is a start.

Much of the empirical data over the last three to four years consistently suggests that when it comes to using their mobile devices to play games, watch video, listen to music, or manage their online social networks that black and Latino youth are much more active than their white and Asian American counterparts. Nielsen recently reported that African Americans are 30 percent more likely to visit Twitter than any other racial or ethnic group. We began reporting two years ago that black and Latino teens were using Twitter largely via their mobile phones.

It is unclear what kinds of phones black and Latino teens from low-income and working-class homes are adopting. Are they more likely to own smartphones or feature phones? The functionalities of the former afford powerful social, recreational, and informational opportunities while the capabilities of the latter are much more limited. And while we know that black and Latino youth have turned to mobile as a source of anytime, anywhere media does this mean that they are largely consumers rather than creators of content?

As we begin to learn more about the media ecologies of black and Latino teens an inevitable question arises: is there any evidence that their engagement with media technology is producing behaviors and learning outcomes that might impact the academic achievement gap? There is an abundance of evidence that suggests that the informal learning environment (i.e., leisure, extracurricular and enrichment opportunities) of middle-income students is just as important as the formal environment (i.e., schools) in their academic achievement.

The academic achievement gap takes root in early childhood and is related to the formal and informal learning ecologies that kids navigate throughout life. Different parenting practices and household resources mean that middle-income kids enter kindergarten with richer language skills and greater exposure to books than their low-income counterparts. Throughout schooling these early learning divides expand. What role, if any, do digital and mobile media platforms play in America's learning divides?

Not All Media Ecologies Are Equal

The issue, of course, is not that young people's adoption of mobile phones causes an achievement gap that began long before any of us ever heard of the Internet or mobile phones. Rather, what is the potential for learning and engagement with mobile media in closing the learning divides that exist between low- and middle-income students? The mere adoption of mobile phones is certainly not the solution to the achievement gap. Technology— social network sites, laptops, smart phones, games, tablets, interactive books and maps—alone will never close America's learning divide. This is the myth of the "digital native" narrative, the notion that youth can thrive in the digital world without any adult support, mentoring, or scaffolding of rich learning experiences. While a greater diversity of young people are using digital and mobile platforms than ever before not all media ecologies are equal. Thus it's very possible that if poor and working-class students adopt technologies like mobile phones in environments that do not offer adult engagement and scaffolding the potential benefits in terms of learning and empowerment may not be realized.

10   Currently, I'm involved in a series of case studies that examine how adult educators and mentors are creating innovative learning experiences that

encourage young people, for example, to view their mobile device as a powerful data-collection resource and gateway to cultivating new literacies and forms of civic engagement. What I see is promising in terms of igniting young minds and young citizens. While only a small percentage of young people are using mobile devices as a powerful learning tool today the percentage is growing. The real challenge is not if rich and meaningful mobile learning ecologies will develop. As a 2011 NMC Horizon report shows, they already exist. Rather, the real challenge is, will they be distributed in ways that close or maintain America's learning divide?

Analyze

1. What are two ways of measuring the "digital divide"?
2. Why do the results of the two measures vary so greatly?
3. According to Watkins, in what ways may the "digital divide" relate to the "learning divide"?
4. How might mobile technologies be used to narrow rather than increase the "digital divide"?

Explore

1. What Watkins refers to as the "learning divide" is often referred to as the "achievement gap." Do some research on this issue by reviewing and analyzing government educational statistics published on the National Center for Education Statistics website (http://nces.ed.gov/ nationsreportcard/studies/gaps/). In a short essay, explain what you learned from this research regarding the "learning divide" in the United States and how it relates to Watkins's essay.
2. Working in groups, design a project for your fellow students in your class that would enable them to use their mobile phones in a way that Watkins believes may be useful and productive to their education, for instance "as a powerful data collection resource," as a tool for exploring new literacies, or for participating in community politics.
3. Visit the Connected Learning website (http://connectedlearning.tv/) and the Digital Media and Learning Research Hub (http://dmlhub .net/). Choose a project from one of the websites and write a two-page profile of it. Then, in one or two pages, explain how the project addresses one or more of the issues Watkins writes about in his essay.

Andrew Delbanco
"MOOCs of Hazard"

Andrew Delbanco is Director of American Studies and Julian Clarence Levi Professor in the Humanities at Columbia University. He is the author of numerous books, including, most recently, *College: What It Was, Is, and Should Be* (2012). Delbanco's essays appear regularly in *The New York Review of Books, The New Republic, Raritan,* and other journals, on topics ranging from American literary and religious history to contemporary issues in higher education. In this essay, Delbanco reviews current and historical technological initiatives in education, assesses their outcomes, and discusses the factors that may eventually make contemporary initiatives more successful than those from the past.

How effective have your Web-based learning experiences been compared to those you've had in a traditional classroom setting?

In the spring of 2011, Sebastian Thrun was having doubts about whether the classroom was really the right place to teach his course on artificial intelligence. Thrun, a computer-science professor at Stanford, had been inspired by Salman Khan, the founder of the online Khan Academy, whose videos and discussion groups have been used by millions to learn about everything from arithmetic to history. And so that summer, Thrun announced he would offer his fall course on Stanford's website for free. He reorganized it into short segments rather than hour-long lectures, included problem sets and quizzes, and added a virtual office hour via Google Hangout. Enrollment jumped from 200 Stanford undergraduates to 160,000 students around the world (only 30 remained in the classroom). A few months later, he founded an online for-profit company called Udacity; his course, along with many others, is now available to anyone with a fast Internet connection.

Meanwhile, two of Thrun's Stanford colleagues, Daphne Koller and Andrew Ng, founded another for-profit company, Coursera, that posts courses taught by faculty from leading universities such as Princeton, Michigan, Duke, and Penn. Three million students have signed on. Not to be outdone, Harvard and MIT announced last spring their own online partnership, edX, a nonprofit with an initial investment of $60 million. A new phenomenon requires a new name, and so MOOC—massive open online course—has now entered the lexicon. So far, MOOCs have been true to the first "o" in the acronym: Anyone can take these courses for free.

Many people outside academia—including *New York Times* columnists David Brooks and Thomas L. Friedman—are gushing that MOOCs are the best thing to happen to learning since movable type. Inside academia, however, they have been met with widespread skepticism. As Joseph Harris, a writing professor at Duke, recently remarked in *The Chronicle of Higher Education*, "I don't see how a MOOC can be much more than a digitized textbook."

In fact, MOOCs are the latest in a long series of efforts to use technology to make education more accessible. Sixty years ago, the Ford Foundation funded a group of academics to study what was then a cutting-edge technology: television. In language almost identical to that used today, a report on the project announced that television had the power to drive down costs, enable the collection of data on how students learn, and extend "the reach of the superior teacher to greater numbers of students." From 1957 to 1982, the local CBS channel in New York City broadcast a morning program of college lectures called "Sunrise Semester." But the sun never rose on television as an educational "delivery system."

In the 1990s, my own university, Columbia, started a venture called Fathom, using the relatively new technology of the Web. The idea was to sell online courses taught by star faculty such as Simon Schama and Brian Greene to throngs of supposedly eager customers. But the paying consumers never showed up in the anticipated numbers, and by the time it was shut down, Fathom had cost Columbia, according to some estimates, at least $20 million. Looking back, the project's director, Ann Kirschner, concluded that she and her colleagues had arrived too soon—"pre-broadband, pre-videocasting and iPods, and all the rest."

Of course, we will always be pre-something. Former University of Michigan President James Duderstadt foresees a technology that will be "totally immersive in all our senses"—something like the "feelies" that Aldous Huxley, in *Brave New World*, imagined would render the "talkies" obsolete. The MIT Media Lab has already developed a vest that gives you a hug when a friend "likes" something you have posted on Facebook. It may not be long before we can log onto a Shakespeare course taught by, say, Stephen Greenblatt and feel the spray of his saliva as he recites "tomorrow and tomorrow and tomorrow." Such technologies will likely find their biggest market through the pornography industry, but there's no reason to doubt that academia will adopt and adapt them.

The Luddite in me is inclined to think that the techno-dreamers are headed for another disappointment. But this time around, something does seem different—and it's not just that the MOOC pioneers have an infectious excitement rarely found in a typical faculty meeting. They also have a striking public-spiritedness. Koller sees a future in which a math prodigy in a developing country might nurture his or her gifts online and then, having been identified by a leading university, enroll in person—on a scholarship, one might imagine, funded by income derived from Coursera. This idea of using online courses as a detection tool is a reprise (on a much larger scale) of the one that spurred the development of standardized tests in the mid-twentieth century, such as the SAT, which was originally envisioned as a means for finding gifted students outside the usual Ivy League "feeder" schools.

Koller speaks with genuine passion about the universal human craving for learning and sees in Internet education a social good that reminds me of Thomas Jefferson's dream of geniuses being "raked from the rubbish"—by which he meant to affirm the existence of a "natural aristocracy" to be nurtured for the sake of humankind. No one knows whether the MOOCs will achieve any of these things, but many academic leaders are certain that, as Stanford President John Hennessy predicts, higher education is about to be hit by a "tsunami."

What's driving all this risk-taking and excitement? Many people are convinced that the MOOCs can rein in the rising costs of colleges and universities. For decades, the price of tuition has outstripped the pace of inflation. Over the past ten years, the average sticker price at private colleges has increased by almost 30 percent (though net tuition has risen less because financial aid has grown even faster). At state universities, the problem has been exacerbated by public disinvestment. For example, less than 6 percent of the annual budget of the University of Virginia is covered by state funds. Last fall, I heard the chief financial officer of an urban public university put the matter succinctly: The difficulty, he said, is not so much the cost of college, but the shift of the financial burden from the state to the student.

10   There are many reasons why college costs continue to soar: the expense of outfitting high-tech science labs, the premium placed on research that lures faculty out of the classroom (and, in turn, requires hiring more faculty

to teach classes), the proliferation of staff for everything from handling government regulation to counseling increasingly stressed students. At some institutions, there are also less defensible reasons, such as wasteful duplication, lavish amenities, and excessive pay and perks for top administrators and faculty.

But the most persuasive account of the relentless rise in cost was made nearly 50 years ago by the economist William Baumol and his student William Bowen, who later became president of Princeton. A few months ago, Bowen delivered two lectures in which he revisited his theory of the "cost disease." "In labor-intensive industries," he explained, "such as the performing arts and education, there is less opportunity than in other sectors to increase productivity by, for example, substituting capital for labor." Technological advances have allowed the auto industry, for instance, to produce more cars while using fewer workers. Professors, meanwhile, still do things more or less as they have for centuries: talking to, questioning, and evaluating students (ideally in relatively small groups). As the Ohio University economist Richard Vedder likes to joke, "With the possible exception of prostitution . . . teaching is the only profession that has had no productivity advance in the 2,400 years since Socrates."

This is a true statement—but it unwittingly undercuts its own point: Most people, I suspect, would agree that there are some activities—teaching and prostitution among them—in which improved productivity and economies of scale are not desirable, at least not from the point of view of the consumer.

True believers think that the new digital technologies will finally enable educators to increase productivity by allowing a smaller number of teachers to produce a larger number of "learning outcomes" (today's term for educated students) than ever before. But it's too soon to say whether MOOCs will really help cure the cost disease. Their own financial viability is by no means certain. The for-profits must make money for their investors, and the non-profits must return revenue to the universities that give them start-up funds.

Coursera has begun to try out a number of different strategies. It provides a matchmaking service for employers looking to hire people with certain demonstrable skills—a logical extension of a role that colleges already play. When a company expresses interest in a top-performing student, Coursera e-mails the student, offering an introduction, and receives a finder's fee from the prospective employer. The college that developed the course also receives a cut. As for Udacity, Thrun says only that it charges companies looking for talent "significantly less than you'd pay for a headhunter, but significantly more than what you'd pay for access to LinkedIn."

15   A few months ago, Coursera also announced a licensing arrangement with Antioch University, which agreed to pay a fee in return for incorporating selected Coursera offerings into its curriculum. The idea is for students to supplement their online experience by working with on-campus faculty—a practice known as "hybrid" or "blended" learning. The college can expand its course offerings without hiring new faculty, and Coursera can earn income that will be shared by the institutions and professors who develop the courses. So far, however, student interest has been low.

Other possible sources of revenue include selling expertise to universities that want to set up their own MOOCs or partnering with textbook publishers willing to share revenue in exchange for selling to online students. Some MOOCs are also beginning to charge fees for proctored exams (in person or by webcam) for students seeking a certificate marking their successful completion of a course.

If new technologies can cure, or even slow down, the cost disease before it kills the patient, that would be a great public service. The dark side of this bright dream is the fear that online education could burst what appears to be a higher education bubble. Consumers, the argument goes, are already waking up to the fact that they're paying too much for too little. If they are priced out of, or flee from, the market, they will find new ways to learn outside the brick-and-mortar institutions that, until now, have held a monopoly on providing credentials that certify what graduates have supposedly learned. If that happens, it would be a classic case of "disruptive innovation"—a term popularized by Harvard Business School Professor Clayton Christensen, who argues that, "in industries from computers to cars to steel those entrants that start at the bottom of their markets, selling simple products to less demanding customers and then improving from that foothold, drive the prior leaders into a disruptive demise."

We've already witnessed the first phase of this process. Early consumers of online courses tended to be students with families or jobs for whom full-time attendance at a residential or even a commuter college was out of the question. As underfunded public colleges struggled to meet the needs of such students, private for-profit "universities" such as Phoenix, Kaplan, DeVry, and Strayer emerged. They offer mainly online courses that serve— some would say exploit—an expanding population of consumers (a word increasingly used as a synonym for students). The first time I heard someone commend for-profit universities was five or six years ago, when a savvy investor said to me, "Look at California—the public system can't meet the demand, so we will step in." He was making the safe, and sad, assumption that public reinvestment is unlikely to restore what was once an unrivaled system of public higher education. Last August, nearly half a million students found themselves on waiting lists for oversubscribed courses at California's community colleges.

Many online students meet the low-income eligibility threshold for federal Pell grants—a ripe market for the for-profit universities. These institutions offer cheaper courses than traditional private colleges, usually in practical or technical subjects such as cosmetology or computer programming. Their business model depends heavily on faculty who receive low compensation and on students with high loan obligations. It's a system that works well for investors. (In 2009, the CEO of Strayer University collected a cool $42 million, mainly in stock options.) How well it works for students is another question. Last summer, a U.S. Senate committee noted that for-profit universities spend more on advertising and recruiting than on instruction and that, without significant reform, they "will continue to turn out hundreds of thousands of students with debt but no degree."

So far, the for-profit sector has been regarded with disdain or indifference by established universities. This fits the Christensen theory of "disruptive innovation": The leap by low-end products into higher-end markets is sudden and surprising because the higher-ups have been lulled into thinking their place in the pecking order is unassailable. What has happened to newspapers and publishing are obvious examples. Suddenly everything changes, and the old is swept away by the new. 20

Because of the durable value of prestige, it will be a long time before Harvard has to fear for its existence. But one reason to think we're on the cusp of major change is that online courses are particularly well-suited to the new rhythms of student life. On traditional campuses, many students already regard time offline as a form of solitary confinement. Classrooms have become battlegrounds where professors struggle to distract students from their smartphones and laptops. Office hours are giving way to e-mail. To the millions who have used sites such as the Khan Academy, the idea of hour-long lectures spread out over 15-week semesters is already anachronistic. "Disruptive innovation" is a variant of Joseph Schumpeter's famous declaration that capitalism works by "creative destruction." What will be innovated and created in our colleges and universities, and what will be disrupted and destroyed?

One vulnerable structure is the faculty itself, which is already in a fragile state. This is especially true of those who teach subjects such as literature, history, and the arts. The humanities account for a static or declining percentage of all degrees conferred, partly because students often doubt their real-world value. And as humanities departments shrink, some institutions are collaborating to shrink them faster (or close them altogether) in order to avoid duplicative hiring in subjects with low student demand. For example, Columbia, Yale, and Cornell have announced a collaboration whereby certain languages—such as Romanian, Tamil, or Yoruba—will be taught via teleconferencing. This is good for students, since the subjects will still be available. But it's bad for aspiring faculty—as the number of positions dwindles, research and scholarship in these fields will dry up.

MOOCs also seem likely to spur more demand for celebrity professors in a teaching system that is already highly stratified. Among tenured faculty, there is currently a small cadre of stars and a smaller one of superstars—and the MOOCs are creating megastars. Michael Sandel, for example, who teaches a famous course on justice at Harvard, has become a global figure with millions of followers, notably in Asia, since his lectures became available online through Harvard's website and at a site called Academic Earth. A few months ago, Harvard announced that Sandel had signed up with edX. Sandel is an exceptional educator, but as master-teachers go global, lesser-known colleagues fear being relegated to a supporting role as glorified teaching assistants.

In some respects, this is the latest chapter in an old story of faculty entrepreneurship. By the mid-twentieth century, the president of the University of California, Clark Kerr, was already describing the Berkeley faculty as "individual entrepreneurs held together by a common grievance over parking." Today, as star professors increasingly work for themselves, more faculty members at less prestigious institutions face low wages, meager benefits, and—since many lack tenure—minimal job security. But if the new technology threatens some professors with obscurity, others face obsolescence. Language instructors may someday be replaced by multilingual versions of Siri on your iPhone. One of my colleagues speaks of the imminent "evisceration" of graduate study, once young people who might have pursued an academic career are deterred as it becomes harder and harder to find a dignified job after years of training.

These prospects raise many pressing questions—not just speculative 25
ones about the future, but actionable ones about the present. What, if anything, can universities do to formulate new rules governing conflicts of
interest? As faculty stars relocate to cyberspace, how can institutions sustain the community of teachers and students that has been the essence of
the university for a thousand years? (The pacesetting Thrun, who is a vice
president of Google, resigned from his tenured teaching post at Stanford,
though he remains a "research professor.") In this brave new world, how can
the teaching profession, already well on its way to "adjunctification," attract
young people with a pastoral impulse to awaken and encourage students
one by one?

There are also unanswered questions about how much students actually
learn from MOOCs. Coursera recently withdrew one course at Georgia
Tech because of student discontent and another, at the University of
California, Irvine, because the professor disputed how much students were
really learning.

So far, most testimonials to the value of online learning come from motivated students, often adults, who seek to build on what they have already
learned in traditional educational settings. These are people with clear
goals and confidence in their abilities. Stanford has even established an
online high school "for gifted students" from around the world (a residential program brings them together in the summers). Its medical school has
introduced "lecture halls without lectures," whereby students use short
videos to master the material on their own, then converge in class for discussion of clinical applications of what they've learned.

And yet it's one thing to expect brilliant teens or medical students to be
self-starters. It's another to teach students who are in need of close guidance. A recent report from the Community College Research Center at
Columbia finds that underprepared students taking online courses are,
according to one of the authors, "falling farther behind than if they were
taking face-to-face courses." Michael Crow, one of the architects of Fathom
and now president of Arizona State University and certainly no tradition-
alist, warns against a future in which "rich kids get taught by professors and
poor kids get taught by computer."

Back in the mid-twentieth century, the Ford Foundation report on
"telecourses" asked the key question about technology and education:
"How effective is this instruction?" When I came upon that sentence, it put
me in mind of something Ralph Waldo Emerson wrote a long time ago.

"Truly speaking," he said, "it is not instruction, but provocation, that I can receive from another soul." I first understood this distinction during my own student days, while struggling with the theologian Jonathan Edwards's predestinarian view of life. Toward the end of the course, my teacher, the scholar of American religion Alan Heimert, looked me in the eye and asked: "What is it that bothers you about Edwards? Is it that he's so hard on self-deception?" This was more than instruction; it was a true provocation. It came from a teacher who listened closely to his students and tried to grasp who they were and who they were trying to become. He knew the difference between knowledge and information. He understood education in the Socratic sense, as a quest for self-knowledge.

30   Nearly 40 years later, in my own course on American literature, one of my gifted teaching assistants received an e-mail from a student after a discussion on Emerson:

> Hi, I just wanted to let you know that our section meeting tonight had a really profound effect on me.... [T]he way you spoke and the energy our class had really moved me.... I walked the whole way home staring at the sky, a probably unsafe decision, but a worthwhile one nonetheless. I actually cannot wait for next week's class just so I can dive even further into this. So I just wanted to send you a quick message thanking you, letting you know that this fifty minutes of class has undeniably affected the rest of my life.... [S]ome fire was lit within me tonight, and I guess I'm blowing the smoke towards you a little bit.

No matter how anxious today's students may be about gaining this or that competence in a ferociously competitive world, many still crave the enlargement of heart as well as mind that is the gift of true education. It's hard for me to believe that this kind of experience can happen without face-to-face teaching and the physical presence of other students.

Yet I'm convinced that those leading us into the digital future truly want to dispense the gift of learning more widely than ever before. Currently, the six-year graduation rate at America's public four-year colleges is approximately 58 percent. It would be a great benefit to society if online education can improve on that record—although it should be noted that, so far, the completion rate by students who sign up for MOOCs is even worse—barely 10 percent.

In one experiment, Udacity is providing remedial courses to students at San Jose State for a much lower price than in-person courses. A bill is now under discussion in the California legislature that would require public colleges to offer online courses to students whom they can't accommodate in their classrooms. If the new technology can bring great teaching to students who would otherwise never encounter it, that could lessen inequities between the haves and have-nots, just as digital technologies now give students and scholars worldwide access to previously locked-up books and documents. But so far, there is scant evidence on which to base these hopes.

Quite apart from the MOOCs, there's an impressive array of new efforts   35
to serve low-income students—including the online public Western Governors University, which charges around $6,000 in tuition and awards reputable degrees in such fields as information technology and business. Southern New Hampshire University—also a nonprofit—has moved aggressively into online learning, which it combines with on-campus programs; and Carnegie Mellon University has launched an "open learning initiative" that offers non-credit free courses, with substantial interactive capabilities, and seems to be working well in science, math, and introductory languages.

The best of the new education pioneers have a truly Emersonian passion for remaking the world, for rejecting the stale conviction that change always means degradation. I sense in them a fervent concurrence with Emerson's refusal to believe "that the world was finished a long time ago" and with his insistence that, "as the world was plastic and fluid in the hands of God, so it is ever to so much of his attributes as we bring to it."

In the face of such exuberance, it feels foolish and futile to demur. In one form or another, the online future is already here. But unless we are uncommonly wise about how we use this new power, we will find ourselves saying, as Emerson's friend Henry David Thoreau said about an earlier technological revolution, "We do not ride the railroad; it rides upon us."

Analyze

1. Who is Salman Khan?
2. What does the acronym MOOC stand for?
3. What was "Sunrise Semester"? How does it relate to Delbanco's argument?

4. What are some reasons why, according to Delbanco, MOOCs may be successful even when past educational technology ventures were not?
5. What are hybrid, or blended, courses?
6. What is "disruptive innovation"? How might MOOCs be an example of this?

Explore

1. In his essay, Delbanco cites an email from a student who explains how inspired he was by a recent class. Have you had the experience of being inspired by a particular teacher or lecture? In one paragraph, describe this experience. Then, develop paragraphs to answer the following questions: When did it take place? Where did it take place? What was the subject of the course or lecture? What did you learn from the experience? Finally, conclude your piece of writing by explaining why or why not you believe it is crucial that this learning experience took place in the setting and under the circumstances it did, and the specific reasons why you believe that the experience could—or could not—have been replicated in a distance learning environment.

2. Reflecting on one of his most memorable educational experiences, Delbanco writes, "this was more than instruction; it was a true provocation. It came from a teacher who listened closely to his students and tried to grasp who they were and who they were trying to become. He knew the difference between knowledge and information. He understood education in the Socratic sense, as a quest for self-knowledge." Free write about why you agree or disagree with Delbanco's proposition that education should be "a quest for self-knowledge," and whether, based on your own educational experiences, you would, like Delbanco, make a distinction between "knowledge and information."

3. Using an online search engine, find three or four images and/or infographics that visually represent some of the issues related to the rising costs of higher education in the United States. Write titles for each image or infographic to help your reader understand the import of the image. Then, arrange the images in such a way that they present either a story or an argument about the current costs of higher education. Write a one-page description of what each image or infographic represents in which you explain the issue or issues it addresses and its source. Finally, write a short essay explaining how the three or four images or infographics relate to one another.

San Jose State University Philosophy Department

"An Open Letter to Professor Michael Sandel [Regarding His JusticeX MOOC] from the Philosophy Department at the San Jose State University"

Professors in the philosophy department at San Jose State University wrote the following letter, which was published in *The Chronicle of Higher Education*, to make a direct appeal to Michael Sandel, a Harvard professor whose Massive Open Online Course (MOOC) JusticeX they were being encouraged to use as part of their courses. In this essay, the authors lay out the reasons why they refused to integrate the online course module, why they believe a traditional lecture model has greater educational benefits for students than a blended online model, and how the decision was made by the San Jose State University to adopt online lectures distributed by edX.

> Have you ever written a letter of complaint or protest? What was your purpose in writing the letter? What happened as a result of writing the letter?

April 29, 2013

Dear Professor Sandel,

San José State University (SJSU) recently announced a contract with edX (a company associated with MIT and Harvard) to expand the use of online blended courses. The SJSU Philosophy Department was asked to pilot your JusticeX course, and we refused. We decided to express to you our reasons for refusing to be involved with this course, and, because we believe that other departments and universities will sooner or later face the same predicament, we have decided to share our reasons with you publicly.

There is no pedagogical problem in our department that JusticeX solves, nor do we have a shortage of faculty capable of teaching our equivalent course. We believe that long-term financial considerations motivate the call for massively open online courses (MOOCs) at public universities such as ours. Unfortunately, the move to MOOCs comes at great peril to our university. We regard such courses as a serious compromise of quality of education and, ironically for a social justice course, a case of social injustice.

What Are the Essential Components of a Good Quality Education in a University?

First, one of the most important aspects of being a university professor is scholarship in one's specialization. Students benefit enormously from interaction with professors engaged in such research. The students not only have a teacher who is passionate, engaged, and current on the topic, but, in classes, independent studies, and informal interaction, they are provided the opportunity to engage a topic deeply, thoroughly, and analytically in a dynamic and up-to-date fashion.

A social justice course needs to be current since part of its mission is the application of conceptions of justice to existing social issues. In addition to providing students with an opportunity to engage with active scholars, expertise in the physical classroom, sensitivity to its diversity, and familiarity with one's own students are simply not available in a one-size-fits-all blended course produced by an outside vendor.

5   Second, of late we have been hearing quite a bit of criticism of the traditional lecture model as a mismatch for today's digital generation. Anat Agarwal, edX President, has described the standard professor as basically just "pontificating" and "spouting content," a description he used ten times in a recent press conference here at SJSU. Of course, since philosophy has traditionally been taught using the Socratic method, we are largely in agreement as to the inadequacy of lecture alone. But, after all the rhetoric questioning the effectiveness of the antiquated method of lecturing and note taking, it is telling to discover that the core of edX's JusticeX is a series of videotaped lectures that include excerpts of Harvard students making comments and taking notes. In spite of our admiration for your ability to lecture in such an engaging way to such a large audience, we believe that having a scholar teach and engage his or her own students in person is far superior to having those students watch a video of another scholar engaging his or her students. Indeed, the videos of you lecturing to and interacting with your students is itself a compelling testament to the value of the in-person lecture/discussion.

In addition, purchasing a series of lectures does not provide anything over and above assigning a book to read. We do, of course, respect your work in political philosophy; nevertheless, having our students read a variety of texts, perhaps including your own, is far superior to having them listen to your lectures. This is especially important for a digital generation that reads far too little. If we can do something as educators we would like to increase literacy, not decrease it.

Third, the thought of the exact same social justice course being taught in various philosophy departments across the country is downright scary—something out of a dystopian novel. Departments across the country possess unique specializations and character, and should stay that way. Universities tend not to hire their own graduates for a reason. They seek different influences. Diversity in schools of thought and plurality of points of view are at the heart of liberal education.

What Would Our Students Learn About Justice Through a Purchased Blended Course from a Private Vendor?

First, what kind of message are we sending our students if we tell them that they should best learn what justice is by listening to the reflections of the largely white student population from a privileged institution like Harvard? Our very diverse students gain far more when their own experience is central to the course and when they are learning from our own very diverse faculty, who bring their varied perspectives to the content of courses that bear on social justice.

Second, should one-size-fits-all vendor-designed blended courses become the norm, we fear that two classes of universities will be created: one, well-funded colleges and universities in which privileged students get their own real professor; the other, financially stressed private and public universities in which students watch a bunch of video-taped lectures and interact, if indeed any interaction is available on their home campuses, with a professor that this model of education has turned into a glorified teaching assistant. Public universities will no longer provide the same quality of education and will not remain on par with well-funded private ones. Teaching justice through an educational model that is spearheading the creation of two social classes in academia thus amounts to a cruel joke.

Can Technology Be Used to Improve Education?

10   Absolutely. Blended courses provide the opportunity to listen to lectures for a second or third time and enable class discussion sessions outside the usual constraints of time and space. For these very reasons many of the faculty in our department offer very high quality online and blended versions of a number of our offerings, including videotaped material we ourselves have developed. All of these offerings are continuously updated and their use includes extensive interaction among students. In addition, they also involve extensive interaction with the professor teaching the course, something that is not available in MOOCs, which rely on videotaped lectures, canned exercises, and automated and peer grading.

When a university such as ours purchases a course from an outside vendor, the faculty cannot control the design or content of the course; therefore, we cannot develop and teach content that fits with our overall curriculum and is based on both our own highly developed and continuously renewed competence and our direct experience of our students' needs and abilities. In the short term, we might be able to preserve our close contact with our students, but, given the financial motivations driving the move to MOOCs, the prognosis for the long term is grim.

The use of technology, as history shows, can improve or worsen the quality of education—but in a high-quality course, the professor teaching it must be able both to design the course and to choose its materials, and to interact closely with the students. The first option is not available in a pre-packaged course, and the second option is at grave risk if we move toward MOOCs.

It Is Time To Call It Like It Is

We believe the purchasing of online and blended courses is not driven by concerns about pedagogy, but by an effort to restructure the U.S. university system in general, and our own California State University system in particular. If the concern were pedagogically motivated, we would expect faculty to be consulted and to monitor quality control. On the other hand, when change is financially driven and involves a compromise of quality it is done quickly, without consulting faculty or curriculum committees, and behind closed doors. This is essentially what happened with SJSU's contract with edX. At a press conference (April 10, 2013 at SJSU) announcing the signing of the contract with edX, California Lieutenant Governor Gavin Newsom acknowledged as much: "The old education financing model, frankly, is no longer sustainable." This is the crux of the problem. It is time to stop masking the real issue of MOOCs and blended courses behind empty rhetoric about a new generation and a new world. The purchasing of MOOCs and blended courses from outside vendors is the first step toward restructuring the CSU.

Good-quality online courses and blended courses (to which we have no objections) do not save money, but purchased-pre-packaged ones do, and a lot. With prepackaged MOOCs and blended courses, faculty are ultimately not needed. A teaching assistant would suffice to facilitate a blended course, and one might argue, paying a university professor just to monitor someone else's material would be a waste of resources. Public universities that have so long and successfully served the students and citizens of California will be dismantled, and what remains of them will become a hodgepodge branch of private companies.

Administrators of the CSU say they do not see a choice; they are trying   15
to admit and graduate as many students as they can with insufficient funds. Whether they are right in complying with rather than resisting this, the discussion has to be honest and to the point. Let's not kid ourselves; administrators at the CSU are beginning a process of replacing faculty with cheap online education. In our case, we had better be sure that this is what we want to do because once the CSU or any university system is restructured in this way it will never recover.

Industry is demanding that public universities devote their resources to providing ready-made employees, while at the same time they are resisting paying the taxes that support public education. (California is the ninth largest economy in the world, yet has one of the most poorly supported public education systems in the nation.) Given these twin threats, the liberal arts are under renewed attack in public universities. We believe that education in a democracy must be focused on responsible citizenship, and general education courses in the liberal arts are crucial to such education. The move to outside vendor MOOCs is especially troubling in light of this—it is hard to see how they can nourish the complex mix of information, attitudes, solidarity and moral commitment that are crucial to flourishing democracies.

We respect your desire to expand opportunities for higher education to audiences that do not now have the chance to interact with new ideas.

We are very cognizant of your long and distinguished record of scholarship and teaching in the areas of political philosophy and ethics. It is in a spirit of respect and collegiality that we are urging you, and all professors involved with the sale and promotion of edX-style courses, not to take away from students in public universities the opportunity for an education beyond mere jobs training. Professors who care about public education should not produce products that will replace professors, dismantle departments, and provide a diminished education for students in public universities.

Sincerely and in solidarity,
The Department of Philosophy
San José State University

Analyze

1. What are the two broad issues that the authors point to for writing their letter?
2. What are the three components of a good-quality education, according to the authors?
3. Why do the authors fear two classes of universities will be created as a result of the use of MOOCs and other technologies in education?
4. Near the end of the letter, the authors make a reference to "empty rhetoric." What are they referring to?
5. What is the "crux of the problem," according to the authors?

Explore

1. Write a letter responding to the authors' argument explaining why you do or do not agree with it, making sure to respond to the specific claims used in support of the original argument in your response.
2. This letter has a "corporate author," meaning it has no single name or group of names attached to it. Although a great deal of writing is done collectively, it is still common for a published piece of writing to be attributed to a single author. Free write in response to the following questions: What does the fact that the authors chose not to list individual names as authors of this article do in relation to the power of the argument presented? Do you believe this decision was a rhetorical or practical one, or both? Then, consider other situations where it

might be more appropriate to use a corporate author. How much of the writing that you do is actually collaborative? Afterward, read over what you have written and write a one- or two-page synopsis of the points you have made, crafting well-developed paragraphs for each point.

3. As a class, or in small groups, write a letter in response to the SJSU letter, making sure to address not only the authors' primary argument, but the three questions posed in three of the four section headings. Afterward, free write about the experience, describing this experience of collective composition. Was it easier or harder than composing on your own? How did it differ from other acts of composing that you've done on your own? What did you learn from it? Would you recommend this as a model for composing? Why or why not?

4. Read the response to the letter published by Michael Sandel, which is available on the Web. Based on this, in a short essay, describe the rhetorical context for each letter. What was the purpose? Who was the audience? What does the style and tone of each letter indicate about the stance of the writer(s)? Finally, in one or two pages, explain why or why not Sandel's response is one the SJSU Philosophy Department's letter intended to elicit.

David Williamson Shaffer, Kurt Squire, Richard Halverson, and James P. Gee
"Video Games and the Future of Learning"

David Williamson Shaffer is a Professor at the University of Wisconsin-Madison (UW-Madison) in the departments of Educational Psychology and Biomedical Engineering, a Game Scientist at the Wisconsin Center for Education Research, and Principal of EFGames, LLC. **Kurt Squire** is an Associate Professor at UW-Madison, Director of the Games, Learning & Society Initiative (GLS) at the university, and the author of *Video Games and Learning: Teaching and Participatory Culture in the Digital Age* (2011). **Richard Halverson** is an Associate Professor in the Department of Education Leadership and Policy Analysis at UW-Madison. A co-founder of the GLS research group, he is a Fellow at the Wisconsin Institutes for Discovery. **James Paul Gee** is the Mary Lou Fulton Presidential Professor of Literacy Studies at Arizona State University and a faculty affiliate of the GLS research group at UW-Madison. He has published several books and articles about video games and education, including *What Video Games Have To Teach Us About Learning and Literacy* (2003). In this essay the authors explore the various reasons that video games may be a particularly effective educational tool.

What have you learned from video games? What would you like to learn from them?

Computers are changing our world: how we work, how we shop, how we entertain ourselves, how we communicate, how we engage in politics, how we care for our health. The list goes on and on. But will computers change the way we learn? The short answer is yes. Computers are already changing the way we learn—and if you want to understand how, just look at video games. Not because the games that are currently available are going to replace schools as we know them any time soon, but because they give a glimpse into how we might create new and more powerful ways to learn in schools, communities, and workplaces—new ways to learn for a new Information Age. Look at video games because, while they are wildly popular with adolescents and young adults, they are more than just toys. Look at video games because they create new social and cultural worlds—worlds that help us learn by integrating thinking, social interaction, and technology, all in service of doing things we care about.

We want to be clear from the start that video games are no panacea. Like books and movies, they can be used in antisocial ways. Games are inherently simplifications of reality, and today's games often incorporate—or are based on—violent and sometimes misogynistic themes. Critics suggest that the lessons people learn from playing video games as they currently exist are not always desirable. But even the harshest critics agree that we learn *something* from playing video games. The question is, How can we use the power of video games as a constructive force in schools, homes, and workplaces?

In answer to that question, we argue here for a particular view of games—and of learning—as activities that are most powerful when they are personally meaningful, experiential, social, and epistemological all at the same time. From this perspective, we describe an approach to the design of learning environments that builds on the educational properties of games but grounds them deeply within a theory of learning appropriate to an age marked by the power of new technologies.

Virtual Worlds for Learning

The first step toward understanding how video games can—and, we argue, will—transform education is changing the widely shared perspective that games are "mere entertainment." More than a multibillion-dollar industry, more than a compelling toy for both children and adults, more than a route to computer literacy, video games are important because they let people participate in new worlds. They let players think, talk, and act in new ways. Indeed, players come to *inhabit* roles that are otherwise inaccessible to them. A 16-year-old in Korea playing *Lineage* can become an international financier, trading raw materials, buying and selling goods in different parts of the virtual world, and speculating on currencies.[1] A *Deus Ex* player can experience life as a government special agent, operating in a world where the lines between terrorism and state-sponsored violence are called into question.

These rich virtual worlds are what make video games such powerful contexts for learning. In game worlds, learning no longer means confronting words and symbols that are separated from the things those words and symbols refer to. The inverse square law of gravitational attraction is no longer something to be understood solely through an equation. Instead, students can gain virtual experience walking in a world with a mass smaller than that of Earth, or they can plan manned space flights—a task that requires understanding the changing effects of gravitational forces in different parts of the solar system. In virtual worlds, learners experience the concrete realities that words and symbols describe. Through these and similar experiences in multiple contexts, learners can understand complex concepts without losing the connection between abstract ideas and the real problems they can be used to solve. In other words, the virtual worlds of games are powerful because they make it possible to develop *situated understanding*.

Although the stereotypical gamer is a lone teenager seated in front of a computer, game playing can also be a thoroughly social phenomenon. The clearest examples are the "massively multiplayer" online games, in which thousands of players are simultaneously online at any given time, participating in virtual worlds with their own economies, political systems, and cultures. Moreover, careful study shows that most games—from console action games to PC strategy games—have robust game-playing communities. Whereas schools largely sequester students from one another and from the outside world, games bring players together—competitively and cooperatively—in the virtual world of the game and in the social community of its players. In schools, students largely work alone, with school-sanctioned materials; avid gamers seek out news sites, read and write FAQs, participate in discussion forums, and become critical consumers of information.[2] Classroom work rarely has an impact outside the classroom; its only real audience is the teacher. Game players, in contrast, develop reputations in online communities, cultivate audiences by contributing to discussion forums, and occasionally even take up careers as professional gamers, traders of online commodities,[3] or game designers and modders (players who use programming tools to modify games). The virtual worlds of games are powerful, in other words, because playing games means developing a set of *effective social practices.*

By participating in these social practices, game players have an opportunity to explore new identities. In one well-publicized case, a heated political contest erupted for the presidency of Alphaville, one of the towns in *The Sims Online.* Arthur Baynes, the 21-year-old incumbent, was running against Laura McKnight, a 14-year-old. The muckraking, accusations of voter fraud, and political jockeying taught young Laura about the realities of politics. The election also gained national attention on National Public Radio, as pundits debated the significance of games that allowed teens not only to argue and debate politics but also to run a political system in which the virtual lives of thousands of real players were at stake. The complexity of Laura's campaign, political alliances, and platform—a platform that called for a stronger police force and a significant restructuring of the judicial system—shows how deep the disconnect has become between the kinds of experiences made available in schools and those available in online worlds. The virtual worlds of games are rich contexts for learning because they make it possible for players to experiment with new and *powerful identities.*[4]

The communities that game players form similarly organize meaningful learning experiences outside of school contexts. In the various websites devoted to the game *Civilization,* for example, players organize themselves around the shared goal of developing the skills, habits, and understandings that are necessary to become experts in the game. At Apolyton.net, one such site, players post news feeds, participate in discussion forums, and trade screenshots of the game. But they also run a radio station, exchange saved game files in order to collaborate and compete, create custom modifications, and, perhaps most unusually, run their own university to teach other players to play the game at deeper levels. Apolyton University shows us how part of expert gaming is developing a set of values—values that highlight enlightened risk taking, entrepreneurship, and expertise rather than the formal accreditation emphasized by institutional education.[5]

If we look at the development of game communities, we see that part of the power of games for learning is the way they *develop shared values*.

In other words, by creating virtual worlds, games integrate knowing and doing. But not just knowing and doing. Games bring together ways of knowing, ways of doing, ways of being, and ways of caring: the situated understandings, effective social practices, powerful identities, and shared values that make someone an expert. The expertise might be that of a modern soldier in *Full Spectrum Warrior*, a zoo operator in *Zoo Tycoon*, or a world leader in *Civilization III*. Or it might be expertise in the sophisticated practices of gaming communities, such as those built around *Age of Mythology* or *Civilization III*.

There is a lot being learned in these games. But for some educators, it is hard to see the educational potential of the games because these virtual worlds aren't about memorizing words or definitions or facts. But video games are about a whole lot more.

From Fact Fetish to Ways of Thinking

A century ago, John Dewey argued that schools were built on a fact fetish, and the argument is still valid today. The fact fetish views any area of learning—whether physics, mathematics, or history—as a body of facts or information. The measure of good teaching and learning is the extent to which students can answer questions about these facts on tests.

But *to know* is a verb before it becomes a noun in *knowledge*. We learn by doing—not just by doing any old thing, but by doing something as part of a larger community of people who share common goals and ways of achieving those goals. We learn by becoming part of a community of practice and thus developing that community's ways of knowing, acting, being, and caring—the community's situated understandings, effective social practices, powerful identities, and shared values.[6]

Of course, different communities of practice have different ways of thinking and acting. Take, for example, lawyers. Lawyers act like lawyers. They identify themselves as lawyers. They are interested in legal issues. And they know about the law. These skills, habits, and understandings are made possible by looking at the world in a particular way—by thinking like a lawyer. Doctors think and act in their own ways, as do architects, plumbers, steelworkers, and waiters or physicists, historians, and mathematicians.

The way of thinking—the epistemology—of a practice determines how someone in the community decides what questions are worth answering, how to go about answering them, and how to decide when an answer is sufficient. The epistemology of a practice thus organizes (and is organized by) the situated understandings, effective social practices, powerful identities, and shared values of the community. In communities of practice, knowledge, skills, identities, and values are shaped by a particular way of thinking into a coherent *epistemic frame*.[7] If a community of practice is a group with a local culture, then the epistemic frame is the grammar of the culture: the ways of thinking and acting that individuals learn when they become part of that culture.

Let's look at an example of how this might play out in the virtual world of a video game. *Full Spectrum Warrior* (Pandemic Studios, for PC and Xbox) is a video game based on a U.S. Army training simulation.[8] But *Full Spectrum Warrior* is not a mere first-person shooter in which the player blows up everything on the screen. To survive and win the game, the player has to learn to think and act like a modern professional soldier.

In *Full Spectrum Warrior*, the player uses the buttons on the controller to give orders to two squads of soldiers, as well as to consult a GPS device, radio for support, and communicate with commanders in the rear. The instruction manual that comes with the game makes it clear from the outset that players must take on the values, identities, and ways of thinking of a professional soldier if they are to play the game successfully. "Everything about your squad," the manual explains, "is the result of careful planning and years of experience on the battlefield. Respect that experience, soldier, since it's what will keep your soldiers alive."[9]

In the game, that experience—the skills and knowledge of professional military expertise—is distributed between the virtual soldiers and the real-world player. The soldiers in a player's squads have been trained in movement formations; the role of the player is to select the best position for them on the field. The virtual characters (the soldiers) know part of the task (various movement formations), and the player knows another part (when and where to engage in such formations). This kind of distribution holds for every aspect of military knowledge in the game. However, the knowledge that is distributed between virtual soldiers and real-world player is not a set of inert facts; what is distributed are the values, skills, practices, and (yes) facts that constitute authentic military professional practice. This simulation of the social context of knowing allows players to act as if in concert with (artificially intelligent) others, even within the single-player context of the game.

In so doing, *Full Spectrum Warrior* shows how games take advantage of situated learning environments. In games as in real life, people must be able to build meanings on the spot as they navigate their contexts. In *Full Spectrum Warrior*, players learn about suppression fire through the concrete experiences they have while playing. These experiences give a working definition of suppression fire, to be sure. But they also let a player come to understand how the idea applies in different contexts, what it has to do with solving particular kinds of problems, and how it relates to other practices in the domain, such as the injunction against shooting while moving.

Video games thus make it possible to "learn by doing" on a grand scale—but not just by wandering around in a rich computer environment to learn without any guidance. Asking learners to act without explicit guidance—a form of learning often associated with a loose interpretation of progressive pedagogy—reflects a bad theory of learning. Learners are novices. Leaving them to float in rich experiences with no support triggers the very real human penchant for finding creative but spurious patterns and generalizations. The fruitful patterns or generalizations in any domain are the ones that are evident to those who already know how to look at the domain and know how complex variables in the domain interrelate. And this is precisely what the learner does not yet know. In *Full Spectrum Warrior*, the player is immersed in activity, values, and ways of seeing but is guided and supported by the knowledge built into the virtual soldiers and the weapons, equipment, and environments in the game. Players are not free to invent everything for themselves. To succeed in the game, they must live by—and ultimately come to master—the epistemic frame of military doctrine. *Full Spectrum Warrior* is an example of what we suggest is the promise of video games and the future of learning: the development of epistemic games.[10]

Epistemic Games for Initiation and Transformation

We have argued that video games are powerful contexts for learning be- cause they make it possible to create virtual worlds and because acting in such worlds makes it possible to develop the situated understandings, effec- tive social practices, powerful identities, shared values, and ways of think- ing of important communities of practice. To build such worlds, one has to understand how the epistemic frames of those communities are developed, sustained, and changed. Some parts of practice are more central to the cre- ation and development of an epistemic frame than others, so analyzing the epistemic frame tells you, in effect, what might be safe to leave out in a re- creation of the practice. The result is a video game that preserves the con- nections between knowing and doing that are central to an epistemic frame and so becomes an epistemic game. Such epistemic games let players par- ticipate in valued communities of practice to develop a new epistemic frame or to develop a better and more richly elaborated version of an already mas- tered epistemic frame.

Initiation

Developing games such as *Full Spectrum Warrior* that simultaneously build situated understandings, effective social practices, powerful identi- ties, shared values, and ways of thinking is clearly no small task. But the good news is that in many cases existing communities of practice have al- ready done a lot of that work. Doctors know how to create more doctors; lawyers know how to create more lawyers; the same is true for a host of other socially valued communities of practice. Thus we can imagine epis- temic games in which players learn biology by working as a surgeon, history by writing as a journalist, mathematics by designing buildings as an archi- tect or engineer, geography by fighting as a soldier, or French by opening a restaurant. More precisely, these players learn by inhabiting virtual worlds based on the way surgeons, journalists, architects, soldiers, and restaura- teurs develop their epistemic frames.

To build such games requires understanding how practitioners develop their ways of thinking and acting. Such understanding is uncovered through *epistemographies* of practice: detailed ethnographic studies of how the epistemic frame of a community of practice is developed by new members. Gathering this information requires more work than is currently invested in most "educational" video games. But the payoff is that such work can become the basis for an alternative educational model. Video games based on the training of socially valued practitioners let us begin to build an education system in which students learn to work (and thus to think) as doctors, lawyers, architects, engineers, journalists, and other important members of the community. The purpose of building such education systems is not to train students for these pursuits in the traditional sense of vocational education. Rather, we develop such epistemic frames because they can provide students with an opportunity to see the world in a variety of ways that are fundamentally grounded in meaningful activity and well aligned with the core skills, habits, and understandings of a postindustrial society.[11]

One early example of such a game is *Madison 2200*, an epistemic game based on the practices of urban planning.[12] In *Madison 2200*, players learn about urban ecology by working as urban planners who are redesigning a downtown pedestrian mall popular with local teenagers. Players get a project directive from the mayor, addressed to them as city planners, including a city budget plan and letters from concerned citizens about crime, revenue, jobs, waste, traffic, and affordable housing. A video features interviews about these issues with local residents, businesspeople, and community leaders. Players conduct a site assessment of the street and work in teams to develop a land use plan, which they present at the end of the game to a representative of the city planning office.

Not surprisingly, along the way players learn a good deal about urban planning and its practices. But something very interesting happens in an epistemic game like *Madison 2200*. When knowledge is first and foremost a form of activity and experience—of doing something in the world within a community of practice—the facts and information eventually come for free. A large body of facts that resists out-of-context memorization and rote learning comes easily if learners are immersed in activities and experiences that use these facts for plans, goals, and purposes within a coherent domain of knowledge. Data show that, in *Madison 2200*, players start to form an epistemic frame of urban planning. But they also develop their understanding of ecology and are able to apply it to urban issues. As one player commented, "I really noticed how urban planners have to think about building things. Urban planners also have to think about how the crime rate might go up or the pollution or waste, depending on choices." Another said about walking on the same streets she had traversed before the workshop, "You notice things, like that's why they build a house there, or that's why they build a park there."

The players in *Madison 2200* do enjoy their work. But more important is that the experience lets them inhabit an imaginary world in which they are urban planners. The world of *Madison 2200* recruits these players to new ways of thinking and acting as part of a new way of seeing the world. Urban planners have a particular way of addressing urban issues. By participating in an epistemic game based on urban planning, players begin to take on that way of seeing the world. As a result, it is fun, too.

Transformation

Games like *Full Spectrum Warrior* and *Madison 2200* expose novices to the ways professionals make sense of typical problems. But other games are designed for those who are already members of a professional community, with the intention of transforming the ways they think by focusing on atypical problems: cases in which established ways of knowing break down in the face of a new or challenging situation.

Just as games that initiate players into an epistemic frame depend on epistemographic study of the training practices of a community, games designed to transform an epistemic frame depend on detailed examination of how the mature epistemic frame of a practice is organized and maintained—and on when and how the frame becomes problematic. These critical moments of "expectation failure" are the points of entry for reorganizing experienced practitioners' ways of thinking.[13] Building the common assumptions of an existing epistemic frame into a game allows experienced professionals to cut right to the key learning moments.

For example, work on military leadership simulations has used *goal-based scenarios* to build training simulations based on the choices military leaders face when setting up a base of operations.[14] In the business world, systems like RootMap (Root Learning, www.rootlearning.com) create graphical representations of professional knowledge, offering suggestions for new practice by highlighting breakdowns in conventional understanding.[15] Studies of school leaders similarly suggest that the way professionals frame problems has a strong impact on the possible solutions they are willing and able to explore.[16] This ability to successfully frame problems in complex systems is difficult to cultivate, but Richard Halverson and Yeonjai Rah have shown that a multimedia representation of successful problem-framing strategies—such as how a principal reorganized her school to serve disadvantaged students—can help school leaders reexamine the critical junctures where their professional understanding is incomplete or ineffective for dealing with new or problematic situations.[17]

Epistemic Games and the Future of Schooling

Epistemic games give players freedom to act within the norms of a valued community of practice—norms that are embedded in nonplayer characters like the virtual soldiers in Full Spectrum Warrior or the real urban planners and planning board members in *Madison 2200*. To work successfully within the norms of a community, players necessarily learn to think as members of the community. Think for a moment about the student who, after playing *Madison 2200*, walked down the same streets she had been on the day before and noticed things she had never seen. This is situated learning at its most profound—a transfer of ideas from one context to another that is elusive, rare, and powerful. It happened not because the student learned more information but because she learned it in the context of a new way of thinking—an epistemic frame—that let her see the world in a new way.

Although there are not yet any complete epistemic games in wide circulation, there already exist many games that provide similar opportunities for deeply situated learning. *Rise of Nations* and *Civilization III* offer rich, interactive environments in which to explore counterfactual historical claims and help players understand the operation of complex historical modeling. *Railroad Tycoon* lets players engage in design activities that draw on the same economic and geographic issues faced by railroad engineers in the 1800s. *Madison 2200*, of course, shows the pedagogical potential of bringing students the experience of being city planners, and we are in the process of developing projects that similarly let players work as biomechanical engineers,[18] journalists,[19] professional mediators,[20] and graphic designers.[21] Other epistemic games might allow a player to experience the world as an evolutionary biologist or as a tailor in colonial Williamsburg.[22]

But even if we had the world's best educational games produced and ready for parents, teachers, and students to buy and play, it's not clear that most educators or schools would know what to do with them. Although the majority of students play video games, the majority of teachers do not. Games, with their anti-authoritarian aesthetics and inherently anti-Puritanical values, can be seen as challenging institutional education. Even if we strip away the blood and guts that characterize some video games, the reality is that, as a form, games encourage exploration, personalized meaning-making, individual expression, and playful experimentation with social boundaries—all of which cut against the grain of the social mores valued in school. In other words, even if we sanitize games, the theories of learning embedded in them run counter to the current social organization of schooling. The next challenges for game and school designers alike is to understand how to shape learning and learning environments to take advantage of the power and potential of games and how to integrate games and game-based learning environments into the predominant arena for learning: schools.

How might school leaders and teachers bring more extended experiments with epistemic games into the culture of the school? The first step will be for superintendents and spokespersons for schools to move beyond the rhetoric of games as violent-serial-killer-inspiring time-wasters and address the range of learning opportunities that games present. Understanding how games can provide powerful learning environments might go a long way toward shifting the current anti-gaming rhetoric. Although epistemic games of the kind we describe here are not yet on the radar of most educators, they are already being used by corporations, the government, the military, and even by political groups to express ideas and teach facts, principles, and world views. Schools and school systems must soon follow suit or risk being swept aside.

A New Model of Learning

The past century has seen an increasing identification of learning with schooling. But new information technologies challenge this union in fundamental ways. Today's technologies make the world's libraries accessible to anyone with a wireless PDA. A vast social network is literally at the fingertips of anyone with a cell phone. As a result, people have unprecedented freedom to bring resources together to create their own learning trajectories.

But classrooms have not adapted. Theories of learning and instruction embodied in school systems designed to teach large numbers of students a standardized curriculum are dinosaurs in this new world. Good teachers and good school leaders fight for new technologies and new practices. But mavericks grow frustrated by the fundamental mismatch between the social organization of schooling and the realities of life in a postindustrial, global, high-tech society. In the push for standardized instruction, the general public and some policy makers may not have recognized this mismatch, but our students have. School is increasingly seen as irrelevant by many students who are past the primary grades.

Thus we argue that, to understand the future of learning, we should be looking beyond schools to the emerging arena of video games. We suggest that video games matter because they present players with simulated worlds—worlds that, if well constructed, are not just about facts or isolated skills but embody particular social practices. And we argue that video games thus make it possible for players to participate in valued communities of practice and so develop the ways of thinking that organize those practices.

Our students will learn from video games. The questions we must ask and answer are: Who will create these games, and will they be based on sound theories of learning and socially conscious educational practices? The U.S. Army, a longtime leader in simulations, is building games like *Full Spectrum Warrior* and *America's Army*—games that introduce civilians to a military world view. Several homeland security games are under development, as are a range of games for health education, from games to help kids with cancer take better care of themselves to simulations to help doctors perform surgery more effectively. Companies are developing games for learning history (*Making History*), engineering (*Time Engineers*), and the mathematics of design (*Homes of Our Own*).[23]

This interest in games is encouraging, but most educational games to date have been produced in the absence of any coherent theory of learning or underlying body of research. We need to ask and answer important questions about this relatively new medium. We need to understand how the conventions of good commercial games create compelling virtual worlds. We need to understand how inhabiting a virtual world develops situated knowledge—how playing a game like *Civilization III*, for example, mediates players' conceptions of world history. We need to understand how spending thousands of hours participating in the social, political, and economic systems of a virtual world develops powerful identities and shared values.[24] We need to understand how game players develop effective social practices and skills in navigating complex systems and how those skills can support learning in other complex domains. And most of all, we need to leverage these understandings to build games that develop for players the epistemic frames of scientists, engineers, lawyers, political activists, and members of other valued communities of practice—as well as games that can help transform those ways of thinking for experienced professionals.

Video games have the potential to change the landscape of education as we know it. The answers to the fundamental questions raised here will make it possible to use video games to move our system of education beyond the traditional academic disciplines—derived from medieval scholarship and constituted within schools developed in the Industrial Revolution— and toward a new model of learning through meaningful activity in virtual worlds. And that learning experience will serve as preparation for meaningful activity in our postindustrial, technology-rich, real world.

NOTES

1. Constance A. Steinkuehler, "Emergent Play," paper presented at the State of Play Conference, New York University Law School, New York City, October 2004.

2. Kurt R. Squire, "Game Cultures, School Cultures," *Innovate*, in press.

3. As Julian Dibbell, a journalist for *Wired* and *Rolling Stone*, has shown, it is possible to make a better living by trading online currencies than by working as a freelance journalist!

4. Constance A. Steinkuehler, "Learning in Massively Multiplayer Online Games," in Yasmin Kafai et al., eds., *Proceedings of the Sixth International Conference of the Learning Sciences* (Mahwah, N.J.: Erlbaum, 2004), pp. 521–28.

5. Kurt R. Squire and Levi Giovanetto, "The Higher Education of Gaming," *eLearning*, in press.

6. Jean Lave and Etienne Wenger, *Situated Learning: Legitimate Peripheral Participation* (Cambridge: Cambridge University Press, 1991).

7. David Williamson Shaffer, "Epistemic Frames and Islands of Expertise: Learning from Infusion Experiences," in Kafai et al., pp. 473–80.

8. The commercial game retains about 15% of what was in the Army's original simulation. For more on this game as a learning environment, see James

P. Gee, "What Will a State of the Art Video Game Look Like?," *Innovate*, in press.

9. *Manual for* Full Spectrum Warrior (Los Angeles: Pandemic Studios, 2004), p. 2.

10. David Williamson Shaffer, "Epistemic Games," *Innovate*, in press.

11. David Williamson Shaffer, "Pedagogical Praxis: The Professions as Models for Postindustrial Education," *Teachers College Record*, July 2004, pp. 1401–21.

12. Kelly L. Beckett and David Williamson Shaffer, "Augmented by Reality: The Pedagogical Praxis of Urban Planning as a Pathway to Ecological Thinking," *Journal of Educational Computing Research*, in press; and Shaffer, "Epistemic Games."

13. Roger C. Schank, *Virtual Learning: A Revolutionary Approach to Building a Highly Skilled Work Force* (New York: McGraw-Hill, 1997).

14. Roger C. Schank et al., "The Design of Goal-Based Scenarios," *Journal of the Learning Sciences*, vol. 3, 1994, pp. 305–45; and A. S. Gordon, "Authoring Branching Storylines for Training Applications," in Kafai et al., pp. 230–38.

15. Kurt R. Squire, "Game-Based Learning: Present and Future State of the Field," e-Learning Consortium, an X-Learn Perspective Paper, Masie Center, February 2005, available at www.masie.com/xlearn/game-based_ learning.pdf, 2005.

16. Richard Halverson, "Systems of Practice: How Leaders Use Artifacts to Create Professional Community in Schools," *Education Policy Analysis Archives*, vol. 11, 2003, p. 37; and idem, "Accessing, Documenting and Communicating Practical Wisdom: The Phronesis of School Leadership Practice," *American Journal of Education*, vol. 111, 2004, pp. 90–121.

17. Richard Halverson and Yeonjai Rah, "Representing Leadership for Social Justice: The Case of Franklin School," *Journal of Cases in Educational Leadership*, Spring 2005.

18. Gina Svarovsky and David Williamson Shaffer, "SodaConstructing Knowledge Through Exploratoids," *Journal of Research in Science Teaching*, in press.

19. Shaffer, "Pedagogical Praxis."

20. David Williamson Shaffer, "When Computer-Supported Collaboration Means Computer-Supported Competition: Professional Mediation as a Model for Collaborative Learning," *Journal of Interactive Learning Research*, vol. 15, 2004, pp. 101–15.

21. David Williamson Shaffer, "Learning Mathematics Through Design: The Anatomy of Escher's World," *Journal of Mathematical Behavior*, vol. 16, 1997, pp. 95–112.

22. Kurt R. Squire and Henry Jenkins, "Harnessing the Power of Games in Education," *Insight*, vol. 3, 2004, pp. 5–33.

23. Ibid.

24. Kurt R. Squire, "Sid Meier's *Civilization III*," *Simulations and Gaming*, vol. 35, 2004, pp. 135-40.

Analyze

1. Explain the reasons why, according to the authors, video games should be seen as more than "mere entertainment"?
2. According to the authors, what happens to learners in virtual worlds?
3. What is the "fact fetish"? How does it relate to the authors' arguments about good teaching and learning?
4. What is an epistemic frame? What is an epistemic game?
5. According to the authors, what types of exploration do video games encourage?

Explore

1. The authors argue that "we learn by becoming part of a community of practice, and thus developing that community's ways of knowing, acting, being, and caring." Describe one community of practice of which you are part. Then, explain what it means to think and act as part of this community. Finally, based on the authors' discussion of the instruction manual developed for the *Full Spectrum Warrior* game, write an instruction manual for the community of practice of which you are a part.
2. Although the potential for the use of video games in higher education appears to be huge, not many of these types of games have yet to be developed. Think about the classes that you are taking this semester and some of the material that has been covered in these courses. Select one discrete unit from one of your courses and write a proposal explaining how a new video game could be used either to teach the material from that unit or as a way for students to apply the knowledge and skills related to it.
3. Do some research on gaming and education. Then, write a letter to the authors in which you explain what you have learned about gaming and education and why you agree or disagree that the virtual world of video games and the attributes of these worlds may be one model for creating effective learning environments.

Forging Connections

1. It is noteworthy that despite the media attention focused on MOOCs, Diane Ravitch does not write specifically about MOOCs in her essay. However, there are many similarities between the issues discussed by

Ravitch and those raised by Andrew Delbanco and the SJSU Philosophy Departments in their essays about MOOCs. Based on Delbanco's essay and the SJSU Philosophy Department's letter, write a short essay explaining the specific ways in which MOOCs relate to the three trends Ravitch identifies.

2. Analyze the argument presented in Andrew Delbanco's essay and in the letter written by the SJSU Philosophy Department. What is the thesis of each essay? What claims are used to support each thesis? Write a one page descriptive overview of each of the two arguments, explaining which you believe is most persuasive and why. Based on your analysis of the two arguments, and your understanding and interpretation of the issues, write an editorial for your college newspaper about the issue of MOOCs and why they should—or should not—be adopted at your college.

Looking Further

1. There are several different ways in which Neil Postman's essay "Five Things We Need To Know About Technological Change" (Chapter 1) can be brought into dialogue with the readings in this chapter. Carefully read Postman's essay and re-write each of his five ideas about technological change in your own words. Once you have done that, review the essays in this chapter and create a list of the benefits that technologies may hold for education. Then, create another list of the possible drawbacks of the use of technologies in education. Using these lists and the key issues discussed in the essays to inform your writing, write a three- to five-page report informing your reader of the connections that could be made between Postman's five ideas about technological change and what may be gained and what may be lost as a result of the increased use of technologies in education. After writing your report, write a one-page abstract of your findings.

2. Although all of the authors in this chapter propose that technologies may be transforming education, none of them includes voices of actual students to assess how well or poorly the current technologies being used in education are working. Choose one specific application that you use regularly as part of your education, for instance Blackboard, email, electronic textbooks, or Web videos. Write a three-page essay describing in detail how this specific technology has been used at your

college, and its benefits and drawbacks. After writing this, write a two-page article for your school newspaper on the topic of "Promise and Peril: Technology in Education." In your article, make sure to refer to at least one essay in this chapter and one essay from another chapter as you explain first the ways in which one specific technology has had positive and negative effects on your educational experience and secondly why and how such a tradeoff has also been a characteristic of the adoption of other specific technologies.

Digital (In)equality and Politics: Can Technology Change the World?

According to the International Telecommunications Union, as of 2014, the estimated world population will total 7.2 billion and the estimated number of cell phone subscriptions will total 7.3 billion. In other words, 2014 marks the first time in history that a single technology—the cell phone subscription—exceeds the estimated global population. This statistic does not mean that every person on the planet owns a cell phone, nor even that every person has a cell phone subscription. In certain countries, cell phone subscriptions exceed the population; in others, cell phone subscriptions do not yet equal the population. Nevertheless, this statistic is noteworthy in the context of other statistics about technology adoption. In the developed world, fixed-line telephone subscriptions never exceeded 50 percent of the population; in the developing world, fixed-line telephone subscriptions never exceeded 15 percent. Such statistics about older and newer technologies in relation to one another can be interpreted in many different ways. Certainly one interpretation is that the world is technically more connected. Beyond that, it is hard to agree on very much. Living conditions continue to vary widely across the globe, and while some people may spend a fraction of their living expenses on cell phone subscriptions, others, mostly those in the developing world, may be spending up to 20 percent of their income on such subscriptions.

Although uneven, the spread of information and communications technologies across the globe has had—and will continue to have—a profound impact on social, political, and economic structures. All of the authors in this chapter address the myriad issues related to technology and sociopolitical economies. Some assess the potential for information and communications technologies to address economic, social, and political issues, while, conversely, others look at how these very technologies are also creating new socioeconomic issues that will need to be addressed.

In this chapter, two authors, Kentaro Toyama and Susan Davis, ask and respond to the question "Can Technology End Poverty?" in essays that share the same title and recount somewhat differently the experiences of each author in global development projects related to technology. In an essay excerpted from his book *Who Owns the Future?* Jaron Lanier explains why information technologies have the power to make the world a very unequal place, and in an article entitled "Digital Capitalism Produces Few Winners," John Naughton reviews some characteristics of today's global economy. In his essay "Why the Revolution Will Not Be Retweeted," Malcolm Gladwell considers how the types of social and political organizing enabled by new information and communication technologies are fundamentally different from what has taken place via nonvirtual sociopolitical organizing networks. Finally, in his essay "It's Time to Work for a Better Internet," Douglas Schuler asks if it might be time to ask not what technology is doing to the world, but what we can do with technology to make the world a better place.

Kentaro Toyama
"Can Technology End Poverty?"

Kentaro Toyama is a researcher in the School of Information at the University of California, Berkeley, and a fellow of the Dalai Lama Center for Ethics and Transformative Values at the Massachusetts Institute of Technology. Having worked for many years as a computer scientist with Microsoft, he is also a co-founder of Microsoft Research India. Focusing his current work on relationships between society and technology, particularly in relation to the challenges of global poverty and development, he is editor of the blog ICT4D Jester (http://blog.ict4djester.org/) and the author of *Human–Computer Interaction and Global Development (Foundations and Trends in Human–Computer Interaction)* (2010). In this essay, Toyama recounts his experiences working on several technology-focused international development projects in South Asia and Africa and what he learned as a result.

Should access to the Internet be a fundamental right of all people? Why or why not?

A ten-year-old boy named Dhyaneshwar looked up for approval after carefully typing the word "Alaska" into a PC.

"Bahut acchaa!" I cheered—"very good."

It was April, 2004, and I was visiting a "telecenter" in the tiny village of Retawadi, three hours from Mumbai. The small, dirt-floored room, lit only by an open aluminum doorway, was bare except for a desk, a chair, a PC, an inverter, and a large tractor battery, which powered the PC when grid electricity was unavailable. Outside, a humped cow chewed on dry stalks, and a goat bleated feebly.

> "Technology has positive effects only to the extent that people are willing and able to use it positively."

As I encouraged the boy, I wondered about the tradeoff his parents had made in order to pay for a typing tutor. Their son was learning to write words he'd never use, in a language he didn't speak. According to the telecenter's owner, Dhyaneshwar's parents paid a hundred rupees—about $2.20—a month for a couple hours of lessons each week. That may not sound like much, but in Retawadi, it's twice as much as full-time tuition in a private school.

5   Such was my introduction to the young field of ICT4D, or Information and Communication Technologies for Development. The goal of ICT4D is to apply the power of recent technologies—particularly the personal computer, the mobile phone, and the Internet—to alleviate the problems of global poverty. ICT4D sprouted from two intersecting trends: the emergence of an international-development community eager for novel solutions to nearly intractable socioeconomic challenges; and the expansion of a brashly successful technology industry into emerging markets and philanthropy.

The latter prompted my own move to India. I was working as a computer scientist for Microsoft Research in the United States during a time when India's rise as an information-technology superpower drew to that country increasing investments from multinational firms. In 2004 I was asked to help start a lab in Bangalore, and I jumped at the opportunity. While the lab's broader mission was to engage India's science and engineering talent in computer-science research, I would have the chance to start an ICT4D research group, where I hoped to devote my expertise to something of wider societal value.

At the time, telecenters were the poster children of ICT4D. Telecenters are like Internet cafés, except they are placed in impoverished communities with the intention of accelerating socioeconomic growth. The telecenters are often sponsored wholly or in part by outside agencies—governments, NGOs, academia, industry—harboring a variety of secondary aims, from profits and publicity to increased interaction with a voting constituency.

In Retawadi the telecenter was created jointly by a for-profit start-up company and a local nonprofit. The partners believed that the telecenter would provide social services to the community and income for a local entrepreneur, and, in fact, it did a bit of both. When I visited, the telecenter had two students. Occasionally, a college-aged youth would come in to use the Internet for the equivalent of $0.25 per hour. And the owner boasted that he earned additional income by using the PC himself to provide a local hospital with data-entry services.

Some telecenters have been successful. One operator in South India reported saving a farmer's okra crop by enabling a timely video teleconference between him and a university agriculture expert. Another boasted a threefold increase in income after opening a computer-training center. The press headlines have been unabashedly flattering: "India's Soybean Farmers Join the Global Village" (*The New York Times*); Village Kiosks Bridge India's

Digital Divide" (*The Washington Post*); "Kenyan Farmer Lauds Internet as Saviour of Potato Crop" (BBC).

These stories have sparked high hopes for telecenters: distance education will make every child a scholar; telemedicine can cure dysfunctional rural health-care systems; citizens will offer each other services locally and directly, bypassing corrupt government officials. Ashok Jhunjhunwala, a member of the Indian Prime Minister's Science Advisory Council, suggested that telecenters could double incomes in rural villages. M.S. Swaminathan, widely credited with India's "Green Revolution" in agriculture, called for a telecenter in each of the country's 640,000 villages. Other countries have followed suit, proclaiming their own national telecenter programs.

The excitement around telecenters has spread to the rest of ICT4D. Prominent people in both the technology and development sectors eagerly fan the flames, and proponents of ICT4D increasingly wrap it in the language of needs and rights. Nicholas Negroponte—founder of One Laptop Per Child (OLPC), a project devoted to getting inexpensive laptops into the hands of every poor child—claims, "Kids in the developing world need the newest technology, especially really rugged hardware and innovative software." Kofi Annan has publicly backed the project. Edward Friedman, director of the Center for Technology Management for Global Development, epitomized engineers involved in ICT4D when he wrote, "There is a pressing need to employ information technology for rural healthcare in sub-Saharan Africa." One recent worldwide survey commissioned by the BBC found that 79 percent of the nearly 28,000 adults polled—mainly from richer countries and those with Internet access—strongly agreed or somewhat agreed with the statement, "Access to the Internet should be a fundamental right of all people."

Yet the successes of ICT4D are few, fleeting, and very far between. In Retawadi the telecenter owner made approximately twenty dollars per month, but monthly costs of hardware, electricity, connectivity, and maintenance were a hundred dollars. The telecenter closed shortly after my visit.

Over a span of five years I traveled to nearly 50 telecenters across South Asia and Africa. The vast majority looked a lot like the one in Retawadi. Locals rarely saw much value in the Internet, and telecenter operators couldn't market even the paltry services available. Most suffered the same fate as the Retawadi telecenter, shutting down soon after they opened. Research on telecenters, though limited in rigor and scale, confirms my observations about consistent underperformance. As I soon discovered, these mostly failed ventures reflect a larger pattern in technology and development, in which new technologies generate optimism and exuberance eventually dashed by disappointing realities.

15   Academic observers have deconstructed telecenters and other ICT4D projects, enumerating the many reasons why the initiatives fail: ICT4D enthusiasts don't design context-appropriate technology, adhere to sociocultural norms, account for poor electrical supply, build relationships with local governments, invite the participation of the community, provide services that meet local needs, consider bad transportation infrastructure, think through a viable financial model, provide incentives for all stakeholders, and so on. These criticisms are each valid as far as they go, and ICT4D interventionists sometimes focus narrowly on addressing them. But this laundry list of foibles ultimately provides no insight into the deeper reasons why ICT4D projects rarely fulfill their promise, even as their cousins in the developed world thrive in the form of netbooks, BlackBerrys, and Facebook.

Nothing would have pleased my group more than finding a way for technology to advance the cause of poverty alleviation. But as we conducted research projects in multiple domains (education, microfinance, agriculture, health care) and with various technologies (PCs, mobile phones, custom-designed electronics), a pattern, having little to do with the technologies themselves, emerged. In every one of our projects, a technology's effects were wholly dependent on the intention and capacity of the people handling it. The success of PC projects in schools hinged on supportive administrators and dedicated teachers. Microcredit processes with mobile phones worked because of effective microfinance organizations. Teaching farming practices through video required capable agriculture-extension officers and devoted nonprofit staff. In our most successful ICT4D projects, the partner organizations did the hard work of real development, and our role was simply to assist, and strengthen, their efforts with technology.

If I were to summarize everything I learned through research in ICT4D, it would be this: technology—no matter how well designed—is only a *magnifier of human intent and capacity*. It is not a substitute. If you have a foundation of competent, well-intentioned people, then the appropriate technology can amplify their capacity and lead to amazing achievements. But, in circumstances with negative human intent, as in the case of corrupt government bureaucrats, or minimal capacity, as in the case of people who have been denied a basic education, no amount of technology will turn things around.

Technology is a magnifier in that its impact is multiplicative, not additive, with regard to social change. In the developed world, there is a tendency to see the Internet and other technologies as necessarily additive, inherent contributors of positive value. But their beneficial contributions are contingent on an absorptive capacity among users that is often missing in the developing world. Technology has positive effects only to the extent that people are willing and able to use it positively. The challenge of international development is that, whatever the potential of poor communities, well-intentioned capability is in scarce supply and technology cannot make up for its deficiency.

This point may sound reasonable enough when stated in the abstract, but it has an important consequence for anyone expecting to save the world with technology: you can't . . . at least, not unless the technology is applied where human intent and capacity are already present, or unless you are willing also to invest heavily in developing human capability and institutions.

The converse belief—accepted as faith by technocrats and techno-   20
utopians—is that the large-scale dissemination of appropriately designed technology, per se, can provide solutions to poverty and other social problems. Believers jump to address the scale of global problems before confirming the value of the solution. They equate technology penetration with progress. For example OLPC seeks to enable "self-empowered learning." Teachers can be altogether absent; OLPC has consistently sold its technology with little discussion of the realities of pedagogy—training teachers, redesigning curricula, strengthening weak school systems. As for technical maintenance, the students are supposed to provide it themselves. OLPC's very name implies that its goal is, primarily, widely disseminated technology. Yet, few of us would choose PC-based education for our own children.

This *myth of scale* is the religion of telecenter proponents, who believe that bringing the Internet into villages is enough to transform them. Most recently, there is the cult of the mobile phone: one *New York Times Magazine* headline ran, "Can the Cellphone Help End Global Poverty?" The article went on to assert, "the possibilities afforded by a proliferation of cellphones are potentially revolutionary."

"Revolutionary." The myth of scale is seductive because it is easier to spread technology than to effect extensive change in social attitudes and human capacity. In other words, it is much less painful to purchase a hundred thousand PCs than to provide a real education for a hundred thousand children; it is easier to run a text-messaging health hotline than to convince people to boil water before ingesting it; it is easier to write an app that helps people find out where they can buy medicine than it is to persuade them that medicine is good for their health. It seems obvious that the promise of scale is a red herring, but ICT4D proponents rely—consciously or otherwise—on it in order to promote their solutions.

Estimates of annual, worldwide ICT4D expenditure are hard to come by, but they range from hundreds of millions to tens of billions of U.S. dollars, depending on what is counted. Given the extent of the investment, the opportunity costs become significant. OLPC's target cost of a hundred dollars or less per laptop (in practice, the machines have been more expensive) sounds affordable, but that's about half of India's per-student education budget, most of which is currently devoted to teachers' salaries. Does a hundred dollars for a computer make sense when $0.50 per year per child for deworming pills could reduce the incidence of illness-causing parasites and increase school attendance by 25 percent?

Despite critical needs in all areas of development, ICT4D proponents tend not only to ignore the opportunity costs of technology, but also to press for funding from budgets allocated to non-technology purposes. Presumably, this was one of the reasons behind OLPC's brazen doublespeak in claiming to be "an education project, not a laptop project," while expecting governments to spend $100 million for a million laptops, the original minimum order. In a fine example of the skewed priorities of ICT4D boosters, Hamadoun Touré, secretary-general of the International Telecommunications Union, suggests, "[governments should] regard the Internet as basic infrastructure—just like roads, waste and water." Of course, in conditions of extreme poverty, investments to provide broad access to the Web will necessarily compete with spending on proper sanitation and the rudiments of transportation.

25   Disseminating a technology would work if, somehow, the technology did more for the poor, undereducated, and powerless than it did for the rich, well-educated, and mighty. But the theory of technology-as-magnifier leads to the opposite conclusion: the greater one's capacity, the more technology delivers; the lesser one's capacity, the less value technology has. In effect, technology helps the rich get richer while doing little for the incomes of the poor, thus widening the gaps between haves and have-nots.

Technology widens the gap through three mechanisms. First, differential access. Technology is consistently more accessible to the rich and the powerful. Technology costs money not only to acquire, but also to operate, maintain, and upgrade. And this "digital divide" persists even when the technology is fully sponsored. For instance, most public libraries in the United States provide free access to the Internet, but poorer residents have less leisure time in which to visit them and a harder time reaching them because of transportation costs. There may be social barriers, too: many of the rural telecenters I've visited in the developing world were not accessible to the least privileged people in their villages due to social injunctions against comingling of caste, tribe, or gender.

Technology producers also reinforce the digital divide. As for-profit companies, by and large, they naturally cater their products toward larger groups of richer customers, who are more likely to buy. Technology amplifies shareholder interest in profit, and, globally, this means hardware tends to be designed for people working in climate-controlled offices with stable AC power; software tends to be developed in languages understood by the world's largest, wealthiest populations; and content tends to be written for audiences with the greatest disposable income. Even when products appear to be free, as with TV or Google, they are frequently supported by advertisers who seek consumers with more disposable income. The result is, again, that the disadvantaged are further disadvantaged. India has more than twenty nationally recognized languages, yet almost all of the software in use there is in English, making it difficult for those literate only in their local languages to use computers. And this inclination reinforces itself: if a technology is not designed for someone, she won't buy it; and if she doesn't buy it, the producers won't design for her.

It is possible to fight against this differential access. Telecenter projects, in fact, typify such efforts, as the centers are always targeted at poorer clients. But progressive practices with respect to technology are not particularly effective on their own because of other differentials that technology doesn't undo. A level playing field doesn't address the underlying issues, which are the inequalities among the players themselves.

This brings us to the second mechanism: even if differential access to technology could be countered through universally distributed technology, differential capacity—in terms of education, social skills, or social connections—remains. Consider the following thought experiment. You and a poor farmer from a remote village are each given 24 hours to raise as much money as you can for the charity of your choice. You are both provided unfettered access to an Internet-connected PC, and nothing else, with which to fulfill the task. Who would be able to raise more money? You would, because of your education, social ties, self-confidence, and organizational capacities. The technology is exactly the same in both cases, so the difference is due to qualities associated with the person. It could be argued that telecenter projects are not far off from a real-life version of this experiment. Clients of telecenters are limited in literacy, education, social ties, political influence, etc., and are therefore constrained in the value they can extract from the Internet. With limited capacity, technology's value is minimal.

30   Along with differential access and capacity, a third mechanism—differential motivation—contributes to the widening divergence between the privileged and the marginalized. What do people want to do with the technology they have access to? Those of us who have worked in interventionist ICT4D have often been surprised to find that poor people don't rush to gain more education, learn about health practices, or upgrade vocational skills. Instead, they seem to use technology primarily for entertainment. Telecenter surveys find that when a village has ready access to a PC—connected to the Internet or otherwise—the dominant use is by young men playing games, watching movies, or consuming adult content. Many become proficient at the software incantations required to download YouTube videos from a PC onto a mobile phone. But these same users typically forsake software-based accounting and language lessons. What interventionists perceive to be "productive" use of technology is trumped by the "frivolous" desires of users. Even users in the developed world rarely take advantage of their technologies for purposes of self-improvement—the most popular iPhone apps are games and other entertainments, nothing that would improve productivity or health—but this tendency is exacerbated among those who have grown up with lessons of learned helplessness and low self-confidence.

I'm not blaming the victim. None of the three mechanisms necessarily speak to failures on the part of those who are poor or poorly educated. Blame, if it must be attributed, falls readily on historical circumstances, social structures, and the rich world's unwillingness to invest in high-quality, universal education. In fact, one reason for valuing education is that it generates the appetite for and capacity to use modern tools—all the more reason to focus on nurturing human capability, rather than trying to compensate for limited capacity with technology.

The problem is that ICT4D assumes the very results it seeks to achieve. The human intent and competence ICT4D aims to generate must already be in place for the technology to work. But if developing economies had the capacity, there would be no need for an external technology push: capable people attract, or develop, their own technology.

North America, Western Europe, Japan, and several other economically blessed regions are cases in point. They attained their status as economic powerhouses well before digital technologies had a measurable impact of any kind. Their advanced production and consumption of information technology can be interpreted more as a result of economic advances than as a primary cause.

There is also evidence that previous applications of information and communications technology in developing countries have not led directly to socioeconomic progress. Consider television. In 1964 Wilbur Schramm, the father of communications studies and a cofounder of Stanford University's Department of Communication, wrote a book eerily prescient of ICT4D discourse, though its focus was on the technologies of its day— print, radio, and television. In one section of *Mass Media and National Development*, Schramm highlights the potential of television:

> What if the full power and vividness of television teaching were to   35
> be used to help the schools develop a country's new educational pattern? What if the full persuasive and instructional power of television were to be used in support of community development and the modernization of farming?

Since then television has had some positive impact. Economists Robert Jensen and Emily Oster have found that exposure to cable television empowers rural women in India. Anthropological evidence suggests that television shows depicting urban values can shift social attitudes in rural areas. One nonprofit organization, the Population Media Center, explicitly applies this principle in order to influence birth rates and health-care practices in developing countries by running soap operas with positive social messaging. These are encouraging points.

Yet the sum total of television's development impact comes nowhere near even Schramm's measured expectations. Half a century later, we find that television has not been consistently beneficial to national education or agriculture, either in the developed or the developing world. A visit to a poor household with a television suggests how appropriate the "boob tube" nickname really is. TV is not an effective guard against illiteracy, poverty, or poor health, as India, where about half of households own TVs, demonstrates. Whatever television's potential, society—both as producer and consumer of technology—has failed to apply it consistently toward development on a large scale.

My point is not that technology is useless. To the extent that we are willing and able to put technology to positive ends, it has a positive effect. For example, Digital Green (DG), one of the most successful ICT4D projects I oversaw while at Microsoft Research, promotes the use of locally recorded how-to videos to teach smallholder farmers more productive practices. When it comes to persuading farmers to adopt good practices, DG is ten times more cost-effective than classical agriculture extension without technology.

But the value of a technology remains contingent on the motivations and abilities of organizations applying it—villagers must be organized, content must be produced, and instructors must be trained. The limiting factor in spreading DG's impact is not how many camcorders its organizers can purchase or how many videos they can shoot, but how many groups are performing good agriculture extension in the first place. Where such organizations are few, building institutional capacity is the more difficult, but necessary, condition for DG's technology to have value. In other words, disseminating technology is easy; nurturing human capacity and human institutions that put it to good use is the crux.

40   The claim that technology is only a magnifier extends beyond international development and beyond information and communication technology. Nobody expects to turn around a loss-making company with the injection of newer computers, but well-run corporations can benefit from, say, computerized supply chains. A gun in the right hands protects citizens and maintains peace; in the wrong hands, it kills and oppresses. (Alas, the gun lobby is right—"guns don't kill people; people kill people.") Modern industrial technology magnifies our ability to produce, but it also magnifies our desire to consume. On a planet with finite resources, the latter could be our ruin. And

history suggests that even the political "technology" of democracy is all too easily subverted in the absence of an educated, self-confident citizenry, willing and able to implement checks and balances against the abuse of power. Computers, guns, factories, and democracy are powerful tools, but the forces that determine how they're used ultimately are human.

This point seems obvious but is forgotten in the rush to scale. Currently the international-development community is having a love affair with the mobile phone. Rigorously executed research by Jensen and by fellow economist Jenny C. Aker demonstrates that cell phones can eliminate certain kinds of information inefficiencies in developing-world markets. Encouraged by such findings and by the sheer depth of mobile-phone penetration, foundations and multilateral agencies have formed task forces and entire departments devoted to mobile phones for international development. In these circles, it is not possible to discuss microfinance without "mobile money," or health care without "mHealth" (short for "mobile health").

The magnification thesis, however, suggests that this is a one-sided view of mobile phones. Certainly talking is something that all human beings, as social animals, not only want to do, but are well equipped for. Phones multiply that intent and capacity, and some of the resulting value is positive—no point in being an indiscriminate Luddite.

But, it's not just productive intentions that are magnified by technology. When a dollar-a-day rickshaw puller pays a large corporation for the privilege of changing his ring tone, does he generate a net benefit to himself or society? Companies pump out such questionable, "value-added" services, and millions of impoverished consumers readily pay for them. Kathleen Diga of the University of KwaZulu Natal observed that some households in Uganda prioritize talk time over family nutrition and clean water. Sociologist Jenna Burrell found that destructive patterns of gender politics are exacerbated by mobile phones, as men wield phones as tools of sexual exchange. Meanwhile, in the developed world, there is mounting evidence that mobile phones contribute to distracted driving, fractured attention, and reduced cognitive ability.

We are in the midst of the largest ICT4D experiment ever. In 2009 there were over 4.5 billion active mobile phone accounts, more than the entire population of the world older than twenty years of age. The cell phone is overtaking both television and radio as the most popular consumer electronic device in history. Some 80 percent of the global population is within range of a cell tower, and mobile phones are increasingly seen in the poorest, remotest communities.

45   These numbers prompt suggestions that there is no longer a "digital divide" for real-time communication. Yet any demographic account of mobile have-nots will show them to be predominantly poor, remote, female, and politically mute. Whatever the case, if the spread of mobile phones is sufficient to help end global poverty, we will know soon enough. But, if it doesn't, should we then pin our hopes on the next new shiny gadget?

Analyze

1. What does ICT4D stand for?
2. What patterns "having little to do with technology" emerged from Toyama's project?
3. List the nine reasons cited by academic observers that ICT4D projects often fail.
4. What does OLPC stand for? How does the OLPC project relate to Toyama's argument?
5. Why, according to Toyama, should "technology penetration not be equated with progress"?
6. What is the "myth of scale"? How does it relate to Toyama's argument?
7. According to Toyama, what are the three mechanisms through which technology widens the gap between haves and have-nots?

Explore

1. Toyama argues that technology is "only a magnifier of human intent and capacity," not a substitute. In a short essay, describe a project involving technology that you have been involved with and explain how your experiences with this project confirm or contest Toyama's argument.
2. Do some research into per capita income by country on the World Bank website: http://data.worldbank.org/indicator/NY.GNP.PCAP .CD. Then, enter the phrase (including the quotation marks) "mobile phone spending per capita" into an Internet search engine. Based on the results of that search, calculate the percentage of mobile phone spending per income for a range of countries, both developing and

developed. Working in small groups, compare your findings with those of your classmates. Then, as a group, develop a five-minute presentation explaining and interpreting the data you have collected and its possible implications.

3. In response to Toyama's 2010 article, the *Boston Review* established a forum for the discussion of the question "Can Technology End Poverty," inviting contributions from a number of prominent individuals working in areas related to technology and global development, including some mentioned in Toyama's article. Look up this forum (http://www.bostonreview.net/forum/can-technology-end-poverty). Read three or four responses to Toyama's article. Then, consider how these responses may have changed, expanded, or altered your understanding of Toyama's article and the issues discussed in it. In a short essay, explain your initial response and interpretation of Toyama's article and how the various responses to the article influenced your later response and interpretation of it.

Susan Davis
"Can Technology End Poverty?"

Susan Davis is the founder, current president, and CEO of BRAC USA, a program started to alleviate global poverty through initiatives related to microfinance, education, healthcare, legal services, and community empowerment. Formerly a founding member and chair of the Grameen Foundation, an economic development organization focused on global poverty alleviation, she is also, along with David Bornstein, the co-author of *Social Entrepreneurship: What Everyone Needs to Know* (2010). In this essay, Davis reviews the global development initiatives related to technology that BRAC has been involved with and some of the factors that made specific projects more successful than others.

Do you believe that information and communications technology can help end global poverty? Why or why not?

If you believe the hype, technology is going to help us end global poverty. Advances have indeed made a huge difference in the lives of the poor, but there's also a healthy amount of skepticism out there. Berkeley researcher Kentaro Toyama has a blog dedicated to calling out naïve or inappropriate uses of information and communication technologies (ICT). Calling himself the ICT4D jester (using the development jargon for "information and communication technologies for development"), he has no shortage of material. We've all heard stories of computers that sit unused in African classrooms; on a recent post, the jester takes aim at texting cows.

The organization I'm part of, BRAC, is known for going to scale with solutions that are often radically low-tech. We're more likely to scale up birthing kits that cost less than 50 cents apiece than mobile apps that might diagnose disease; more likely to open one-room schools in rented spaces or even boats, where children sit on the floor and learn to think creatively, than insist that every pupil have Internet access.

But I'm hardly a naysayer when it comes to tech. I agree with Peter Diamandis and Steven Kotler, who write in *Abundance: The Future Is Better Than You Think*, that higher productivity associated with the falling cost of technology is leading us to a world of plenty.

The trick is making sure everyone shares in the coming abundance—or at least has a fair shot at doing so.

5   To do that, it's vital that technology be suitable and relevant to the lives of its users. That's easier said than done in a world where most product innovations are geared toward the rich.

We can take some lessons from Bangladesh, where BRAC is heading full steam into mobile banking with bKash (*bikash* means "growth" in Bengali), which is now the largest mobile banking provider in the country. BRAC Bank (the commercial bank owned by BRAC) launched the service as a pilot in five branches in November 2011, asking small enterprise borrowers to make repayments via local agents—who would send a receipt via text message—rather than in person at branch offices.

Even though it was designed to save time for hard-working families, asking borrowers to forego their passbooks in favor of SMS confirmations made them extremely uncomfortable. Shameran Abed, who runs BRAC's microfinance program, explains what happened: "In the first couple months, a lot of our borrowers would send the money through their mobile phones and then physically show up at the branch to check with the accountant that the money had turned up."

You may chuckle at that, but consider things from the point of view of a Bangladeshi smallholder farmer. "In a country where most people think that the only thing that is irrefutable is hard copy documentation with someone's signature affixed to it, we were asking our borrowers to take a major leap of faith," Abed says. "Some of them said to us: 'If ever there is a dispute and we end up in court, no magistrate or judge will want to see an SMS confirmation. They'll want to see proof'—meaning a hard-copy passbook."

BKash is now advertised widely, with 30,000 agents and 2.2 million users. We're confident in the cautious approach we've taken, and more importantly, the clients seem so, too.

But what happens when you ask customers to make a leap of faith and the chasm proves too wide? The consequences can be harmful—often more so for poorer clients than the ones pushing the solution.

BRAC learned this lesson from its foray into community-owned tube wells and irrigation pumps in the 1990s, documented in Ian Smillie's *Freedom From Want*. Since water deep in the ground doesn't belong to anybody, we thought of giving loans to organizations of the landless poor to drill and manage deep tube wells and sell the water to rice farmers, who would in turn benefit from higher yields.

The promise was exciting—the details far less so. The project depended on sufficient demand from farmers, which depended on ensuring they had access to high-yield seeds, fertilizer, and pesticides. It also meant gauging demand for irrigation with a certain level of precision, which meant accurately forecasting the sale price of rice.

In the end, the program had far too many moving parts over which BRAC and the borrowers had insufficient control. At the program's peak, 700 pumps covered 27,000 acres, with the loans constituting 9% of BRAC's total microfinance portfolio. By the end of 1993, half of the pumps were operating at a loss and many loans were in arrears. The program was shut down in 1996, and although it refunded 100% of the loan repayments, it went down as one of BRAC's biggest failures.

If details about fertilizers and crop yields seem tedious, that's part of my point. We need to learn to hang on to the positive energy of the tech-innovation movement—in the words of Steve Jobs, stay hungry and foolish—even when the complexities don't exactly liven up our cocktail party chatter (or, for that matter, galvanize investors).

15   In that regard, social entrepreneurs should heed the following:

- **Invest in local innovation.** The poor and marginalized may not have been to school, but that doesn't mean they're uneducated. They're often experts at *jugaad*, the Hindi word for "frugal innovation." Piecemeal, low-tech solutions often go further—and are more easily scaled-up—than anything dreamed up by R&D-centric outsiders.
- **Grapple with the human dimensions of the problem.** Understand not just the thrill of empowering people in principle, but the challenges in practice. To really know what managing a well means for a group of landless villagers, one needs to understand workaday hassles easily overlooked in the excitement of helping people. One must be sensitive to the stress of uncertainty with new innovations, such as replacing cumbersome microfinance passbooks with digital money.
- **Immerse yourself in the details.** If you find yourself frustrated, bored, or driven to distraction by the nitty-gritty (the financial yields of improved rice varietals, say), that's a sign you may be on the right track—and safer from the jester's taunts.

The prospect of billions rising up from poverty with nothing more than gadgets is indeed a fanciful notion—and not a helpful one, either. But the evidence says that when we tether enthusiasm to reality, the reality starts to budge.

Analyze

1. What is bKash?
2. What is microfinance?
3. According to Davis, what are the three key issues that every social entrepreneur needs to keep in mind when thinking about the potential for technological applications in the developing world?

Explore

1. Davis writes that it is "vital that technology be suitable and relevant to the lives of its users." Make an inventory of the information and communications technology devices that you use on a daily basis. Describe in detail the functions of one or two of these devices and how each is designed to be suitable and relevant to you.

2. Are there any "radically low-tech" solutions that you have used to complete certain tasks or address certain problems that work as well as, or possibly even better than, some "high-tech" solutions? Describe two or three of these low-tech solutions and the problem each addresses. Then, describe the high-tech solutions also available to address each problem. As a class, discuss the benefits and drawbacks of the low-tech compared with the high-tech solutions.

3. Do some research into a specific global development project related to microfinance and mobile phone technology. In a three- to five-page report, describe the project and its aims. Did the project accomplish its aims? If yes, why? If no, why not? Assess the success or lack of success of the project in relation to Davis's article and the issues she believes are most important to the success of technology-focused global development projects.

Jaron Lanier
"The Problem in Brief"

Jaron Lanier is a computer scientist, composer, visual artist, and author. His scientific interests include biometrics, user interfaces, and advanced information systems for medicine. Lanier is considered a pioneer in the field of virtual reality (VR). In the 1980s he founded VPL Research, which was the first company to sell VR products. A frequent contributor to national debates about the societal impact of technology, he is also the author of the books *You Are Not a Gadget* (2010) and *Who Owns the Future?* (2014), from which the following essay is excerpted. In this essay, Lanier considers the economic implications of continuing to treat information as a free resource, and the consequences of this model in a future where more and more of the economy is based solely on information.

Have you ever contributed information to a website for free? What types of knowledge and skills were required for you to develop and contribute that information?

We're used to treating information as "free,"* but the price we pay for the illusion of "free" is only workable so long as most of the overall economy *isn't* about information. Today, we can still think of information as the intangible enabler of communications, media, and software. But as technology advances in this century, our present intuition about the nature of information will be remembered as narrow and shortsighted. We can think of information narrowly only because sectors like manufacturing, energy, health care, and transportation aren't yet particularly automated or 'net-centric.

But eventually most productivity probably *will* become software-mediated. Software could be the final industrial revolution. It might subsume all the revolutions to come. This could start to happen, for instance, once cars and trucks are driven by software instead of human drivers, 3D printers magically turn out what had once been manufactured goods, automated heavy equipment finds and mines natural resources, and robot nurses handle the material aspects of caring for the elderly. (These and other examples will be explored in detail later on.) Maybe digital technology won't advance enough in this century to dominate the economy, but it probably will.

Maybe technology will then make all the needs of life so inexpensive that it will be virtually free to live well, and no one will worry about money, jobs, wealth disparities, or planning for old age. I strongly doubt that neat picture would unfold.

Instead, if we go on as we are, we will probably enter into a period of hyperunemployment, and the attendant political and social chaos. The outcome of chaos is unpredictable, and we shouldn't rely on it to design our future.

5   The wise course is to consider in advance how we can live in the long term with a high degree of automation.

Put Up or Shut Up

For years I have presented complaints about the way digital technology interfaces with people. I love the technology and doubly love the people; it's the connection that's out of whack. Naturally, I am often asked, "What

---

*As exemplified by free consumer Internet services, or the way financial services firms can often gather and use data without having to pay for it.

would you do instead?" If the question is framed on a personal level, such as "Should I quit Facebook?" the answer is easy. You have to decide for yourself. I am not trying to be anyone's guru.

On the level of economics, though, I ought to provide an answer. People are not just pointlessly diluting themselves on cultural, intellectual, and spiritual levels by fawning over digital superhuman phenomena that don't necessarily exist. There is also a material cost.

People are gradually making themselves poorer than they need to be. We're setting up a situation where better technology in the long term just means more unemployment, or an eventual socialist backlash. Instead, we should seek a future where more people will do well, without losing liberty, even as technology gets much, much better.

Popular digital designs do not treat people as being "special enough." People are treated as small elements in a bigger information machine, when in fact people are the *only* sources or destinations of information, or indeed of any meaning to the machine at all. My goal is to portray an alternate future in which people are treated appropriately as being special.

How? Pay people for information gleaned from them if that information turns out to be valuable. If observation of you yields data that makes it easier for a robot to seem like a natural conversationalist, or for a political campaign to target voters with its message, then you ought to be owed money for the use of that valuable data. It wouldn't exist without you, after all. This is such a simple starting point that I find it credible, and I hope to persuade you about that as well.

The idea that mankind's information should be made free is idealistic, and understandably popular, but information wouldn't need to be free if no one were impoverished. As software and networks become more and more important, we can either be moving toward free information in the midst of insecurity for almost everyone, or toward paid information with a stronger middle class than ever before. The former might seem more ideal in the abstract, but the latter is the more realistic path to lasting democracy and dignity.

An amazing number of people offer an amazing amount of value over networks. But the lion's share of wealth now flows to those who aggregate and route those offerings, rather than those who provide the "raw materials." A new kind of middle class, and a more genuine, growing information economy, could come about if we could break out of the "free information" idea and into a universal micropayment system. We might even be able to strengthen individual liberty and self-determination even when the machines get very good.

This is a book about futuristic economics, but it's really about how we can remain human beings as our machines become so sophisticated that we can perceive them as autonomous. It is a work of non-narrative science fiction, or what could be called speculative advocacy. I'll argue that the particular way we're reorganizing our world around digital networks is not sustainable, and that there is at least one alternative that is more likely to be sustainable.

Moore's Law Changes the Way People Are Valued

The primary influence on the way technologists have come to think about the future since the turn of the century is their direct experience of digital networks through consumer electronics. It only takes a few years, not a lifetime, for a young person to experience Moore's Law–like changes.

15   Moore's Law is Silicon Valley's guiding principle, like all ten commandments wrapped into one. The law states that chips get better at an accelerating rate. They don't just accumulate improvements, in the way that a pile of rocks gets higher when you add more rocks. Instead of being added, the improvements *multiply*. The technology seems to always get twice as good every two years or so. That means after forty years of improvements, microprocessors have become *millions* of times better. No one knows how long this can continue. We don't agree on exactly why Moore's Law or other similar patterns exist. Is it a human-driven, self-fulfilling prophecy or an intrinsic, inevitable quality of technology? Whatever is going on, the exhilaration of accelerating change leads to a religious emotion in some of the most influential tech circles. It provides a meaning and context.

Moore's Law means that more and more things can be done practically for free, if only it weren't for those people who want to be paid. People are the flies in Moore's Law's ointment. When machines get incredibly cheap to run, people seem correspondingly expensive. It used to be that printing presses were expensive, so paying newspaper reporters seemed like a natural expense to fill the pages. When the news became free, that anyone would want to be paid at all started to seem unreasonable. Moore's Law can make salaries—and social safety nets—seem like unjustifiable luxuries.

But our immediate experience of Moore's Law has been cheap treats. Yesterday's unattainably expensive camera becomes just one of today's throwaway features on a phone. As information technology becomes millions of times more powerful, any particular use of it becomes correspondingly cheaper. Thus, it has become commonplace to expect online services (not just news, but 21st century treats like search or social networking) to be given for free, or rather, in exchange for acquiescence to being spied on.

Analyze

1. If, as Lanier believes, more and more of the economy will be based on information, what does he recommend as the "wise course" in response to this?
2. Why, according to Lanier, may better technology "mean more unemployment"?
3. What is one answer Lanier proposes as a way to prevent mass unemployment in an information economy?
4. What is Moore's Law? What have been some of the consequences of Moore's Law for the consumer electronics industry and for consumers?

Explore

1. Lanier uses a unique structure for his essay, writing in short, interconnected sections rather than in a traditional essay form. How effective is this structure for the argument he is presenting? Explain some of the possible advantages and disadvantages of employing such a structure with regard to audience considerations and the overall purpose(s) of the piece. Could you imagine adopting this type of structure for one of your own writing projects? Why or why not?
2. Lanier proposes that "it only takes a few years, not a lifetime, for a young person to experience Moore's Law–like changes." Describe a process, function, or device that in your experience has been transformed over the span of a few years as a result of increased automation, or integration (i.e., the incorporation of one stand-alone device into another [for instance, a smart phone, which may incorporate features that make it usable as a calculator, date book, camera, watch, music player, video recorder, alarm clock, and ebook reader], the giving away of services that at one time required payment, the dramatic decrease in

price and widespread adoption of technological devices that were once prohibitively expensive). Then, create a storyboard or comic strip in which you depict and tell the story of that change, making sure to take into consideration what happened to the people and products formerly involved in the creation, manufacturing, and distribution of the process or device.

3. The profound effects of Internet technology on the musical recording industry are well known and are discussed briefly by Lanier in his essay. Do some research into the changes that have taken place in the musical recording industry over the past ten years. Write a three-page report describing your findings. Finally, write two pages reflecting on how these findings relate to various issues discussed by Lanier in his essay.

John Naughton
"Digital Capitalism Produces Few Winners"

John Naughton is an Irish academic, journalist, and author. Currently holding faculty and research appointments at several universities, including Cambridge, the British Open University, and University College, Cork, Naughton is also the technology columnist for the London *Observer* newspaper. The author of several books and articles, Naughton's books about technology include *A Brief History of the Future: Origins of the Internet* (2000) and *From Gutenberg to Zuckerberg: What You Really Need to Know About the Internet* (2012). In this essay, Naughton reviews and analyzes some characteristics of "digital capitalism."

What do you now regularly purchase via the Web that you used to purchase in a brick-and-mortar store?

Need a crash course in digital capitalism? Easy: you just need to understand four concepts—margins, volume, inequality and employment. And if you need more detail, just add the following adjectives: thin, vast, huge and poor.

First, margins. Once upon a time, there was a great company called Kodak. It dominated its industry, which happened to be chemistry-based photography. And in its dominance, it enjoyed very fat profit margins—up to 70% in some cases. But somewhere in the depths of Kodak's R&D labs, a few researchers invented digital photography. When they put it to their bosses, the conversation went something like this. Boss: "What are the margins likely to be on this stuff?" Engineers: "Well, it's digital technology so maybe 5% at best." Boss: "Thank you and goodbye."

Actually, it turned out to be goodbye Kodak: those fat margins on an obsolete technology blindsided the company's leaders. Kodak's engineers were right, of course. Anything that involves computers and mass production is destined to be commoditised. My first mobile phone (purchased in the 1980s) cost nearly £1,000. I've just seen a handset for sale in Tesco for £9.95. (And, yes, I know that Apple currently earns fat margins on its hardware, but that's because it's usually ahead of the competition and it won't last. What's happening in the much bigger Android market is a better guide.) And, if anything, the trend towards thin margins in non-hardware businesses is even more pronounced because online markets are relatively frictionless. Just ask anyone who's trying to compete with Amazon.

Then there's volume, which in the online world is astronomical. For example: 72 hours of video uploaded to YouTube every minute; more than 100bn photographs have been uploaded to Facebook; during the Christmas period, Amazon.co.uk dispatched a truck filled with parcels every three minutes; to date, more than 40bn apps have been downloaded from Apple's iTunes store. And so on. Margins may be thin, but when you multiply them by these kinds of numbers you get staggering amounts of revenue.

These vast revenues, however, are not being widely shared. Instead, they are mostly enriching the founders and shareholders of Apple, Amazon, Google, Facebook et al. Of course, those who work at the heart of these organisations—the engineers, developers and the executives who manage them, for example—are richly rewarded in salaries, stock options and lavish perks. But these gilded employees constitute only a minority of the workforces of the big tech companies and most of their colleagues have decidedly more mundane terms of employment—and remuneration.

Take Apple, for example. It makes grandiose claims about the number of jobs that it "directly or indirectly" creates or supports. But about two-thirds of the company's 50,000 American employees work in the US

Apple stores, where many of them were earning about $25,000 a year in 2012—when the mean annual personal income in the US was $38,337 (2010 figure).

Then there's the question of employment, a topic on which the big technology companies seem exceedingly sensitive. Facebook, for example, is given to engaging fancy consultants to produce preposterous claims about the number of jobs it creates. One such "report" claimed that the company, which at the time had a global workforce of about 3,000, indirectly helped create 232,000 jobs in Europe in 2011 and enabled more than $32bn in revenues. And Apple, stung by criticism about all the work it has outsourced to Foxconn in China, is now driven to claiming it has "created or supported" nearly 600,000 jobs in the US.

The really tough question that none of these companies really wants to answer is: what kinds of jobs exactly? Anyone seeking an insight into this would do well to consult a terrific report by Sarah O'Connor, the *Financial Times*'s economics correspondent. She visited Amazon's vast distribution centre at Rugeley in Staffordshire and her account of what she found there makes sobering reading.

She saw hundreds of people in orange vests pushing trolleys around a space the size of nine football pitches, glancing down at the screens of their handheld satnav computers for directions on where to walk next and what to pick up when they get there. They do not dawdle because "the devices in their hands are also measuring their productivity in real time." They walk between seven and 15 miles a day and everything they do is determined by Amazon's software. "You're sort of like a robot, but in human form," one manager told Ms O'Connor. "It's human automation, if you like."

10   Still, it's a job. Until it's replaced by a robot.

Analyze

1. Explain how and why the four concepts, "vast, volume, poor, employment," listed by Naughton at the beginning of his essay are key to understanding digital capitalism.

2. What evidence does Naughton provide to support his claim that the "vast revenues" of certain companies are not being shared widely with their employees?

3. Why, according to Naughton, should readers question the basis and findings of some reports about job creation in a digital economy?

4. Describe the working conditions of Amazon employees in Rugeley. Why might such conditions lead some employees to report that they feel "sort of like a robot"?

Explore

1. If, as Naughton proposes, digital capitalism is based on thin margins, vast volume, huge inequality, and poor employment, what might companies or government bodies do to ensure that wealth created in the digital economy is fairly distributed? Write an opinion/editorial piece for your school newspaper in which you respond to Naughton's essay, explaining why it is important for students to be aware of it and what might be done in response to these issues.

2. In his essay, Naughton provides some details related to salaries and job creation for Apple Computer. However, he does not report similar statistics for Facebook, Amazon or Google. Choose one of these companies and compile salary and job creation statistics for it. Then, compare the findings you have collected with Naughton's.

3. Using either a library database or the Web, look up Sarah O'Connor's *Financial Times* article entitled "Amazon Unpacked" on working conditions at an Amazon warehouse in Britain and Spencer Soper's article entitled "Inside Amazon's Warehouse" on working conditions at an Amazon warehouse in Pennsylvania. In a short essay, compare and contrast the findings reported in the two articles to each other and to Naughton's essay.

Malcolm Gladwell
"Why the Revolution Will Not Be Retweeted"

Malcolm Gladwell is a Canadian journalist and the author of several books, including *The Tipping Point: How Little Things Can Make a Big Difference* (2000), *Blink: The Power of Thinking Without Thinking* (2005), *Outliers: The Story of Success* (2008), and *What the Dog Saw: And Other Adventures* (2009). A staff writer at *The New Yorker* since 1996, Gladwell's work covers diverse topics and trends in social psychology, economics, and sociology. In this essay, Gladwell compares the Civil Rights sit-ins in the early 1960s to the organizing activity that takes place today via social media, exploring the differences between "strong" and "weak" ties in the success of social and political movements.

Have you used social media to either participate in or organize a political event? Is organizing around social and political causes an important part of why you use social media? Could it be?

At four-thirty in the afternoon on Monday, February 1, 1960, four college students sat down at the lunch counter at the Woolworth's in downtown Greensboro, North Carolina. They were freshmen at North Carolina A. & T., a black college a mile or so away.

"I'd like a cup of coffee, please," one of the four, Ezell Blair, said to the waitress.

"We don't serve Negroes here," she replied.

The Woolworth's lunch counter was a long L-shaped bar that could seat sixty-six people, with a standup snack bar at one end. The seats were for whites. The snack bar was for blacks. Another employee, a black woman who worked at the steam table, approached the students and tried to warn them away. "You're acting stupid, ignorant!" she said. They didn't move. Around five-thirty, the front doors to the store were locked. The four still didn't move. Finally, they left by a side door. Outside, a small crowd had gathered, including a photographer from the Greensboro *Record*. "I'll be back tomorrow with A. & T. College," one of the students said.

15   By next morning, the protest had grown to twenty-seven men and four women, most from the same dormitory as the original four. The men were dressed in suits and ties. The students had brought their schoolwork, and studied as they sat at the counter. On Wednesday, students from Greensboro's "Negro" secondary school, Dudley High, joined in, and the number of protesters swelled to eighty. By Thursday, the protesters numbered three hundred, including three white women, from the Greensboro campus of the University of North Carolina. By Saturday, the sit-in had reached six hundred. People spilled out onto the street. White teen-agers waved Confederate flags. Someone threw a firecracker. At noon, the A. & T. football team arrived. "Here comes the wrecking crew," one of the white students shouted.

By the following Monday, sit-ins had spread to Winston-Salem, twenty-five miles away, and Durham, fifty miles away. The day after that, students at Fayetteville State Teachers College and at Johnson C. Smith College, in Charlotte, joined in, followed on Wednesday by students at St. Augustine's College and Shaw University, in Raleigh. On Thursday and Friday, the protest crossed state lines, surfacing in Hampton and Portsmouth, Virginia, in Rock Hill, South Carolina, and in Chattanooga, Tennessee. By the end of the month, there were sit-ins throughout the South, as far west as Texas. "I asked every student I met what the first day of the sitdowns had been like on his campus," the political theorist Michael Walzer wrote in *Dissent*. "The answer was always the same: 'It was like a fever. Everyone wanted to go.'" Some seventy thousand students eventually took part. Thousands were arrested and untold thousands more radicalized. These events in the early sixties became a civil-rights war that engulfed the South for the rest of the decade—and it happened without e-mail, texting, Facebook, or Twitter.

The world, we are told, is in the midst of a revolution. The new tools of social media have reinvented social activism. With Facebook and Twitter and the like, the traditional relationship between political authority and popular will has been upended, making it easier for the powerless to collaborate, coördinate, and give voice to their concerns. When ten thousand protesters took to the streets in Moldova in the spring of 2009 to protest against their country's Communist government, the action was dubbed the Twitter Revolution, because of the means by which the demonstrators had been brought together. A few months after that, when student protests rocked Tehran, the State Department took the unusual step of asking Twitter to suspend scheduled maintenance of its Web site, because the Administration didn't want such a critical organizing tool out of service at the height of the demonstrations. "Without Twitter the people of Iran would not have felt empowered and confident to stand up for freedom and democracy," Mark Pfeifle, a former national-security adviser, later wrote, calling for Twitter to be nominated for the Nobel Peace Prize. Where activists were once defined by their causes, they are now defined by their tools. Facebook warriors go online to push for change. "You are the best hope for us all," James K. Glassman, a former senior State Department official, told a crowd of cyber activists at a recent conference sponsored by Facebook, A. T. & T., Howcast, MTV, and Google. Sites like Facebook, Glassman said, "give the U.S. a significant competitive advantage over terrorists. Some time ago, I said that Al Qaeda was 'eating our lunch on the

Internet.' That is no longer the case. Al Qaeda is stuck in Web 1.0. The Internet is now about interactivity and conversation."

These are strong, and puzzling, claims. Why does it matter who is eating whose lunch on the Internet? Are people who log on to their Facebook page really the best hope for us all? As for Moldova's so-called Twitter Revolution, Evgeny Morozov, a scholar at Stanford who has been the most persistent of digital evangelism's critics, points out that Twitter had scant internal significance in Moldova, a country where very few Twitter accounts exist. Nor does it seem to have been a revolution, not least because the protests—as Anne Applebaum suggested in the *Washington Post*—may well have been a bit of stagecraft cooked up by the government. (In a country paranoid about Romanian revanchism, the protesters flew a Romanian flag over the Parliament building.) In the Iranian case, meanwhile, the people tweeting about the demonstrations were almost all in the West. "It is time to get Twitter's role in the events in Iran right," Golnaz Esfandiari wrote, this past summer, in *Foreign Policy*. "Simply put: There was no Twitter Revolution inside Iran." The cadre of prominent bloggers, like Andrew Sullivan, who championed the role of social media in Iran, Esfandiari continued, misunderstood the situation. "Western journalists who couldn't reach—or didn't bother reaching?—people on the ground in Iran simply scrolled through the English-language tweets post with tag #iranelection," she wrote. "Through it all, no one seemed to wonder why people trying to coordinate protests in Iran would be writing in any language other than Farsi."

Some of this grandiosity is to be expected. Innovators tend to be solipsists. They often want to cram every stray fact and experience into their new model. As the historian Robert Darnton has written, "The marvels of communication technology in the present have produced a false consciousness about the past—even a sense that communication has no history, or had nothing of importance to consider before the days of television and the Internet." But there is something else at work here, in the outsized enthusiasm for social media. Fifty years after one of the most extraordinary episodes of social upheaval in American history, we seem to have forgotten what activism is.

10   Greensboro in the early nineteen-sixties was the kind of place where racial insubordination was routinely met with violence. The four students who first sat down at the lunch counter were terrified. "I suppose if anyone had come up behind me and yelled 'Boo,' I think I would have fallen off my seat," one of them said later. On the first day, the store manager notified the

police chief, who immediately sent two officers to the store. On the third day, a gang of white toughs showed up at the lunch counter and stood ostentatiously behind the protesters, ominously muttering epithets such as "burr-head nigger." A local Ku Klux Klan leader made an appearance. On Saturday, as tensions grew, someone called in a bomb threat, and the entire store had to be evacuated.

The dangers were even clearer in the Mississippi Freedom Summer Project of 1964, another of the sentinel campaigns of the civil-rights movement. The Student Nonviolent Coordinating Committee recruited hundreds of Northern, largely white unpaid volunteers to run Freedom Schools, register black voters, and raise civil-rights awareness in the Deep South. "No one should go *anywhere* alone, but certainly not in an automobile and certainly not at night," they were instructed. Within days of arriving in Mississippi, three volunteers—Michael Schwerner, James Chaney, and Andrew Goodman—were kidnapped and killed, and, during the rest of the summer, thirty-seven black churches were set on fire and dozens of safe houses were bombed; volunteers were beaten, shot at, arrested, and trailed by pickup trucks full of armed men. A quarter of those in the program dropped out. Activism that challenges the status quo—that attacks deeply rooted problems—is not for the faint of heart.

What makes people capable of this kind of activism? The Stanford sociologist Doug McAdam compared the Freedom Summer dropouts with the participants who stayed, and discovered that the key difference wasn't, as might be expected, ideological fervor. "*All* of the applicants—participants and withdrawals alike—emerge as highly committed, articulate supporters of the goals and values of the summer program," he concluded. What mattered more was an applicant's degree of personal connection to the civil-rights movement. All the volunteers were required to provide a list of personal contacts—the people they wanted kept apprised of their activities—and participants were far more likely than dropouts to have close friends who were also going to Mississippi. High-risk activism, McAdam concluded, is a "strong-tie" phenomenon.

This pattern shows up again and again. One study of the Red Brigades, the Italian terrorist group of the nineteen-seventies, found that seventy per cent of recruits had at least one good friend already in the organization. The same is true of the men who joined the mujahideen in Afghanistan. Even revolutionary actions that look spontaneous, like the demonstrations in East Germany that led to the fall of the Berlin Wall, are, at core, strong-tie phenomena. The opposition movement in East Germany consisted of several hundred groups, each with roughly a dozen members. Each group was in limited contact with the others: at the time, only thirteen per cent of East Germans even had a phone. All they knew was that on Monday nights, outside St. Nicholas Church in downtown Leipzig, people gathered to voice their anger at the state. And the primary determinant of who showed up was "critical friends"—the more friends you had who were critical of the regime the more likely you were to join the protest.

So one crucial fact about the four freshmen at the Greensboro lunch counter—David Richmond, Franklin McCain, Ezell Blair, and Joseph McNeil—was their relationship with one another. McNeil was a roommate of Blair's in A. & T.'s Scott Hall dormitory. Richmond roomed with McCain one floor up, and Blair, Richmond, and McCain had all gone to Dudley High School. The four would smuggle beer into the dorm and talk late into the night in Blair and McNeil's room. They would all have remembered the murder of Emmett Till in 1955, the Montgomery bus boycott that same year, and the showdown in Little Rock in 1957. It was McNeil who brought up the idea of a sit-in at Woolworth's. They'd discussed it for nearly a month. Then McNeil came into the dorm room and asked the others if they were ready. There was a pause, and McCain said, in a way that works only with people who talk late into the night with one another, "Are you guys chicken or not?" Ezell Blair worked up the courage the next day to ask for a cup of coffee because he was flanked by his roommate and two good friends from high school.

15   The kind of activism associated with social media isn't like this at all. The platforms of social media are built around weak ties. Twitter is a way of following (or being followed by) people you may never have met. Facebook is a tool for efficiently managing your acquaintances, for keeping up with the people you would not otherwise be able to stay in touch with. That's why you can have a thousand "friends" on Facebook, as you never could in real life.

This is in many ways a wonderful thing. There is strength in weak ties, as the sociologist Mark Granovetter has observed. Our acquaintances—not our friends—are our greatest source of new ideas and information. The Internet lets us exploit the power of these kinds of distant connections with marvelous efficiency. It's terrific at the diffusion of innovation, interdisciplinary collaboration, seamlessly matching up buyers and sellers, and the logistical functions of the dating world. But weak ties seldom lead to high-risk activism.

In a new book called *The Dragonfly Effect: Quick, Effective, and Powerful Ways to Use Social Media to Drive Social Change*, the business consultant Andy Smith and the Stanford Business School professor Jennifer Aaker tell the story of Sameer Bhatia, a young Silicon Valley entrepreneur who came down with acute myelogenous leukemia. It's a perfect illustration of social media's strengths. Bhatia needed a bone-marrow transplant, but he could not find a match among his relatives and friends. The odds were best with a donor of his ethnicity, and there were few South Asians in the national bone-marrow database. So Bhatia's business partner sent out an e-mail explaining Bhatia's plight to more than four hundred of their acquaintances, who forwarded the e-mail to their personal contacts; Facebook pages and YouTube videos were devoted to the Help Sameer campaign. Eventually, nearly twenty-five thousand new people were registered in the bone-marrow database, and Bhatia found a match.

But how did the campaign get so many people to sign up? By not asking too much of them. That's the only way you can get someone you don't really know to do something on your behalf. You can get thousands of people to sign up for a donor registry, because doing so is pretty easy. You have to send in a cheek swab and—in the highly unlikely event that your bone marrow is a good match for someone in need—spend a few hours at the hospital. Donating bone marrow isn't a trivial matter. But it doesn't involve financial or personal risk; it doesn't mean spending a summer being chased by armed men in pickup trucks. It doesn't require that you confront socially entrenched norms and practices. In fact, it's the kind of commitment that will bring only social acknowledgment and praise.

The evangelists of social media don't understand this distinction; they seem to believe that a Facebook friend is the same as a real friend and that signing up for a donor registry in Silicon Valley today is activism in the same sense as sitting at a segregated lunch counter in Greensboro in 1960. "Social networks are particularly effective at increasing motivation," Aaker and Smith write. But that's not true. Social networks are effective at increasing *participation*—by lessening the level of motivation that participation requires. The Facebook page of the Save Darfur Coalition has 1,282,339 members, who have donated an average of nine cents apiece. The next biggest Darfur charity on Facebook has 22,073 members, who have donated an average of thirty-five cents. Help Save Darfur has 2,797 members, who have given, on average, fifteen cents. A spokesperson for the Save Darfur Coalition told *Newsweek,* "We wouldn't necessarily gauge someone's value to the advocacy movement based on what they've given. This is a powerful mechanism to engage this critical population. They inform their community, attend events, volunteer. It's not something you can measure by looking at a ledger." In other words, Facebook activism succeeds not by motivating people to make a real sacrifice but by motivating them to do the things that people do when they are not motivated enough to make a real sacrifice. We are a long way from the lunch counters of Greensboro.

20   The students who joined the sit-ins across the South during the winter of 1960 described the movement as a "fever." But the civil-rights movement was more like a military campaign than like a contagion. In the late nineteen-fifties, there had been sixteen sit-ins in various cities throughout the South, fifteen of which were formally organized by civil-rights organizations like the N.A.A.C.P. and CORE. Possible locations for activism were scouted. Plans were drawn up. Movement activists held training sessions and retreats for would-be protesters. The Greensboro Four were a product of this groundwork: all were members of the N.A.A.C.P. Youth Council. They had close ties with the head of the local N.A.A.C.P. chapter. They had been briefed on the earlier wave of sit-ins in Durham, and had been part of a series of movement meetings in activist churches. When the sit-in movement spread from Greensboro throughout the South, it did not spread indiscriminately. It spread to those cities which had preëxisting "movement centers"—a core of dedicated and trained activists ready to turn the "fever" into action.

The civil-rights movement was high-risk activism. It was also, crucially, strategic activism: a challenge to the establishment mounted with precision and discipline. The N.A.A.C.P. was a centralized organization, run from New York according to highly formalized operating procedures. At the Southern Christian Leadership Conference, Martin Luther King, Jr., was the unquestioned authority. At the center of the movement was the black church, which had, as Aldon D. Morris points out in his superb 1984 study, "The Origins of the Civil Rights Movement," a carefully demarcated division of labor, with various standing committees and disciplined groups. "Each group was task-oriented and coordinated its activities through authority structures," Morris writes. "Individuals were held accountable for their assigned duties, and important conflicts were resolved by the minister, who usually exercised ultimate authority over the congregation."

This is the second crucial distinction between traditional activism and its online variant: social media are not about this kind of hierarchical organization. Facebook and the like are tools for building *networks*, which are the opposite, in structure and character, of hierarchies. Unlike hierarchies, with their rules and procedures, networks aren't controlled by a single central authority. Decisions are made through consensus, and the ties that bind people to the group are loose.

This structure makes networks enormously resilient and adaptable in low-risk situations. Wikipedia is a perfect example. It doesn't have an editor, sitting in New York, who directs and corrects each entry. The effort of putting together each entry is self-organized. If every entry in Wikipedia were to be erased tomorrow, the content would swiftly be restored, because that's what happens when a network of thousands spontaneously devote their time to a task.

There are many things, though, that networks don't do well. Car companies sensibly use a network to organize their hundreds of suppliers, but not to design their cars. No one believes that the articulation of a coherent design philosophy is best handled by a sprawling, leaderless organizational system. Because networks don't have a centralized leadership structure and clear lines of authority, they have real difficulty reaching consensus and setting goals. They can't think strategically; they are chronically prone to conflict and error. How do you make difficult choices about tactics or strategy or philosophical direction when everyone has an equal say?

The Palestine Liberation Organization originated as a network, and   25 the international-relations scholars Mette Eilstrup-Sangiovanni and Calvert Jones argue in a recent essay in *International Security* that this is why it ran into such trouble as it grew: "Structural features typical of networks—the absence of central authority, the unchecked autonomy of rival groups, and the inability to arbitrate quarrels through formal mechanisms—made the P.L.O. excessively vulnerable to outside manipulation and internal strife."

In Germany in the nineteen-seventies, they go on, "the far more unified and successful left-wing terrorists tended to organize hierarchically, with professional management and clear divisions of labor. They were concentrated geographically in universities, where they could establish central leadership, trust, and camaraderie through regular, face-to-face meetings." They seldom betrayed their comrades in arms during police interrogations. Their counterparts on the right were organized as decentralized networks, and had no such discipline. These groups were regularly infiltrated, and members, once arrested, easily gave up their comrades. Similarly, Al Qaeda was most dangerous when it was a unified hierarchy. Now that it has dissipated into a network, it has proved far less effective.

The drawbacks of networks scarcely matter if the network isn't interested in systemic change—if it just wants to frighten or humiliate or make a splash—or if it doesn't need to think strategically. But if you're taking on a powerful and organized establishment you have to be a hierarchy. The Montgomery bus boycott required the participation of tens of thousands of people who depended on public transit to get to and from work each day. It lasted a *year*. In order to persuade those people to stay true to the cause, the boycott's organizers tasked each local black church with maintaining morale, and put together a free alternative private carpool service, with forty-eight dispatchers and forty-two pickup stations. Even the White Citizens Council, King later said, conceded that the carpool system moved with "military precision." By the time King came to Birmingham, for the climactic showdown with Police Commissioner Eugene (Bull) Connor, he had a budget of a million dollars, and a hundred full-time staff members on the ground, divided into operational units. The operation itself was divided into steadily escalating phases, mapped out in advance. Support was maintained through consecutive mass meetings rotating from church to church around the city.

Boycotts and sit-ins and nonviolent confrontations—which were the weapons of choice for the civil-rights movement—are high-risk strategies. They leave little room for conflict and error. The moment even one protester deviates from the script and responds to provocation, the moral legitimacy of the entire protest is compromised. Enthusiasts for social media would no doubt have us believe that King's task in Birmingham would have been made infinitely easier had he been able to communicate with his followers through Facebook, and contented himself with tweets from a Birmingham jail. But networks are messy: think of the ceaseless pattern of correction and revision, amendment and debate, that characterizes Wikipedia. If Martin Luther King, Jr., had tried to do a wiki-boycott in Montgomery, he would have been steamrollered by the white power structure. And of what use would a digital communication tool be in a town where ninety-eight per cent of the black community could be reached every Sunday morning at church? The things that King needed in Birmingham—discipline and strategy—were things that online social media cannot provide.

The bible of the social-media movement is Clay Shirky's *Here Comes Everybody*. Shirky, who teaches at New York University, sets out to demonstrate the organizing power of the Internet, and he begins with the story of Evan, who worked on Wall Street, and his friend Ivanna, after she left her smart phone, an expensive Sidekick, on the back seat of a New York City taxicab. The telephone company transferred the data on Ivanna's lost phone to a new phone, whereupon she and Evan discovered that the Sidekick was now in the hands of a teenager from Queens, who was using it to take photographs of herself and her friends.

When Evan e-mailed the teen-ager, Sasha, asking for the phone back, 30 she replied that his "white ass" didn't deserve to have it back. Miffed, he set up a Web page with her picture and a description of what had happened. He forwarded the link to his friends, and they forwarded it to their friends. Someone found the MySpace page of Sasha's boyfriend, and a link to it found its way onto the site. Someone found her address online and took a video of her home while driving by; Evan posted the video on the site. The story was picked up by the news filter Digg. Evan was now up to ten e-mails a minute. He created a bulletin board for his readers to share their stories, but it crashed under the weight of responses. Evan and Ivanna went to the police, but the police filed the report under "lost," rather than "stolen," which essentially closed the case. "By this point millions of readers were watching," Shirky writes, "and dozens of mainstream news outlets had covered the story." Bowing to the pressure, the N.Y.P.D. reclassified the item as "stolen." Sasha was arrested, and Evan got his friend's Sidekick back.

Shirky's argument is that this is the kind of thing that could never have happened in the pre-Internet age—and he's right. Evan could never have tracked down Sasha. The story of the Sidekick would never have been publicized. An army of people could never have been assembled to wage this fight. The police wouldn't have bowed to the pressure of a lone person who had misplaced something as trivial as a cell phone. The story, to Shirky, illustrates "the ease and speed with which a group can be mobilized for the right kind of cause" in the Internet age.

Shirky considers this model of activism an upgrade. But it is simply a form of organizing which favors the weak-tie connections that give us access to information over the strong-tie connections that help us persevere in the face of danger. It shifts our energies from organizations that promote strategic and disciplined activity and toward those which promote resilience and adaptability. It makes it easier for activists to express themselves, and harder for that expression to have any impact. The instruments of social media are well suited to making the existing social order more efficient. They are not a natural enemy of the status quo. If you are of the opinion that all the world needs is a little buffing around the edges, this should not trouble you. But if you think that there are still lunch counters out there that need integrating it ought to give you pause.

Shirky ends the story of the lost Sidekick by asking, portentously, "What happens next?"—no doubt imagining future waves of digital protesters. But he has already answered the question. What happens next is more of the same. A networked, weak-tie world is good at things like helping Wall Streeters get phones back from teen-age girls. *Viva la revolución.*

Analyze

1. Where and when did the Civil Rights sit-in described by Gladwell at the beginning of his article take place?
2. Who was Ezell Blair?
3. Who is Golnaz Esfandiari? How do his findings relate to Gladwell's argument?
4. What, according to the sociologist Doug McAdam, explained the key difference between Freedom Summer dropouts and the participants who stayed? What characteristics did the two groups share?
5. How does Gladwell define "strong ties"? How does he define "weak ties"?

Explore

1. Based on the claims presented by Gladwell and on your own experiences with using social media, hold a debate in class regarding the effectiveness of in-person organizing versus organizing via social media.
2. In a three- to five-page essay, explain the difference between hierarchical and networked organizations. Which organizations or groups discussed by Gladwell were structured hierarchically? Which were networked? Compare and contrast the characteristics of these organizational structures. Then, explain why, according to Gladwell, one organizational structure may be more effective than another in relation to social activism. Do you agree with his assessment? Why or why not?
3. Do some research on the reported "Twitter Revolution" in Iran and the use of Twitter as an organizing tool in the Occupy Wall Street

movement. How do your findings relate to Gladwell's? Write a short essay in which you describe why and how your findings support or question those of Gladwell.

Douglas Schuler
"It's Time to Work for a Better Internet"

Douglas Schuler is a faculty member at Evergreen State College, where he currently teaches courses in Community Information Systems, Global Citizenship, and Civic Intelligence in the Real World. His writing and teaching are often focused on the concept of society's civic intelligence, or the collective capability of society to address its problems. He is the co-founder of the Seattle Community Network, a free public-access computer network, and the author of *Liberating Voices: A Pattern Language for Communication Revolution* (2008). In this essay, Schuler proposes that it is time to stop taking sides with regard to the promise and perils of Internet technology and begin working together to imagine "what the Internet *could* be and to work for those *possible* outcomes."

> How might the Internet be used as a tool to help people work together to address their shared concerns regarding sociopolitical, economic, and environmental issues?

Far from the public eye, a battle is raging over abstractions. It touches our hearts and minds. And although it's a battle with consequences, it's a battle that really shouldn't be fought at all.

The battle I'm referring to is the one between the optimists and the pessimists.

On one side are the optimists. They believe that in spite of everything, things are getting better. The pessimists, as everybody knows, believe that things are inevitably getting worse.

Ironically, it's the point that both sides agree on that's the most dangerous: *that historical momentum makes human effort unnecessary*. Both views imply an inevitability that is not only inaccurate, but paralyzing. In short, they offer excuses that many people are consciously or subconsciously looking for, reasons for not getting involved.

5   But, with apologies to Shakespeare, *if neither an optimist nor a pessimist be*, who or what *should* we be? Is there a word for a better way to think about the future?

Luckily, such a word exists. The word is *meliorism*—the belief that the world can be made better by human effort. (But note that the flip side—that human effort can make the world *worse*—is also true.)

What does all of this have to do with the evolution of the Internet? Plenty.

For one thing, the Internet inspired the optimists to some of the greatest rhetorical heights of all times. The optimists convinced many people that a Golden Age was imminent. The governed would achieve parity with the governors. Knowledge would flow equally to all and education would be transformed. The *wisdom of crowds* would rule the land. And censorship was impossible because information *wants to be free*.

On the other hand, cynical utopia deniers—dour pessimists—continued to assert that things will *always* be unequal, the Internet will change nothing at all, and that the human race will never develop the civic intelligence that it needs, Internet or no Internet.

10   But little-by-little, people are breaking free of the optimism/pessimism trap. They are realizing the Internet is not magic after all. They are learning that it's not immune to the forces that created the commercial television or radio we know today.

The fact remains that the Internet represents an extremely rare opportunity. For one thing, it's a meta-medium that can assume many shapes. Because it's becoming a tool that billions of people use, it *could* help people of the world work together to address their shared concerns.

The "coulds" could be multiplied *ad infinitum*: The Internet *could* be used to help mediate discussions between adversaries; it *could* be used to develop solutions to problems of environmental degradation, oppression and intolerance, and violence. It *could* . . .

A critical question surfaces in relation to these issues: Is there a role for business in building the information and communication infrastructure that promotes the civic intelligence that the world needs? And if not, why not?

Unfortunately, the standard rules might not apply. For one thing, who is interested in building capabilities for people with few economic resources? And while the costs of despotism and anarchy are high indeed, democracy has no immediate ROI. And would venture capitalists bother with ventures that have dubious aims like developing *social* imagination or improving collective problem-solving capabilities?

Clearly, people in business can be counted on for innovation for eco-   15
nomic gain. My presumption is that they could retool themselves intellectually for *social* innovation as well.

Meliorism, unlike optimism or pessimism, doesn't allow us to wriggle out of our responsibilities. In the case of the Internet, meliorism compels us to imagine what the Internet *could* be and to work for those *possible* outcomes.

We have the imagination and the resources to build the Internet that the utopians may have envisioned and the dystopians swore we'd never see. It will take the meliorists who have gotten tired of the silly debate over optimism and pessimism to roll up their sleeves and actually make it happen.

Analyze

1. What is meliorism?
2. Explain what the optimists and pessimists respectively claim regarding the possibilities for the Internet.
3. Schuler writes, "democracy has no ROI." Explain what this means in the context of Schuler's argument.
4. What is the "major presumption" Schuler makes for meliorism to succeed?
5. List the examples of "civic intelligence" cited by Schuler in his essay.

Explore

1. Construct a brief summary of the article in which you explain what the author is doing—what his purpose is for writing—and what kinds of information or evidence he uses to achieve his goal.
2. The words "pessimism" and "optimism" are ones that just about everyone clearly understands. However, the word "meliorism," which is an important one in Schuler's argument, is not as familiar. Free write

about this word "meliorism." How does Schuler define it? What does it mean to you? What are some synonyms for "meliorism" that Schuler could use in place of that word and that might be more effective in persuading his audience why "meliorism," as opposed to "pessimism" or "optimism," is a stance that should be adopted in relation to the Internet?

3. Do a search for "Douglas Schuler" in a library database or on Google Scholar. Locate and read one of his articles on the subject of community networks. Based on your reading of that article and this one, write an article for your student newspaper about how information and communications technologies could be used to build community networks at your college, in your community, or in your city.

Forging Connections

1. At the end of the introduction to his book *Who Owns the Future?*, Jaron Lanier writes, "The story of our times is that humanity is deciding how to be as our technological abilities increase. When will we grow proud enough to be a match for our own inventions?" You have read a number of essays in this chapter that raise concerns over whether current technological developments are adequately taking into consideration concerns for human welfare. Two authors in particular, John Naughton and Jaron Lanier, raise the question of whether today's technological innovations may be exacting a very high cost in terms of what is socially and economically in the best interest of humans. Write an article for your school newspaper in which you incorporate evidence from both Lanier's and Naughton's essays to explain the current and future costs of technological innovation and why your fellow students should be concerned about both.

2. Although Douglas Schuler is optimistic about the potential for Internet technologies to be used in the interest of community and political organization, Malcolm Gladwell seems to take the opposite position in his essay. Write a letter to Schuler explaining the issues Gladwell describes in his essay that make Internet technologies and social media a poor choice for social organizing. Then, write a letter to Gladwell in which you explain why Schuler would characterize the position Gladwell takes as one reflective of "Internet pessimism" and the reasons why it may be important and worthwhile for him to adopt a

stance informed more by "Internet meliorism." Afterward, read over what you have written and write a one page cover letter to your instructor discussing and synthesizing what you have learned as a result of writing these letters.

Looking Further

1. Civic intelligence is defined by Douglas Schuler as "the ability of humankind to use information and communication in order to engage in collective problem solving" (2001). Design an Internet-based project or application focused on increasing civic intelligence either on your campus or in your community. Write a proposal describing this project, its purpose, its characteristics, and its proposed outcomes.

2. Several authors in this chapter make explicit or implicit references to *Wikipedia*, which is considered by some to be one of the most successful crowd-sourced projects on the Internet. However, both Malcolm Gladwell and Jaron Lanier are, for their own unique reasons, both critical of crowd-sourced projects like *Wikipedia*. Their opinions stand in marked contrast to those in William Cronon's essay "Scholarly Authority in a Wikified World" (Chapter 4). Write a blog post for your fellow classmates in which you lay out the arguments of the three authors and explain why—or why not—it may be possible to synthesize their three unique perspectives regarding crowd-sourced projects.

3. In his essay, Douglas Naughton focuses his attention on digital capitalism, which is increasingly a global enterprise. But how does digital capitalism affect local business practices? Every time each one of us purchases something from an online merchant, we are not buying something from a local business. This has financial consequences for the local community with respect to tax revenues, rents, and wages. Many people, given the choice, would always buy from a local merchant. However, Amazon and other online merchants make it very easy to purchase things online. Furthermore, part of what makes the online shopping experience so convenient is that all of the activities related to actually getting the purchase home are invisible to the online shopper. But what actually happens when you press that "Buy it Now" button? Develop a "visual map" depicting the logistics and individuals involved in buying a book from Amazon. This project involves a lot of research, so it may be best to work in groups to pool your resources.

Once you have constructed your map for an Amazon purchase, create another "visual map" of the logistics and individuals involved in buying a book from a local bookstore. Compare and contrast these two maps from the perspective of how much revenue is generated for your local community based on a purchase from Amazon versus a purchase made at a local bookstore. After you have completed your group work for this project, write two pages reflecting on what you have learned from the project and how it may or may not have changed the number of online purchases you make.

Can Humans Live Forever?
Healthcare, Technology, and the Environment

When it comes to medicine and healthcare, it is difficult to think of a type or sector of technology that is not in some way either directly or indirectly involved in both. Whether it is transportation technologies used to convey patients to healthcare facilities, pharmaceutical technologies to treat diseases, medical devices and tools used by surgeons, x-ray and photographic technologies used in imaging, or electrical systems to power hospitals and the various technologies contained in them, it is fairly easy to envision the many relationships connecting technology with medicine and healthcare. Furthermore, the fact that various technologies have been part of medicine and healthcare for some time does not mean that technological development is slowing down. On the contrary, such development is ongoing.

Nowadays, when we talk about pressing issues of medicine or healthcare, we often have in mind some specific technology or scientific advancement that may greatly enhance or prolong life. But consider this thought experiment: Say that advances in nanotechnology and biotechnology lead to a kind of virtual immortality, or to the ability to genetically design offspring. What ethical and regulatory issues might arise as the result of such technologies? What are the effects on today's healthcare system of a focus on the latest medical technologies, when, in fact, these may be used by only a small portion of the population?

Balancing current realities with future possibilities, the authors in this chapter all remind us of how changes and practices in healthcare and medicine may relate as much to sociocultural practices and beliefs as to the technological tools available at any given time. The political scientist Francis Fukuyama writes about potential applications of biotechnology in relation to controlling or altering elements of what it means to be human—how we think and behave, how we age, how we reproduce—and asks whether such broad-reaching technologies necessitate government regulation on an international level. Daniel Callahan and Sherwin B. Nuland review the dominant beliefs and metaphors guiding healthcare and the treatment of disease in the United States in the late twentieth and early twenty-first century and ask whether it may be time to reassess the benefits of these investments, which may very well extend but not improve the lives of those being treated. Cardiologist Eric Topol takes a very optimistic view of the potential for technology to transform healthcare and explains how the convergence of various technologies may accelerate this process, while Atul Gawande considers just how slowly technological changes may happen in the fields of medicine and healthcare, as well as the conditions required for the adoption of even those not-so-high-tech solutions that can save millions of lives. Finally, Francisco Seijo in his essay "When Worlds Collide" reflects on the current state of climate change and the complexity of using technologies to expand the capacities of an ever more populous planet and thereby sustain the life-spans of its residents.

Francis Fukuyama
"Our Posthuman Future"

Francis Fukuyama is a political scientist and social philosopher who is currently the Olivier Nomellini Senior Fellow at the Freeman Spogli Institute for International Studies at Stanford University. He has written widely on technology, democratization, and international political economy and is the author of several books, including *The End of History and the Last Man* (1992) and *The Origins of Political Order: From Prehuman Times to the French Revolution* (2012). In the following excerpt from his 2002 book *Our Posthuman Future: Consequences of the Biotechnology Revolution*, Fukuyama considers the potential impact of biotechnologies on human nature and liberal democracy and why regulation of such technologies may be both possible and necessary.

Should technologies related to biology and healthcare be more highly regulated than developments in other technological sectors? Why or why not?

I was born in 1952, right in the middle of the American baby boom. For any person growing up as I did in the middle decades of the twentieth century, the future and its terrifying possibilities were defined by two books, George Orwell's *1984* (first published in 1949) and Aldous Huxley's *Brave New World* (published in 1932).

The two books were far more prescient than anyone realized at the time, because they were centered on two different technologies that would in fact emerge and define the world over the next two generations. The novel *1984* was about what we now call information technology: central to the success of the vast, totalitarian empire that had been set up over Oceania was a device called the telescreen, a wall-sized flat-panel display that could simultaneously send and receive images from each individual household to a hovering Big Brother. The telescreen was what permitted the vast centralization of social life under the Ministry of Truth and the Ministry of Love, for it allowed the government to banish privacy by monitoring every word and deed over a massive network of wires.

Brave New World, by contrast, was about the other big technological revolution about to take place, that of biotechnology. Bokanovskification, the hatching of people not in wombs but, as we now say, in vitro; the drug soma, which gave people instant happiness; the Feelies, in which sensation was simulated by implanted electrodes; and the modification of behavior through constant subliminal repetition and, when that didn't work, through the administration of various artificial hormones were what gave this book its particularly creepy ambiance.

"Medical technology offers us in many cases a devil's bargain."

With at least a half century separating us from the publication of these books, we can see that while the technological predictions they made were startlingly accurate, the political predictions of the first book, *1984*, were entirely wrong. The year 1984 came and went, with the United States still locked in a Cold War struggle with the Soviet Union. That year saw the introduction of a new model of the IBM personal computer and the beginning of what became the PC revolution. As Peter Huber has argued, the personal computer, linked to the Internet, was in fact the realization of Orwell's telescreen. But instead of becoming an instrument of centralization and tyranny, it led to just the opposite: the democratization of access to information and the decentralization of politics. Instead of Big Brother watching everyone, people could use the PC and Internet to watch Big Brother, as governments everywhere were driven to publish more information on their own activities.

5   Just five years after 1984, in a series of dramatic events that would earlier have seemed like political science fiction, the Soviet Union and its empire collapsed, and the totalitarian threat that Orwell had so vividly evoked vanished. People were again quick to point out that these two events—the collapse of totalitarian empires and the emergence of the personal computer, as well as other forms of inexpensive information technology, from TVs and radios to faxes and e-mail—were not unrelated. Totalitarian rule depended on a regime's ability to maintain a monopoly over information, and once modern information technology made that impossible, the regime's power was undermined.

The political prescience of the other great dystopia, *Brave New World*, remains to be seen. Many of the technologies that Huxley envisioned, like in vitro fertilization, surrogate motherhood, psychotropic drugs, and genetic engineering for the manufacture of children, are already here or just over the horizon. But this revolution has only just begun; the daily avalanche of announcements of new breakthroughs in biomedical technology and achievements such as the completion of the Human Genome Project in the year 2000 portend much more serious changes to come.

Of the nightmares evoked by these two books, *Brave New World*'s always struck me as more subtle and more challenging. It is easy to see what's wrong with the world of *1984*: the protagonist, Winston Smith, is known to hate rats above all things, so Big Brother devises a cage in which rats can bite at Smith's face in order to get him to betray his lover. This is the world of classical tyranny, technologically empowered but not so different from what we have tragically seen and known in human history.

In *Brave New World*, by contrast, the evil is not so obvious because no one is hurt; indeed, this is a world in which everyone gets what they want. As one of the characters notes, "The Controllers realized that force was no good," and that people would have to be seduced rather than compelled to live in an orderly society. In this world, disease and social conflict have been abolished, there is no depression, madness, loneliness, or emotional distress, sex is good and readily available. There is even a government ministry to ensure that the length of time between the appearance of a desire and its satisfaction is kept to a minimum. No one takes religion seriously any longer, no one is introspective or has unrequited longings, the biological family has been abolished, no one reads Shakespeare. But no one (save John the Savage, the book's protagonist) misses these things, either, since they are happy and healthy.

Since the novel's publication, there have probably been several million high school essays written in answer to the question, "What's wrong with this picture?" The answer given (on papers that get A's, at any rate) usually runs something like this: the people in *Brave New World* may be healthy and happy, but they have ceased to be human beings. They no longer struggle, aspire, love, feel pain, make difficult moral choices, have families, or do any of the things that we traditionally associate with being human. They no longer have the characteristics that give us human dignity. Indeed, there is no such thing as the human race any longer, since they have been bred by the Controllers into separate castes of Alphas, Betas, Epsilons, and Gammas who are as distant from each other as humans are from animals. Their world has become unnatural in the most profound sense imaginable, because human nature has been altered. In the words of bioethicist Leon Kass, "Unlike the man reduced by disease or slavery, the people dehumanized à la

Brave New World are not miserable, don't know that they are dehumanized, and, what is worse, would not care if they knew. They are, indeed, happy slaves with a slavish happiness."

10   But while this kind of answer is usually adequate to satisfy the typical high school English teacher, it does not (as Kass goes on to note) probe nearly deeply enough. For one can go on to ask, What is so important about being a human being in the traditional way that Huxley defines it? After all, what the human race is today is the product of an evolutionary process that has been going on for millions of years, one that with any luck will continue well into the future. There are no fixed human characteristics, except for a general capability to choose what we want to be, to modify ourselves in accordance with our desires. So who is to tell us that being human and having dignity means sticking with a set of emotional responses that are the accidental byproduct of our evolutionary history? There is no such thing as a biological family, no such thing as human nature or a "normal" human being, and even if there were, why should that be a guide for what is right and just? Huxley is telling us, in effect, that we should continue to feel pain, be depressed or lonely, or suffer from debilitating disease, all because that is what human beings have done for most of their existence as a species. Certainly, no one ever got elected to Congress on such a platform. Instead of taking these characteristics and saying that they are the basis for "human dignity," why don't we simply accept our destiny as creatures who modify themselves?

Huxley suggests that one source for a definition of what it means to be a human being is religion. In *Brave New World*, religion has been abolished and Christianity is a distant memory. The Christian tradition maintains that man is created in God's image, which is the source of human dignity. To use biotechnology to engage in what another Christian writer, C. S. Lewis, called the "abolition of man" is thus a violation of God's will. But I don't think that a careful reading of Huxley or Lewis leads to the conclusion that either writer believed religion to be the only grounds on which one could understand the meaning of being human. Both writers suggest that nature itself, and in particular human nature, has a special role in defining for us what is right and wrong, just and unjust, important and unimportant. So our final judgment on "what's wrong" with Huxley's brave new world stands or falls with our view of how important human nature is as a source of values.

The aim of this book is to argue that Huxley was right, that the most significant threat posed by contemporary biotechnology is the possibility that it will alter human nature and thereby move us into a "posthuman" stage of history. This is important, I will argue, because human nature exists, is a meaningful concept, and has provided a stable continuity to our experience as a species. It is, conjointly with religion, what defines our most basic values. Human nature shapes and constrains the possible kinds of political regimes, so a technology powerful enough to reshape what we are will have possibly malign consequences for liberal democracy and the nature of politics itself.

It may be that, as in the case of *1984*, we will eventually find biotechnology's consequences are completely and surprisingly benign, and that we were wrong to lose sleep over it. It may be that the technology will in the end prove much less powerful than it seems today, or that people will be moderate and careful in their application of it. But one of the reasons I am not quite so sanguine is that biotechnology, in contrast to many other scientific advances, mixes obvious benefits with subtle harms in one seamless package.

Nuclear weapons and nuclear energy were perceived as dangerous from the start, and therefore were subject to strict regulation from the moment the Manhattan Project created the first atomic bomb in 1945. Observers like Bill Joy have worried about nanotechnology—that is, molecular-scale self-replicating machines capable of reproducing out of control and destroying their creators. But such threats are actually the easiest to deal with because they are so obvious. If you are likely to be killed by a machine you've created, you take measures to protect yourself. And so far we've had a reasonable record in keeping our machines under control.

There may be products of biotechnology that will be similarly obvious in   15 the dangers they pose to mankind—for example, superbugs, new viruses, or genetically modified foods that produce toxic reactions. Like nuclear weapons or nanotechnology, these are in a way the easiest to deal with because once we have identified them as dangerous, we can treat them as a straightforward threat. The more typical threats raised by biotechnology are those captured so well by Huxley, and are summed up in the title of an article by novelist Tom Wolfe, "Sorry, but Your Soul Just Died." Medical technology offers us in many cases a devil's bargain: longer life, but with reduced mental capacity; freedom from depression, together with freedom from creativity or spirit; therapies that blur the line between what we achieve on our own and what we achieve because of the levels of various chemicals in our brains.

Consider the following three scenarios, all of which are distinct possibilities that may unfold over the next generation or two.

The first has to do with new drugs. As a result of advances in neuropharmacology, psychologists discover that human personality is much more plastic than formerly believed. It is already the case that psychotropic drugs such as Prozac and Ritalin can affect traits like self-esteem and the ability to concentrate, but they tend to produce a host of unwanted side effects and hence are shunned except in cases of clear therapeutic need. But in the future, knowledge of genomics permits pharmaceutical companies to tailor drugs very specifically to the genetic profiles of individual patients and greatly minimize unintended side effects. Stolid people can become vivacious; introspective ones extroverted; you can adopt one personality on Wednesday and another for the weekend. There is no longer any excuse for anyone to be depressed or unhappy; even "normally" happy people can make themselves happier without worries of addiction, hangovers, or long-term brain damage.

In the second scenario, advances in stem cell research allow scientists to regenerate virtually any tissue in the body, such that life expectancies are pushed well above 100 years. If you need a new heart or liver, you just grow one inside the chest cavity of a pig or cow; brain damage from Alzheimer's and stroke can be reversed. The only problem is that there are many subtle and some not-so-subtle aspects of human aging that the biotech industry hasn't quite figured out how to fix: people grow mentally rigid and increasingly fixed in their views as they age, and try as they might, they can't make themselves sexually attractive to each other and continue to long for partners of reproductive age. Worst of all, they just refuse to get out of the way, not just of their children, but their grandchildren, and great-grandchildren. On the other hand, so few people have children or any connection with traditional reproduction that it scarcely seems to matter.

In a third scenario, the wealthy routinely screen embryos before implantation so as to optimize the kind of children they have. You can increasingly tell the social background of a young person by his or her looks and intelligence; if someone doesn't live up to social expectations, he tends to blame bad genetic choices by his parents rather than himself. Human genes have been transferred to animals and even to plants, for research purposes and to produce new medical products; and animal genes have been added to certain embryos to increase their physical endurance or resistance to disease. Scientists have not dared to produce a full-scale chimera, half human and half ape, though they could; but young people begin to suspect that classmates who do much less well than they do are in fact genetically not fully human. Because, in fact, they aren't.

Sorry, but your soul just died . . .   20

Toward the very end of his life, Thomas Jefferson wrote, "The general spread of the light of science has already laid open to every view the palpable truth, that the mass of mankind has not been born with saddles on their backs, nor a favored few booted and spurred, ready to ride them legitimately, by the grace of God." The political equality enshrined in the Declaration of Independence rests on the empirical fact of natural human equality. We vary greatly as individuals and by culture, but we share a common humanity that allows every human being to potentially communicate with and enter into a moral relationship with every other human being on the planet. The ultimate question raised by biotechnology is, What will happen to political rights once we are able to, in effect, breed some people with saddles on their backs, and others with boots and spurs?

A Straightforward Solution

What should we do in response to biotechnology that in the future will mix great potential benefits with threats that are either physical and obvious or spiritual and subtle? The answer is obvious: We should use the power of the state to regulate it. And if this proves to be beyond the power of any individual nation-state to regulate, it needs to be regulated on an international basis. We need to start thinking concretely now about how to build institutions that can discriminate between good and bad uses of biotechnology, and effectively enforce these rules both nationally and internationally.

This obvious answer is not obvious to many of the participants in the current biotechnology debate. The discussion remains mired at a relatively abstract level about the ethics of procedures like cloning or stem cell research, and divided into one camp that would like to permit everything, and another camp that would like to ban wide areas of research and practice. The broader debate is of course an important one, but events are moving so rapidly that we will soon need more practical guidance on how we can direct future developments so that the technology remains man's servant rather than his master. Since it seems very unlikely that we will either permit everything or ban research that is highly promising, we need to find a middle ground.

The creation of new regulatory institutions is not something that should be undertaken lightly, given the inefficiencies that surround all efforts at regulation. For the past three decades, there has been a commendable worldwide movement to deregulate large sectors of every nation's economy, from airlines to telecommunications, and more broadly to reduce the size and scope of government. The global economy that has emerged as a result is a far more efficient generator of wealth and technological innovation. Excessive regulation in the past, however, led many to become instinctively hostile to state intervention in any form, and it is this knee-jerk aversion to regulation that will be one of the chief obstacles to getting human biotechnology under political control.

25   But it is important to discriminate: what works for one sector of the economy will not work for another. Information technology, for example, produces many social benefits and relatively few harms and therefore has appropriately gotten by with a fairly minimal degree of government regulation. Nuclear materials and toxic waste, on the other hand, are subject to strict national and international controls because unregulated trade in them would clearly be dangerous.

One of the biggest problems in making the case for regulating human biotechnology is the common view that even if it were desirable to stop technological advance, it is impossible to do so. If the United States or any other single country tries to ban human cloning or germline genetic engineering or any other procedure, people who wanted to do these things would simply move to a more favorable jurisdiction where they were permitted. Globalization and international competition in biomedical research ensure that countries that hobble themselves by putting ethical constraints on their scientific communities or biotechnology industries will be punished.

The idea that it is impossible to stop or control the advance of technology is simply wrong. We in fact control all sorts of technologies and many types of scientific research: people are no more free to experiment in the development of new biological warfare agents than they are to experiment on human subjects without the latter's informed consent. The fact that there are some individuals or organizations that violate these rules, or that there are countries where the rules are either nonexistent or poorly enforced, is no excuse for not making the rules in the first place. People get away with robbery and murder, after all, which is not a reason to legalize theft and homicide.

We need at all costs to avoid a defeatist attitude with regard to technology that says that since we can't do anything to stop or shape developments we don't like, we shouldn't bother trying in the first place. Putting in place a regulatory system that would permit societies to control human biotechnology will not be easy: it will require legislators in countries around the world to step up to the plate and make difficult decisions on complex scientific issues. The shape and form of the institutions designed to implement new rules is a wide-open question; designing them to be minimally obstructive of positive developments while giving them effective enforcement capabilities is a significant challenge. Even more challenging will be the creation of common rules at an international level, the forging of a consensus among countries with different cultures and views on the underlying ethical questions. But political tasks of comparable complexity have been successfully undertaken in the past.

Analyze

1. Explain the reasons why Fukuyama begins and frames his essay with the two novels *1984* and *Brave New World*.
2. Why does Fukuyama consider biotechnology unique from other powerful and potentially hazardous or destructive technologies?
3. List and briefly summarize the three scenarios that Fukuyama believes may unfold as a result of new biotechnologies.
4. Why does Fukuyama differentiate between biotechnology and other sectors of the economy with regard to government regulation?

Explore

1. The opening paragraph of Fukuyama's essay presents an interesting model for writers to follow in thinking about their own relationships to technologies and their socio-cultural implications. Using Fukuyama's essay as a template, rewrite his first paragraph from your own perspective: "I was born in _____, right in the middle of _____. For any person growing up when I did and in the

_____ decades of the _____ century, the future and its _____ possibilities were defined by _____, _____, and _____." Write a short essay in which you reflect on this introductory paragraph and explain how your generational perspective and the technologies and/or books about technologies you grew up with relate to contemporary social issues and your understanding of the future.

2. Explain how the term "posthuman" is defined by Fukuyama. Then, do some research on the history and current usage of the term. Where does this term come from? How widespread has it become? What are some of the ways in which the term is defined? What similarities and differences exist among Fukuyama's definition and those of other writers?

3. Summarize the three scenarios Fukuyama writes about related to the potential hazards of biotechnologies. Then, perform a Web search on each of the three search terms: neuropharmacology, stem cell research, and reprogenetics. Review the search results from each and read and summarize one article from each search. Write a three- to five-page essay explaining how researching the current state of biotechnology has or has not changed your understanding of Fukuyama's essay.

Daniel Callahan and Sherwin B. Nuland
"The Quagmire: How American Medicine Is Destroying Itself"

Daniel Callahan is a philosopher in the field of biomedical ethics. He is President Emeritus of the Hastings Center, where his research covers end-of-life issues, ethics, and health policy. Callahan has written over forty books, including most recently *Taming the Beloved Beast: Why Medical Technology Costs Are Destroying Our Health Care System* (2009). **Sherwin B. Nuland** (1930–2014) was a surgeon, writer, and educator. He taught bioethics, the history of medicine, and medicine at Yale University and was also a fellow at the Hastings Center. Nuland's articles on medicine and healthcare have been published in *The New York Times*, *The New Republic*, and *Time*. He is also the author of several books, including *How We Die: Reflections on Life's Final Chapter* (1994) and *The Soul of Medicine* (2009). In this essay, originally published in *The New Republic*, Callahan and Nuland reflect on the state and the culture of healthcare in the United States in the twenty-first century.

In what ways could the healthcare system in the United States be improved?

In 1959, the great biologist René Dubos wrote a book called *Mirage of Health*, in which he pointed out that "complete and lasting freedom from disease is but a dream remembered from imaginings of a Garden of Eden." But, in the intervening decades, his admonition has largely been ignored by both doctors and society as a whole. For nearly a century, but especially since the end of World War II, the medical profession has been waging an unrelenting war against disease—most notably cancer, heart disease, and stroke. The ongoing campaign has led to a steady and rarely questioned increase in the disease-research budget of the National Institutes of Health (NIH). It has also led to a sea change in the way Americans think about medicine in their own lives: We now view all diseases as things to be conquered. Underlying these changes have been several assumptions: that medical advances are essentially unlimited; that none of the major lethal diseases is in theory incurable; and that progress is economically affordable if well managed.

But what if all this turns out not to be true? What if there are no imminent, much less foreseeable cures to some of the most common and most lethal diseases? What if, in individual cases, not all diseases should be fought? What if we are refusing to confront the painful likelihood that our biological nature is not nearly as resilient or open to endless improvement as we have long believed?

Let us begin by pointing to some unpleasant realities, starting with infectious disease. Forty years ago, it was commonly assumed that infectious disease had all but been conquered, with the eradication of smallpox taken as the great example of that victory. That assumption has been proved false—by the advent, for example, of HIV as well as a dangerous increase in antibiotic-resistant microbes. Based on what we now know of viral disease and microbial genetics, it is reasonable to assume that infectious disease will never be eliminated but only, at best, become less prevalent.

Then there are chronic diseases, now the scourge of industrialized nations. If the hope for eradication of infectious disease was misplaced, the hopes surrounding cures for chronic diseases are no less intoxicated. Think of the "war on cancer," declared by Richard Nixon in 1971. Mortality rates for the great majority of cancers have fallen slowly over the decades, but we remain far from a cure. No one of any scientific stature even predicts a cure for heart disease or stroke. As for Alzheimer's, not long before President Obama recently approved a fresh effort to find better treatments, a special panel of the NIH determined that essentially little progress has been made in recent years toward finding ways to delay the onset of major symptoms. And no one talks seriously of a near-term cure.

5   One of the hardiest hopes in the chronic-disease wars has been that of a compression of morbidity—a long life with little illness followed by a brief period of disability and then a quick death. A concept first introduced by James Fries in 1980, it has had the special attraction of providing a persuasively utopian view of the future of medicine. And it has always been possible to identify very old people who seemed to have the good fortune of living such a life—a kind of end run on medicine—and then dying quickly. But a recent and very careful study by Eileen Crimmins and Hiram Beltran-Sanchez of the University of Southern California has determined that the idea has no empirical support. Most of us will contract one or more chronic diseases later in life and die from them, slowly. "Health," Crimmins and Beltran-Sanchez write, "may not be improving with each generation" and "compression of morbidity may be as illusory as immortality. We do not appear to be moving to a world where we die without experiencing disease, functioning loss, and disability."

Average life expectancy, moreover, steadily increasing for many decades, now shows signs of leveling off. S. Jay Olshansky, a leading figure in longevity studies, has for some years expressed skepticism about the prospect of an indefinite increase in life expectancy. He calls his position a "realist" one, particularly in contending that it will be difficult to get the average beyond 85. He also writes that it is "biased" to assume that "only positive influences on health and longevity will persist and accelerate." That view, he notes, encompasses a belief that science will surely keep moving on a forward track—a projection that is not necessarily true. Simply look at the "breakthroughs" that have been predicted for such scientific sure things as stem-cell technology and medical genetics—but have yet to be realized. These breakthroughs may eventually happen, but they are chancy bets. We have arrived at a moment, in short, where we are making little headway in defeating various kinds of diseases. Instead, our main achievements today consist of devising ways to marginally extend the lives of the very sick.

There are many ways of responding to this generally pessimistic reading of medical innovation in recent years. The most common is simply to note all the progress that has been made: useful new drugs, helpful new devices and technologies, decreased disability, better ways of controlling pain, and so on. And it is certainly true that some aspects of medicine have made enormous strides over the past few decades. Some of these strides, in fact, have taken place in the very areas—such as cardiac and infectious diseases (for instance, treatment of HIV)—in which so much of the outlook remains otherwise unpromising. One of us was the beneficiary of a life-saving heart operation at age 78, of a kind that did not exist a decade ago (and both of us celebrated our eightieth birthdays this past year). Americans do live longer, by eight to nine years since 1960; a great range of treatments are available for our illnesses, mild or severe; our pain is better relieved; and our prospects for living from youth to old age have never been greater.

It might also be said that there is no reason to believe that cures for infectious and chronic diseases cannot eventually be found; it is just taking longer than expected and the necessary knowledge for breakthroughs seems to be slowly accumulating. Or it might be said that more people living longer, though sick, is a not inconsiderable triumph.

These advances, however, should be balanced against another factor: the insupportable, unsustainable economic cost of this sort of success. Twenty years from now, the maturation of the baby boom generation will be at flood tide. We will have gone from 40 million Americans over the age of 65 in 2009 to 70 million in 2030. This will put enormous pressure on the health care system, regardless of whether Obama's reform efforts, or even Paul Ryan's, prove successful. The chronic diseases of the elderly will be the front line. Because we cannot cure those diseases at present, nor reasonably hope for cures over the next few decades, the best we will be able to do in many cases, especially those of the elderly and frail, is extend people's lives for a relatively short period of time—at considerable expense and often while causing serious suffering to the person in question.

Consider that a National Cancer Institute study projects a 39 percent   10
increase in cancer costs between 2010 and 2020. That figure represents in great part our success in extending the lives of those already afflicted with the disease. Kidney dialysis also has become an economic quagmire.

A 150 percent increase in the number of such patients is expected over the next decade. The cost of Alzheimer's disease is projected to rise from $91 billion in 2005 to $189 billion in 2015 to $1 trillion in 2050 (twice the cost of Medicare expenditures for all diseases now).

In a 2006 article, Harvard economist David Cutler and colleagues wrote, "Analyses focused on spending and on the increase in life expectancy beginning at 65 years of age showed that the incremental cost of an additional year of life rose from $46,800 in the 1970s to $145,000 in the 1990s. . . . If this trend continues in the elderly, the cost-effectiveness of medical care will continue to decrease at older ages." Emory professor Kenneth Thorpe and colleagues, summing up some Medicare data, note that "more than half of beneficiaries are treated for five or more chronic conditions each year." Among the elderly, the struggle against disease has begun to look like the trench warfare of World War I: little real progress in taking enemy territory but enormous economic and human cost in trying to do so.

In the war against disease, we have unwittingly created a kind of medicine that is barely affordable now and forbiddingly unaffordable in the long run. The Affordable Care Act might ease the burden, but it will not eliminate it. Ours is now a medicine that may doom most of us to an old age that will end badly: with our declining bodies falling apart as they always have but devilishly—and expensively—stretching out the suffering and decay. Can we conceptualize something better? Can we imagine a medicine that is more affordable—that brings our health care system's current cost escalation, now in the range of 6 percent to 7 percent per year, down to 3 percent, which would place it in line with the annual rise in GDP? Can we imagine a system that is less ambitious but also more humane—that better handles the inevitable downward spiral of old age and helps us through a somewhat more limited life span as workers, citizens, and parents?

The answer to these questions is yes. But it will require—to use a religious term in a secular way—something like a conversion experience on the part of physicians, researchers, industry, and our nation as a whole.

Vannevar Bush, a scientific advisor to President Franklin D. Roosevelt, famously said that science is an "endless frontier." He was right then and that is still true now. But scientific progress to extend that frontier is not an endlessly affordable venture. Health care, like the exploration of outer space, will always be open to progress, but we understand that putting humans on Mars is not at present economically sensible. We have settled for a space station and the Hubble telescope. We must now comparably scale down our ambitions for medicine, setting new priorities in light of the obstacles we have encountered.

We need, first of all, to change our approach to research. A key ingredient of the economic engine of medical progress has been the endless issuing of promissory notes by scientists and the medical industry, which are then amplified by the media. The human genome project, stem-cell research, highly touted "breakthroughs"—all have raised hopes that we are on the verge of saving hundreds of millions of lives. But these promises have not materialized. A more realistic rhetoric is necessary, one that places a heavier emphasis on caring for the sick, not curing them.

The traditional open-ended model of medical research, with the war against death as the highest priority, should give way to a new goal: aiming to bring everyone's life expectancy up to an average age of 80 years (already being approached), reducing early death, and shifting the emphasis in the direction of improving the quality of life of those in every age group. The highest priority should be given to children, the next-highest to those in their adult years (the age group responsible for managing society), and the lowest to those over 80.

In light of the fact that we are not curing most diseases, we need to change our priorities for the elderly. Death is not the only bad thing that can happen to an elderly person. An old age marked by disability, economic insecurity, and social isolation are also great evils. Instead of a medical culture of cure for the elderly we need a culture of care, notably a stronger Social Security program and a Medicare program much more heavily weighted toward primary care. Less money, that is, for late-life technological interventions and more for preventive measures and independent living. Some people may die earlier than now, but they will die better deaths.

Bringing about these changes would require shifts in the medical profession. Imagine a health care pyramid. At the lowest and broadest level is public health (health promotion and disease prevention). The next level is primary medicine and emergency care. The level above that consists of short-term hospital care for acute illness. And the top, narrowest level is high-technology care for the chronically ill. It is essential that we find ways to push down the ever-expanding kind of care at the highest level to lower levels, and particularly to the public-health and primary-care levels. The standards for access to care at the highest levels should be strict, marked by a decent chance of good outcomes at a reasonable cost.

Along these lines, one obvious step is to encourage more medical students to become primary-care physicians rather than specialists. Though there is nothing new or radical in such a proposal, it will not be easy to implement. Medical education must be better subsidized to reduce the debt of young doctors, which discourages many from entering family practice and tempts them toward ever-narrowing and more lucrative specialties.

20   Yet the most difficult shift will have to take place not among doctors, but among the public as a whole. The institution of medicine is enormously popular with the public. None of us likes being sick or threatened with death. Modern technology has brought us many benefits that enhance the prestige and social power of medicine. But the public must be persuaded to lower its expectations. We must have a society-wide dialogue on what a new model of medicine will look like: a model that will be moderate in its research aspirations, and dominated by primary care and neighborhood clinics staffed mainly by family physicians, paramedics and nurses for routine health needs, and organized teams for acute care. If this society-wide dialogue is to be successful, doctors will have to call repeated attention to the economic and social realities of the endless war on disease. They will have to remind the public that this war cannot be won—or can achieve small, incremental victories only—and if we are not careful, we can harm ourselves trying.

Finally, we need a health care system that is far more radically reformed than the system envisioned by the Affordable Care Act (ACA). Should the ACA be successful down to the last detail, it is still unlikely to succeed in bringing the annual rise in health care costs down to the annual GDP increase. In their 2011 yearly report, the Medicare program trustees project insolvency by 2024. The only reliable way of controlling costs has been the method used by most other developed countries: a centrally directed and budgeted system, oversight in the use of new and old technologies, and price controls. Medicine cannot continue trying to serve two masters, that of providing affordable health care and turning a handsome profit for its middlemen and providers.

Even so, those countries with less costly but more effective health care systems are in trouble as well—not as much as we are, but enough to inspire constant reforms. Every health care system has to cope with aging populations, new technologies, and high patient expectations. However a health care system is organized, the open-ended idea of medical progress is the deepest driver of health care costs. It dooms us to live too much of our later years in poor and declining health, and to die inch by inch from failure of one organ after another. Is it really a medical benefit, for ourselves or our families, to be doomed by frailty to a life that makes even walking a hazard? Or to spend our last years in and out of doctors' offices and ICUs? Those results are what progress has given us—a seeming benefit that has become a serious economic and personal burden.

"All politics," the late and wise Tip O'Neill once said, "is local." It can no less be said that "all medicine is personal." Our own experience in trying to talk about the kind of wholesale reforms we think necessary for medicine's future is that people are far more concerned about what it will mean for themselves and their families than for something as general and abstract as the health care system. Their heads tell them that rationing and limits will probably be necessary, but they reject these ideas if it means that a loved one might not have what is needed to be kept alive, even if in a bad or terminal state. Unhappily, however, some rationing and limit-setting will be necessary. There is no way the Medicare program can survive unless it both sharply cuts benefits and raises taxes. Certain benefits can be cut directly or indirectly—directly by reducing payments for treatments, or indirectly by increasing co-payments and deductibles to a painful level, sufficient to discourage people from insisting on them.

But our broader point is not really about policy changes such as rationing. It is, put simply, that substantial shifts will be needed in the way our culture thinks about death and aging. There is good evidence that if physicians talk candidly and with empathy to critically ill patients and their families, telling them what they are in for if they want a full-court press, minds can be changed. That, in turn, means that physicians themselves will have to acknowledge their limits, explore their own motivations, and be willing to face patients with bad news as a way of avoiding even worse treatment outcomes. The ethic of medicine has long been to inspire unbounded hope in the sick patient and the same kind of hope in medical research. Sobriety and prudence must now take their place.

The problems we are describing are, of course, hardly the only flaws   25
within the U.S. medical system. Among the spheres of concern most commonly cited for major criticism are: the perception of significant deterioration in the doctor–patient relationship; the state of care at the end of life; maldistribution of health care availability among geographic locations; malpractice and tort law; physician entrepreneurship; emphasis on profit motive by the insurance and pharmaceutical industries; duplication of resources among competing health facilities; multiple tiers of access and care,

largely determined by income; wasting of money, resources, and personnel within the system; and costly overspecialization.

Sometimes—at all times, actually—the problems seem overwhelming. Not only does the complexity of the issues make them appear insoluble, but so does the way in which each seems to intertwine with all the others, inevitably to exacerbate the whole. The entire web of interconnected, complicating factors has long since reached the bewildering point where no issue can be addressed, or so much as approached, in isolation. The complexities are enough to make every stakeholder in American medicine—namely all of us—throw up our hands in desperation.

But there is, in fact, a solution: a top-down, bottom-up study of the entire U.S. health system, with a view toward taking it apart and reconstructing it in a manner adapted to our nation's needs—a multiyear, multidisciplinary project whose aim would be to change the very culture of American medicine. The inadequate, inequitable, and financially insupportable system that has been jerry-built and constantly band-aided during recent decades will no longer do. Nor will incremental policy reforms, no matter how well-intentioned.

There is a historical precedent for such a project. At the turn of the twentieth century, U.S. medical education was a disgrace, and care of the sick, except in a certain few facilities, was almost as bad. Something had to be done. In 1908, the newly founded Carnegie Foundation for the Advancement of Teaching stepped in, hiring a 42-year-old educator named Abraham Flexner to embark on a study of medical education in North America. His report, published two years later, became a clarion call for drastic change. Subsequently, armed with a total of $600 million provided by the Carnegie and Rockefeller philanthropies and other contributors, Flexner visited 35 schools in the United States and Canada, and provided the financial wherewithal for the changes so desperately needed. The result of this remarkable effort was that, within ten years, U.S. medical schools became the prototype upon which all others tried to fashion themselves; our nation's medicine, like the vastly improved institutions that gave it new life, became the gold standard for the world.

We can do this kind of thing again. It will take political will; unyielding leadership; vast amounts of money, both from government and private philanthropy; and extreme patience. Above all, it will take the confidence of the American people that a more humane, more affordable kind of medicine is possible.

Analyze

1. Who was René Dubos? Why do Callahan and Nuland begin their essay with a reference to him and his book?

2. What three key assumptions do the authors argue have been underlying the current, widely held belief that all disease can be conquered?

3. In your own words, briefly explain James Fries's concept of "compression of morbidity."

4. How does Crimmins and Beltran-Sanchez's study relate to Fries's concept?

5. What, according to the authors, have the "main achievements today" in medical technology accomplished?

6. Why is the projected 2020 population of the American population over 65 of particular concern to the authors?

7. Explain the reasons mentioned in the essay to support the authors' proposition that "scientific progress" is "not an endlessly affordable venture."

Explore

1. In their essay, Callahan and Nuland write, "In the war against disease, we have unwittingly created a kind of medicine that is barely affordable now and forbiddingly unaffordable in the long run." Although Callahan and Nuland then refer to numerous statistics to support their claim, it is often easy to simply pass over the import of the data reported. Choose two instances where the authors cite data to support this claim. Write a paragraph explaining how the data reported relates to the claim. Then, figure out a way to explain the importance of the data reported to your classmates by describing it in terms that they can easily understand and relate to.

2. Based on your own experience or the experience of a close friend or family member, would you agree with the authors' assessment that most Americans "view diseases as things to be conquered"? Describe a disease or medical condition that you or a friend or family member contracted and that required treatment. What were the possible approaches to this treatment? Which was recommended? Which taken? In what ways did the language used to discuss the condition and the approach to treating it both reflect the idea of conquest?

3. Do some research into the Affordable Care Act passed in 2010. How well does this Act address some of the issues raised by Callahan and Nuland? Prepare a two-page report to explain and introduce the Act to your classmates. Make sure to include two sections: an overview of the Act and an assessment of the Act based on how well it addresses numerous issues raised by Callahan and Nuland.

Eric Topol
"How Technology Is Transforming Healthcare"

Eric Topol is a cardiologist, geneticist, and researcher. In 2006, he started the Scripps Genomic Medicine program to advance individualized medicine using genomic approaches. In this essay, an excerpt from his book *The Creative Destruction of Healthcare: How the Digital Revolution Will Create Better Healthcare* (2013) published in *Psychology Today*, Topol considers the ways in which information, communications, medical, and genomic technologies may converge to affect how healthcare is delivered in the twenty-first century.

How might the portable electronic devices that you use daily better assist you in tracking health information and accessing healthcare?

In the mid-20th century Joseph Schumpeter, the noted Austrian economist, popularized the term "creative destruction" to denote transformation that accompanies radical innovation. In recent years, our world has been "Schumpetered."

By virtue of the intensive infiltration of digital devices into our daily lives, we have radically altered how we communicate with one another and with our entire social network at once. Everywhere we go, we take pictures and videos with our cellphone, the one precious object that never leaves our side. Forget about going to a video store to rent a movie and finding out it is not in stock. Just download it at home and watch it on television, a computer monitor, a tablet or even your phone. The Web lets us sample nearly all books in print without even making a purchase and efficiently download the whole book in a flash. Our lives have been radically transformed through digital innovation. Radically transformed. Creatively destroyed.

But the most precious part of our existence—our health—has thus far been largely unaffected, insulated and almost compartmentalized from this digital revolution. How could this be? Medicine is remarkably conservative to the point of being properly characterized as sclerotic, even ossified. Beyond the reluctance and resistance of physicians to change, the life science industry (companies that develop and commercialize drugs, devices or diagnostic tests) and government regulatory agencies are in a near-paralyzed state, unable to break out of a broken model determining how their products are developed or commercially approved. But that is about to change. Medicine is about to go through its biggest shakeup in history.

For the first time we can digitize humans. We can remotely and continuously monitor each heartbeat, moment-to-moment blood pressure readings, the rate and depth of breathing, body temperature, oxygen concentration in the blood, glucose, brain waves, activity, mood—all the things that make us tick. We can image any part of the body and do a three-dimensional reconstruction, eventually leading to the capability of printing an organ. Or, we can use a miniature, handheld, high-resolution imaging device that rapidly captures critical information anywhere, such as the scene of a motor vehicle accident or a person's home in response to a call of distress. We can determine all 6 billion letters ("life codes") of a person's genome sequence.

And all of this information about an individual can be assembled from wireless biosensors, genome sequencing or imaging to be readily available, integrated with all the traditional medical data and constantly updated. We now have the technology to digitize a human being in highest definition, in granular detail, and in ways that most people thought would not be possible.

This reflects an unprecedented super-convergence. It would not be possible were it not for the maturation of the digital world technologies—the ubiquity of smartphones, bandwidth, pervasive connectivity and social networking. Beyond this, the perfect digital storm includes immense, seemingly unlimited, computing power via cloud server farms, remarkable biosensors, genome sequencing, imaging capabilities and formidable health information systems.

Think of the cellphone, which is not only a hub of telecommunications convergence, but also a remarkable number of devices all rolled into one gadget: camera, video recorder, GPS, calculator, watch, alarm clock, music player, voice recorder, photo album and library of books—like a pluripotent stem cell. Armed with apps, it carries out diverse functions from flashlight to magnifying glass. Then connect it to a wireless network, and this tiny device is a web surfer, word processor, video player, translator, dictionary, encyclopedia and gateway to the world's knowledge base. And, by the way, it even texts, emails and provides phone service. But now picture this device loaded for medicine, capable of displaying all of one's vital signs in real time, conducting laboratory analyses, sequencing parts of one's genome, or even acquiring ultrasound images of one's heart, abdomen or unborn baby.

These are the collective tools that lay the groundwork for digitizing humans. This is a new era of medicine, in which each person can be near fully defined at the individual level, instead of how we practice medicine at a population level, with mass screening policies for such conditions as breast or prostate cancer and use of the same medication and dosage for a diagnosis rather than for a patient. We are each unique human beings, but up until now there was no way to establish one's biologic or physiologic individuality. There was no way to determine a relevant metric like blood pressure around the clock while a person is sleeping, or at work, or in the midst of an emotional upheaval. This represents the next frontier of the digital revolution, finally getting to the most important but heretofore insulated domain—preserving our health.

We have early indicators that this train has left the station. The first individual, a five-year-old boy who had his life saved by genome sequencing, was recently documented. But it's not just about finding the root molecular cause of why an individual is sick. We can now perform whole genome sequencing of a fetus to determine what conditions should be watched for postnatally. At the other end of the continuum of life, we can do DNA sequencing to supplant a traditional physical autopsy, to determine the cause of death. We can dissect, decode and define individual granularity at the molecular level, from womb to tomb.

10   That's just the start of illuminating the human black box. Recognizing that we are walking event recorders and that we just need biosensors to capture the data, and algorithms to process it, sets up the ability to track virtually any metric. Today, these sensors are wearable, like Band-Aids or

wristwatches. But soon enough they will also be embedded into our circulation in the form of nanosensors, the size of a grain of sand, providing continuous surveillance of our blood for the earliest possible detection of cancer, an impending heart attack or the likelihood of a forthcoming autoimmune attack.

Yes, this does ring in the sci-fi concept of cyborgs, the fusion of artificial and biological parts in humans. We've already been there with cochlear implants for hearing loss, a trachea transplant, and we're going there in the creation of embedded sensors that talk to our cellphones via wireless body area networks in the future. With it comes the familiar "check engine" capability that we are accustomed to in our cars but never had before for our bodies. Think true, real prevention for the first time in medical history.

We live in an extraordinary data-rich universe, a world that had only accumulated 1 billion gigabytes (10^9 or 1,000,000,000 bytes of data) from the dawn of civilization until 2003. But now, we are generating multiple zettabytes—each representing 1 trillion gigabytes—each year and will exceed 35 zettabytes by 2020, roughly equivalent to the amount of data on 250 billion DVDs. Sensors are now the dominant source of worldwide-generated data, with 1,250 billion gigabytes in 2010, representing more bits than all of the stars in the universe.

The term "massively parallel" is an important one that, in part, accounts for this explosion of data and brings together the computer, digital and life science domains. Note the convergence: from single chips that contain massively parallel processor arrays, to supercomputers with hundreds of thousands of central processing units, to whole-genome sequencing that is performed by breaking the genomes into tiny pieces and determining the life codes in a massively parallel fashion. In 2011, the Watson IBM computer system beat champion humans on the game show "Jeopardy!". Watson is equipped with a 15-terabyte (10^{12}) or 15,000,000,000,000-byte databank and massively parallel 2,880-processor cores.

So, beyond its television premiere and victory, where was Watson first deployed? At Columbia University and the University of Maryland medical centers to provide a cybernetic assistant service to doctors. David Gelernter's February 2011 op-ed in *The Wall Street Journal*, "Coming Next: A Supercomputer Saves Your Life," introduced the concept of a WikiWatson supercomputer that could bring together the whole world's medical literature and clinical expertise. Putting a massive databank to use to improve health care is emblematic of the overlay of the digital and medical worlds.

15   In some health care systems, patients can now directly download their laboratory reports and medical records, which they were never allowed to do in the past. Any consumer with adequate funds can have his or her genome scanned or even wholly sequenced.

But just having these technological capabilities will not catapult medicine forward. The gridlock of the medical community, government and the life science industry will not facilitate change or a willingness to embrace and adopt innovation. The U.S. government has been preoccupied with health care "reform," but this refers to improving access and insurance coverage and has little or nothing to do with innovation. Medicine is currently set up to be maximally imprecise. Private practice physicians render "by the yard" and are rewarded for doing more procedures. Medical care is largely shaped by guidelines, indexed to a population rather than an individual. And the evidence from clinical research is derived from populations that do not translate to the real world of persons. The life science industry has no motivation to design drugs or devices that are only effective, however strikingly, for a small, well-defined population segment. At the same time, the regulatory agencies are entirely risk-averse and, as a result, are suppressing remarkably innovative, and even frugal, opportunities to change medicine. The end result is that most of our screening tests and treatments are overused and applied to the wrong individuals, promoting vast waste. And virtually nothing is being done to accelerate true prevention of disease.

In fact, consumers must provide the impetus for new medicine—a new medicine that is no longer paternalistic, since the doctor does not necessarily know best anymore. The American Medical Association has lobbied the government hard for consumers not to have direct access to their genomic data, asserting that this must be mediated through physicians.

We know that 90 percent of physicians are uncomfortable and largely unwilling to make decisions based on their patients' genomic information. But it is your DNA, your cellphone and your right to have all of your medical data and information. With a medical profession particularly incapable of making a transition to practicing individualized medicine, despite a new array of powerful tools, isn't it time for consumers to drive this capability?

A revolution in technology that is based on the primacy of individuals mandates a revolution by consumers in order for new medicine to take hold. We desperately need medicine to be Schumpetered, to be radically transformed. We need the digital world to invade the medical cocoon and to exploit the newfound and exciting technological capabilities of digitizing human beings.

Analyze

1. Why, according to Topol, is medicine "about to go through its biggest shakeup in history"?
2. What is Watson? How does Topol envision Watson being used in healthcare?
3. List the types of technologies that Topol believes will be part of the technological convergence that will profoundly affect medicine.

Explore

1. Research genomics and its possible applications in healthcare. Describe one to three potential genomic applications. Have any of these yet reached the consumer market? What are some of the obstacles standing in the way? What are the potential benefits of these applications?
2. Working in small groups and using Topol's discussion as a guide, brainstorm some possible healthcare-related applications for mobile phones that could be developed. Select one. Then, develop a brochure for consumers describing what your proposed mobile digital application is, the problem or problems it addresses, and how, specifically, it could help consumers become more empowered regarding the management and oversight of their healthcare.
3. Perform an Internet search using the phrase "mobile healthcare applications." Based on your findings, write a two-page report describing the types of mobile healthcare applications that are currently available and how they are being used. Then, write a short essay explaining how your findings may add support or raise questions regarding Topol's argument.

Atul Gawande
"Slow Ideas"

Atul Gawande is a surgeon and a journalist. A practitioner of general and endocrine surgery at Brigham and Women's Hospital in Boston, he is also a staff writer for *The New Yorker*, where he has been contributing articles on global healthcare and medicine since 1998. His books include *The Checklist Manifesto: How to Get Things Right* (2011) and *Complications: A Surgeon's Notes on an Imperfect Science* (2003). In this essay, Gawande reviews the history of two important medical technologies, considering why the adoption of one far outpaced the other, and what that fact may help us understand more generally about technology adoption and healthcare.

Have you noticed that some innovations spread more quickly than others? What are some of the characteristics of those that are rapidly adopted?

Why do some innovations spread so swiftly and others so slowly? Consider the very different trajectories of surgical anesthesia and antiseptics, both of which were discovered in the nineteenth century. The first public demonstration of anesthesia was in 1846. The Boston surgeon Henry Jacob Bigelow was approached by a local dentist named William Morton, who insisted that he had found a gas that could render patients insensible to the pain of surgery. That was a dramatic claim. In those days, even a minor tooth extraction was excruciating. Without effective pain control, surgeons learned to work with slashing speed. Attendants pinned patients down as they screamed and thrashed, until they fainted from the agony. Nothing ever tried had made much difference. Nonetheless, Bigelow agreed to let Morton demonstrate his claim.

On October 16, 1846, at Massachusetts General Hospital, Morton administered his gas through an inhaler in the mouth of a young man undergoing the excision of a tumor in his jaw. The patient only muttered to himself in a semi-conscious state during the procedure. The following day, the gas left a woman, undergoing surgery to cut a large tumor from her upper arm, completely silent and motionless. When she woke, she said she had experienced nothing at all.

Four weeks later, on November 18th, Bigelow published his report on the discovery of "insensibility produced by inhalation" in the *Boston Medical and Surgical Journal*. Morton would not divulge the composition of the gas, which he called Letheon, because he had applied for a patent. But Bigelow reported that he smelled ether in it (ether was used as an ingredient in certain medical preparations), and that seems to have been enough. The idea spread like a contagion, travelling through letters, meetings, and periodicals. By mid-December, surgeons were administering ether to patients in

Paris and London. By February, anesthesia had been used in almost all the capitals of Europe, and by June in most regions of the world.

There were forces of resistance, to be sure. Some people criticized anesthesia as a "needless luxury"; clergymen deplored its use to reduce pain during childbirth as a frustration of the Almighty's designs. James Miller, a nineteenth-century Scottish surgeon who chronicled the advent of anesthesia, observed the opposition of elderly surgeons: "They closed their ears, shut their eyes, and folded their hands. . . . They had quite made up their minds that pain was a necessary evil, and must be endured." Yet soon even the obstructors, "with a run, mounted behind—hurrahing and shouting with the best." Within seven years, virtually every hospital in America and Britain had adopted the new discovery.

Sepsis—infection—was the other great scourge of surgery. It was the single biggest killer of surgical patients, claiming as many as half of those who underwent major operations, such as a repair of an open fracture or the amputation of a limb. Infection was so prevalent that suppuration—the discharge of pus from a surgical wound—was thought to be a necessary part of healing.

In the eighteen-sixties, the Edinburgh surgeon Joseph Lister read a paper by Louis Pasteur laying out his evidence that spoiling and fermentation were the consequence of microorganisms. Lister became convinced that the same process accounted for wound sepsis. Pasteur had observed that, besides filtration and the application of heat, exposure to certain chemicals could eliminate germs. Lister had read about the city of Carlisle's success in using a small amount of carbolic acid to eliminate the odor of sewage, and reasoned that it was destroying germs. Maybe it could do the same in surgery.

During the next few years, he perfected ways to use carbolic acid for cleansing hands and wounds and destroying any germs that might enter the operating field. The result was strikingly lower rates of sepsis and death. You would have thought that, when he published his observations in a groundbreaking series of reports in *The Lancet*, in 1867, his antiseptic method would have spread as rapidly as anesthesia.

Far from it. The surgeon J. M. T. Finney recalled that, when he was a trainee at Massachusetts General Hospital two decades later, hand washing was still perfunctory. Surgeons soaked their instruments in carbolic acid, but they continued to operate in black frock coats stiffened with the blood and viscera of previous operations—the badge of a busy practice. Instead of using fresh gauze as sponges, they reused sea sponges without sterilizing them. It was a generation before Lister's recommendations became routine and the next steps were taken toward the modern standard of asepsis—that is, entirely excluding germs from the surgical field, using heat-sterilized instruments and surgical teams clad in sterile gowns and gloves.

In our era of electronic communications, we've come to expect that important innovations will spread quickly. Plenty do: think of in-vitro fertilization, genomics, and communications technologies themselves. But there's an equally long list of vital innovations that have failed to catch on. The puzzle is why.

10   Did the spread of anesthesia and antisepsis differ for economic reasons? Actually, the incentives for both ran in the right direction. If painless surgery attracted paying patients, so would a noticeably lower death rate. Besides, live patients were more likely to make good on their surgery bill. Maybe ideas that violate prior beliefs are harder to embrace. To nineteenth-century surgeons, germ theory seemed as illogical as, say, Darwin's theory that human beings evolved from primates. Then again, so did the idea that you could inhale a gas and enter a pain-free state of suspended animation. Proponents of anesthesia overcame belief by encouraging surgeons to try ether on a patient and witness the results for themselves—to take a test drive. When Lister tried this strategy, however, he made little progress.

The technical complexity might have been part of the difficulty. Giving Lister's methods "a try" required painstaking attention to detail. Surgeons had to be scrupulous about soaking their hands, their instruments, and even their catgut sutures in antiseptic solution. Lister also set up a device that continuously sprayed a mist of antiseptic over the surgical field.

But anesthesia was no easier. Obtaining ether and constructing the inhaler could be difficult. You had to make sure that the device delivered an adequate dosage, and the mechanism required constant tinkering. Yet most surgeons stuck with it—or else they switched to chloroform, which was found to be an even more powerful anesthetic, but posed its own problems. (An imprecise dosage killed people.) Faced with the complexities, they didn't give up; instead, they formed an entire new medical specialty—anesthesiology.

So what were the key differences? First, one combatted a visible and immediate problem (pain); the other combatted an invisible problem (germs) whose effects wouldn't be manifest until well after the operation. Second, although both made life better for patients, only one made life better for doctors. Anesthesia changed surgery from a brutal, time-pressured assault on a shrieking patient to a quiet, considered procedure. Listerism, by contrast, required the operator to work in a shower of carbolic acid. Even low dilutions burned the surgeons' hands. You can imagine why Lister's crusade might have been a tough sell.

This has been the pattern of many important but stalled ideas. They attack problems that are big but, to most people, invisible; and making them work can be tedious, if not outright painful. The global destruction wrought by a warming climate, the health damage from our over-sugared modern diet, the economic and social disaster of our trillion dollars in unpaid student debt—these things worsen imperceptibly every day. Meanwhile, the carbolic-acid remedies to them, all requiring individual sacrifice of one kind or another, struggle to get anywhere.

The global problem of death in childbirth is a pressing example. Every year, three hundred thousand mothers and more than six million children die around the time of birth, largely in poorer countries. Most of these deaths are due to events that occur during or shortly after delivery. A mother may hemorrhage. She or her baby may suffer an infection. Many babies can't take their first breath without assistance, and newborns, especially those born small, have trouble regulating their body temperature after birth. Simple, lifesaving solutions have been known for decades. They just haven't spread.

Many solutions aren't ones you can try at home, and that's part of the problem. Increasingly, however, women around the world are giving birth in hospitals. In India, a government program offers mothers up to fourteen hundred rupees—more than what most Indians live on for a month—when they deliver in a hospital, and now, in many areas, the majority of births are in facilities. Death rates in India have fallen, but they're still ten times greater than in high-income countries like our own.

Not long ago, I visited a few community hospitals in north India, where just one-third of mothers received the medication recommended to prevent hemorrhage; less than ten per cent of the newborns were given adequate warming; and only four per cent of birth attendants washed their hands for vaginal examination and delivery. In an average childbirth, clinicians followed only about ten of twenty-nine basic recommended practices.

Here we are in the first part of the twenty-first century, and we're still trying to figure out how to get ideas from the first part of the twentieth century to take root. In the hopes of spreading safer childbirth practices, several colleagues and I have teamed up with the Indian government, the World Health Organization, the Gates Foundation, and Population Services International to create something called the BetterBirth Project. We're working in Uttar Pradesh, which is among India's poorest states. One afternoon in January, our team travelled a couple of hours from the state's capital, Lucknow, with its bleating cars and ramshackle shops, to a rural hospital surrounded by lush farmland and thatched-hut villages. Although the sun was high and the sky was clear, the temperature was near freezing. The hospital was a one-story concrete building painted goldenrod yellow. (Our research agreement required that I keep it unnamed.) The entrance is on a dirt road lined with rows of motorbikes, the primary means of long-distance transportation. If an ambulance or an auto-rickshaw can't be found, women in labor sit sidesaddle on the back of a bike.

The hospital delivers three thousand newborns a year, a typical volume in India but one that would put it in the top fifth of American hospitals. Yet it had little of the amenities that you'd associate with a modern hospital. I met the physician in charge, a smart and capable internist in his early thirties who had trained in the capital. He was clean-shaven and buzz-cut, with an Argyle sweater, track shoes, and a habitual half smile. He told me, apologetically, that the hospital staff had no ability to do blood tests, to give blood transfusions, or to perform emergency obstetrics procedures such as Cesarean sections. There was no electricity during the day. There was certainly no heating, even though the temperature was barely forty degrees that day, and no air-conditioning, even though summer temperatures routinely reach a hundred degrees. There were two blood-pressure cuffs for the entire facility. The nurse's office in my neighborhood elementary school was better equipped.

20   The hospital was severely understaffed, too. The doctor said that half of the staff positions were vacant. To help with child deliveries for a local population of a quarter of a million people, the hospital had two nurses and one obstetrician, who happened to be his wife. The nurses, who had six months of childbirth training, did most of the deliveries, swapping shifts year-round. The obstetrician covered the outpatient clinic, and helped with complicated births whenever she was required, day or night. During holidays or sickness, the two nurses covered for each other, but, if no one was available, laboring women were either sent to another hospital, miles away, or an untrained assistant might be forced to step in.

It may be surprising that mothers are better off delivering in such places than at home in a village, but studies show a consistently higher survival rate when they do. The staff members I met in India had impressive experience. Even the youngest nurses had done more than a thousand child deliveries. They've seen and learned to deal with countless problems—a torn placenta, an umbilical cord wrapped around a baby's neck, a stuck shoulder. Seeing the daily heroism required to keep such places going, you feel foolish and ill-mannered asking how they could do things better.

But then we hung out in the wards for a while. In the delivery room, a boy had just been born. He and his mother were lying on a cot, bundled under woollen blankets, resting. The room was coffin-cold; I was having trouble feeling my toes. I tried to imagine what that baby must have felt like. Newborns have a high body-surface area and lose heat rapidly. Even in warm weather, hypothermia is common, and it makes newborns weak and less responsive, less able to breast-feed adequately and more prone to infection. I noticed that the boy was swaddled separately from his mother. Voluminous evidence shows that it is far better to place the child on the mother's chest or belly, skin to skin, so that the mother's body can regulate the baby's until it is ready to take over. Among small or premature babies, kangaroo care (as it is known) cuts mortality rates by a third.

So why hadn't the nurse swaddled the two together? She was a skilled and self-assured woman in her mid-thirties with twinkly eyes, a brown knit hat, and a wool sweater over her shalwar kameez. Resources clearly weren't the issue—kangaroo care costs nothing. Had she heard of it? Oh, yes, she said. She'd taken a skilled-birth-attendant class that taught it. Had she forgotten about it? No. She had actually offered to put the baby skin to skin with the mother, and showed me where she'd noted this in the record.

"The mother didn't want it," she explained. "She said she was too cold."

The nurse seemed to think it was strange that I was making such an issue of this. The baby was fine, wasn't he? And he was. He was sleeping sweetly, a tightly wrapped peanut with a scrunched brown face and his mouth in a lowercase "o."

But had his temperature been taken? It had not. The nurse said that she had been planning to do so. Our visit had disrupted her routine. Suppose she had, though, and his temperature was low. Would she have done anything differently? Would she have made the mom unswaddle the child and put him to her chest?

Everything about the life the nurse leads—the hours she puts in, the circumstances she endures, the satisfaction she takes in her abilities—shows that she cares. But hypothermia, like the germs that Lister wanted surgeons to battle, is invisible to her. We picture a blue child, suffering right before our eyes. That is not what hypothermia looks like. It is a child who is just a few degrees too cold, too sluggish, too slow to feed. It will be some time before the baby begins to lose weight, stops making urine, develops pneumonia or a bloodstream infection. Long before that happens—usually the morning after the delivery, perhaps the same night—the mother will have hobbled to an auto-rickshaw, propped herself beside her husband, held her new baby tight, and ridden the rutted roads home.

From the nurse's point of view, she'd helped bring another life into the world. If four per cent of the newborns later died at home, what could that possibly have to do with how she wrapped the mother and child? Or whether she washed her hands before putting on gloves? Or whether the blade with which she cut the umbilical cord was sterilized?

We're infatuated with the prospect of technological solutions to these problems—baby warmers, say. You can still find high-tech incubators in rural hospitals that sit mothballed because a replacement part wasn't available, or because there was no electricity for them. In recent years, though, engineers have produced designs specifically for the developing world. Dr. Steven Ringer, a neonatologist and BetterBirth leader, was an adviser for a team that made a cheap, ingenious, award-winning incubator from old car parts that are commonly available and easily replaced in low-income environments. Yet it hasn't taken off, either. "It's in more museums than delivery rooms," he laments.

30   As with most difficulties in global health care, lack of adequate technology is not the biggest problem. We already have a great warming technology: a mother's skin. But even in high-income countries we do not consistently use it. In the United States, according to Ringer, more than half of newborns needing intensive care arrive hypothermic. Preventing hypothermia is a perfect example of an unsexy task: it demands painstaking effort without immediate reward. Getting hospitals and birth attendants to carry out even a few of the tasks required for safer childbirth would save hundreds of thousands of lives. But how do we do that?

The most common approach to changing behavior is to say to people, "Please do X." Please warm the newborn. Please wash your hands. Please follow through on the twenty-seven other childbirth practices that you're not doing. This is what we say in the classroom, in instructional videos, and in public-service campaigns, and it works, but only up to a point.

Then, there's the law-and-order approach: "You must do X." We establish standards and regulations, and threaten to punish failures with fines, suspensions, the revocation of licenses. Punishment can work. Behavioral economists have even quantified how averse people are to penalties. In experimental games, they will often quit playing rather than risk facing negative consequences. And that is the problem with threatening to discipline birth attendants who are taking difficult-to-fill jobs under intensely trying conditions. They'll quit.

The kinder version of "You must do X" is to offer incentives rather than penalties. Maybe we could pay birth attendants a bonus for every healthy child who makes it past a week of life. But then you think about how hard it would be to make a scheme like that work, especially in poor settings. You'd need a sophisticated tracking procedure, to make sure that people aren't gaming the system, and complex statistical calculations, to take prior risks into account. There's also the impossible question of how you split the reward among all the people involved. How much should the community health worker who provided the prenatal care get? The birth attendant who handled the first twelve hours of labor? The one who came on duty and handled the delivery? The doctor who was called in when things got complicated? The pharmacist who stocked the antibiotic that the child required?

Besides, neither penalties nor incentives achieve what we're really after: a system and a culture where X is what people do, day in and day out, even when no one is watching. "You must" rewards mere compliance. Getting to "X is what we do" means establishing X as the norm. And that's what we want: for skin-to-skin warming, hand washing, and all the other lifesaving practices of childbirth to be, quite simply, the norm.

To create new norms, you have to understand people's existing norms   35 and barriers to change. You have to understand what's getting in their way. So what about just working with health-care workers, one by one, to do just that? With the BetterBirth Project, we wondered, in particular, what would happen if we hired a cadre of childbirth-improvement workers to visit birth attendants and hospital leaders, show them why and how to follow a checklist of essential practices, understand their difficulties and objections, and help them practice doing things differently. In essence, we'd give them mentors.

The experiment is just getting under way. The project has recruited only the first few of a hundred or so workers whom we are sending out to hospitals across six regions of Uttar Pradesh in a trial that will involve almost two hundred thousand births over two years. There's no certainty that our approach will succeed. But it seemed worth trying.

Reactions that I've heard both abroad and at home have been interestingly divided. The most common objection is that, even if it works, this kind of one-on-one, on-site mentoring "isn't scalable." But that's one thing it surely is. If the intervention saves as many mothers and newborns as we're hoping—about a thousand lives in the course of a year at the target hospitals—then all that need be done is to hire and develop similar cadres of childbirth-improvement workers for other places around the country and potentially the world. To many people, that doesn't sound like much of a solution. It would require broad mobilization, substantial expense, and perhaps even the development of a new profession. But, to combat the many antisepsis-like problems in the world, that's exactly what has worked. Think about the creation of anesthesiology: it meant doubling the number of doctors in every operation, and we went ahead and did so. To reduce illiteracy, countries, starting with our own, built schools, trained professional teachers, and made education free and compulsory for all children. To improve farming, governments have sent hundreds of thousands of agriculture extension agents to visit farmers across America and every corner of the world and teach them up-to-date methods for increasing their crop yields. Such programs have been extraordinarily effective. They have cut the global illiteracy rate from one in three adults in 1970 to one in six today, and helped give us a Green Revolution that saved more than a billion people from starvation.

In the era of the iPhone, Facebook, and Twitter, we've become enamored of ideas that spread as effortlessly as ether. We want frictionless, "turnkey" solutions to the major difficulties of the world—hunger, disease, poverty. We prefer instructional videos to teachers, drones to troops, incentives to institutions. People and institutions can feel messy and anachronistic. They introduce, as the engineers put it, uncontrolled variability.

But technology and incentive programs are not enough. "Diffusion is essentially a social process through which people talking to people spread an innovation," wrote Everett Rogers, the great scholar of how new ideas are communicated and spread. Mass media can introduce a new idea to people. But, Rogers showed, people follow the lead of other people they know and trust when they decide whether to take it up. Every change requires effort, and the decision to make that effort is a social process.

40   This is something that salespeople understand well. I once asked a pharmaceutical rep how he persuaded doctors—who are notoriously stubborn—to adopt a new medicine. Evidence is not remotely enough, he said, however

strong a case you may have. You must also apply "the rule of seven touches." Personally "touch" the doctors seven times, and they will come to know you; if they know you, they might trust you; and, if they trust you, they will change. That's why he stocked doctors' closets with free drug samples in person. Then he could poke his head around the corner and ask, "So how did your daughter Debbie's soccer game go?" Eventually, this can become "Have you seen this study on our new drug? How about giving it a try?" As the rep had recognized, human interaction is the key force in overcoming resistance and speeding change.

In 1968, *The Lancet* published the results of a modest trial of what is now regarded as among the most important medical advances of the twentieth century. It wasn't a new drug or vaccine or operation. It was basically a solution of sugar, salt, and water that you could make in your kitchen. The researchers gave the solution to victims of a cholera outbreak in Dhaka, the capital of what is now Bangladesh, and the results were striking.

Cholera is a violent and deadly diarrheal illness, caused by the bacterium *Vibrio cholera*, which the victim usually ingests from contaminated water. The bacteria secrete a toxin that triggers a rapid outpouring of fluid into the intestine. The body, which is sixty per cent water, becomes like a sponge being wrung out. The fluid pouring out is a cloudy white, likened to the runoff of washed rice. It produces projectile vomiting and explosive diarrhea. Children can lose a third of their body's water in less than twenty-four hours, a fatal volume. Drinking water to replace the fluid loss is ineffective, because the intestine won't absorb it. As a result, mortality commonly reached seventy per cent or higher. During the nineteenth century, cholera pandemics killed millions across Asia, Europe, Africa, and North America. The disease was dubbed the Blue Death because of the cyanotic blue-gray color of the skin from extreme dehydration.

In 1906, a partially effective treatment was found: intravenous fluid solutions reduced mortality to thirty per cent. Prevention was the most effective approach. Modern sewage and water treatment eliminated the disease in affluent countries. Globally, though, millions of children continued to die from diarrheal illness each year. Even if victims made it to a medical facility, the needles, plastic tubing, and litres of intravenous fluid required for treatment were expensive, in short supply, and dependent on medical workers who were themselves in short supply, especially in outbreaks that often produced thousands of victims.

Then, in the nineteen-sixties, scientists discovered that sugar helps the gut absorb fluid. Two American researchers, David Nalin and Richard Cash, were in Dhaka during a cholera outbreak. They decided to test the scientific findings, giving victims an oral rehydration solution containing sugar as well as salt. Many people doubted that victims could drink enough of it to restore their fluid losses, typically ten to twenty litres a day. So the researchers confined the Dhaka trial to twenty-nine patients. The subjects proved to have no trouble drinking enough to reduce or even eliminate the need for intravenous fluids, and none of them died.

45   Three years later, in 1971, an Indian physician named Dilip Mahalanabis was directing medical assistance at a West Bengal camp of three hundred and fifty thousand refugees from Bangladesh's war of independence when cholera struck. Intravenous-fluid supplies ran out. Mahalanabis instructed his team to try the Dhaka solution. Just 3.6 per cent died, an unprecedented reduction from the usual thirty per cent. The solution was actually better than intravenous fluids. If cholera victims were alert, able to drink, and supplied with enough of it, they could almost always save their own lives.

One might have expected people to clamor for the recipe after these results were publicized. Oral rehydration solution seems like ether: a miraculous fix for a vivid, immediate, and terrifying problem. But it wasn't like ether at all.

To understand why, you have to imagine having a child throwing up and pouring out diarrhea like you've never seen before. Making her drink seems only to provoke more vomiting. Chasing the emesis and the diarrhea seems both torturous and futile. Many people's natural inclination is to not feed the child anything.

Furthermore, why believe that this particular mixture of sugar and salt would be any different from water or anything else you might have tried? And it *is* particular. Throw the salt concentration off by a couple of teaspoons and the electrolyte imbalance could be dangerous. The child must also keep drinking the stuff even after she feels better, for as long as the diarrhea lasts, which is up to five days. Nurses routinely got these steps wrong. Why would villagers do any better?

A decade after the landmark findings, the idea remained stalled. Nothing much had changed. Diarrheal disease remained the world's biggest killer of children under the age of five.

In 1980, however, a Bangladeshi nonprofit organization called BRAC 50
decided to try to get oral rehydration therapy adopted nationwide. The
campaign required reaching a mostly illiterate population. The most recent
public-health campaign—to teach family planning—had been deeply un-
popular. The messages the campaign needed to spread were complicated.

Nonetheless, the campaign proved remarkably successful. A gem of a
book published in Bangladesh, *A Simple Solution*, tells the story. The organization didn't launch a mass-media campaign—only twenty per cent of
the population had a radio, after all. It attacked the problem in a way that is
routinely dismissed as impractical and inefficient: by going door to door,
person by person, and just talking.

It started with a pilot project that set out to reach some sixty thousand
women in six hundred villages. The logistics were daunting. Who, for instance, would do the teaching? How were those workers going to travel?
How was their security to be assured? The BRAC leaders planned the best
they could and then made adjustments on the fly.

They recruited teams of fourteen young women, a cook, and a male
supervisor, figuring that the supervisor would protect them from others as
they travelled, and the women's numbers would protect them from the supervisor. They travelled on foot, pitched camp near each village, fanned out
door to door, and stayed until they had talked to women in every hut. They
worked long days, six days a week. Each night after dinner, they held a
meeting to discuss what went well and what didn't and to share ideas on
how to do better. Leaders periodically debriefed them, as well.

The workers were only semi-literate, but they helped distill their sales
script into seven easy-to-remember messages: for instance, severe diarrhea
leads to death from dehydration; the signs of dehydration include dry
tongue, sunken eyes, thirst, severe weakness, and reduced urination; the
way to treat dehydration is to replace salt and water lost from the body,
starting with the very first loose stool; a rehydration solution provides the
most effective way to do this. BRAC's scientists had to figure out how
the workers could teach the recipe for the solution. Villagers had no precise
measuring implements—spoons were locally made in nonstandard sizes.
The leaders considered issuing special measuring spoons with the recipe on
the handle. But these would be costly; most people couldn't read the recipe;
and how were the spoons to be replaced when lost? Eventually, the team hit
upon using finger measures: a fistful of raw sugar plus a three-finger pinch

of salt mixed in half a "seer" of water—a pint measure commonly used by villagers when buying milk and oil. Tests showed that mothers could make this with sufficient accuracy.

55   Initially, the workers taught up to twenty mothers per day. But monitors visiting the villages a few weeks later found that the quality of teaching suffered on this larger scale, so the workers were restricted to ten households a day. Then a new salary system was devised to pay each worker according to how many of the messages the mothers retained when the monitor followed up. The quality of teaching improved substantially. The field workers soon realized that having the mothers make the solution themselves was more effective than just showing them. The workers began looking for diarrhea cases when they arrived in a village, and treating them to show how effective and safe the remedy was. The scientists also investigated various questions that came up, such as whether clean water was required. (They found that, although boiled water was preferable, contaminated water was better than nothing.)

Early signs were promising. Mothers seemed to retain the key messages. Analysis of their sugar solutions showed that three-quarters made them properly, and just four in a thousand had potentially unsafe salt levels. So BRAC and the Bangladeshi government took the program nationwide. They hired, trained, and deployed thousands of workers region by region. The effort was, inevitably, imperfect. But, by going door to door through more than seventy-five thousand villages, they showed twelve million families how to save their children.

The program was stunningly successful. Use of oral rehydration therapy skyrocketed. The knowledge became self-propagating. The program had changed the norms.

Coaxing villagers to make the solution with their own hands and explain the messages in their own words, while a trainer observed and guided them, achieved far more than any public-service ad or instructional video could have done. Over time, the changes could be sustained with television and radio, and the growth of demand led to the development of a robust market for manufactured oral rehydration salt packets. Three decades later, national surveys have found that almost ninety per cent of children with severe diarrhea were given the solution. Child deaths from diarrhea plummeted more than eighty per cent between 1980 and 2005.

As other countries adopted Bangladesh's approach, global diarrheal deaths dropped from five million a year to two million, despite a fifty-per-cent increase in the world's population during the past three decades. Nonetheless, only a third of children in the developing world receive oral rehydration therapy. Many countries tried to implement at arm's length, going "low touch," without sandals on the ground. As a recent study by the Gates Foundation and the University of Washington has documented, those countries have failed almost entirely. People talking to people is still how the world's standards change.

Surgeons finally did upgrade their antiseptic standards at the end of the   60
nineteenth century. But, as is often the case with new ideas, the effort required deeper changes than anyone had anticipated. In their blood-slick, viscera-encrusted black coats, surgeons had seen themselves as warriors doing hemorrhagic battle with little more than their bare hands. A few pioneering Germans, however, seized on the idea of the surgeon as scientist. They traded in their black coats for pristine laboratory whites, refashioned their operating rooms to achieve the exacting sterility of a bacteriological lab, and embraced anatomic precision over speed.

The key message to teach surgeons, it turned out, was not how to stop germs but how to think like a laboratory scientist. Young physicians from America and elsewhere who went to Germany to study with its surgical luminaries became fervent converts to their thinking and their standards. They returned as apostles not only for the use of antiseptic practice (to kill germs) but also for the much more exacting demands of aseptic practice (to prevent germs), such as wearing sterile gloves, gowns, hats, and masks. Proselytizing through their own students and colleagues, they finally spread the ideas worldwide.

In childbirth, we have only begun to accept that the critical practices aren't going to spread themselves. Simple "awareness" isn't going to solve anything. We need our sales force and our seven easy-to-remember messages. And in many places around the world the concerted, person-by-person effort of changing norms is under way.

I recently asked BetterBirth workers in India whether they'd yet seen a birth attendant change what she does. Yes, they said, but they've found that it takes a while. They begin by providing a day of classroom training for birth attendants and hospital leaders in the checklist of practices to be followed. Then they visit them on site to observe as they try to apply the lessons.

Sister Seema Yadav, a twenty-four-year-old, round-faced nurse three years out of school, was one of the trainers. (Nurses are called "sisters" in India, a carryover from the British usage.) Her first assignment was to follow a thirty-year-old nurse with vastly more experience than she had. Watching the nurse take a woman through labor and delivery, she saw how little of the training had been absorbed. The room had not been disinfected; blood from a previous birth remained in a bucket. When the woman came in—moaning, contractions speeding up—the nurse didn't check her vital signs. She didn't wash her hands. She prepared no emergency supplies. After delivery, she checked the newborn's temperature with her hand, not a thermometer. Instead of warming the baby against the mother's skin, she handed the newborn to the relatives.

65   When Sister Seema pointed out the discrepancy between the teaching and the practice, the nurse was put out. She gave many reasons that steps were missed—there was no time, they were swamped with deliveries, there was seldom a thermometer at hand, the cleaners never did their job. Sister Seema—a cheerful, bubbly, fast talker—took her to the cleaner on duty and together they explained why cleaning the rooms between deliveries was so important. They went to the medical officer in charge and asked for a thermometer to be supplied. At her second and third visits, disinfection seemed more consistent. A thermometer had been found in a storage closet. But the nurse still hadn't changed much of her own routine.

By the fourth or fifth visit, their conversations had shifted. They shared cups of chai and began talking about why you must wash hands even if you wear gloves (because of holes in the gloves and the tendency to touch equipment without them on), and why checking blood pressure matters (because hypertension is a sign of eclampsia, which, when untreated, is a common cause of death among pregnant women). They learned a bit about each other, too. Both turned out to have one child—Sister Seema a four-year-old boy, the nurse an eight-year-old girl. The nurse lived in the capital, a two-hour bus ride away. She was divorced, living with her mother, and struggled with the commute. She'd been frustrated not to find a hospital posting in the city. She worked for days at a stretch, sleeping on a cot when she got a break. Sister Seema commiserated, and shared her own hopes for her family and her future. With time, it became clearer to the nurse that Sister Seema was there only to help and to learn from the experience herself. They even exchanged mobile-phone numbers and spoke between visits. When Sister Seema didn't have the answer to a question, she made sure she got one.

Soon, she said, the nurse began to change. After several visits, she was taking temperatures and blood pressures properly, washing her hands, giving the necessary medications—almost everything. Sister Seema saw it with her own eyes.

She'd had to move on to another pilot site after that, however. And although the project is tracking the outcomes of mothers and newborns, it will be a while before we have enough numbers to know if a difference has been made. So I got the nurse's phone number and, with a translator to help with the Hindi, I gave her a call.

It had been four months since Sister Seema's visit ended. I asked her whether she'd made any changes. Lots, she said.

"What was the most difficult one?" I asked.   70

"Washing hands," she said. "I have to do it so many times!"

"What was the easiest?"

"Taking the vital signs properly." Before, she said, "we did it haphazardly." Afterward, "everything became much more systematic."

She said that she had eventually begun to see the effects. Bleeding after delivery was reduced. She recognized problems earlier. She rescued a baby who wasn't breathing. She diagnosed eclampsia in a mother and treated it. You could hear her pride as she told her stories.

Many of the changes took practice for her, she said. She had to learn, for   75
instance, how to have all the critical supplies—blood-pressure cuff, thermometer, soap, clean gloves, baby respiratory mask, medications—lined up and ready for when she needed them; how to fit the use of them into her routine; how to convince mothers and their relatives that the best thing for a child was to be bundled against the mother's skin. But, step by step, Sister Seema had helped her to do it. "She showed me how to get things done practically," the nurse said.

"Why did you listen to her?" I asked. "She had only a fraction of your experience."

In the beginning, she didn't, the nurse admitted. "The first day she came, I felt the workload on my head was increasing." From the second time, however, the nurse began feeling better about the visits. She even began looking forward to them.

"Why?" I asked.

All the nurse could think to say was "She was nice."

"She was nice?"   80

"She smiled a lot."

"That was it?"

"It wasn't like talking to someone who was trying to find mistakes," she said. "It was like talking to a friend."

That, I think, was the answer. Since then, the nurse had developed her own way of explaining why newborns needed to be warmed skin to skin. She said that she now tells families, "Inside the uterus, the baby is very warm. So when the baby comes out it should be kept very warm. The mother's skin does this."

85   I hadn't been sure if she was just telling me what I wanted to hear. But when I heard her explain how she'd put her own words to what she'd learned, I knew that the ideas had spread. "Do the families listen?" I asked.

"Sometimes they don't," she said. "Usually, they do."

Analyze

1. What is anesthesia? What are antiseptics?
2. Explain the reasons why Gawande believes anesthesia was adopted so quickly and antiseptics were adopted so slowly.
3. Gawande points to several important ideas that have been stalled by their invisibility. List them.
4. What is the Better Birth Project?
5. Why is cholera dubbed "the blue death"?
6. Describe Nalin and Cash's Dhaka experiment. Why is this important to Gawande's argument?
7. What is BRAC? What is significant about the BRAC project Gawande describes in the context of the overall argument he is making in the essay?

Explore

1. Working in small groups, discuss and analyze the rhetorical context (audience[s], purpose[s]) for this essay and Gawande's argument. Then, assess Gawande's title for this essay. How accurately and completely does it represent and reflect the ideas presented in the essay? Brainstorm and discuss some other possible titles that would be appropriate for this essay. Afterward, develop a two-page report that you write collectively as a group or that you each contribute to explaining your findings from these discussions.

2. In his comparison of anesthesia and antiseptics, Gawande proposes that one key reason anesthesia was adopted more rapidly than antiseptics was that it had a visible impact, whereas the benefits of antiseptics were mostly invisible. Have you observed this phenomenon? First, free write about phenomena that may be analogous to the ones described in Gawande's essay. Then, in a three-page essay, explain and describe the visible problem and invisible problem. Describe the time and place where these problems arose. Which one was solved first? Discuss the ways in which the dynamics that you observed were similar or dissimilar to those proposed by Gawande.

3. In his essay, Gawande writes about BRAC's oral rehydration therapy (ORT) campaign in Bangladesh. Re-read Gawande's description of this project, paying particular attention to the ways in which the highly effective campaign combined low-tech solutions with unique communications, training, and compensations strategies to achieve its ends. Using the ORT campaign as a model, think of a persistent health-related problem in your community or at your college that needs to be addressed. Create a booklet modeled on the one workers developed to teach people about severe diarrhea and how to treat it to explain the import and possible treatment of the health-related problem you hope to address. Afterwards, create a two- to three-page plan describing the problem, the possible impact of your solution for addressing it, and a method for distributing the booklet and the information contained in it in an effective manner.

Francisco Seijo
"When Worlds Collide"

Francisco Seijo is an adjunct professor of political science for various U.S. undergraduate programs in Spain, including those affiliated with Middlebury College, New York University, Stanford University, Fundacion IES, and the University of Southern California. His current research, which concerns climate change and environmental politics, is affiliated with The Breakthrough Institute, an environmental think tank that publishes the online journal *The Breakthrough,* where this essay was originally published. In this essay, Seijo reviews the current status and potential impact of anthropogenic climate change and considers the types of changes—political, social, and technological—that will be necessary to confront climate change.

How much do you know about the most current research into climate change?

Anthropogenic climate change represents one of the greatest and swiftest transformations the earth has experienced. Some scientists argue that since the advent of the industrial era, humanity has caused enough biotic, sedimentary and geochemical changes to the planet that we have left the Holocene and entered a new geological phase: the Anthropocene. The implications of this geologic event for the future of life on earth are unclear. Understandably, some scientists have interpreted this wholesale transformation of the planet's climate and biosphere systems as a sign that humanity is reaching, or has already exceeded, the limits of the planet's carrying capacity.

In "The Planet of No Return," Erle Ellis takes issue with this position and argues that human systems have proven resilient to all sorts of natural system transformations including climatic fluctuations. Successful adaptation to global warming, however, requires a transformation of human systems concomitant with the scale of transformation taking place in the planet's natural systems. While Ellis outlines some developments in agricultural systems, he fails to appreciate or take full account of the transformations needed on our warming planet.

Ellis simplifies humanity's agricultural prowess. Large-scale geoengineering of terrestrial ecosystems is only part of the story. Humanity's agricultural systems do not operate in a vacuum. They are embedded in complex cultural, economic and political systems whose interactions and feedbacks are impossible to disentangle. The success of Rome's agricultural systems, for example, was due less to the Roman plough than the influence of the Roman state. The same can be said of America's formidable agricultural systems. Without the large-scale intervention of the US Army Corps of Engineers during the Great Depression in Florida's natural water systems, the state would still be an impenetrable marsh rather than the agricultural powerhouse it is today. Indeed, throughout recorded history natural and human systems have often decoupled with complex consequences for carrying capacity. Witness North Korea—a political system capable of producing the atomic bomb but incapable of feeding its population.

In fact, institutional innovation in the political and economic spheres may well be the single most important factor explaining the resilience of the most successful human systems on the planet. The level of reorganization needed for agricultural systems to adapt to and mitigate climate change will only be achieved when it is matched by an equally large leap in humanity's political, economic, social and cultural systems. This has been the case throughout humanity's past and will continue to be so in the future.

In the 1951 science fiction film *When Worlds Collide*, humanity is given a second chance, following the earth's destruction, on the planet Zyra. As the spaceship with a chosen few lands on Zyra, the survivors discover the planet is not only inhabitable but that the ruins of an ancient civilization lie semi-hidden in luxuriant vegetation. The film provides a prescient metaphor for the crossroads at which humanity stands today.

We possess an incredibly sophisticated knowledge about our past and present. We have even reached the point where, through computer models, we can catch a glimpse of our possible futures. Yet never has humanity had access to so much information and proven so incapable of reaching an imaginative conclusion about what ought to be done. It is as if the capacity to know has stunted the capacity to imagine. This is unfortunate because imagination, above all, is what we need to redesign our human systems to make it possible for the human species to thrive beyond the 21st century.

Finally, while Ellis's point is well taken regarding the remarkable ability of human agricultural systems to adapt to change in the earth's natural systems, one wonders whether our current political systems will show identical stamina in confronting the advent of the Anthropocene. In the 1967 Star Trek episode, "Planet of No Return," Captain Kirk, the foremost political authority aboard the Starship Enterprise, orders the destruction of the planet in question. Let us work, through the exercise of political and technological imagination, to avoid a similar fate for our planet.

Analyze

1. The title of Seijo's article has multiple references. Explain what these are.
2. According to Seijo, what is Erle Ellis's central argument in "The Planet of No Return"?

3. What is Seijo's response to Ellis? Why does he respond in the way he does?
4. Explain why Seijo proposes that the film *When Worlds Collide* may be a "prescient metaphor for the crossroads at which humanity stands today."

Explore

1. Look up the term "Anthropocene" on *Wikipedia*. Read the entry. Based on what you have read, write a one-paragraph definition of the term. Then, write one page reflecting on why Seijo may have decided to use this term in the introductory paragraph of his essay.
2. Do some research into the types of local government initiatives related to climate change that are taking place near you. Locate one document or report published by your local government about climate change. Compare and contrast this document or report to Seijo's article. Do both discuss climate change in similar ways? What similarities and differences exist between these two documents, the style and tone of the writing, and their assessment of how pressing a threat climate change may be? Prepare a short presentation for your class in which you review and discuss your findings.
3. Visit the Intergovernmental Panel on Climate Change website (www.ipcc.ch) and do some research on climate change. Based on your findings from this research, write a two-page response to Seijo, explaining why or why not you agree with his proposition that "never has humanity had access to so much information and proven so incapable of reaching an imaginative conclusion about what ought to be done."

Forging Connections

1. In two or three pages, describe one or two specific experiences that you have had in relation to the healthcare system. Based on your experience, do you tend to agree more with the assessment of healthcare and medicine provided by Daniel Callahan and Sherwin B. Nuland in their essay "The Quagmire," or the one provided by Eric Topol in his essay "How Technology Is Transforming Healthcare"? In a short essay, explain how your experience relates to these articles, your understanding of each, and the arguments presented in them.

2. In his essay "Slow Ideas," Atul Gawande proposes that one key reason anesthesia was adopted more rapidly than antiseptics was that it had a visible impact, whereas the benefits of antiseptics were mostly invisible. But Gawande's discussion of how visible versus invisible problems get addressed is actually much broader and can be applied to several different essays in this chapter. Write a blog post in which you use Gawande's discussion of visible and invisible problems as a framework for helping your readers understand some of the issues related to healthcare technology discussed in Daniel Callahan and Douglas Nuland's essay "The Quagmire."

Looking Further

1. Concerns about ethics and the possible need to regulate technology arise in relation not only to biotechnologies but also to advances in artificial intelligence and robotics. Compare and contrast Francis Fukuyama and Gary Marcus's essays. What similar concerns do both express? Do they advocate for a similar course of action? Write a three- to five-page essay in which you compare the ethical issues related to biotechnologies with those that arise in relation to automated technologies, and explain the ways in which the advancement of ethical policies in the two fields might benefit from being in dialogue with one another.

2. All of the readings in this chapter, and many in this book, discuss and often critique the idea that technologies of various kinds will solve some very large and important issues—climate change, disease, economic inequality. This phenomenon can be described as "technological solutionism" or "technological utopianism," which promotes the idea that the latest technologies will simply make some of the world's major problems go away. This is a story that we all frequently tell ourselves and is one that is very appealing. So appealing, in fact, that many people simply hope that it may be possible to construct a giant shield to protect the Earth from the effects of climate change, or to develop a pill that will cure every disease. Instead, the reality is that technologies are embedded in social processes and systems that are enormously complex, and that every technology both solves a problem and creates others. How can you begin to change the perspective that many of your classmates and fellow citizens may have from one that is characterized

by "technological solutionism" to one that is more realistic? This new perspective, which you may want to refer to as "technological realism," takes into consideration the fact that technologies solve some problems while creating others and that some of the very problems that we may hope that technologies will solve were ultimately made worse by technologies in the first place. Drawing on evidence from several readings in this anthology, draft an editorial that persuades your fellow students that it is time to give up the overly simplistic notion that technologies will simply solve the world's problems. In your editorial, cite evidence from specific essays to clearly show your readers how technological innovation is never simply a solution, but always involves some type of compromise that may or may not be worth the costs extracted. End your editorial by outlining and describing your model for addressing one major sociocultural or economic issue and your vision of how technologies may—or may not—play a role.

Researching and Writing About Technology

Barbara Rockenbach and Aaron Ritzenberg[1]

Research-based writing lies at the heart of the mission of higher education: to discover, transform, and share ideas. As a college student, it is through writing and research that you will become an active participant in an intellectual community. Doing research in college involves not only searching for information but also digesting, analyzing, and synthesizing what you find in order to create new knowledge. Your most successful efforts as a college writer will report on the latest and most important ideas in a field as well as make new arguments and offer fresh insights.

It may seem daunting to be asked to contribute new ideas to a field in which you are a novice. After all, creating new knowledge seems to be the realm of experts. In this guide, we offer strategies that demystify the research and writing process, breaking down some of the fundamental steps that scholars take when they do research and make arguments. You'll see that contributing to scholarship involves strategies that can be learned and practiced.

Throughout this guide we imagine doing research and writing as engaging in a scholarly conversation. When you read academic writing, you'll see that scholars reference the studies that came before them and allude to the studies that will grow out of their research. When you think of research as engaging in a conversation, you quickly realize that scholarship always has a social aspect. Even if you like to find books in the darkest corners of the library, even if you like to draft your essays in deep solitude, you will always be awake to the voices that helped you form your ideas and to the audience who will receive your ideas. As if in a conversation at a party, scholars mingle: They listen to others and share their most recent ideas, learning and teaching at the same time. Strong scholars, like good conversationalists, will listen and speak with an open mind, letting their own thoughts evolve as they encounter new ideas.

You may be wondering, "What does it mean to have an open mind when I'm doing research? After all, aren't I supposed to find evidence that supports my thesis?" We'll be returning to this question soon, but the quick answer is: To have an open mind when you're doing research means that you'll be involved in the research process well before you have a thesis. We realize this may be a big change from the way you think about research. The fact is, though, that scholars do research well before they know any of the arguments they'll be making in their papers. Indeed, scholars do research even before they know what specific topic they'll be addressing and what questions they'll be asking.

When scholars do research they may not know exactly what they are hunting for, but they have techniques that help them define projects, identify strong interlocutors, and ask important questions. This guide will help you move through the various kinds of research that you'll need at the different stages of your project. If writing a paper involves orchestrating a conversation within a scholarly community, there are a number of important questions you'll need to answer: How do I choose what to write about? How do I find a scholarly community? How do I orchestrate a conversation that involves this community? Whose voices should be most prominent? How do I enter the conversation? How do I use evidence to make a persuasive claim? How do I make sure that my claim is not just interesting but important?

GETTING STARTED

You have been asked to write a research paper. This may be your first research paper at the college level. Where do you start? The important thing when embarking on any kind of writing project that involves research is to find something that you are interested in learning more about. Writing and research is easier if you care about your topic. Your instructor may have given you a topic, but you can make that topic your own by finding something that appeals to you within the scope of the assignment.

Academic writing begins from a place of deep inquiry. When you are sincerely interested in a problem, researching can be a pleasure, since it will satisfy your own intellectual curiosity. More important, the intellectual problems that seem most difficult—the questions that appear to resist obvious answers—are the very problems that will often yield the most surprising and most rewarding results.

Presearching to Generate Ideas

When faced with a research project, your first instinct might be to go to Google or Wikipedia, or even to a social media site. This is not a bad instinct. In fact, Google, Wikipedia, and social media can be great places to start. Using Google, Wikipedia, and social media to help you discover a topic is what we call "presearch"—it is what you do to warm up before the more rigorous work of academic research. Academic research and writing will require you to go beyond these sites to find resources that will make the work of researching and writing both easier and more appropriate to an academic context.

Google   Let's start with Google. You use Google because you know you are going to find a simple search interface and that your search will produce many results. These results may not be completely relevant to your topic, but Google helps in the discovery phase of your work. For instance, you are asked to write about technology and literacy practices.

This Google search will produce articles from many diverse sources—magazines, government sites, and corporate reports among them. It's not a bad start. Use these results to begin to home in on a topic you are interested in pursuing. A quick look through these results may yield a more focused topic such as how information and communication technologies are affecting written communication. A particular source mentions this impact in the context of writing across genres and populations, while others examine how student writing is being affected in particular.

Wikipedia   A Wikipedia search on technology and writing will lead you to several articles that address both concepts. The great thing about Wikipedia is that it is an easy way to gain access to a wealth of information about thousands of topics. However, it is crucial to realize that Wikipedia itself is not an authoritative source in a scholarly context. Even though you may see Wikipedia cited in mainstream newspapers and popular magazines,

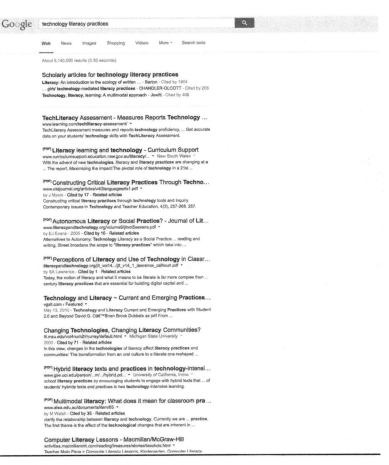

Image 1.1   A standard Google search.

academic researchers do not consider Wikipedia a reliable source and do not consult or cite it in their own research. Wikipedia itself says that "Wikipedia is not considered a credible source . . . This is especially true considering that anyone can edit the information given at any time." For research papers in college, you should use Wikipedia only to find basic information about your topic and to point you toward scholarly sources. Wikipedia may be a great starting point for presearch, but it is not an adequate ending point for research. Use the References section at the bottom of the Wikipedia article to find other, more substantive and authoritative resources about your topic.

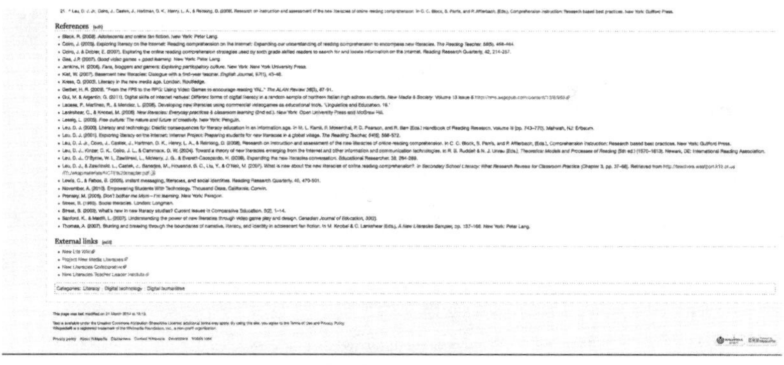

Image 1.2 References section on Wikipedia.

Using Social Media Social media such as Facebook and Twitter can be useful in the presearch phase of your project, but you must start thinking about these tools in new ways. You may have a Facebook or Twitter account and use it to keep in touch with friends, family, and colleagues. These social networks are valuable, and you may already use them to gather information to help you make decisions in your personal life and your workplace. Although social media is not generally useful to your academic research, both Facebook and Twitter have powerful search functions that can lead you to resources and help you refine your ideas.

After you log in to Facebook, use the "Search for people, places, and things" bar at the top of the page to begin. When you type search terms into this bar, Facebook will first search your own social network. To extend beyond your own network, try adding the word "research" after your search terms. For instance, a search on Facebook for "technology research" will lead you to a Facebook page for the *MIT Technology Review.* The posts on the page link to current news stories on technology, links to other similar research centers, and topics of interest in the field of technology research. You can use these search results as a way to see part of the conversation about a particular topic. This is not necessarily the scholarly conversation we referred to at the start of this guide, but it is a social conversation that can still be useful in helping you determine what you want to focus on in the research process.

Twitter is an information network where users can post short messages (or "tweets"). While many people use Twitter simply to update their friends

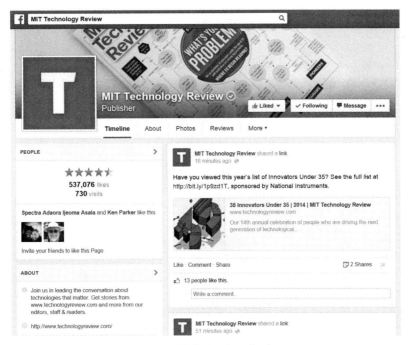

Image 1.3   Facebook page for *MIT Technology Review*.

("I'm going to the mall" or "Can't believe it's snowing!"), more and more individuals and organizations use Twitter to comment on noteworthy events or link to interesting articles. You can use Twitter as a presearch tool because it aggregates links to sites, people in a field of research, and noteworthy sources. Communities, sometimes even scholarly communities, form around topics on Twitter. Users group posts together by using hashtags—words or phrases that follow the "#" sign. Users can respond to other users by using the @ sign followed by a user's Twitter name. When searching for specific individuals or organizations on Twitter, you search using their handle (such as @barackobama or @whitehouse). You will retrieve tweets that were created either by the person or organization, or tweets that mention the person or organization. When searching for a topic to find discussions, you search using the hashtag symbol, #. For instance, a search on #technology will take you to tweets and threaded discussions on the topic of technology.

There are two ways to search Twitter. You can use the search book in the upper right-hand corner and enter either a @ or # search as described above.

Once you retrieve results, you can search again by clicking on any of words that are hyperlinked within your results, such as #antitechnology.

If you consider a hashtag (the # sign) as an entry point into a community, you will begin to discover a conversation around topics. For instance, a search on Twitter for #technology leads you to *Wired* (@Wired), a technology magazine, and TechCrunch (@TechCrunch), a technology news feed. Evaluating information and sources found in social media is similar to how you evaluate any information you encounter during the research process. And, as with Wikipedia and Google searches, this is just a starting point to help you get a sense of the spectrum of topics. This is no substitute for using library resources. Do not cite Facebook, Twitter, or Wikipedia in a research paper; use them to find more credible, authoritative sources. We'll talk about evaluating sources in the sections that follow.

Create a Concept Map

Once you have settled on a topic that you find exciting and interesting, the next step is to generate search terms, or keywords, for effective searching. Keywords are the crucial terms or phrases that signal the content of any given source. Keywords are the building blocks of your search for information. One way to generate keywords is to tell a friend or classmate what you are interested in. What words are you using to describe your research project? You may not have a fully formed idea or claim, but you have a vague sense of your interest. A concept map exercise can help you generate more keywords and, in many cases, narrow your topic to make it more manageable.

A concept map is a way to visualize the relationship between concepts or ideas. You can create a concept map on paper, or there are many free programs online that can help you do this (see, for instance http://vue.tufts .edu/, http://wisemapping.org, or http://freeplane.sourceforge.net). There are many concept mapping applications available for mobile devices; the concept map here was created using the app SimpleMind.

Here is how you use a concept map. First, begin with a term like "technology and literacy practices." Put that term in the first box. Then think of synonyms or words related to this topic, such as "reading," "writing," "visual literacy," "digital literacy," "blogging," and "texting." This brainstorming process will help you develop keywords for searching. Notice that keywords can also be short phrases.

After some practice, you'll discover that some phrases make for excellent keywords and others make for less effective search tools. The best keywords

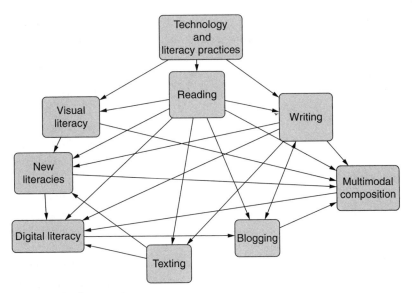

Image 1.4 A concept map.

are precise enough to narrow your topic so that all of your results are relevant, but are not so specific that you might miss helpful results. Concept maps created using apps such as SimpleMind allow you to use templates, embed hyperlinks, and attach notes, among other useful functions.

Keyword Search

One of the hardest parts of writing is coming up with something to write about. Too often, we make the mistake of waiting until we have a fully formed idea before we start writing. The process of writing can actually help you discover what your idea is, and most important, what is interesting about your idea.

Keyword searches are most effective at the beginning stages of your research. They generally produce the most results and can help you determine how much has been written on your topic. You want to use keyword searches to help you achieve a manageable number of results. What is manageable? This is a key question when beginning research. Our keyword search in Google on technology and literacy practices produced over 18 million results. The same search in JSTOR.org also produces tens of thousands of results. These are not manageable results sets. Let's see how we can narrow our search.

Keyword searches, in library resources or on Google, are most effective if you employ a few search strategies that will focus your results.

1. Use AND when you are combining multiple keywords. We have used this search construction previously:

technology AND literacy

The AND ensures that all your results will contain "technology" and "literacy." Many search engines and databases will assume an AND search, meaning if you type

technology literacy

the search will automatically look for both terms. However, in some cases the AND will not be assumed, and "technology literacy" will be treated as a phrase. This means that "technology" will have to be next to the word "literacy" to return results. Worse yet, sometimes the search automatically assumes an OR. That would mean that all your results would come back with either "technology" or "literacy." This will produce a large and mostly irrelevant set of results. Therefore, use AND whenever you want two or more words to appear in a result.

2. Using OR can be very effective when you want to use several terms to describe a concept, such as:

literacy OR reading OR writing

A search on technology and literacy can be broadened to include specific digital literacies. The following search casts a broader net because results will come back with "technology" and either "digital," "texting," or "blogging":

(technology OR digital OR texting OR blogging) AND literacy

Not all of these words will appear in each record. Note also that the parentheses set off the OR search, indicating that "literacy" must appear in each record and then either "technology," "digital," "texting," or "blogging" needs to appear along with literacy.

3. Use quotation marks when looking for a phrase. For instance, if you are looking for information on technology and literacy in an educational context, you can ensure that the search results will include all of

these concepts and increase the relevance by using the following search construction:

Technology AND literacy AND "schools and education"

This phrasing will return results that contain both the words "technology" and "literacy" and the phrase "schools and education."

4. Use NOT to exclude terms that will make your search less relevant. You may find that a term keeps appearing in your search that is not useful. Try this:

Technology AND literacy AND "schools and education" NOT K-12

If you are interested in the looking at the impact of technology on literacy only in higher education, by excluding the keyword "K-12," you will retrieve far fewer sources and ideally more relevant results.

Researchable Question

In a college research paper, it is important that you make an argument, not just offer a report. In high school you may have found some success by merely listing or cataloging the data and information you found; you might have offered a series of findings to show your teacher that you investigated your topic. In college, however, your readers will not be interested in data or information merely for its own sake; your readers will want to know what you make of this data and why they should care.

To satisfy the requirements of a college paper, you'll need to distinguish between a topic and a research question. You will likely begin with a topic, but it is only when you move from a topic to a question that your research will begin to feel motivated and purposeful. A topic refers only to the general subject area that you'll be investigating. A researchable question, on the other hand, points toward a specific problem in the subject area that you'll be attempting to answer by making a claim about the evidence you examine.

"Technology and literacy" is a topic but not a researchable question. It is important that you ask yourself, "What aspect of the topic is most interesting to me?" It is even more important that you ask, "What aspect of the topic is it most important that I illuminate for my audience?" Ideally, your presearch phase of the project will yield questions about technology and literacy that you'd like to investigate.

A strong researchable question will not lead to an easy answer, but rather will lead you into a scholarly conversation in which there are many competing claims. For instance, the question, "Has technology effected literacy?" is not a strong research question, because there is only one correct answer and thus there is no scholarly debate surrounding the topic. It is an interesting question (the answer is: yes), but it will not lead you into a scholarly conversation.

When you are interested in finding a scholarly debate, try using the words "why" and "how" rather than "what." Instead of leading to a definitive answer, the words "why" and "how" will often lead to complex, nuanced answers for which you'll need to marshal evidence in order to be convincing. "Why did the printing press have such widespread effects on literacy practices?" is a question that has a number of complex and competing answers that might draw from a number of different disciplines (education, history, political science, economics, linguistics, and geography, among others). If you can imagine scholars having an interesting debate about your researchable question, it is likely that you've picked a good one.

Once you have come up with an interesting researchable question, your first task as a researcher is to figure out how scholars are discussing your question. Many novice writers think that the first thing they should do when beginning a research project is to articulate an argument, then find sources that confirm their argument. This is not how experienced scholars work. Instead, strong writers know that they cannot possibly come up with a strong central argument until they have done sufficient research. So, instead of looking for sources that confirm a preliminary claim you might want to make, look for the scholarly conversation.

Looking at the scholarly conversation is a strong way to figure out if you've found a research question that is suitable in scope for the kind of paper you're writing. Put another way, reading the scholarly conversation can tell you if your research question is too broad or too narrow. Most novice writers begin with research questions that are overly broad. If your question is so broad that there are thousands of books and articles participating in the scholarly conversation, it's a good idea for you to focus your question so that you are asking something more specific. If, on the other hand, you are asking a research question that is so obscure that you cannot find a corresponding scholarly conversation, you will want to broaden the scope of your project by asking a slightly less specific question.

Keep in mind the metaphor of a conversation. If you walk into a room and people are talking about technology and literacy, it would be out of place for you to begin immediately by making a huge, vague claim, like, "New technology affects the way that people read and write around the world." It would be equally out of place for you to begin immediately by making an overly specific claim, such as "The growth of Kindle usage in Doha is a strong indicator of an increase in ebook reading in Qatar." Rather, you would gauge the scope of the conversation and figure out what seems like a reasonable contribution.

Your contribution to the conversation, at this point, will likely be a focused research question. This is the question you take with you to the library. In the next section, we'll discuss how best to make use of the library. Later, we'll explore how to turn your research question into an argument for your essay.

Your Campus Library

You have probably used libraries all your life, checking out books from your local public library and studying in your high school library. The difference between your previous library experiences and your college library experience is one of scale. Your college library has more stuff. It may be real stuff like books, journals, and videos, or it may be virtual stuff, like online articles, ebooks, and streaming video. Your library pays a lot of money every year to buy or license content for you to use for your research. By extension, your tuition dollars are buying a lot of really good research material. Resorting to Google and Wikipedia means you are not getting all you can out of your college experience.

Not only will your college library have a much larger collection, it will have a more up-to-date and relevant collection than your high school or community public library. Academic librarians spend considerable time acquiring research materials based on classes being taught at your institution. You may not know it, but librarians carefully monitor what courses are being taught each year and are constantly trying to find research materials appropriate to those courses and your professor's research interests. In many cases, you will find that the librarians will know about your assignment and will already have ideas about the types of sources that will make you most successful.

Get To Know Your Librarians! The most important thing to know during the research process is that there are people to help you. While you may not yet be in the habit of going to the library, there are still many ways in which librarians and library staff can be helpful. Most libraries now have an email or chat service set up so you can ask questions without even setting foot in a library. No question is too basic or too specific. It's a librarian's job to help you find answers, and all questions are welcome. The librarian can even help you discover the right question to ask given the task you are trying to complete.

Help can also come in the form of consultations. Librarians will often make appointments to meet one-on-one to offer in-depth help on a research paper or project. Chances are you will find a link on your library website for scheduling a consultation.

Among the many questions fielded by reference librarians, three stand out as the most often asked. Because librarians hear these questions with such regularity, we suggest that students ask these questions when they begin their research. You can go to the library and ask these questions in person, or you can ask via email or online chat.

1. How do I find a book relevant to my topic?

The answer to this question will vary from place to place, but the thing to remember is that finding a book can be either a physical process or a virtual process. Your library will have books on shelves somewhere, and the complexity of how those shelves are organized and accessed depends on factors of size, number of libraries, and the system of organization your library uses. You will find books by using your library's online catalog and carefully noting the call number and location of a book.

Your library is also increasingly likely to offer electronic books or ebooks. These books are discoverable in your library's online catalog as well. When looking at the location of a book you will frequently see a link for ebook versions. You will not find an ebook in every search, but when you do the advantage is that ebook content is searchable, making your job of finding relevant material in the book easier.

If you find one book on your topic, use it as a jumping-off point for finding more books or articles on that topic. Most books will have bibliographies either at the end of each chapter or at the end of the book in which the author has compiled all the sources he or she used. Consult these bibliographies to find other materials on your topic that will help support your claim.

Another efficient way to find more sources once you've identified a particularly authoritative and credible book is to go back to the book's listing in your library's online catalog. Once you find the book, look carefully at the record for links to subjects. By clicking on a subject link you are finding other items in your library on the same subject. For instance, a search on

technology AND literacy practices

will lead you to items with subjects such as

digital literacy

multimodal composition

English language—computer-assisted instruction

2. What sources can I use as evidence in my paper?

There are many types of resources out there to use as you orchestrate a scholarly conversation and support your paper's argument. Books, which we discussed earlier, are great sources if you can find them on your topic, but often your research question will be something that is either too new or too specific for a book to cover. Books are very good for historical questions and overviews of large topics. For current topics, you will want to explore articles from magazines, journals, and newspapers.

Magazines or periodicals (you will hear these terms interchangeably) are published on a weekly or monthly schedule and contain articles of popular interest. These sources can cover broad topics, like the news in magazines

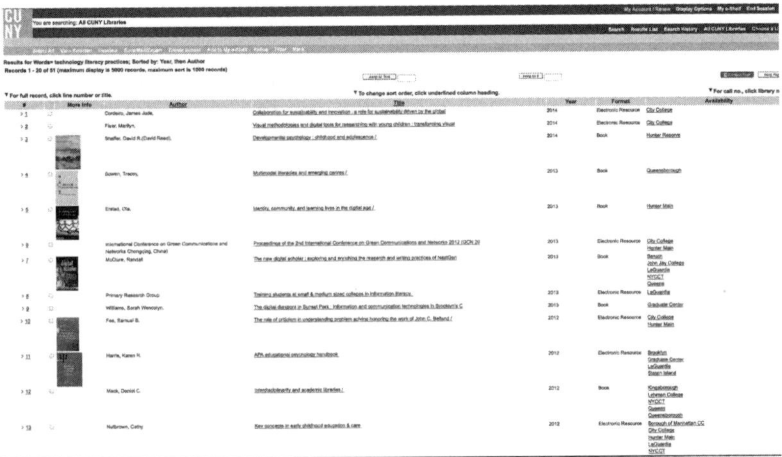

Image 1.5   College library online catalog search.

such as *Newsweek, Time,* and *U.S. News and World Report.* They can also be more focused for particular groups like farmers (*Dairy Farmer*) or photographers (*Creative Photography*). Articles in magazines or periodicals are by professional writers who may or may not be experts. Magazines typically are not considered scholarly and generally do not contain articles with bibliographies, endnotes, or footnotes. This does not mean they are not good sources for your research. In fact, there may be very good reasons to use a magazine article to help support your argument. Magazines capture the point of view of a particular group on a subject, like how farmers feel about increased technology of food production. This point of view may offer support for your claim or an opposing viewpoint to counter. Additionally, magazines can highlight aspects of a topic at a particular point in time. Comparing a *Newsweek* article from 1989 on Japan and technology to an article on the same topic in 2009 allows you to draw conclusions about the changing relationship between the United States and Japan over that 20-year period.

Journals are intended for a scholarly audience of researchers, specialists, or students of a particular field. Journals such as *Technology and Health, Modern Language Journal,* or *Anthropological Linguistics* are all examples of scholarly journals focused on a particular field or research topic. You may hear the term "peer-reviewed" or "refereed" in reference to scholarly journals. This means that the articles contained in a journal have been reviewed by a group of scholars in the same field before the article is published in the journal. This ensures that the research has been vetted by a group of peers before it is published. Articles from scholarly journals can help provide some authority to your argument. By citing experts in a field you are bolstering your argument and entering into the scholarly conversation we talked about at the beginning of this guide.

Newspaper articles are found in newspapers that are generally published daily. There is a broad range of content in newspapers, ranging from articles written by staff reporters, to editorials written by scholars, experts, and general readers, to reviews and commentary written by experts. Newspapers are published more frequently and locally than magazines or journals, making them excellent sources for very recent topics and events as well as those with regional significance. Newspaper articles can provide you with a point of view from a particular part of the country or world (how do Texans feel about technology vs. New Yorkers) or a strong opinion on a topic from an expert (an economist writing an editorial on the effects of technology on the Chinese economy).

A good argument uses evidence from a variety of sources. Do not assume you have done a good job if your paper only cites newspaper articles. You need a broad range of sources to fill out your argument. Your instructor will provide you with guidelines about the number of sources you need, but it will be up to you to find a variety of sources. Finding two or three sources in each of the categories above will help you begin to build a strong argument.

3. Where should I look for articles on my topic?

The best way to locate journal, magazine, or newspaper articles is to use a database. A database is an online resource that organizes research material of a particular type or content area. For example, *PsycINFO* is a psychology database where you would look for journal articles (as well as other kinds of sources) in the discipline of psychology. Your library licenses or subscribes to databases on your behalf. Finding the right database for your topic will depend upon what is available at your college or university because every institution has a different set of resources. Many libraries will provide subject or research guides that can help you determine what database would be best for your topic. Look for these guides on your library website. Your library's website will have a way to search databases. Look for a section of the library website on databases, and look for a search box in that section. For instance, if you type "language" in a database search box, you may find that your library licenses a database called *MLA International Bibliography* (Modern Language Association). A search for "history" in the database search box may yield *American History and Life* or *Historical Abstracts*. In most instances, your best bet is to ask a librarian which database or databases are most relevant to your research.

When using these databases that your library provides for you, you will know that you are starting to sufficiently narrow or broaden your topic when you begin to retrieve thirty to fifty sources during a search. This kind of narrow result field will rarely occur in Google, which is one of the reasons why using library databases is preferable to Google when doing academic research. Databases will help you determine when you have begun to ask a manageable question.

When you have gotten down to thirty to fifty sources in your result list, begin to look through those results to see what aspects of your topic are being written about. Are there lots of articles on technology, language, and China? If so, that might be a topic worth investigating since there is a lot of information for you to read. This is where you begin to discover where your voice might add to the ongoing conversation on the topic.

Using Evidence

The quality of evidence and how you deploy the evidence is ultimately what will make your claims persuasive. You may think of evidence as that which will help prove your claim. But if you look at any scholarly book or article you'll see that evidence can be used in a number of different ways. Evidence can be used to provide readers with crucial background information. It can be used to tell readers what scholars have commonly thought about a topic (but which you may disagree with). It can offer a theory that you use as a lens. It can offer a methodology or an approach that you would like to use. And finally, evidence can be used to back up the claim that you'll be making in your paper.

Novice researchers begin with a thesis and try to find all the evidence that will prove that their claim is valid or true. What if you come across evidence that doesn't help with the validity of your claim? A novice researcher might decide not to take this complicating evidence into account. Indeed, when you come across complicating evidence, you might be tempted to pretend you never saw it! But rather than sweeping imperfect evidence under the rug, you should figure out how to use this evidence to complicate your own ideas.

The best scholarly conversations take into account a wide array of evidence, carefully considering all sides of a topic. As you probably know, often the most fruitful and productive conversations occur not just when you are talking to people who already agree with you, but when you are fully engaging with the people who might disagree with you.

Coming across unexpected, surprising, and contradictory evidence, then, is a good thing! It will force you to make a complex, nuanced argument and will ultimately allow you to write a more persuasive paper.

Other Forms of Evidence

We've talked about finding evidence in books, magazines, journals, and newspapers. Here are a few other kinds of evidence you may want to use.

Interviews   Interviews can be a powerful form of evidence, especially if the person you are interviewing is an expert in the field that you're investigating. Interviewing can be intimidating, but it might help to know that many people (even experts!) will feel flattered when you ask them for an interview. Most scholars are deeply interested in spreading knowledge, so you should feel comfortable asking a scholar for his or her ideas. Even if the scholar doesn't know the specific answer to your question, he or she may be able to point you in the right direction.

Remember, of course, to be as courteous as possible when you are planning to interview someone. This means sending a polite email that fully introduces yourself and your project before you begin asking questions. Email interviews may be convenient, but an in-person interview is best, since this allows for you and the interviewee to engage in a conversation that may take surprising and helpful turns.

It's a good idea to write down a number of questions before the interview. Make sure not just to get facts (which you can likely get somewhere else). Ask the interviewee to speculate about your topic. Remember that "why" and "how" questions often yield more interesting answers than "what" questions.

If you do conduct an in-person interview, act professionally. Be on time, dress respectfully, and show sincere interest and gratitude. Bring something to record the interview. Many reporters still use pens and a pad, since these feel unobtrusive and are very portable.

Write down the interviewee's name, the date, and the location of the interview, and have your list of questions ready. Don't be afraid, of course, to veer from your questions. The best questions might be the follow-up questions that couldn't have occurred to you before the conversation began. You're likely to get the interviewee to talk freely and openly if you show real intellectual curiosity. If you're not a fast writer, it's certainly OK to ask the interviewee to pause for a moment while you take notes. Some people like to record their interviews. Just make sure that you ask permission if you choose to do this. It's always nice to send a brief thank-you note or email after the interview. This would be a good time to ask any brief follow-up questions.

Images   Because we live in a visual age, we tend to take images for granted. We see them in magazines, on TV, and on the Internet. We don't often think about them as critically as we think about words on a page. Yet, a critical look at an image can uncover helpful evidence for a claim. For example, if you are writing about the impact of technology on writing, you could introduce an image such as the one pictured below to illustrate literacy practices in a networked world.

Image 1.6   The cognitive demands involved with multitasking.

This is an image of the cognitive demands involved with multitasking, which is often part of contemporary reading and writing practices. This image enables you to discuss the ways in which information and communications technologies may increase our access to information while also limiting our ability to read and process that information. Images can add depth and variety to your argument and they are generally easy to find on the Internet. Use Google Image search or flickr.com to find images using the same keywords you used to find books and articles. Ask your instructor for guidance on how to properly cite and acknowledge the source of any images you wish to use. If you want to present your research outside of a classroom project (for example, publish it on a blog or share it at a community event), ask a research librarian for guidance on avoiding any potential copyright violations.

Multimedia   Like images, multimedia such as video, audio, and animations are increasingly easy to find on the Internet and can strengthen your claim. For instance, if you are working on technology and literacy practices, you could find audio or video news clips illustrating the effects of technology on reading and writing. There are several audio and video search engines available, such as Vimeo (vimeo.com) or Blinkx (blinkx.com), a search engine featuring audio and video from the BBC, Reuters, and the Associated Press among others. As with images, ask your instructor for guidance on how to properly cite and acknowledge the source of any multimedia you wish to use. If you want to present your research outside of a classroom project (for example, publish it on a blog or share it at a community event), ask a research librarian for guidance on avoiding any potential copyright violations.

Evaluating Sources

A common problem in research isn't a lack of sources, but an overload of information. Information is more accessible than ever. How many times have you done an online search and asked yourself the question: "How do I know what is good information?" Librarians can help. Evaluating online sources is more challenging than traditional sources because it is harder to make distinctions between good and bad online information than with print sources. It is easy to tell that *Newsweek* magazine is not as scholarly as an academic journal, but online everything may look the same. There are markers of credibility and authoritativeness when it comes to online information, and you can start to recognize them. We'll provide a few tips here, but be sure to ask a librarian or your professor for more guidance whenever you're uncertain about the reliability of a source.

1. **Domain**—The "domain" of a site is the last part of its URL. The domain indicates the type of website. Noting the web address can tell you a lot. A .edu site indicates that an educational organization created that content. This is no guarantee that the information is accurate, but it does suggest less bias than a .com site, which will be commercial in nature with a motive to sell you something, including ideas.

2. **Date**—Most websites include a date somewhere on the page. This date may indicate a copyright date, the date something was posted, or the date the site was last updated. These dates tell you when the content on the site was last changed or reviewed. Older sites might be outdated or contain information that is no longer relevant.

3. **Author or editor**—Does the online content indicate an author or editor? Like print materials, authority comes from the creator or the content. It is now easier than ever to investigate an author's credentials. A general Google search may lead you to a Wikipedia entry on the author, a LinkedIn page, or even an online résumé. If an author is affiliated with an educational institution, try visiting the institution's website for more information.

Managing Sources

Now that you've found sources, you need to think about how you are going to keep track of the sources and prepare the bibliography that will accompany your paper. Managing your sources is called "bibliographic citation management," and you will sometimes see references to bibliographic citation management on your library's website. Don't let this complicated phrase deter you—managing your citations from the start of your research will make your life much easier during the research process and especially the night before your paper is due when you are compiling your bibliography.

EndNote and RefWorks Chances are your college library provides software, such as EndNote or RefWorks, to help you manage citations. These are two commercially available citation management software packages that are not freely available to you unless your library has paid for a license. EndNote or RefWorks enables you to organize your sources in personal libraries. These libraries help you manage your sources and create bibliographies. Both EndNote and RefWorks also enable you to insert endnotes and footnotes directly into a Microsoft Word document.

Zotero If your library does not provide EndNote or RefWorks, a freely available software called Zotero (Zotero.org) will help you manage your sources. Zotero helps you collect, organize, cite, and share your sources, and it lives right in your Web browser where you do your research. As you are searching Google, your library catalog, or library database, Zotero enables you to add a book, article, or website to a personal library with one click. As you add items to your library, Zotero collects both the information you need for your bibliography and any full-text content. This means that the content of journal articles and ebooks will be available to you right from your Zotero library.

To create a bibliography, simply select the items from your Zotero library you want to include, right click and select "Create Bibliography from Selected Items . . . ," and choose the citation style your instructor has asked you to use for the paper. To get started, go to Zotero.org and download Zotero for the browser of your choice.

Taking Notes It is crucial that you take good, careful notes while you are doing your research. Not only is careful note taking necessary to avoid plagiarism, it can also help you think through your project while you are doing research.

While many researchers used to take notes on index cards, most people now use computers. If you're using your computer, open a new document for each source that you're considering using. The first step in taking notes is to make sure that you gather all the information you might need in your bibliography or works cited. If you're taking notes from a book, for instance, you'll need the author, the title, the place of publication, the press, and the year. Be sure to check the style guide assigned by your instructor to make sure you're gathering all the necessary information.

After you've recorded the bibliographic information, add one or two keywords that can help you sort this source. Next, write a one- or two-sentence summary of the source. Finally, have a section on your document that is reserved for specific places in the text that you might want to work with. When you write down a quote, remember to be extra careful that you are capturing the quote exactly as it is written—and that you enclose the quote in quotation marks. Do not use abbreviations or change the punctuation. Remember, too, to write down the exact page numbers from the source you are quoting. Being careful with small details at the beginning of your project can save you a lot of time in the long run.

WRITING ABOUT TECHNOLOGY

In your writing, as in your conversations, you should always be thinking about your audience. While your most obvious audience is the instructor, most college instructors will want you to write a paper that will be interesting and illuminating for other beginning scholars in the field. Many students are unsure of what kind of knowledge they can presume of their audience. A good rule of thumb is to write not only for your instructor but also for other students in your class and for other students in classes similar to yours. You can assume a reasonably informed audience that is curious but also skeptical.

Of course it is crucial that you keep your instructor in mind. After all, your instructor will be giving you feedback and evaluating your paper. The best way to keep your instructor in mind while you are writing is to periodically reread the assignment while you are writing. Are you answering the assignment's prompt? Are you adhering to the assignment's guidelines? Are you fulfilling the assignment's purpose? If your answer to any of these questions is uncertain, it's a good idea to ask the instructor.

From Research Question to Thesis Statement

Many students like to begin the writing process by writing an introduction. Novice writers often use an early draft of their introduction to guide the shape of their paper. Experienced scholars, however, continually return to their introduction, reshaping it and revising it as their thoughts evolve. After all, since writing is thinking, it is impossible to anticipate the full thoughts of your paper before you have written it. Many writers, in fact, only realize the actual argument they are making after they have written a draft or two of the paper. Make sure not to let your introduction trap your thinking. Think of your introduction as a guide that will help your readers down the path of discovery—a path you can only fully know after you have written your paper.

A strong introduction will welcome readers to the scholarly conversation. You'll introduce your central interlocutors and pose the question or problem that you are all interested in resolving. Most introductions contain a thesis statement, which is a sentence or two that clearly states the main argument. Some introductions, you'll notice, do not contain the argument, but merely contain the promise of a resolution to the intellectual problem.

Is Your Thesis an Argument?

So far, we've discussed a number of steps for you to take when you begin to write a research paper. We started by strategizing about ways to use presearch to find a topic and ask a researchable question, then we looked at ways to find a scholarly conversation by using your library's resources. Now we'll discuss a crucial step in the writing process: coming up with a thesis.

Your thesis is the central claim of your paper—the main point that you'd like to argue. You may make a number of claims throughout the paper; when you make a claim, you are offering a small argument, usually about a piece of evidence that you've found. Your thesis is your governing claim, the central argument of the whole paper. Sometimes it is difficult to know if you have written a proper thesis. Ask yourself, "Can a reasonable person disagree with my thesis statement?" If the answer is no, then you likely have written an observation rather than an argument. For instance, the statement, "There are six official languages of the UN" is not a thesis, since this is a fact. A reasonable person cannot disagree with this fact, so it is not an argument. The statement, "Arabic became an official language of the UN for economic reasons" is a thesis, since it is a debatable point. A reasonable person might disagree (by arguing, for instance, that "Arabic became an official language of the UN for political reasons"). Remember to keep returning to your thesis statement while you are writing. Not only will you be thus able to make sure that your writing remains on a clear path, but you'll also be able to keep refining your thesis so that it becomes clearer and more precise.

Make sure, too, that your thesis is a point of persuasion rather than one of belief or taste.

"Chinese food tastes delicious" is certainly an argument you could make to your friend, but it is not an adequate thesis for an academic paper, because there is no evidence that you could provide that might persuade a reader who doesn't already agree with you.

Organization

For your paper to feel organized, readers should know where they are headed and have a reasonable idea of how they are going to get there. An introduction will offer a strong sense of organization if it:

- introduces your central intellectual problem and explains why it is important
- suggests who will be involved in the scholarly conversation
- indicates what kind of evidence you'll be investigating; and
- offers a precise central argument.

Some readers describe well-organized papers as having a sense of flow. When readers praise a sense of flow, they mean that the argument moves easily from one sentence to the next and from one paragraph to the next. This allows your reader to follow your thoughts easily. When you begin writing a sentence, try using an idea, keyword, or phrase from the end of the previous sentence. The next sentence, then, will appear to have emerged smoothly from the previous sentence. This tip is especially important when you move between paragraphs. The beginning of a paragraph should feel like it has a clear relationship to the end of the previous paragraph.

Keep in mind, too, a sense of wholeness. A strong paragraph has a sense of flow and a sense of wholeness: not only will you allow your reader to trace your thoughts smoothly, but you will ensure that your reader understands how all your thoughts are connected to a large, central idea. Ask yourself, as you write a paragraph: What does this paragraph have to do with the central intellectual problem that I am investigating? If the relationship isn't clear to you, then your readers will likely be confused.

Novice writers often use the form of a five-paragraph essay. In this form, each paragraph offers an example that proves the validity of the central claim. The five-paragraph essay may have worked in high school, since it meets the minimum requirement for making an argument with evidence. You'll quickly notice, though, that experienced writers do not use the five-paragraph essay. Indeed, your college instructors will expect you to move beyond the five-paragraph essay. This is because a five-paragraph essay relies on static examples rather than fully engaging new evidence. A strong essay will grow in complexity and nuance as the writer brings in new evidence. Rather than thinking of an essay as something that offers many examples to back up the same static idea, think of an essay as the evolution of an idea that grows ever more complex and rich as the writer engages with scholars who view the idea from various angles.

Integrating Your Research

As we have seen, doing research involves finding an intellectual community by looking for scholars who are thinking through similar problems and may be in conversation with one another. When you write your paper, you will not merely be reporting what you found; you will be orchestrating the conversation that your research has uncovered. To orchestrate a conversation involves asking a few key questions: Whose voices should be most prominent? What is the relationship between one scholar's ideas and another scholar's ideas? How do these ideas contribute to the argument that your own paper is making? Is it important that your readers hear the exact words of the conversation, or can you give them the main ideas and important points of the conversation in your own words? Your answers to these questions will determine how you go about integrating your research into your paper.

Using evidence is a way of gaining authority. Even though you may not have known much about your topic before you started researching, the way you use evidence in your paper will allow you to establish a voice that is authoritative and trustworthy. You have three basic choices to decide how best you'd like to present the information from a source: summarize, paraphrase, or quote. Let's discuss each one briefly.

Summary You should summarize a source when the source provides helpful background information for your research. Summaries do not make strong evidence, but they can be helpful if you need to chart the intellectual terrain of your project. Summaries can be an efficient way of capturing the main ideas of a source. Remember, when you are summarizing, to be fully sympathetic to the writer's point of view. Put yourself in the scholar's shoes. If you later disagree with the scholar's methods or conclusions, your disagreement will be convincing because your reader will know that you have given the scholar a fair hearing. A summary that is clearly biased is not only inaccurate and ethically suspect, but it will make your writing less convincing because readers will be suspicious of your rigor.

Let's say you come across the following quote that you'd like to summarize. Here's an excerpt from *The Language Wars: A History of Proper English*, by Henry Hitchings:

> No language has spread as widely as English, and it continues to spread. Internationally the desire to learn it is insatiable. In the twenty-first century the world is becoming more urban and more middle class, and the adoption of English is a symptom of this, for increasingly English serves as the lingua franca of business and popular culture. It is dominant or at least very prominent in other areas such as shipping, diplomacy, computing, medicine and education. (300)

Consider this summary:

> In *The Language Wars*, Hitchings says that everyone wants to learn English because it is the best language in the world (300). I agree that English is the best.

If you compare this summary to what Hitchings actually said, you will see that this summary is a biased, distorted version of the actual quote. Hitchings did not make a universal claim about whether English is better or worse than other languages. Rather, he made a claim about why English is becoming so widespread in an increasingly connected world.

Now let's look at another summary:

> According to Hitchings, English has become the go-to choice for global communications and has spread quickly as the language of commerce and ideas (300).

This is a much stronger summary than the previous example. The writer shortens Hitchings's original language, but he or she is fair to the writer's original meaning and intent.

Paraphrase   Paraphrasing involves putting a source's ideas into your own words. It's a good idea to paraphrase if you think you can state the idea more clearly or more directly than the original source does. Remember that if you paraphrase you need to put the entire idea into your own words. It is not enough for you to change one or two words. Indeed, if you only change a few words, you may put yourself at risk of plagiarizing.

Let's look at how we might paraphrase the Hitchings quote that we've been discussing. Consider this paraphrase:

> Internationally the desire to learn English is insatiable. In today's society, the world is becoming wealthier and more urban, and the use of English is a symptom of this (Hitchings 300).

You will notice that the writer simply replaced some of Hitchings's original language with synonyms. Even with the parenthetical citation, this is unacceptable paraphrasing. Indeed, this is a form of plagiarism, because the writer suggests that the language is his or her own, when it is in fact an only slightly modified version of Hitchings's own phrasing.

Let's see how we might paraphrase Hitchings in an academically honest way:

> Because English is used so frequently in global communications, many people around the world want to learn English as they become members of the middle class (Hitchings 300).

Here the writer has taken Hitchings's message but has used his or her own language to describe what Hitchings originally wrote. The writer offers Hitchings's ideas with fresh syntax and new vocabulary, and the writer is sure to give Hitchings credit for the idea in a parenthetical citation.

Quotation   The best way to show that you are in conversation with scholars is to quote them. Quoting involves capturing the exact wording and punctuation of a passage. Quotations make for powerful evidence, especially in humanities papers. If you come across evidence that you think will be helpful in your project, you should quote it. You may be tempted to quote only those passages that seem to agree with the claim that you are working with. But remember to write down the quotes of scholars who may not seem to agree with you. These are precisely the thoughts that will help you build a powerful scholarly conversation. Working with fresh ideas that you may not agree with can help you revise your claim to make it even more persuasive, since it will force you to take into account potential counterarguments. When your readers see that you are grappling with an intellectual problem from all sides and that you are giving all interlocutors a fair voice, they are more likely to be persuaded by your argument.

To make sure that you are properly integrating your sources into your paper, remember the acronym ICE: Introduce, Cite, and Explain. Let's imagine that you've found an idea that you'd like to incorporate into your paper. We'll use a quote from David Harvey's *A Brief History of Neoliberalism* as an example. On page 7, you find the following quote that you'd like to use: "The assumption that individual freedoms are guaranteed by freedom of the market and of trade is a cardinal feature of neoliberal thinking, and it has long dominated the US stance towards the rest of the world."

1. The first thing you need to do is **introduce** the quote ("introduce" gives us the "I" in ICE). To introduce a quote, provide context so that your readers know where it is coming from, and you must integrate the quote into your own sentence. Here are some examples of how you might do this:

   > In his book *A Brief History of Neoliberalism*, David Harvey writes . . .
   > One expert on the relationship between economics and politics claims . . .
   > Professor of Anthropology David Harvey explains that . . .
   > In a recent book by Harvey, he contends . . .

   Notice that each of these introduces the quote in such a way that readers are likely to recognize it as an authoritative source.

2. The next step is to **cite** the quote (the C in ICE). Here is where you indicate the origin of the quotation so that your readers can easily look up the original source. Citing is a two-step process that varies slightly depending on the citation style that you're using. We'll offer an

example using MLA style. The first step involves indicating the author and page number in the body of your essay. Here is an example of a parenthetical citation that gives the author and page number after the quote and before the period that ends the sentence:

> One expert on the relationship between economics and politics claims that neoliberal thinking has "long dominated the US stance towards the rest of the world" (Harvey 7).

Note that if it is already clear to readers which author you're quoting, you need only to give the page number:

> In *A Brief History of Neoliberalism*, David Harvey contends that neoliberal thinking has "long dominated the US stance towards the rest of the world" (7).

The second step of citing the quote is providing proper information in the works cited or bibliography of your paper. This list should include the complete bibliographical information of all the sources you have cited. An essay that includes the quote by David Harvey should also include the following entry in the works cited:

> Harvey, David. *A Brief History of Neoliberalism*. New York: Oxford UP, 2005. Print.

3. Finally, the most crucial part of integrating a quote is **explaining** it. The E in ICE is often overlooked, but a strong explanation is the most important step to involve yourself in the scholarly conversation. Here is where you will explain how you interpret the source you are citing, what aspect of the quote is most important for your readers to understand, and how the source pertains to your own project. For example:

> David Harvey writes, "The assumption that individual freedoms are guaranteed by freedom of the market and of trade is a cardinal feature of neoliberal thinking, and it has long dominated the US stance towards the rest of the world" (7). As Harvey explains, neoliberalism suggests that free markets do not limit personal freedom but actually lead to free individuals.

Or:

> David Harvey writes, "The assumption that individual freedoms are guaranteed by freedom of the market and of trade is a cardinal feature of neoliberal thinking, and it has long dominated the US stance towards the rest of the world" (7). For Harvey, before we understand the role of the United States in global politics, we must first understand the philosophy that binds personal freedom with market freedom.

Novice writers are sometimes tempted to end a paragraph with a quote that they feel is especially compelling or clear. But remember that you should never leave a quote to speak for itself (even if you love it!). After all, as the orchestrator of this scholarly conversation, you need to make sure that readers are receiving exactly what you'd like them to receive from each quote. Notice, in the above examples, that the first explanation suggests that the writer quoting Harvey is centrally concerned with neoliberal philosophy, while the second explanation suggests that the writer is centrally concerned with U.S. politics. The explanation, in other words, is the crucial link between your source and the main idea of your paper.

Avoiding Plagiarism

Scholarly conversations are what drive knowledge in the world. Scholars using each other's ideas in open, honest ways form the bedrock of our intellectual communities and ensure that our contributions to the world of thought are important. It is crucial, then, that all writers do their part in maintaining the integrity and trustworthiness of scholarly conversations. It is crucial that you never claim someone else's ideas as your own, and that you always are extra careful to give the proper credit to someone else's thoughts. This is what we call responsible scholarship.

The best way to avoid plagiarism is to plan ahead and keep careful notes as you read your sources. Remember the advice (above) on Zotero and taking notes: find the way that works best for you to keep track of what ideas are your own and what ideas come directly from the sources you are reading. Most acts of plagiarism are accidental. It is easy when you are drafting a paper to lose track of where a quote or idea came from; plan ahead and this won't happen. Here are a few tips for making sure that confusion doesn't happen to you.

1. Know what needs to be cited. You do not need to cite what is considered common knowledge such as facts (the day Lincoln was born), concepts (the Earth orbits the sun), or events (the day Martin Luther King was shot). You do need to cite the ideas and words of others from the sources you are using in your paper.
2. Be conservative. If you are not sure if you should cite something, either ask your instructor or a librarian, or cite it. It is better to cite something you don't have to than not cite something you should.
3. Direct quotations from your sources need to be cited as well as anytime you paraphrase the ideas or words from your sources.
4. Finally, extensive citation not only helps you avoid plagiarism, but it also boosts your credibility and enables your reader to trace your scholarship.

Citation Styles

It is crucial that you adhere to the standards of a single citation style when you write your paper. The most common styles are MLA (Modern Language Association, generally used in the humanities), APA (American Psychological Association, generally used in the social sciences), and Chicago (*Chicago Manual of Style*). If you're not sure which style you should use, you must ask your instructor. Each style has its own guidelines regarding the format of the paper. While proper formatting within a given style may seem arbitrary, there are important reasons behind the guidelines of each style. For instance, while MLA citations tend to emphasize authors' names, APA citations tend to emphasize the date of publications. This distinction makes sense, especially given that MLA standards are usually followed by departments in the humanities and APA standards are usually followed by departments in the social sciences. While papers in the humanities value original thinking about arguments and texts that are canonical and often old, papers in the social sciences tend to value arguments that take into account the most current thought and the latest research.

There are a number of helpful guidebooks that will tell you all the rules you need to know in order to follow the standards for various citation styles. If your instructor hasn't pointed you to a specific guidebook, try the following online resources:

Purdue Online Writing Lab: owl.english.purdue.edu/
Internet Public Library: www.ipl.org/div/farq/netciteFARQ.html
Modern Language Association (for MLA style): www.mla.org/style
American Psychological Association (for APA style): www.apastyle.org/
The Chicago Manual of Style Online: www.chicagomanualofstyle.org/
  tools_citationguide.html

NOTE

1. BarbaraRockenbach, Director of Humanities & History Libraries, Columbia University. Aaron Ritzenberg, Associate Director of First-Year Writing, Columbia University.

SAMPLE STUDENT RESEARCH PAPER

Pichardo   1

Riki Pichardo

Professor Rodgers

English 1101

March 3, 2014

This Is Your Brain on Google: Diverse Perspectives
on How Internet Usage Affects Reading Habits

The Internet has become so prominent and widely used in today's society that much of the reading that people are doing is taking place online. The effects of reading online are only now being closely studied and opinions differ as to what the effects may be. Some, such as the media theorist Marshall McLuhan, who has famously proclaimed, "the medium is the message," believe the changes will be significant (203). His view that media may shape thinking appears to be backed up by the research of Maryanne Wolf, my own experiences reading online, and the experiences described by Nicholas Carr in his article "Is Google Making Us Stupid?" However, two writers, N. Katherine Hayles and Ursula K. Le Guin, offer different perspectives on the issue. In her essay "The Death of the Book," Le Guin focuses more on readers and the fact that they are continuing to read than on how the technologies they are using for reading may have changed what they are doing. Hayles, in her essay "How We Read: Close, Hyper, Machine," does not see online reading and print reading as being in opposition to one another, but instead sees a place for both types of literacy practices to supplement one another. Reviewing all of these essays, it appears that the Internet has expanded our access to information, and that it may be changing our ability to process and understand that information. In other words, the Internet may be increasing the amount of information available while at the same time limiting our minds because of the ways in which it makes that information available. Though some writers, such as Le Guin and Hayles, believe online reading will only enhance our reading practices, others, including Carr, Wolf, and McLuhan, believe online reading could change how we read. Based on my reading and my own experiences reading online, I find the arguments of Carr, Wolf, and McLuhan the most convincing.

Many years ago books were the only primary source of information. This is obviously not the case anymore, with the Internet at center stage in everyone's lives. In his article Carr explains the vigorous hours people used to spend on finding information in libraries and in books. He states, "Research that once required days in the stack of periodical rooms of libraries can be done in minutes" (101). While this is beneficial, Carr also sees some trade-offs between easy access to information online. For example, people who read books were more likely to get lost in them, absorbing information they may not necessarily think is useful. On the Internet everything you search for is so narrowed down that there is no space—and less and less time—to pay attention to anything other than what you are looking for.

Carr also explains how he is finding long articles becoming more challenging to read, as we expect to locate in

Pichardo   3

minutes what it used to take long hours to find. Carr writes, "Immersing myself in a book or lengthy articles used to be easy . . . I'd spend hours strolling through long stretches of prose. Now my concentration often starts to drift after two or three pages" (102). I have had a similar experience. I no longer enjoy taking the time to look for information by reading an entire book. I want the information I seek on demand and I want it quickly. Google has captured our minds by training us to expect instant information at our fingertips. We no longer want to read everything we can and immerse ourselves in a new topic along the way, perhaps finding that what we were looking for was not as important or relevant as what we ended up finding.

Skimming seems to be the new way of reading, whether it is in a book or an article on the Internet. Carr quotes a blogger by the name of Bruce Friedman, who stated that "Even a blog post of more than three or four paragraphs is too much to absorb. I skim it" (104). Writing about his own reading, Carr states that "once I was a scuba diver in the sea of words. Now I zip along the surface like a guy on a Jet Ski," once again proving how the Internet has affected the way that we read (101). We are all slowly becoming Jet Skiers; we no longer scuba dive into information for new discoveries. Our treasure now is information, rather than exploration. Opposed to taking the time to read every bit of information we can, we skim to find what we need and get the reading over with. Carr states, "My mind now expects to take in information the way the net distributes it: in a swiftly moving stream of particles" (101).

Pichardo   4

Carr refers to the research of Maryanne Wolf in his essay to support his argument that reading practices may be changing as a result of the amount of time spent searching and reading online. Carr cites research from Wolf's book- *Proust and the Squid: The Story and Science of the Reading Brain* (2008). In Wolf's more recent 2010 essay "Our 'Deep Reading' Brain: Its Digital Evolution Poses Questions," she writes more about the possible effects of online reading on the brain and explains what happens in the brain when we learn to read. Wolf states that

> Whenever we learn something new, the brain forms a new circuit that connects some of the brain's original struc- tures. In the case of learning to read, the brain builds con- nections between and among the visual, language and conceptual areas that are part of our genetic heritage, but that were never woven together in this way before.

But Wolf goes on to explain that

> The reading circuit's very plasticity is also its Achilles' heel. It can be fully fashioned over time and fully implemented when we read, or it can be short-circuited—either early on in its formation period or later, after its formation, in the execution of only part of its potentially available cognitive resources. Because we literally and physiologically can read in multiple ways, how we read—and what we absorb from our reading—will be influenced by both the content of our reading and the medium we use.

What Wolf is saying is that without practice in certain types of reading, our brains could be "short-circuited," or rewired. Our brains can change if we do not read in the same way as we have. Thus, when Carr states that "over the past few years I've had an uncomfortable sense that someone, or something, has been tinkering with my brain," he may not just be imagining things.

Le Guin offers a very different perspective in her essay, "The Death of the Book." Instead of seeing the Internet as taking away from our ability to read, Le Guin asks what people do on computers other than read. She states that

> Reading is undeniably one of the things people do on the computer. And also, on the various electronic devices that are capable of and may be looked upon as "for" telephoning, taking photographs, playing music and games, etc, people may spend a good while texting sweetiepie, or looking up recipes for authentic Cajun gumbo, or checking out the stock report—all of which involve reading. People use computers to play games or wander through picture galleries or watch movies, and to do computations and make spreadsheets and pie charts, and a few lucky ones get to draw pictures or compose music, and so on, but mostly, am I wrong? isn't an awful lot of what people do with computers either word-processing (writing) or processing words (reading)? (130)

Although I agree with Le Guin that people may be doing a lot of reading and writing on the computer, in her own description of how people are reading, she suggests that people are reading while doing many other things. Although she may not have intended for someone to interpret her paragraph to be about a distracted person reading, one who is texting and looking up recipes and researching the stock report all at the same time, this is what her paragraph implies. This is also what most people do when they are reading online. Even if they are reading, they are reading in a distracted way. Instead of focusing on one thing—writing to someone, or reading a cookbook, or researching stocks—they are doing several things at once. This means that they are training their brains to be distracted while they read.

Despite the fact that Le Guin admits in her essay that "Reading on a screen is certainly different from reading a page," she does not seem to agree with Wolf or Carr or McLuhan that the differences are "so great as to justify giving the two kinds of reading different names, or saying that an ebook isn't a book at all" (130; 132). Based on Carr's experiences of reading online and Wolf's essay, which stresses the importance of how we read and the media used for reading to specific brain functions, it seems that the differences between reading online and reading in print may be so great as to "justify giving the two kinds of reading different names" (132). It seems that Le Guin is trying to be optimistic by proposing that great literature will continue to be read on computer screens and may even be read with greater frequency because people are reading more and eBooks are widely available. But in my experience, the type of reading that I do in front of a screen and in front of a book are different. What is more, I am finding it harder and harder to not fall into the same reading habits I have formed in response to reading on a screen when I am reading a printed book.

In her essay, "How We Read: Close, Hyper, Machine," Hayles, like Le Guin, is more optimistic about reading in a digital age, but not for the same reasons as Le Guin. Hayles proposes that new technologies mean that new reading practices will develop and that these can supplement traditional reading practices. Hayles asks two questions at the beginning of her essay, "how to convert the increased digital reading into increased reading ability and how to make effective bridges between digital reading and the literacy traditionally associated with print." In asking these questions, Hayles seems to be agreeing with Le Guin that people are reading more online and also agreeing with Carr, Wolf, and McLuhan that there may be differences between how people read online and how they read in print. Although Hayles makes some interesting suggestions about how print and digital reading practices may supplement each other and how educators can do a better job teaching both print and digital reading practices, the fact remains that she still separates the two mediums. She also seems to suggest that we can have the best of both worlds: that we can have access to all of the information that we have today and still learn how to read as people read when information was only available via print media. But as James Paul Gee stated in his book *What Video Games Have To Teach Us About Learning and Literacy*, "Reading and writing in any domain . . . are not just ways of decoding print, they are also caught up with and

Pichardo   8

in social practices" (18). It may be necessary therefore to maintain not only print reading practices but some of the other social practices related to print reading.

Although Hayles' idea that there can be some kind of compromise reached between print and digital literacy practices is interesting, I have found, based on my own experiences, that my reading is less focused than it used to be. Even reading Hayles' essay, which I did online, I found myself simultaneously reading Kirsty Hawthorne's "A Response to Hayles' 'How We Read: Close, Hyper, Machine.'" Hawthorne's essay helped me better understand Hayles' essay. However, at some point, because I was going back and forth between the two, I began confusing one for the other. As much as I try to focus my reading when I am online, I find it difficult to do so. I'm not sure if this is because of bad habits that I've developed or because of how the Internet is built. At this point, I feel the Internet is winning and I am beginning to read more and more the way that it has trained me to read, which is in a distracted and fragmented way.

The Internet has been a great help to the world in terms of saving time doing research, but the fact that we can access so much information in such a short span of time may have drawbacks. As Wolf states,

My major worry is that, confronted with a digital glut of immediate information that requires and receives less and less intellectual effort, many new (and many older) readers will have neither the time nor the motivation to think through the possible layers of meaning in what they read. The omnipresence of multiple distractions for attention—and the brain's own natural attraction to novelty—contribute to a mindset toward reading that seeks to reduce information to its lowest conceptual denominator. Sound bites, text bites, and mind bites are a reflection of a culture that has forgotten or become too distracted by and too drawn to the next piece of new information to allow itself time to think.

Both Carr and Wolf present convincing evidence that the Internet may be changing the way we read and in the process changing our brains. Before reading these essays, I knew something was going with the way that I am now reading. Even if I want to read a book that has over 30 chapters, for example, after the first two pages my mind begins to wander. I am looking for information rather than immersing myself in what I am reading. I am looking for the "sound bites, text bites, and mind bites" Wolf refers to in her essay. After reading some of the research, I understand as Wolf states that it may be too early to know exactly what the consequences of reading online may be. Nevertheless, based on my own experiences and the findings presented by Carr and Wolf, the risks seem real enough. As a result, I plan to push myself back into the wonderful world of deep reading. I plan on actually taking my time to read from now on, as opposed to trying to save time with my usual skim reading. I also plan on doing as much reading offline as I possibly can.

Pichardo   10

Works Cited

Carr, Nicholas. "Is Google Making Us Stupid?" *Technology: A Reader for Writers*. Ed. Johannah Rodgers. New York: OUP, 2015. Print.

Gee, James Paul. *What Video Games Have To Teach Us About Learning and Literacy*. New York: Macmillan, 2007. Print.

Hawthorn, Kirsty. "A Response to Katherine Hayles' 'How We Read: Close, Hyper, Machine.'" *Digital Literary Studies Blog*. Web. 10 February 2014.

Hayles, K. "How We Read: Close, Hyper, Machine." *Association of Departments of English Bulletin* 150 (2010): 62–79. Print.

Le Guin, Ursula. "The Death of the Book." *Technology: A Reader for Writers*. Ed. Johannah Rodgers. New York: OUP, 2015. Print.

McLuhan, Marshall. "The Medium is the Message." *The New Media Reader*. Eds. Noah Wardrip-Fruin and Nick Montfort. Cambridge: MIT Press, 2003. Print.

Wolf, Maryanne. *Proust and the Squid: The Story and Science of the Reading Brain*. New York: Harper Collins, 2008. Print.

——. "Our 'Deep Reading' Brain: Its Digital Evolution Poses Questions." *Nieman Reports*. Summer 2010. Web.

credits

Chapter 1: Which Came First, Technology or Society?

Page 3 Hughes, Thomas. From *Human-Built World: How to Think about Technology and Culture*. © 2004 by The University of Chicago. Reprinted by permission of The University of Chicago Press.

Page 7 Schatzberg, Eric. "What Is Technology?" From *Rethinking Technology* Blog, June 26, 2012. © Eric Schatzberg 2012. Reprinted by permission of the author.

Page 10 Murray, Sarah. "Transition: Technology Puts Power in the Hands of Many" by Sarah Murray, from the *Financial Times,* June 5, 2013. © The Financial Times Limited 2013. All rights reserved. Reprinted by permission.

Page 15 Marx, Leo. "Technology: The Emergence of a Hazardous Concept." *Technology and Culture* 51:3 (2010), 561–563. ©2010 The Society for the History of Technology. Reprinted with permission of Johns Hopkins University Press.

Page 20 Kelly, Kevin. "What Technology Wants," posted Jan. 27, 2009, at http://www.kk.org/thetechnium/archives/2009/01/what_technology.php? © Kevin Kelly. Reprinted by permission of the author.

Page 26 Postman, Neil. "Five Things We Need to Know About Technological Change" by Neil Postman, from a speech delivered in Denver, Colorado, March 28, 1998. Reprinted by permission of Elaine Markson Literary Agency.

Chapter 2: Imagining Worlds: Does Science Fiction Inform Our Technological Reality?

Page 39 Sawyer, Robert J. "The Purpose of Science Fiction" Copyright 2011 by Robert J. Sawyer, as first published in *Slate™ Magazine* (www.slate.com). Reprinted by permission of the author.

Page 42 Stephenson, Neal. "Innovation Starvation" *World Policy Journal* 28, pp. 11–16. © 2011 by SAGE Publications. Reprinted by Permission of SAGE Publications.

Page 50 Turney, Jon. "Imagining Technology," originally published in NESTA Working Paper 13/06, http://www.nesta.org.uk/publications/imagining-technology. Reprinted by permission of the author.

Page 54 Cramer, Kathryn. "On Science and Science Fiction" by Kathryn Cramer, from *Hieroglyph,* 1995. Copyright © 1995 Kathryn Cramer. Reprinted by permission of the author.

Chapter 3: (Dis)Connecting in a Digital Age: What Does It Mean to Be Human in an Age of Social Media and "Intelligent" Machines?

Chapter 4: Digital Literacies and Identities: Is Technology Changing Readers and Writers?

Chapter 5: Digital Education: What Can Technology Teach Us?

Chapter 6: Digital (In)Equality and Politics: Can Technology Change the World?

New Yorker Magazine/Malcolm Gladwell/Condé Nast. Reprinted by permission of Condé Nast.

Page 247 Schuler, Douglas. "It's Time to Work for a Better Internet" by Douglas Schuler, online at Internet Evolution, Sept. 7, 2010. Used by permission. Copyrighted 2014. UBM-TechWeb. 109932:614BC.

Chapter 7: Can Humans Live Forever? Healthcare, the Environment, and Technology

Page 255 For **Print**: Fukuyama, Francis. From *Our Posthuman Future*. *Our Posthuman Future* appeared in The New York Time Magazine, May 5 2002 and was adapted from the chapter "A Tale of Two Dystopias" from the book from Our Posthuman Future: Consequences of the Biotechnology Revolution by Francis Fukuyama. Copyright © 2002 by Francus Fukuyama. Reprinted by permission of Farrar, Straus and Giroux, LLC. For **Electronic** editions: Fukuyama, Francis. From *Our Posthuman Future*. © 2002 by Francus Fukuyama. Used by Permission. All rights reserved.

Page 264 Callahan, Daniel, and Sherwin B. Nuland. "The Quagmire: How American Medicine Is Destroying Itself" from *The New Republic*, May 19, 2011. Reprinted by permission of The New Republic.

Page 274 Topol, Eric. From *The Creative Destruction of Medicine* by Eric Topol, copyright © 2011. Reprinted by permission of Basic Books, a member of The Perseus Books Group.

Page 279 Gawande, Atul. "Slow Ideas" by Atul Gawande, originally published in *The New Yorker*, July 29, 2013. Reprinted by permission of the author.

Page 297 Seijo, Francisco. "When Worlds Collide" from *Breakthrough Journal*, March 2012. Reprinted by permission of the author and the publisher.

index